The Aging Workforce: Challenges and Opportunities for Human Resource Professionals

Bahaudin G. Mujtaba
Frank J. Cavico

ILEAD Academy, LLC
Davie, Florida. United States of America
www.ileadacademy.com

Bahaudin G. Mujtaba and Frank J. Cavico, 2010. *The Aging Workforce: Challenges and Opportunities for Human Resource Professionals*

Cover Design: By Cagri Tanyar

© ILEAD Academy, LLC (2010)

ISBN-13: 978-1-936237-01-2

ISBN-10: 1-936237-01-6

	Subject Code	Description
1:	SEL005000	Self-Help : Aging
2:	LAW094000	Law : Discrimination
3:	SOC031000	Social Science : Discrimination & Racism

Printed in the United States of America by ILEAD Academy, LLC. Davie, Florida.

International

ILEAD ACADEMY

Leadership Education and Associate Development Academy

* Dedication*

This book is dedicated to those
who strive and push for a just
society though knowing that
perfect justice will not come
until the world hereafter!

Acknowledgements

Since there are many individuals that have contributed to this volume, *first,* we would like to especially thank our students and workshop participants, and especially the following colleagues, for their formal and informal contributions to the content of this book:

- Adam Kinney, Nova Southeastern University
- Albert Williams, Nova Southeastern University
- Cagri Tanyar, Nova Southeastern University
- Carrol Pickersgill, Nova Southeastern University
- Cuneyt Oskal, Nova Southeastern University
- Donovan A. McFarlane, City College of Fort Lauderdale
- Harriette Carlton, Nova Southeastern University
- Jatuporn Sungkhawan, Southeast Bangkok College
- Marissa Samuels, Nova Southeastern University
- Mele K. Akuna, University of Phoenix- Hawaii
- Pamela Blount, University of Phoenix-Tampa
- Rose Marie Edwards, University of West Indies
- Stephanie Ferrari, Nova Southeastern University
- Cagri Tanyar, Nova Southeastern University
- Trevor Pendleton, Nova Southeastern University
- William Richardson, University of Phoenix-Tampa

In particular, the authors want to note that the technological component of the original survey was developed, organized and made ready for global distribution by Cuneyt Oskal and Trevor Pendleton. The authors wish to express their gratitude for this contribution.

Second, we would like to thank all those "younger" and "older" professionals and family members who have helped us both personally and professionally get to this point.

Third, we thank you for reading this material and we trust you will find this book interesting, thought-provoking, useful, and beneficial. You can always contact us at work: (954) 262-5000. Thank you!

Bahaudin and Frank

TABLE OF CONTENTS

Preface

Today, not only is the global workforce getting older, but concomitantly very large numbers of older people are staying in the workplace or are attempting to enter or reenter the workforce. This phenomenon presents serious challenges to government and business leaders. People, of course, are living longer; and many are working well past the typical retirement age. They desire to remain challenged, involved, stimulated, as well as productive, in the work environment. Moreover, the severe financial crisis, deteriorating economy, poor stock market, imploding housing sector, and consequent recession, now have impelled many older people to stay employed or to return to the job market. Many people in the United States who recently were retired have found themselves in serious financial difficulties. They had depended on their house, the typical primary asset of most people, as well as their stock investments, for the major source of income. Now many people are very low on income and as a result are seeking to return to the workforce. The number of older workers thus is growing larger and larger. Many challenges confront older workers who remain employed or who seek to reenter the job market. One, unfortunately, is age discrimination in employment.

Age discrimination has many causes; and one of them seems to be cultural conditioning based on stereotyping of older workers (Posthuma and Campion, 2009). The word "stereotype" comes from two Greek words: *stereo* meaning "solid," and *typos* meaning "a model." Initially the term was used to refer to metal plates that were used for printing pages of the same writing or diagrams. When applied to people, the word symbolizes rigid, repetitive, and formalized behavior. Schneider (2004) indicates that stereotypes have been asserted to be "bad" because they are created, or at least supported, by cultures that are prejudiced and discriminatory. Of course, the problem is that in adopting and using stereotypes, people can let their cultures "do their thinking for them," instead of using factual information or evidence to be their guide (Mujtaba, 2010). Schneider (2004) asks the question of whether stereotypes regarding age and other such characteristics are "merely" cultural products. The answer, according to Schneider as well as many other experts, is "yes." Schneider (2004) also states that cultures provide many "accurate generalizations" but also some "really faulty ones" too. Stereotypes become bad, ugly, and ineffective when people use them to discriminate against a person or groups of individuals without considering the prevailing facts and evidence. The word "discrimination" takes its root from the Latin word *discrimino*, which means "to divide or separate" into a division or category. Discrimination has it positive meanings, such as in the statement that one has "discriminating tastes." Yet in many cases the word is used to refer to making judgments about an individual's or people's behaviors, not based on their unique characteristics, but based solely or mainly on stereotypes or generalizations. Such is the typical case about age discrimination, which negatively impacts many "older workers" in the twenty-first century's work environment.

Through personal observations and conscious thinking about employment practices, one can tell that it is not unusual to quickly find several headlines each week about employment discrimination cases through various genres and media outlets. Even several years ago, Jeffrey M. Bernbach (1996), in a book entitled "*Job*

Discrimination: How to Fight, How to Win," states: "Job-related bias, unfortunately, is big news…and big business." Today, there are many age discrimination cases, as the following chapters will point out, that are keeping lawyers, law firms, and the court system busy as they attempt to bring about fair employment practices.

Gregory (2001) states: "Discrimination against middle-aged and older workers has long been a common practice of American business firms. Nearly all middle-aged and older workers, at some time during their work careers, will suffer the consequences of an age-biased employment-related action." It should be noted that while the law in the United States prohibits age discrimination in the workplace, workers over the age of 40 are nonetheless subjected to adverse employment decisions motivated by false and stereotypical views regarding the physical and mental abilities of older workers. As such, older workers in the U.S. workplace are often "encouraged" into premature retirements, denied developmental opportunities that can lead to promotions, denied deserved transfers or job promotions, or terminated for causes that have little or nothing to do with their performance; and consequently are excluded from long-term decision-making due to biases and assumptions (Posthuma and Campion, 2009). Gregory (2001) underscores that age discrimination continues to be a common practice in business firms in the United States. Gregory (2001), though, does possess a positive view, by stating that isolated instance of enlightened thinking on age discrimination might very well be a harbinger of fairer days for older workers. Gregory (2001) concludes by saying that the world will be an even better place once unfair age discrimination in the workplace is eliminated.

The authors also hope that the elimination of age discrimination in the workplace comes faster; and, of course, you (the reader) can be a huge factor in this process by doing your part to become aware of such biases, and not allowing false and inaccurate stereotypes and myths about older workers to negatively impact your hiring and other management decisions. Managers and leaders, furthermore, are advised to take the time to think about their lives, their attitudes toward others and, most importantly, to determine how they want to live their lives, and how they want to be remembered by their family members, friends, and colleagues. In other words, take the time to determine your life's purpose, which is really the secret to the "fountain of youth"; and that "first step" can be the beginning of your journey to living purposefully. According to Sophia Loren, the actress, "There is a fountain of youth: it is your mind, your talents, the creativity you bring to your life and the lives of the people you love. When you learn to tap this source, you will have truly defeated age."

The purposes of this book, therefore, are to examine the important and challenging topics of the aging workforce, and particularly of age discrimination in employment, in a variety of contexts–legal, cultural, ethical, organizational, managerial, and practical - across various countries, including: Jamaica, Afghanistan, Turkey, Thailand, the Bahamas, and the United States. A cross cultural comparison is provided whereby the laws, moral beliefs, social norms, and employment practices of these countries are compared and contrasted. An additional cross cultural comparison regarding age and value difference between Asians and the United States is provided.

An examination of the relationship between age and morality is also presented. The objectives of the authors are to determine the laws prohibiting age discrimination in employment, ascertain the moral standards regarding age discrimination, and to discuss current employment practices regarding older workers. An important goal of the authors is to provide appropriate recommendations to employers to help them deal with the challenge of attracting, hiring, retaining, and developing older workers in the workforce in a value-maximizing manner for all the organization's stakeholders. Another complementary goal of the authors is to provide suggestions and advice to older workers as to how to find, obtain, and keep employment.

This book is the second the authors have written on the topic of age, older workers, and discrimination. The first book was titled *Age Discrimination in Employment: Cross Cultural Comparison and Management Strategies* (BookSurge, 2006). This second work is a continuation, update, as well as a major expansion and development of the authors' original work. Age discrimination is still covered, naturally; and actually the topic of age discrimination in employment has been materially increased in the second work. Specifically, the authors have significantly expanded the legal analysis of age discrimination in employment, both in the U.S. and especially globally. Furthermore, the authors also have materially increased the coverage of practical management advice, recommendations, and strategies to help employers as well as employees deal with the challenges of an aging workforce in a legal, moral, and efficacious manner. The authors have also presented, albeit in a summary format, the scholarly research on the relationship between age and morality and ethics. The authors in the second work, in addition, have substantially increased the coverage of age, aging, and older workers in the workforce, beyond the original subjects of discrimination and the cross cultural analysis, by incorporating scientific, psychological, cultural, organizational, and human resources components into the book. Regarding the latter element, the authors have provided an extensive chapter examining how employers can recruit, retain, and develop older workers. Finally, very practical advice is offered to the older worker himself or herself as to how to look for and to secure employment.

Overall, the authors hope that all the aforementioned purposes and goals are achieved in a stimulating, thought-provoking, perhaps at times provocative, and enjoyable manner. And as a result, we hope that the knowledge of the reader is increased, the mental acuity of the reader is enhanced, and the mental discipline of the reader is strengthened.

Finally, the authors wish you, the readers, to know that they have created a scholarship at their school, The H. Wayne Huizenga School of Business and Entrepreneurship, Nova Southeastern University, called The Business Ethics and Global Corporate Social Responsibility Scholarship, to which they donate a material portion of their royalties from the sale of all their books.

Bahaudin and Frank

All's the world a stage,

And all the men and women merely players;
They have their exits and entrances,
And one man in his time plays many parts,
His acts being seven stages. At first, the infant,
Mewling and puking in the nurse's arms.
Then the whining school boy with his satchel
And shining morning face, creeping like snail
Unwillingly to school. And then the lover,
Sighing like furnace with a woeful ballad
Made to his mistress' eyebrow. Then a soldier,
Full of strange oaths and bearded like the leopard,
Jealous in honor, sudden and quick in quarrel,
Seeking the bubble reputation
Even in the canon's mouth. And then the justice,
In fair round belly with good capon lined.
With eyes severe and beard of formal cut,
Full of wise saws and modern instances;
And so he plays his part. The sixth stage shifts
Into the lean and slippered pantaloon,
With spectacles on nose and pouch on side;
His youthful hose, well saved, a world too wide
For his shrunk shank, and his big manly voice,
Turning again to childish treble, pipes
And whistles in his sound. Last scene of all,
That ends this strange eventful history,
Is second childishness and mere oblivion,
Sans teeth, sans eyes, sans taste, sans everything.

William Shakespeare;
As You Like It—Scene II, Act VII

CHAPTER 1

INTRODUCTION

Age discrimination, as emphasized in the Preface, has many causes, and one of them seems to be cultural conditioning based on stereotyping of older workers. First the definitions of the key words "older" and "stereotype" must be ascertained. Regarding the word "older" as in the phrase "older worker," there are many opinions as to when a person progresses from middle-age to being "older." *HR Magazine* noted that there are different conceptions of "old" and "older" (Grossman, 2008). To illustrate the diversity of viewpoints, Grossman related: "Professional football players grow old in their 30s; air traffic controllers face mandatory retirement at 56, pilots at 65 and federal law enforcement officers at 57. The Age Discrimination in Employment Act...begins protecting workers at age 40. AARP, seniors' formidable lobbying organization, clusters mature workers in one category: 55-plus. Company officials...- from Borders; Vanguard Group in Valley Forge, Pa.; and Bon Secours Richmond Hospital District in Richmond, Va. – use 50 as the tipping point. Labor economists and gerontologists voice preference for 50 as well" (Grossman, 2008, p. 40). According to others, an older worker is one who is over 60 years of age (Santora and Seaton, 2008, p. 103). Since this book has primarily a practical business focus, as well as an inclusive "theme," the authors will use the 40 years of age to signify that a worker is now an "older" worker, unless of course there is a superseding legal definition, such as when the Age Discrimination in Employment Act, which will be extensively covered in this book, is applicable, or another age meaning for "older" is specifically designated. Nevertheless, it would be remiss of the authors not to relate a very practical "real-world" point made by *HR Magazine*; that is, when most people think of the term "older worker," their image is not of a 40 year old person; rather most likely it is a person in his or her 70s; yet nonetheless a 70 year old person is viewed as "alert, spry, with an inner drive that keeps him going" (Grossman, 2008, p. 41).

The word "stereotype" comes from two Greek words: *stereo* meaning "solid," and *typos* meaning "a model." When applied to people, the term symbolizes rigid, repetitive, and formalized behavior (Posthuma and Campion, 2009). Schneider (2004) relates that stereotypes have been wrong due to the fact that they may be created or at least supported by individuals or cultures that are in fact prejudicial and discriminatory. When using stereotypes, people allow their cultures to "do their thinking for them" instead of using factual information to be their guide. Schneider (2004) asks the question of whether stereotypes regarding age and other such characteristics are cultural products. The answer is "yes." Schneider (2004) indicates that cultures provide many accurate generalizations, but some really faulty ones too. One point is clear – right or wrong - about the "American" culture, as succinctly and plainly stated by *Newsweek* magazine: "Our culture relentlessly celebrates youth" (Gross, 2008, p. 18.). Youth is fine; however, stereotypes about age can become bad, ugly, and ineffective when people use them to discriminate against a person or groups of individuals without considering the current facts or evidence. The word discrimination takes its root from the Latin word *discrimino*, which means "to divide or separate" into a division or category. While discrimination has its positive meanings, in most cases it is used to refer to making judgment about an individual's or people's behaviors based not on their unique characteristics but based on stereotypes or generalizations. Posthuma and Campion (2009) explain further that "managers can hold negative stereotypes about older workers that are subtle or unconscious, yet they may affect how they think about their workers. The result can be discrimination against older workers when they are not hired, are not selected for training, or are targeted for lay-offs. Thus, although the influence may be subtle, the cause may be age stereotypes and the effect, discrimination" (Posthuma and Campion, p. 160).

The American Association of Retired Persons (AARP) also commences its examination of age discrimination in its 2008 report, *Reassessing the Age Discrimination in Employment Act*, by first defining the key term "discrimination":

> Before discussing evidence of age discrimination, it is first necessary to define what is meant by the term. Economic theory, beginning with Becker (1957), holds that a group suffers from discrimination if employers, other workers, or consumers have distaste for contact with the group, which ends up being reflected in market transactions. Thus, for example, if consumers value interactions with young workers more than with older workers, older workers will be hired at lower wages or will less likely be hired. Discriminatory tastes like these are interpreted as 'animus' toward a group. An alternative definition that may have similar observable consequences, but that might be more relevant to the case of older workers, is that economic agents – most likely employers – hold incorrect negative stereotypes about the ability of older individuals to perform on the job (Neumark, 2008, p. 11).

Finally, others believe that "age stereotypes are often connected to work competencies - in short, older workers may be perceived as less able to 'do the job' (Santora and Seaton, 2008, p. 103)." Such clearly is the case about age discrimination, which negatively impacts many "older workers" in the twenty-first century's work environment.

Through personal observations and conscious thinking about employment practices, one can tell that it is not unusual to quickly find several headlines each week about employment discrimination cases through various genres and media outlets. There are many discrimination cases currently that are keeping lawyers, law firms, and the court system very busy as they attempt to bring about fair employment practices. Posthuma and Campion (2009) note that "...at the time when older worker are most needed, there is growing evidence of discrimination against older workers in terms of higher verdicts against employers" (Posthuma and Campion, 2009, p. 159). Gregory (2001) states that discrimination against older workers has been a common practice of American businesses. Nearly all older workers, at some time during their work careers, will suffer the consequences of an age-biased decision. Gregory (2001) continues to state that while the law prohibits age discrimination in the U.S. workplace, workers over the age of 40 are nevertheless subjected to adverse employment decisions driven by false, stereotypical thoughts concerning the physical and mental abilities of older workers. As such, older workers in the "American" workplace are often "encouraged" into premature retirements, denied developmental opportunities that can lead to promotions, denied deserved transfers or job promotions, terminated for causes that have little to nothing with their performance, and are excluded from long-term decision-making due to biases and assumptions. Gregory (2001) points out "without fear of contradiction" that age discrimination continues to be a common practice in the United States today. Santora and Seaton concur; and assert that "...age discrimination is unfortunately alive and well in the workplace" in the United States (2008, p. 104). Posthuma and Campion (2009) most interestingly point out that "despite the importance of the topic, there has been less focus on preventing discrimination from age stereotypes than on discrimination from race and gender stereotypes. This is ironic because stereotypes about older workers have the potential to affect everyone as we get older, not just the members of one race or sex group" (p. 159).

The Components of the Book

The aging global workforce presents many challenges and opportunities for societies, governments, and employers; therefore, this topic is a multi-faceted subject matter that emerges as a most important challenge to the modern-day, global executive, manager, entrepreneur, and government leader. Accordingly, this book will cover the phenomena of an aging global workforce, especially age discrimination in employment, from a variety of perspectives. There are 11 chapters to the book. Each chapter commences with an *Introduction* section, followed by the substantive subsections; and the chapter is concluded with a brief *Summary* section. At the end of each chapter the authors have provided several pertinent *Questions for Discussion* based on the material in the chapter, which the authors hope will be thought-provoking and thus which will elicit spirited, though reasoned, discussion and debate.

This first chapter – *Chapter 1 – Introduction* – provides an introduction and overview of the topic, and states the purposes of the book and the importance and relevance of the subject matter. This first chapter also furnishes the chapter-by-chapter components of the book.

Chapter 2 – Culture and Discrimination – treats the subjects of culture, cultural differences, and culture and discrimination in the contexts of age, aging, and older workers. The chapter also examines appearance-based discrimination and stereotyping generally and as specifically related to age discrimination. As will be seen, stereotyping and perceptions, "Machiavellian" mind-sets, clashing societal norms, cultural conditioning, and conflicts in legal systems will present the international business person with a major test; that is, how to attract, retain, and develop an increasingly aging, as well as a diverse, workforce.

Chapter 3 – Diversity and Aging Challenges – is one that deals with the increasing diverse nature of the workforce today. The chapter also examines the cultural challenges associated with aging. Particular attention is paid to the concept of "unearned advantages" based on culture and some of the challenges confronted by older persons, especially in the workplace.

Chapter 4 of the book - *Legal Analysis of Age Discrimination in Employment* – provides detailed legal analysis of age discrimination laws in the United States and also presents certain "global perspectives" of age discrimination laws, including the extraterritorial effect of U.S. anti-discrimination law. The manager of the U.S. multinational firm, moreover, not only must be concerned with the laws regulating his or her business, but also with ethics, and especially with the ethical norms of the U.S. and the host country. The U.S. multinational business manager, therefore, must be sensitive to not only the legal ramifications of business decision-making, but also the moral consequences.

One purpose of this book, therefore, is to present traditional ethical schools of moral philosophy in a practical international business context. Accordingly, the ethical section to this book is presented in *Chapter 5 – Ethical Analysis of Age Discrimination in Employment*. This chapter presents two traditional, secular, ethical theories – ethical relativism and Kantian ethics – which are examined in depth in the context of age discrimination in employment. Ethical egoism also is examined and then applied to the age discrimination in employment issue in the recommendations section to the book. Ethically, the practice of employment discrimination overseas will be explored in depth pursuant to the doctrine of ethical relativism. A determination will be made regarding the moral norms of selected countries concerning age discrimination in employment. Next, as a balance to and "check" against ethical relativism, the ethics of the German philosopher, Immanuel Kant, will be explicated and applied to the topic. The ethics discussed herein thus will provide a foundation for the business person to more intelligently and skillfully apply ethical theories and engage in ethical reasoning so as to arrive at moral solutions to problems in the international business arena.

Chapter 6 – Views of Aging in Different Cultures – presents cultural perspectives of aging, older workers, and age discrimination in the workforce of various countries. The countries were selected to the availability of information from the authors' and their colleagues' own research, experiences, and contacts as well as from traditional scholarly sources. Chapter 6 also includes scholarly work regarding the perspectives of younger workers in the United States, as well as scholarly research on the relationship between age and morality and ethics.

Chapter 7 - Cross Cultural Comparison and Employment Practices – is based on a survey conducted by the authors: their Age and Cultural Values Questionnaire. The chapter relates the nature, purposes, and methodology of the authors' studies, presents the survey results and the implications thereof, states the limitations of the studies, and indicates some future directions for scholarly research. The countries chosen for the surveys were the United States, Afghanistan, Turkey, Bahamas, Thailand, and Jamaica. As will be seen, of particular interest in the chapter will be the respondents' comments on age discrimination in the workplace from the various countries.

Chapter 8 – Recruiting, Retaining, and Developing Older Workers – is a very practical management chapter as the title to the chapter concisely indicates. The chapter examines the training of older workers, the value-maximizing function of older workers as coaches and mentors, particularly the role that older workers can play in dispelling workplace rumors and in solving workplace problems and avoiding conflict. An important feature of the chapter is the technology material. The benefits of technology for the elderly and especially for older workers are covered, including how employers can involve and develop older workers in technology. Finally, the chapter addresses the issue of the personal responsibility of older workers, and accordingly provides some practical information on job opportunities for older people.

Chapter 9 – The Philosophy and Science of Aging – examines aging from philosophical, scientific, as well as historical vantage points. The chapter compares and contrasts nurture versus nature in the aging process, old age versus young age, and discusses the notions of aging hierarchies and age and privilege. The aforementioned examinations are conducted principally in a business and employment context. The chapter concludes with a spiritual affirmation of aging healthfully and harmoniously.

Chapter 10 – Management Strategies – Age Discrimination and an Aging Workforce – is a very substantive chapter that presents many detailed recommendations, strategies, tactics, and suggestions for managers to use to avoid age discrimination in the workplace, and also to deal effectively with an actual age discrimination lawsuit pursuant to the laws of the United States. The chapter also provides practical suggestions and creative techniques for managers to deal with older workers and to cope with an aging workforce. Furthermore, the chapter provides certain global practical perspectives on how employers deal with the preceding aging workforce issues.

Chapter 11 – Conclusion – is the final chapter to the book. The authors conclude their work by providing a brief overall summary of the work, underscoring certain important issues, and making certain critical points. The authors emphasize the need for legal and ethical conduct in the workplace, and extol the benefits of acting in such a proper, right, and smart manner. The book then offers some hopefully inspirational and reflective lyrics from a poem and a song, as well as a strong declarative statement from the authors underscoring a fundamental point made in the work. Next the book provides a series of *Cases and Case Studies* on age discrimination in employment topics. Each case is followed by a series of discussion questions stemming from the case and relating to material and principles found in the book. The book ends with the *References and Bibliography* section, the *Appendices*, *Index*, and the *Authors' Biographies*.

The cover for the book – a picture of the Venetian Grand Canal and the Rialto Bridge - was selected not "merely" because Venice is a beautiful city – a United Nations World Heritage City actually. Venice is today a major tourist site, naturally; and the Venice of "yesterday," that is, during the Middle Ages and the Renaissance, was a principal international business, trade, banking, and finance center – the "bridge" and trans-shipment point between Europe and the Middle East and Asia; moreover, Venice during its historical greatness was ruled by a very powerful leader, the Doge, who was selected by the Ducal Council, the primary representative body in the Venetian government, which was an elected body as Venice was a republic. The members of the Ducal Council always chose as the Doge to rule the city an older person, actually a very old person, who was selected for his demonstrated long experience, accumulated knowledge, maturity, and wisdom. The Doge was elected as the chief executive official of Venice for a lifetime term.

Summary

This first chapter to this book set forth the purposes of the book and provided a brief introduction to, and overview of, the subject matter, emphasizing the importance of culture to the forthcoming analysis. The chapter also stated the importance and relevance of the subject matter to the global business manager, delineated the chapter-by-chapter coverage of the book, and briefly described all the components of the book.

Questions for Discussion
1. Do you agree with the Gregory's statement (which he asserts, he says, "without fear of contradiction") that age discrimination continues to be a "common practice" in U.S. business firms? Why or why not?
2. Do you agree with Schneider's statement that age stereotypes are cultural products? Why or why not?
3. Does that statement that one has "discriminating tastes" carry negative, prejudicial implications? What about the statement that one is a "discriminating" individual? Why or why not?

CHAPTER 2

CULTURE AND DISCRIMINATION

This chapter examines culture and discrimination, and particularly focuses on one of the significant cultural challenges in international management – dealing with age discrimination in employment. A starting place is to understand culture as a way of attaining better management practices in the international work environment. The chapter, therefore, commences with a discussion of culture and cultural differences in the workplace. The chapter also examines culture and discrimination, stereotypes and age discrimination, and the relationship between appearance-based discrimination and age. The chapter also discusses cultural differences in time orientation and their relationship to age and aging.

Culture and Cultural Differences

Generational differences and discrimination naturally affect the employment setting, but cultural differences are also an important reality of today's workforce. Cultural differences, such as languages spoken, clothing designs, and music played are often apparent among people living in different cities, countries, or continents. Yet, certain cultural differences such as beliefs and values are not always apparent at the surface level, but they are practiced among different human groups. People's views regarding aging and older workers emerge as one prime example of such cultural differences that "lie beneath the surface," but which are experienced in day-to-day activities. Employers in the United States as well as globally are dealing with such views regarding age, and thus are confronting the challenges and opportunities that come with an aging workforce. As matter of fact, the average age of the U.S. workforce is higher than previous years, and the workers now are much more diverse. In the next forty years, the percentage of Caucasian (White non-Hispanic) workers in the United States is expected to see at least a 25% percent reduction, while the percentage of Asian and Hispanic workers is very likely to rise. Due to generational differences, some occupations and industries in the United States are likely to see fewer numbers of experienced and skilled individuals in the labor pool. Due to globalization and limited resources, some organizations have fewer numbers of managers and hierarchal levels in their organizational charts. So, there are many changes that employers have to tackle in the coming decades as they now must be prepared to deal with a much more diverse workforce. Some of the differences in the workforce stem from cultural backgrounds, while others come from generational upbringing. There have been more individuals who retire earlier than previous generations in order to have more time for some of their favorite activities and to fulfill their dreams. The U.S. workforce is seeing a larger percentage of "baby-boomers" retiring, which means that organizations are dealing with a shortage of experienced workers. The second decade of this new century and millennium is going to see more U.S. workers retire as they reach the traditional retirement age of 65 years. As such, employers ultimately will have fewer choices of candidates seeking jobs, as they seek to recruit, attract, and hire qualified individuals for various positions. Thus, employers will have to find various means of competing to acquire a larger percentage of this limited resource - skilled workers; and many of these valuable experienced workers fall into the category of older workers. Accordingly, the attraction, recruitment, retention, and development of older workers have become critical to competing successfully in the "new economy" which promises fast and rapid changes. Employee retention programs for experienced workers will not only work for gaining older workers, but will also increase the likelihood of getting more applicants from all generations of the available labor pool. However, in an effort to attract, hire, and retain older workers, many organizations in the United States as well as globally face the challenges of cultural or generational biases and stereotypes that negatively impact even experienced workers. Therefore, it is important to understand culture and cultural views related to age, stereotypes, biases, and particularly the impact of culture on people's behavior in the workplace.

Culture is a way of life; and culture conditions people's behavior toward specific norms, customs, and societal expectations. One function of culture, therefore, is to regularize behavior within the society. As such, by understanding the culture, one can predict the individual's behavior within that culture toward dilemmas, employment practices, and day-to-day activities. Every individual comes from a society that conditions the person to respond to challenges based on the specific values and morals of his or her upbringing. People of some cultures value experience and age, while at other times and locations people are conditioned in stereotypes and myths. Such stereotypes and conditioning, unfortunately, accompany individuals in the workplace, thus leading to prejudice and discrimination of various forms, including based on age. It should be noted, however, that while years of conditioning can be a very strong influence on a person's behavior, each person can think for him- or herself, and thus make decisions according to the situational factors surrounding a dilemma. This result is especially true in the workplace, as managers and professionals are expected to treat each other with respect and dignity, as well as according to legal, "industry," and organizational standards and practices. Therefore, it is extremely important for professionals, managers, and leaders to have a clear understanding of culture, especially discrimination, stereotypes, laws, and industry practices, in order to make legal, ethical and moral, and efficacious decisions. In particular, possessing a strong moral foundation will enable every worker and manager to become a transformational leader by thinking critically and helping others to reflect upon the facts before making important decisions that impact their future, their organization's future, and the future of current and prospective employees. Denis Waitley, speaker and author, once said: "Don't dwell on what went wrong. Instead, focus on what to do next. Spend your energies on moving forward toward finding the answer." This book, therefore, is not only about reviewing the past, but also understanding the current policies and circumstances, and most importantly moving forward by planning for the future to minimize or eliminate age-related biases in the workplace.

Stereotypes and Age Discrimination

The word stereotype, as noted, comes from two Greek words: *stereo* meaning "solid," and *typos* meaning "a model." Initially the term was used to refer to metal plates that were used for printing pages of the same writing or diagrams. When applied to people, according to experts, it symbolized rigid, repetitive, and formalized behavior. Schneider (2004) states that stereotypes are often based on prejudiced and discriminatory thoughts. Of course, as underscored, the impact is that in adopting and using stereotypes, people can let their cultures "do their thinking for them," instead of using factual information and evidence to be their guide. Schneider (2004) asks the question of whether stereotypes regarding age and other such characteristics are cultural products. The answer, according to Schneider and many other experts, is "yes." Schneider (2004) goes on to say that cultures provide many accurate generalizations and some faulty ones. Stereotypes become bad, ugly, and ineffective when people use them to discriminate against a person or groups of individuals without considering the current facts or evidence. The word discrimination takes it root from the Latin word *discrimino*, which means "to divide or separate" into a division or category. While discrimination has it positive meanings, in most cases it is used to refer to making judgment about and individual's or people's behaviors not based not on their unique characteristics, but rather based on stereotypes or generalizations.

Such is the case about age discrimination, which negatively impacts many "older workers" in today's work environment. To illustrate, Floyd (2008) indicates that the downturn in the economy and lack of jobs has caused an increase in age discrimination suits. In September 2008, a news anchor for BBC, age 57 years, filed a lawsuit because she was overlooked to replace another anchor going on maternity leave with younger anchors ages 32 and 28. Another case was filed against The South Charleston Police Department for not allowing a 37 year applicant to take the physical ability test. Upon reviewing the case the rules set forth by the department were ruled unconstitutional and violated the young woman's civil rights (Floyd, 2008). To further illustrate, according to the American Association of Retired Persons (AARP) study, called "*Staying Ahead of the Curve: The AARP Work and Career Study,*" many older workers in the U.S. perceive age discrimination in employment to be a serious problem. The study indicated that two-thirds of workers aged 45-74 replied affirmatively to the question that "based on what you have seen or experienced, do you think workers face age discrimination in the workplace today" (Neumark, 2008, p. iii). Even more dramatically, *HR Magazine's* declared that "the scourge of age discrimination continues to be endemic" (Grossman, 2008, p. 64.). *HR Magazine* provided two examples. The first was a survey of 5000 workers age 50 and over conducted for Retirement.Jobs.com in Waltham, Massachusetts, in which 77% of the respondents have either experienced or observed age discrimination and bias in the workplace. In a companion survey of 165 employees, 78% indicated that discrimination based on age was a "a fact of life" in the workplace. Secondly, all these findings, related *HR Magazine*, paralleled a survey conducted by the Roper polling organization for the American Association of Retired Persons where two-thirds of the workers aged 45 to 74 indicated that they had experienced or observed age discrimination in the workplace, and, even more disturbingly, 80% of job seekers stated that they were facing age discrimination. Similarly, *Newsweek* magazine reported that "there is still enormous resistance and unwillingness to consider older workers for job hires" (Gross, 2008, p. 18). *Newsweek* quoted a corporate executive recruiter who stated that corporate boards look askance or suspiciously at older candidates because "somebody in their mid-60s isn't going to take an 18 hour-a-day job" (Gross, 2008, p. 18). What makes age discrimination an even greater problem than prejudice based on race and gender is the presence of "...unsubstantiated claims that old age reduces performance. In addition, age discrimination is inextricable from the economic argument because older employees through years of service and experience demand higher wages than newer employees. Accordingly, employers in order to reduce the payroll expense may replace older employees with younger employees" (Khan, 2009, n193).Yet, perhaps in the future, such discrimination, prejudices, and stereotypes may become eroded due to demographic trends, specifically due to the fact that as the "baby-boomers" get older, and carry their social attitudes with them, the acceptance of older workers in the workforce may grow.

Appearance-Based and Disability Discrimination

There are many forms of discrimination in addition to age, including gender, body size, race, appearance, and other dimensions of diversity. Discriminating on the basis of appearance emerges as a difficult area – legally, morally, and practically – and especially in the context of age since of course the aging process affects one's appearance. Appearance is a very widespread form of discrimination that impacts people of all backgrounds. Employers and customers in the business world regularly make decisions based on appearance. Yet, there is no law explicitly prohibiting the use of appearance as a consideration for hiring or other employment decisions. Nevertheless, appearance issues increasingly are arising in the context of conventional employment discrimination law cases.

Employers realize that an employee with a professional, clean, and neat appearance may make the difference in making a big sale or securing an important deal. Employers understand that persons who do not look like they can take care of themselves will not elicit confidence that they can take care of a client's or customer's business. Consequently, employers frequently attempt to control appearance in the workplace. For example, employers will institute dress codes, appearance guidelines, and grooming policies in order to ensure a minimum appearance level. Employees often have challenged these policies with many companies and organizations.

Accordingly, courts in the U.S. have been asked to become considerably more involved in appearance-based questions. Although there is no law that prohibits discrimination based on personal appearance, appearance-based discrimination arises pursuant to several discrimination laws, especially the Civil Rights Act, the Americans with Disabilities Act, and the Age Discrimination in Employment Act. The legal theory is for the employee to connect his or her appearance case, based on unprotected physical characteristics, to a protected category, such as age, race, national origin, sex, religion, or disability. Thus, by utilizing an expansive legal approach, the employee attempts to get his or her appearance-based claim to a court and before a judge and jury as a traditional civil rights discrimination case. The results, however, at best, have been mixed for employees.

Dress codes, grooming requirements, or other appearance-based employment policies generally are permitted under discrimination laws so long as they are enforced in a fair and even-handed manner. These policies, in order to be legal, must not have a disparate impact on any particular protected class, either on its face or in its application. Yet, some variations in requirements may be permissible. For example, in one case, a male employee was discharged for wearing an earring to work in violation of the employer's dress code. The federal district court rejected the employee's discrimination claim. The court explained that minor differences in appearance regulations that reflect "customary modes of grooming" do not constitute sex discrimination within the meaning of Title VII of the Civil Rights Act. In the court's view, so long as both men and women were held to similar standards of professionalism, gender-based differences in standards were not discriminatory, presuming they complied with traditional or customary practices. In another case, two men were fired when they wore ponytails after the effective date of a revised grooming policy that required hair to be clean, neatly combed, and arranged in a traditional style, and for men, no longer than mid-collar in the back. The terminated male employees asserted that because their former employer applied its hair length and style rules differently for men and women, they were discriminated against on the basis of their sex. The court, the New Jersey appeals court, relying on federal precedent, determined that hair length policies generally do not constitute sex discrimination under Title VII of the Civil Rights Act. In yet another case, this one by female Department of Corrections (DOC) officers, who filed a class action in federal court contending that the DOC's dress code policy of requiring men and women officers to wear trousers violated their 1st Amendment rights under the Constitution. In particular, the women claimed that their religious beliefs prohibited them from wearing pants. The court decision, affirmed by the U.S. court of appeals, rejected the women's claims, citing emergency and safety reasons for a rule prohibiting skirts, and also noting that the DOC should be given great latitude in determining the dress code for its correctional employees.

Similar to the sex discrimination cases, the U.S. courts have held that grooming and dress code policies must also be fair and even-handed in their treatment and enforcement between majority and minority races. In one case, an African-American woman brought a racial discrimination case against her employer because it required her to seek prior approval of hairstyles she planned to wear at work. The policy also required hairstyles to be neat and well-groomed. When she wore a "finger wave" style, the employer revised its policy to prohibit "eye-catching" styles. The federal court allowed the woman's discrimination case to proceed on race discrimination grounds, because of evidence that Caucasian women were not subject to the prior approval or "eye-catching" requirements. In another appearance-race case, an African-American woman wanted to display her heritage through her choice of clothing by wearing African-styled attire and also by wearing her hair in dreadlocks and braids. The woman, however, was terminated; but she was replaced by another African-American woman. The terminated employee contended that because of her choice of clothing and hairstyle, she represented a subset of African-Americans whose claim of race discrimination could not be defeated by the hiring of another minority woman whose appearance was more typical of corporate America. The federal district court, however, refused to find that her claim was actionable, and stated that she had failed to provide sufficient evidence for a court to infer discrimination.

Even when employers do not have an established dress code or grooming policy, employers can still be subject to appearance-based lawsuits. In one case, a female employee wore skirts and blouses that, in the employer's opinion, were too tight, short, shear, and revealing. The employee was repeatedly counseled, especially by the firm's chief financial officer, a male, as to the inappropriateness of her clothing. The employee eventually was fired, and her appearance was a contributing factor in the termination decision. The employee sued for sex discrimination, but the federal appeals court upheld her discharge. The appeals court emphasized that there was no evidence that the chief financial officer had ever sexually harassed the employee. Moreover, the court underscored that in addition to the CFO, two female supervisors had informally counseled the employee as to the inappropriateness and unprofessional nature of her attire, thus indicating that she had not been singled out by the male CFO. In another case, an employee was fired for failing to cover a racially offensive tattoo on his arm. The employee was a member of the Ku Klux Klan, and the tattoo showed a hooded figure and a burning cross. The employee sued, contending religious discrimination, but lost. The court pointed out that even if the employee could show a sincere religious belief, it nonetheless would be an undue hardship for the employer to have an employee in the workplace with a racially offensive tattoo.

The U.S. cases indicate that the courts are reluctant to accept appearance as a legitimate basis for discrimination claims. However, if an employee can successfully tie appearance to a protected class, such as being an older worker, and there is evidence that the protected class is treated differently from the majority, such claims may be successful. Although employers are prohibited from unevenly enforcing their dress codes or grooming policies, such policies may reflect differences that are considered reflections of customary appearance standards. Based on the foregoing legal considerations, employers in the U.S. can take precautions to prevent appearance-based lawsuits. If an employer does promulgate appearance and grooming standards as well as a dress code, the employer must make sure that discriminatory standards are not built into the policies. Most importantly, men and women, as well as the young and old, must be treated comparably. The exact requirements may be different, but they must be similar and fair. Any differences in the standards between men and women, as well as the young and old, however, must reflect what is considered customary and proper in society. The development and implementation of rational, fair, and objective policies and standards, and consistency in the treatment of employees, especially between men and women, and the young and the old, are the employer's "best practices" to ensure a successful defense to an appearance-based discrimination lawsuit in the U.S. court.

There is also a relationship between disability discrimination under the Americans with Disabilities Act (ADA) and age discrimination – a relationship that has become even more pronounced with the passage by the U.S. Congress of the ADA Amendments Act of 2008 (ADAAA). This act significantly expanded the definition of the key word "disability" in the ADA, and thereby has materially increased the number of people protected by the ADA. As noted in the *Legal Report of the Society of Human Resource Professionals* (Postol, 2009, p. 2), the ADAAA mandates that a person's disability now must be construed without reference to corrective measures (except for ordinary eye glasses and contact lenses). So now, for example, a person with a moderate hearing loss would be considered "disabled" even though he or she may be using a hearing aid. Furthermore, medications are deemed to be corrective measures, thereby greatly increasing the number of people protected by the ADA. In addition, the ADAAA extends the definition of disability to encompass impairments that are episodic or in remission. The act also extends the definition of the major life activities covered by the act to include "eating, sleeping, walking, standing, lifting, bending, reading, concentrating, thinking, and communicating" (Postol, 2009, p. 2). Thus, if these activities are substantially limited, then a person will be viewed as disabled, and protected. Finally, the act directs the EEOC to interpret "substantially limited" to mean "significantly restricted," with the latter being construed by Congress as a more broad, as well as more favorable to the employee, interpretation. Of course, the employee still must be able to perform the essential duties of the job, such as regular attendance, and if the employee cannot do so with a reasonable accommodation or there is not one that will allow him or her to do so, then the employee is not protected by the ADA. Nonetheless, examining these recent changes, "…most individuals over 50 years old seem likely to be covered by the ADA, since most individuals who are older than 50 have some deterioration in their body, and that is all that is required to fall under the new and improved ADA" (Postol, 2009, p. 1).

Culture and Discrimination

Hodgetts and Luthans (2003) defined international management as "the process of applying management concepts and techniques in a multinational environment" (p. 5). They further said that "culture is acquired knowledge that people use to interpret experience and generate social behavior (p. 5)." Of course, this acquired knowledge forms people's values, creates their attitudes, and influences their behavior in a predictable pattern (Hodgetts and Luthans, 2003, p. 108). Hofstede (1980) defined culture as the collective programming of the mind through locally held value systems, which distinguishes one group of people from another. Today's managers possess diverse value systems; and thus are truly global managers; and also they mostly manage people of diverse beliefs in an international environment. As such, understanding culture plays such a critical role in international management. For an organization to operate in several countries with different cultures, such as Jamaica, Turkey, Bahamas, Thailand, Afghanistan, and the United States, it is important for the "management team" to understand the culture of these countries in order to efficiently and effectively operate interdependently among them. The norms and practices of one culture, including moral beliefs and precepts, may not be the norms and practices of another.

Hall and Hall (1987) stated that each culture operates according to its own internal dynamic, its own principles, and its own laws - written and unwritten. However, there are some common threads that run through all cultures. *Culture* can be likened to a giant, extraordinary complex, yet subtle, computer. Its programs guide the actions and responses of human beings in every walk of life. This process requires attention to everything people do - to survive, advance in the world, and gain satisfaction from life. Furthermore, cultural programs will not work if crucial steps are omitted, which happens when people unconsciously apply their own "rules" to another system. Culture and cultural conditioning of people can affect technology transfer, managerial attitudes, managerial ideology, and even business-government relations. Furthermore, and perhaps most importantly, "culture affects how people think and behave" (Hodgetts and Luthans, 2003, p. 109). An example of observing the differences in cultures is when researchers and managers compare the priorities of cultural values. Time and time again, it has been shown that there are differences in priorities of cultural values between the United States, Japan, and Arab Countries (Elashmawi and Harris, 1996, p. 63). For example while people in the U.S. often rank freedom as their first value, Japanese tend to choose "belongingness," and Arabs choose family security first. Of course, similar differences exist among the cultures of Jamaica, Turkey, Afghanistan, Thailand, the Bahamas, and the United States, which naturally can impact employment practices in and among these cultures.

From the comparison of cultural values by Elashmawi and Harris (1996), one can observe that freedom and independence are the two main priorities in the U.S. culture; whereas in Japan the focus is belonging and group harmony; and in Arab countries it is family security and harmony. In the United States, the Constitution stands for freedom and independence; whereas in Arab countries, it is taught that family is the most important aspect of life. While "age" or seniority was ranked as fourth by the Japanese and Arab respondents, it did not even make the "top ten" list in the United States. Of course, such values and orientations toward age come from society; and society conditions human behavior, which might lead to discriminatory decisions. One behavior "driver" is the belief that older workers are not interested in technology. This technological issue will be directly addressed by the authors in the chapter revealing the results of their age and cultural values survey.

While culture can condition individuals both positively and negatively, at times the conditioning can be stereotypical and consequently lead to illegal or unethical discrimination. The word discrimination is synonymous with acting with bias, as well as making an invidious distinction, or engaging favoritism, bigotry, inequality, injustice, prejudice, unfairness, and intolerance. While many of these synonyms are negative, it is important to note that not all forms of discrimination are illegal or unethical. In society, a man may choose to discriminate against women who do not have a high school education when he decides to marry a woman; thus he may marry someone who has a college degree, while not even considering those who have not acquired this status. Similarly, a female might choose to marry a male who earns a comfortable salary and one who owns a house; as such, she may not even consider those who are unemployed, employed in low paying jobs, or those who have chosen to spend their money in other means versus owning a house. These forms of discrimination are based on personal values and preferences. However, it is important to note that such personal values and preferences do not always apply in the workplace, particularly when one is deciding whom to hire, since hiring practices are to be based on one's ability to perform the job. Professionally, managers and leaders may discriminate based on organizational values, educational qualifications related to the job, the level of experience, as well as many other legal factors, when looking for potential candidates in the workplace. However, these decisions do not always negatively impact others based on their age, gender, or race when properly practiced as intended by the organizational values and job qualifications. Yet, societal stereotypes and myths do lead some individuals to discriminate against others based on their gender, race, age, or other such non-job related variables that are not necessarily indicative of a potential candidate's level of performance. These forms of discrimination are illegal in the United States as well as many other nations and, certainly, highly unethical too. Another important point is to understand that cultures do not discriminate, but people do in terms of their thoughts, words, actions, and behaviors. While cultures cannot be changed easily, people's thoughts, words, actions, and behaviors can be changed; and this change takes place best when it is intrinsically initiated through knowledge, education, awareness, critical thinking, and self-reflection. Overall, each person is likely to achieve fairness in the hiring, development, and promotion of individuals according to his or her own efforts, education, self-reflections, behaviors, and ability to effectively work with others. George Adams, a philosopher, is reported to have said: "There is no such thing as a 'self-made' man. We are made up of thousands of others. Everyone who has ever done a kind deed for us, or spoken one word of encouragement to us, has entered into the make-up of our character and of our thoughts, as well as our success."

Self-reflection about national and international issues is critical for personal growth and development as a global leader. Hopefully, all scholars and practitioners of management, human resources management, and global leadership do this often; and accordingly evaluate their actions and progress on a daily, weekly, monthly, and yearly basis. Of course, one way to answer the question of why study age discrimination issues or global human resources management is to say that continuously getting more education in today's complex world allows for better performance, enhanced leadership, as well as concomitant upward mobility, which can provide for a greater financial reward in today's changing and at times uncertain economic and political environment. While these are good goals, oftentimes they are not the primary motivators for making key decisions in such challenging endeavors. The opportunity to learn and grow personally tends to be the deciding factor for many individuals who choose to continue learning. As has been said many times, global knowledge can open many avenues and also prevent many embarrassments. Phillips (1999-2000) said that the opportunity to learn, enhance one's ability as a self-learner, and explore new information is one that highly qualified students should not miss. Therefore, it is the vast amount of knowledge to be acquired in this world that continues to provide motivation and excitement for many people.

Today's world is a fast-moving and ever-changing place, providing avenues of learning at a pace where many people cannot keep up. These changes can only occur as a result of continued learning. It is the need to question that drives change. It is always easy to "do it the way that it has always been done," but if one "never looks beyond the obvious," then how does one know what lies ahead. To truly learn, one must open one's mind and try to put away preconceived notions. People must become and be critical thinkers in order to continuously learn and grow and to better understand national and international human resource and business practices. The goal of a formal education program is to increase one's knowledge and insight. It allows people to increase their understanding of business management by expanding on subjects that were studied during the completion of a previous degree. A formal program allows one to take "real life" experiences and learn from them. The people participating in a formal program each bring a different background to the group, which allows for new perceptions to be shared and new interactions to occur. Such a program provides a support group to "bounce ideas off each other," and thereby gather knowledge and obtain encouragement from these diverse perspectives.

With the current economic conditions, international firms are looking to fill positions, especially leadership ones, with people that have global experience and cultural sensitivity with regard to gender, age, local norms, and other issues related to hiring practices. They are looking for the candidate that has the "edge," that is, the ability to understand and manage the business in a fair, practical, and efficacious manner. These cultural competency points were underscored by Carlos Ghosn, the very successful, simultaneous CEO of Nissan and Renault. In an interview with *Newsweek* magazine (Smith, 2008), Ghosn, whom *Newsweek* called "an extreme example of a global executive," stated:

> More and more, in any company, managers are dealing with different cultures. Companies are going global, but the teams are being divided and scattered all over the planet. If you're head of engineering, you have to deal with divisions in Vietnam and China, and you have to work across cultures. You have to know how to motivate people who think very differently than you, who have different kinds of sensitivities, so I think the most important message is to get prepared to deal with teams who are multicultural, who do not think the same way (Smith, 2008, p. E10).

Formal and informal education, especially in the area of international business and human resources, provide the framework for these cultural sensitivity qualities. For those already with a company, senior management often sends the message that a degree is needed to move up the corporate "ladder." While promotion is a good reason to obtain global awareness, sensitivity, and an education, the desire to be a business leader and to accomplish one's tasks as a manager in a fair, just, ethical, and moral manner must come from a personal place – the inner-self. The opportunity for personal and professional growth should be a secondary accomplishment, not the primary one.

Understanding cultural differences, therefore, is a necessity for the growth and success of doing business with others throughout the world, and as a result is critical to serving each market in an effective and efficient manner. International expansions have been on the rise in the past few decades; and they present managers with new challenges on how to deal with the differences in culture. One of the benefits that such expansions offer is the access to new markets for economies of scale. With globalization of markets, competition, and organizations, individuals increasingly interact, manage, negotiate, and compromise with people from a variety of cultures.

Many economies are shaping their management practices to model those of the United States. This trend ultimately may transform their national cultures as well. According to some experts and writers, the "export" of U.S. management theories and practices through universities and management development workshops in other countries assumes that other countries are eager to become "Americanized," that is, to converge with the culture of the United States. Other researchers, however, think that there is a general lack of success in countries adopting the so-called "Western" management practices to develop their economy (Hofstede, 1993; Dastoor *et al*, 2005). Many "Third World" countries, including Jamaica and Afghanistan, have adopted Western management practices to achieve economic stability. Many foreign nationals work in the United States; and many students study there as well. The diversity of the cultures within the U.S. presents opportunities and challenges as foreign students and workers are exposed to the "American" culture for a prolonged period of time. According to Dastoor, Roofe, and Mujtaba (2005), when expatriates return to their home country they sometimes discover that they no longer fit into the culture, and many end up on a permanent basis.

Global Thinking and Learning

Managers, particularly leaders and all human resources managers, need to concern themselves with more than "mere" profits or "making the bottom-line numbers" at the end of each week, month, or year. They need to concern themselves with the well-being of their people. Carol Hymowitz (2005) indicated that when companies become fixated on "hitting" quarterly or daily targets, oftentimes they do not produce sustainable profit growth. She quoted organizational psychologist Richard Hagberg, who said "It's hard to capture employees' hearts, and best efforts, with numbers alone." In a recent study of 31 corporations, Hagberg's staff found that the highest returns were achieved at companies whose CEOs not only set challenging financial goals, but also articulated a purpose beyond profit-making, such as creating a great product, and thereby convinced employees their work mattered. Similarly, Susan Annunzio, CEO of the Hudson Highland Center for High Performance in Chicago, found that the biggest impediment to high performance–defined by her as making money for the company and developing new products, services and markets – is short-term focus. She and her staff in 2003 researched 3,000 managers and knowledge workers at global companies, such as Microsoft, Intel, and J.P. Morgan Chase. About 10% of the respondents said they worked in high-performing groups; and 38% said they worked in "nonperforming groups." Yet almost one-third of the non-performers said their businesses used to be high-performing. Annunzio and her staff asked what had happened; and the respondents had said top management raised our targets, cut budgets and staff, and they could not sustain results.

Global managers and leaders, therefore, need to concern themselves with the "people" side of the business. They need to be concerned with "culture shock" - both upon arrival and departure, issues to be considered when relocating to another country, family issues, health care issues, education of children and family members, taxes, living quarters, salary, cost of living equity, transportation, local laws, etc. Besides culture, a country's political and economical consideration further complicates the equation for international human resources managers. Cross-cultural training is a mandatory activity for all employees involved in international business. For expatriates, it is also critical to train the immediate family members and relatives. Otherwise, failure could come not only from the economic activities, but also from political, marketing, interpersonal, and cultural differences. With the convergence of a global workplace, there is a need to ensure that people are not discriminated against nationally as well as internationally. So, to ensure continuity throughout the company, everyone should be required to attend diversity and sensitivity training. These types of training involve understanding different cultures and how people of different cultures act in various situations, including interacting with other people.

Diversity in the workplace is becoming more and more common in today's society. Especially in the United States where more and more businesses are becoming global, the diverse workplace is becoming much more apparent. Moreover, most firms are becoming a "melting pot" of different cultures, ages, genders, and ethnic backgrounds. This global diversity and the increase in import penetration in the United States are forcing more and more companies to create a diverse workplace, and accordingly to have diversity training to promote a wide range of different cultures, yet without the participants being afraid of expressing their views or risk losing business unnecessarily. Therefore, companies will continue to conduct cultural awareness training that will create awareness of the different cultures and the diverse generations of workers, and how the appreciation of these differences are an asset to the overall success of the company in the long-term. Greater awareness of diversity and cultural differences should provide time for personal reflection on how age is an important dimension of today's diverse workforce, and how aging is a normal part of human growth and development. An Indian writer, J. Krishnamurti, said: "In oneself lies the whole world, and if you know how to look and learn, then the door is there and the key is in your hand. Nobody on earth can give you either that key or the door to open, except yourself." Living with honor and integrity often requires learning, patience, and standing for what is right, which are all virtuous endeavors. However, living with honor, by being honest and standing up for what is right, is the only way that one can remain truly happy in the long term and become successful in the business of life. After all, as Khushal Khan Khatak once said: "Without honor and glory-What is this life's story," which relates to a leader's character and integrity. Character and integrity mean living what one preaches, and not cheating others or oneself in this life. The poem entitled "*The Man in the Glass*," written by Dr. Dale Wimbrow, emphasizes that living with integrity requires personal reflection and looking at the mirror every day, while communicating with oneself by asking and honestly answering the questions: Am I doing what is right? Did I do what is right? Am I doing all that I can do for me, my family, my community, and this society?

Summary
This chapter examined culture and discrimination. In particular, the chapter addressed some of the most significant cultural challenges in international management; that is, how to deal with and an aging workforce and age discrimination in employment. A starting place was, and is, to understand cultures as a way of improving management practices in the international work environment. The chapter, therefore, commenced with a discussion of culture and cultural differences in the workplace. The chapter focused on culture and discrimination, stereotypes and age discrimination, and the relationship between appearance-based discrimination and age. The chapter also discussed cultural differences in time orientation and their relationship to age and aging as well as the need for global thinking and learning.

Questions for Discussion
1. What is culture and how does it affect one's behavior? Provide examples with explanations thereof.
2. What is age discrimination; and how can it be culturally based? Provide examples with explanations thereof.
3. Is there a relationship between culture and age discrimination? Why or why not?
4. What is the relationship between appearance-based discrimination and age discrimination? Explain.
5. How are cultures conditioning people regarding age discrimination? Provide examples with explanations thereof.
6. Is there a tendency to view "older" workers differently in individualistic cultures as opposed to collective cultures? Why or why not?
7. Is there developing a global or world culture that condemns age discrimination? Why or why not? Provide examples with explanations thereof.

CHAPTER 3

DIVERSITY AND AGING CHALLENGES

Naturally and spiritually, every human being is a child at heart. Some people associate aging with wisdom and spirituality; yet others relate aging to a deterioration of physical and mental capacities. Of course, there is probably some truth to both views. However, it must be noted that a twenty-five-year old person might be much more spiritually mature than a sixty year-old man or woman. Similarly, a sixty year-old man or woman can be physically healthier than many twenty-five year olds. So, aging cannot be a predictor of each unique individual's level of knowledge, maturity, or capacity to perform at certain standards. Therefore, theoretically, age should not be a factor in employment practices. However, realistically and practically speaking, age has become a major aspect of employment decisions in many modernized and developed countries.

This chapter first discusses the increasing diversity of today's workforce and the concomitant challenges confronting managers who must manage such a workforce in a culturally changing environment. The chapter then addresses two thought-provoking and difficult subject matters – "unearned advantages," which may be predicated on culture, and "daily indignities," which may be suffered by many employees in the workplace. The chapter discusses ways for managers to deal with these two aforementioned problematical areas.

Workforce Diversity and Expectations

Age discrimination and bias in the U.S. workplace and globally impact people of all sizes, races, colors, religions, and ethnicities. Such forms of discrimination, which can be highly unethical, are causing many managers a great deal of anxiety, and are also forcing many of them into court. One of the greatest fears of company officials and individual managers is the likelihood of either being sued for something they have done intentionally or unintentionally, or for something they should have considered doing but did not. It is no secret that age-related lawsuits are proliferating; and more recently age related claims have been on the rise due to layoffs, which, even though may not target older workers, nonetheless may have an impermissible disparate impact on them. Juries, perhaps due to sympathy, often side with aggrieved employees, even if the evidence is flimsy. Because of these trends, companies and their managers are realizing the need to protect themselves by periodically reviewing workforce diversity and examining the workplace for latent signs of discrimination.

The focus of such discussions on discrimination based on age is to create awareness and to reduce the negative impact of stereotypes associated regarding "older workers." Yet how many "older workers" are there in the U.S. workforce? The U.S. population as whole is certainly "graying." *Newsweek* magazine reported in 2009 that in 1960 only one in 11 Americans was aged 65 or older, but now the ratio is only one in seven, and, moreover, by 2030 the ratio is predicted to be merely one in five (Samuelson, 2009). Specifically regarding workers, the *Sun-Sentinel* newspaper of Ft. Lauderdale, Florida, reported in 2008 that based on U.S. Bureau of Labor Statistics, workers aged 65 and older are expected to account for 6.1% of the workforce by 2016, which percentage is a very large increase from the 3.6% in 2006 (Carpenter, 2008). *HR Magazine* in 2008 reported the "numbers" from the U.S. Bureau of Labor Statistics: In 2007, there were 146 million people working full-time or part-time in the United States. Thirteen percent of this workforce was 65 years of age or older; and within that 13%, approximately 20%, or 1.1 million, were still working on a full-time basis. Also, and very significantly, there are 36.4 million predominantly full-time workers who are between the ages of 50 and 64, which figure represents one-quarter of the U.S. workforce (Grossman, 2008). Furthermore, *HR Magazine* states: "Undoubtedly, this number will increase in coming years as people choose to delay retirement for personal reasons or as a result of changes in government policy such as reductions in social security benefits" (Grossman, 2008, p. 42). Therefore, it is imperative that older workers are kept in the workforce as long as possible, as there will be a shortage of skilled labor in the near future, especially if older workers continue to retire early (Harvey and Allard, 2002). According to former Secretary of Labor, Elaine L. Chao, "Nowhere is the case stronger for tapping the strengths of older workers than with employers facing the skills gap. Everywhere I go, employers tell me they are having difficulty finding workers with the right skill sets for the jobs they have to offer" (Allard, 2002, p. 45). Of course, this shortage of experienced labor presents a great opportunity for focusing on the recruitment, development, and retention of older workers, particularly at a time where an unprecedented number of "Americans" are rapidly approaching retirement in today's workforce.

Today's population is more diverse than ever before; and the workforce population has been changing rapidly along with it. Being an effective manager and educator in a diverse environment requires expecting the same standards from all employees regardless of their race, gender, age, language, and general background. Managers should not evaluate workers differently because of their age, gender, nationality, or language, since such differences have a negative consequence as a result of the "self-fulfilling prophecy" syndrome. One of the needed skills for all managers is to acknowledge differences, and then actively incorporate each worker's experiences into the work environment and decision-making process. Recognizing and understanding these differences are neither easy nor automatic, since they require conscious focus and a good level of "comfort" on the part of the manager with cultural and generational diversity issues. In order for managers and workers to be successful, they thus need to become "culturally competent." *Cultural competency* for all practical purposes refers to the continuous learning process that enables one to function effectively in the context of cultural differences in the workforce.

Culturally competent managers should be aware of and eliminate the presence of a "hostile learning environment" in their organization. A *hostile learning environment* can be described as a situation where inappropriate remarks related to age, gender, sexual orientation, etc. consistently take place; and this deleterious situation is not corrected by managers and leaders. This consequence is a situation that demands that insensitive and inappropriate remarks should be addressed publicly by the manager, so everyone in the department understands the "ground rules" and the fact that inappropriate/insensitive comments are neither appreciated nor tolerated. Today, there is a very diverse workforce population in terms of the employees' backgrounds, abilities, age, language, body size, geographic location, culture, desires, learning styles, cultural conditioning, etc. Diversity describes the many unique characteristics and qualities that make a person, employee, or student similar to or different from others. Some of these characteristics might be apparent, such as skin color, hair color, body size, and general appearance. Yet other characteristics such as age, ethnicity, disability, religion, financial status, values, cultural background, and many others may not be apparent based on first impressions. It is imperative, therefore, that one does not judge workers based on assumptions; and accordingly one must treat everyone fairly and equitably.

Research has shown that homogeneous teams are neither as creative nor as productive as heterogeneous teams when dealing with or solving complex problems. Diverse teams can achieve synergistic results if they appreciate, understand, and value their differences effectively. *Synergy* is where the whole is greater than the sum of its parts. Ultimately, synergy is the performance gains that result when individuals, teams, and departments coordinate their actions toward the same goals. Synergistic teams, colleagues, peers, and departments tend to function more cooperatively and productively than if they were operating in isolation. Synergy happens when two or more individuals working together produce more than their combined efforts individually. For example, a team of four workers should produce a final project (or product) that is much better than the combined results of each of their work that is produced individually. Diversity awareness can help teams function harmoniously in the context of cultural differences, and also can produce synergistic results. On the other hand, lack of diversity awareness and lack of respect for diversity can lead to negative synergy. Negative synergy is when two or more people working together produce less than what they could produce individually. According to Stephen R. Covey, author of *"The Seven Habits of Highly Effective People,"* negative synergy takes place when people do not respect and appreciate each other's differences. Stereotyping, prejudice, or biases about aging and other diversity characteristics negatively impact the society in many ways. One way is that human beings, as individuals, may not treat some people very well because of societal conditioning and faulty perceptions. Many people experience unpleasant and unjust incidents daily solely due to some readily apparent physical characteristics. These incidents are referred to as "daily indignities." Business leaders and educators must make sure that such unpleasant and unjust incidents do not exist in their classrooms and work environments.

The Society for Human Resource Management (SHRM) reported in 2008 in its Workplace Forecast survey on the "Top Ten Trends" for 2008-2009:

1. Continuing high care of health cost in the United States;
2. Large numbers of "baby-boomers" (1945-1964) retiring at the same time;
3. Threat of increased health care/medical costs on the economic competitiveness of the United States;
4. Aging population;
5. Growing need to develop retention strategies for current and future workers;
6. Federal health care legislation;
7. Preparing organizations for an older workforce and the next wave of retirements;
8. Threat of recession in the U.S. and globally;
9. Labor shortages at all skills levels;
10. Demographic shifts leading to a shortage of high-skilled workers (Workplace Trends, Workplace Vision, SHRM, 2008, p. 3).

As one can discern from the preceding SHRM "trends" list, the aging of the population and concomitantly of the workforce is emerging as a very significant demographic change as well as challenge confronting the United States.

To corroborate the SHRM forecast, the American Association of Retired Persons (AARP) reported that in 2007 there were more than 80 million people aged 40 or older in the U.S. labor force. Moreover, the AARP cited Bureau of Labor Statistics projections that indicated an increase in this age category to more than 88 million people by 2015 (Neumark, 2008, p. iii). The AARP disclosed that based on its surveys eight in ten "boomers" have indicated that they expect that they will work to retirement. The obvious reason cited was the need for money, mainly caused by inadequate retirement savings, a lack of pension coverage, and economic uncertainty regarding investments. Yet other reasons cited were that work was fulfilling and stimulating "and often fun" (Newmark, 2008, p. iii). The AARP cited a Congressional Budget Office (CBO) study showing how financially beneficial it would be for older workers to continue working and to delay retirement. According to the CBO study, "...continuing to work and delaying receipt of Social Security benefits until age 70 would result in a social security benefit that is 90% larger than it would be if taken at age 62. The AARP also reported that "from 1990 to 2000, the share of the aged 20 and over population in the 45-64-year-old age range grew from about 26 percent to 31 percent...while that aged 65 and over will rise sharply (from 17 percent in 2000 to 28 percent in 2050). The two shares will approach equality by the middle of the century" (Neumark, 2008, p. vii). Furthermore, census data indicates that by the year 2030, nearly 20% of the population will be age 65 or older, compared with about 12% in 2000 (King, 2008). The *Wall Street Journal* reported in May of 2009 that the April labor data revealed that workers aged over 65 accounted for almost 17% of the workforce, which is the highest monthly figure since 1971 (Evans, 2009). A major concern in the U.S. is that the retiring of the "baby-boomers" will leave a gaping hole in the workforce. To illustrate, approximately 80 million "baby-boomers" will be leaving the U.S. workforce in the next 15 to 20 years; and by 2010, the U.S. is expected to confront a shortage of about 10 million workers (Lee, 2008). For example, the Connecticut Department of Labor found that the number of retirement age Connecticut residents is projected to increase 72% by 2030, while the age bracket between 30 and 65 is expected to decrease 4%. Between 2003 and 2006, the percentage of Connecticut jobs held by workers at least 62 years of age increased 16%, whereas that of workers between 25 and 34 years of age declined by 6% (Soule, 2007). Health care organizations had the highest percentage of workers age 62 or older as of 2006 at 14.3% (Soule, 2007).

As one can see, the challenge for businesses will be immense. Educational institutions, governments, corporations, leaders, managers, and communities are now recognizing the necessity of valuing diversity to remain competitive in today's complex global world of business. Since the current workforce is indeed demographically diverse, leadership and management techniques underscoring inclusion are imperative. Creating an inclusive environment and eliminating the "exclusive world" of bias and stereotypes are necessary for an effective workplace. Managers must create an inclusive work environment for people of all ages, characteristics, and differences.

Keep Them Talking and Laughing

Workers, as they get older, tend to have better interpersonal and reflective skills. This is why older workers and senior citizens tend to be better speakers, better listeners, and better overall communicators. As a matter of fact, many older individuals enjoy talking with and listening to others. For example, National Public Radio's Susan Stamberg did an interview with a former interpreter to see why she is at the center of so many conversations. According to Susan Stamberg (2005), Miss Lilly is a senior citizen who thinks seniors have much to offer the world based on their years of experience, interpersonal relationships skills, and very effective listening abilities. As such, Miss Lilly's goal is to get strangers to talk with one another whenever she can. If there are to be "designated smoking" areas throughout airports and other public areas, then why not, she asks, have designated "talking areas" where people can just talk with each other? Miss Lilly has the advantage of speaking at least four languages based on the needs of others as she speaks English, German, Dutch, and her native Hungarian. She can also converse in Spanish. Miss Lilly is in France, which is said to be a nation of talkers. According to Stamberg (2005), in Paris intense one-on-one conversations take place everywhere, all the time. To a "foreign ear" this sounds like pigeons cooing. In the Luxembourg Gardens, perhaps the most beautiful park in Paris, a small white-haired woman sits in the sun inviting conversation. She holds a sign in her lap that reads "Hello! Let's talk." Miss Lilly wants people to talk to each other. She suggests that people avoid conversations related to religion and politics since these two subjects are the cause of much war, animosity, and hatred in the society. Perhaps, she is saying that senior citizens and older workers tend to be great listeners and, overall, good communicators. As such, it is best that they use such capabilities and speak with others who need to just talk. Of course, business leaders and managers can create an infrastructure for their older workers to have time for "idle" conversations which can serve as networking opportunities and better interpersonal relationships among all workers. Certainly, there are productivity benefits to the organization when workers speak openly and have strong bonds with each other. As a matter-of-fact, many "older" individuals now continue to work for its fun, write interesting books, get involved in their favorite hobbies, and stand up for good causes in the society, and they do all this way after their retirement age.

At the ripe age of 88 years, Phyllis Diller published a memoir and appeared in the film *The Aristocrats*. As related by Simon (2005), there was a recent documentary focused on her last stand-up act. Even at this age, retirement has not dulled Diller's sharp wit as she continues to make people laugh and enjoy life's wonderful insights. According to Phyllis Diller and many other comedians, "you know you are old when":

- You bend down to tie your shoe laces, and you wonder "what else can I do while I am down here."
- Your walker has its own airbag.
- They discontinue your blood type.
- Someone compliments you on your shoes, and you are barefoot.
- Your favorite drink is prune juice.

Cultural Challenges Associated with Aging

Cultural and generational differences convey themselves in various forms. For example, in the Afghan culture people respect and cherish age and older individuals. Accordingly, older workers and older members of the community often serve as coaches, mentors, and advisors in settling disputes and guiding major decisions. Many Afghans tend to view the progression of life as a continuum of beginning, growth, and ending with the latter part being the most valuable due to the impact of accumulated experience. Perhaps, this mentality comes from the spiritual lessons of continuous development each day, as many Afghans believe that "if today one is not better than yesterday then a whole day has been wasted." The accumulated lessons of many days and years cannot be gained through quick or unrealistic expectations. As such, age has its value; and there is no effective substitute for life's learning experiences. However, despite the fact that aging is inevitable, the old age is not necessarily something that many American people look forward to as they grow up. Another way to look at it is how people view the ending of movies. In the Afghan culture, it is not rude to tell others what happened in a movie that they just saw, while in the United States, discussing the end of a movie is plainly not recommended unless both parties have seen the movie. Perhaps people in Afghanistan see movies for enjoying the process of reflecting on what leads to the ending, while Americans may have a tendency to see movies with the expectation of a "surprise ending." Whatever the case or differences with regard to old age, education and training are not always good substitutes for years of personal experience and intrinsic reflections.

The Society for Human Resource Management (SHRM, 2002) stated that the education system in the United States has failed to deliver graduates who are perceived to be qualified to successfully enter and meet the demands of today's labor market. Consequently, more and more organizations are trying to retain, recruit, and hire senior citizens because of their skills and accumulated knowledge. Many of the best firms in the world are in search of wisdom, particularly the type of wisdom that comes with age and experience that made people at first successful. Plato, the ancient Greek philosopher, said: "It gives me great pleasure to converse with the aged. They have been over the road that all of us must travel and know where it is rough and difficult and where it is level and easy." The demand for the aged and wise, especially with corporate, management, and leadership experience, is thus on the rise. While there seems to be a long-term trend to a global decrease in the labor supply, there is a rise in demand for experienced workers. Jamrog and McCann (2003) mentioned that about 43% of the civilian labor force will be eligible for retirement by 2013. Therefore, there will be a shortage of talented and skilled professionals that accompany top leadership.

It is thus evident that the pace of change in today's post-industrial organizational environment is increasing. These changes are dynamic and evolutionary, yet not always predictable. Such evolutionary and dynamic changes can include or be caused by the increase in mergers, downsizing, flattening of organizational structures, increased globalization of businesses, increased complexities dealing with cultural and gender differences, increased aging or longevity of the population, and an increase in the number of employees working past the retirement age. These changes have created added responsibilities for managers who now have a significantly more diverse generation of employees with varied cultural backgrounds. While managers attempt to juggle an overwhelming number of changes, priorities, and demands on their time, developmental activities for the aging workforce often have fallen to the bottom of the priority list, even though developing these experienced employees has been found to be a key factor in maintaining an organization's strategic advantage, and thus such efforts are critical to developing a learning, and earning, organization.

The United States has a diverse population of over 300 million diverse individuals. A culture's perspective on aging in the United States can be seen from "American" comedy. The comedian, George Carlin, used aging in his comedic appearances, and he related:

> If you're less than 10 years old, you're so excited about aging that you think in fractions. "How old are you?" "I'm four and a half!" You're never thirty-six and a half. You're four and a half, going on five! That's the key. You get into your teens, now they can't hold you back. You jump to the next number, or even a few ahead. "How old are you?" "I'm gonna be 16!" You could be 13, but hey, you're gonna be 16! And then the greatest day of your life . . . you become 21. Even the words sound like a ceremony . . . YOU BECOME 21. . . YESSSS!!! But then you turn 30. Oooohh, what happened there? Makes you sound like bad milk. He TURNED, we had to throw him out. There's no fun now, you're just a sour-dumpling. What's wrong? What's changed? You BECOME 21, you TURN 30, then

you're PUSHING 40. Whoa! Put on the brakes, it's all slipping away. Before you know it, you REACH 50 . . . and your dreams are gone. But wait!!! You MAKE it to 60. You didn't think you would! So you BECOME 21, TURN 30, PUSH 40, REACH 50 and MAKE it to 60. You've built up so much speed that you HIT 70! After that it's a day-by-day thing; you HIT Wednesday! You get into your 80s and every day is a complete cycle; you HIT lunch; you TURN 4:30; you REACH bedtime. And it doesn't end there. Into the 90s, you start going backwards; "I was JUST 92." Then a strange thing happens. If you make it over 100, you become a little kid again. "I'm 100 and a half!" May you all make it to a healthy 100 and a half!!

Such views, expressed by certain "American" comedians, are associated with aging and are common in the United States. They are representative of how the "American" society feels about aging; and as such youthfulness is valued, and "older age" is not. These mindsets are causing an increasing number of the aging "baby-boomers" to constantly search for the "fountain of youth" when in reality there is no such panacea. Nonetheless, such societal views tend to impact the workplace since senior executives and managers that make hiring decisions do come from the society, but they do not always "check" such mindsets and stereotypes associated with aging "at the door." This societal conditioning is like personal traveling luggage that accompanies a person from one airport to another, and from one hotel to another, and finally back home. Unlike one's luggage, stereotypes and biases do not become lost, at least not automatically. They must be consciously replaced by appropriate new "luggage" or new "paradigms and mindsets."

The "American" culture seems to be obsessed with youth (Kelly, 2003), as can be seen from the increasing number of cosmetic surgeries and by the fact that members of the media are fully capitalizing on such obsessions in their ads and marketing, advertising, and selling efforts. Such youth-mindedness is also accompanied by a concomitant negative perception of aging in the society, which includes the workplace. While many of the Asian cultures value and respect older individuals (both in their personal and professional lives), "Americans" view aging from a negative perspective as if it was a "bad" thing. These negative perceptions tend to convey the message that older workers are not able to keep up with new technology or new ways of doing things because they are not open minded. Besides the perception of not being open-minded, older workers in the American society are seen as: deadwood, incompetent, closed-minded, un-trainable, and less productive (Kelly, 2003). Of course, these are stereotypes and myths that are not factual; and individuals disproving these myths are obvious and ubiquitous in today's workplace. Nonetheless, such views tend to put older individuals at a huge disadvantage as they attempt to compete in the job market with their younger counterparts. Moreover, young "Americans" tend to have this "unearned privilege" or "unearned advantage" of being young that comes to them naturally but at a severe cost to "older workers." This focus on youth, according to the Academy of Management article by Santora and

Seaton, is woefully short-sighted "…in the face of overwhelming evidence that older people (over the age of 60) are more active and more fit than ever before, and are living longer as a result of better health care. So why should older people, a talented and experienced segment of the population, be eliminated from the workplace when there is a tremendous need for highly qualified, committed, and motivated employees" (2008, p. 103)?

Unearned Advantages and Culture

With regard to "unearned advantage," young people are also affected in ways that are very subtle. The term often used to refer to this concept is *unearned privilege*. *Unearned privileges* are advantages given to some individuals and withheld from others, without regard to their efforts or abilities, because of their perceived differences. Every individual falls into a group/club based on his or her age, gender, body size, skin color, culture, ethnicity, race, and other characteristics. If one's group has large numbers or power and prestige, one fits right in the middle of the curve, that is, right in the "norm." Those people in the norm have some privileges that those outside the norm do not have. In real life terms, they get a little boost, a leg-up, a "bennie," or a little extra. This does *not* mean that life is handed to them on a "silver platter" and they do not work hard. Despite the fact that they work hard for what they get, in addition to that effort, they may still get a little boost. The paradox is that they do not even know it. When told of it, they might even disbelieve it. When one is in the "norm" one thinks that is the way it is *for everybody*. It is not!

The existence of unearned privilege for younger workers can lead to increased tension, stress, and frustration because it usually comes at a cost to others, which in this case are older workers. Sometimes, the society automatically affords one an unearned privilege because one falls in the norm (for a specific characteristic such as age, gender, or body size), and sometimes one may have to work harder because the society is not structured toward one's needs. It is helpful to focus on something other than age to demonstrate unearned privilege. For example, society structures everything for right-handed persons, which means that left-handed individuals have to function in a right-handed world. The school desks, manufacturing machines, scissors, doorknobs, and other necessities of life are usually built for right-handed individuals. Many people can think of their own characteristics that have earned certain privileges without any effort or work on their part. For example, being a male can have certain advantages as well as certain disadvantages. Also, being "short" or "vertically challenged" can have many advantages, but at other times many disadvantages. In the case of age in the "American" society, it is an advantage until one gets to be an "older worker." During young age, people enjoy "unearned advantages/privileges" and tend to lose them as they become older. Unearned privilege is a subject that requires deep and introspective thought, but one can conclude that those who have unearned privileges are seldom aware that they have it. Those who do not have the privilege are very much aware that they do not have it. Unearned privileges are very subtle in society and such advantages can create tension, stress, and frustration in diverse environments. When people are aware of such advantages, they can personally assist in making sure another person is not impacted negatively at work. So, refuse accepting privileges that one has done nothing to earn (that is, if one is ever offered a job simply because one is young when a more deserving person who happens to be an "older worker" did not get it because of his/her age), and become a "cultural" ally for those who are not in the norm. Sometimes when one thinks about the magnitude of the challenges that exist in the society, one may feel that he or she cannot make a difference. However, educated and trained individuals can make a difference by becoming cultural allies when they see instances of unfair employment practices in the workplace. Companies should expect their leaders and managers to be allies in the workplace in order to eliminate age discrimination. As one becomes more culturally competent with regard to age discrimination, one will find more and more opportunities to be a cultural ally. *Cultural ally* refers to those individuals who intervene or intercede in order to stop mistreatment or injustice from occurring to other individuals. Such mistreatments can be as subtle as age discrimination toward "older workers" that cannot be seen, but nevertheless are very widespread in the "American" workplace. So, one solution for eliminating age discrimination is for everyone to personally become a cultural ally, which will eventually replace the stereotypes with the truth about "older workers."

It may not always be obvious to some people how important older workers are to the economy and businesses; yet older workers contribute immensely to the success of not only the United States, but also to other countries of the world too. In a national survey, older workers were found to possess the following qualities: functioning well in crisis; possessing basic skills in writing, reading, and arithmetic; loyal; "solid" performers; and good interpersonal skills (Harvey and Allard, 2002). Older workers have various talents that are vital to many businesses in the world today; and those skills are not just restricted to multinational or huge corporations only, but they also apply to smaller and specialized organizations. For example, a company by the name of Vita Needle, in Needham, Massachusetts, manufactures stainless steel tubing and needles, and has a reputation of employing mainly older workers, with an average age of 35. This company hires older workers because utilizing older workers is part of its core competency. There are certain qualities that the older workers possess that fit into the goals and policies of the company. When the President of the company, Fred Hartman, was interviewed by Tom Brokaw, of NBC Nightly News, he said that the primary reason he continuously recruits older workers was because the assembly of their metal components was done by hand, and older employees were "extremely conscientious employees: loyal, dedicated, aware of quality requirements, and very reliable" (Harvey and Allard, 2002). Another example of a company that has benefited immensely from managing older employees is the Aerospace Corporation in El Segundo, California. The company has a "Retirement Transition Program" which makes available to its highly skilled employees four different options, namely: 1) pre-retirement leaves of absence, 2) part-time status working towards retirement, 3) post-retirement employment based on consultancy, and 4) post-retirement in the form casual employment.

Daily Indignities in the Workplace

Thinking back to one's life experiences, one will recall that all people, at some point in time, have undergone experiences when they were treated differently because of age, physical differences, and other such characteristics. While all have experienced unfair treatment and behavior at one time or another, one surely can see how some individuals in society may be exposed to this type of treatment on a more consistent basis. In fact, some individuals may experience such unfair treatment on a daily basis. This unfair treatment is called *daily indignities,* that is, negative things that individuals do or say to or about one another on a continuous basis, because of their biases and perceived differences.

These daily indignities are demonstrated in many different forms, and age discrimination is one of them. Several documentaries have been created that show these various forms of daily indignities or discrimination. These documentaries depict various forms of discrimination in actual work and daily life situations. Typically, two people, called "testers" are used. The testers are equal in all characteristics except the chosen "discriminatory" one, like age, appearance, skin color, or gender. Usually the testers are sent to a location to check on public response to a diversity characteristic in real life settings, such as applying for a job, buying a car, or making a major purchase, using the services of an employment agency, renting an apartment, and shopping in a store. An example of such a documentary that focuses on age discrimination is titled *"Age and Attitude,"* which was aired several times to national and international audiences on ABC's "Prime Time" in the 1990s. The *Age and Attitude* documentary focused on discrimination based on age and attitude. In this documentary, a single male tester assumes two identities. He is "made up" to be a 27-year old candidate (named Joseph) and a 53-year old candidate (named Michael) seeking employment. Michael, the older tester, possesses slightly better job qualifications than Joseph. They enter into identical employment opportunity situations with the following results. The 27-year old tester consistently received various employment offers, even though the 53 year old tester possessed better qualifications. In one instance, the older tester is told during the interview, "this is a young boy's game!" When the employers were confronted and asked to explain these results, they could not offer any logical explanation as to why the younger tester was consistently offered the employment opportunity over the older tester. Some of these decisions may be attributed to the myth that older workers are more "sickly," not as committed, and will not stay with the company as long. Once again, facts prove these myths are all false! Based on the authors' and their colleagues combined years of corporate, management, and educational experience throughout Afghanistan, Jamaica, Turkey, Thailand, the Bahamas, and the United States, associates over the age of 40 tend to be much more experienced and oftentimes more dependable than younger associates who are in their early twenties. They also tend to be mature, more "customer savvy", loyal, honest, quality focused, relationship oriented, and skilled in positive interpersonal communication. Nonetheless, data shows that age discrimination is such an integral part of "American" society that it is even more difficult to detect than either racial or gender discrimination. It is also a fact that older workers (over 40) usually require 64% more time to obtain employment than their younger counterparts. It should also be mentioned that discrimination did not occur every time in this *Age and Attitude* documentary; and that some of the discrimination might have been unintentional; and it is possible that some of the discrimination that occurred was not because of the particular characteristic being tested. However, such forms of age discrimination are prevalent in the United States and, as will be seen, are widespread in the workplace.

Summary

This chapter first discussed the increasing diversity of today's workforce and the concomitant challenges confronting managers who must manage such a workforce in a culturally changing environment. The chapter then addressed two thought-provoking and difficult subject matters – "unearned advantages," which may be predicated on culture, and "daily indignities," which may be suffered by many employees in the workplace. The chapter discussed ways for managers to deal with these two aforementioned problematic areas. The chapter also examined the roles that culture, values, and morals play in decision-making. This chapter revealed one very evident point; that is, in the future, organizations and businesses will have to learn how to manage and deal with an increasingly diverse workforce, including workers who keep growing and learning even as they get older.

Questions for Discussion

1. Discuss the impact of the trends of an aging workforce, as well as retirement, especially of the "baby-boomers" in the United States.
2. What is meant by the term "cultural competency" and how does it relate to managing a diverse workforce in a global economy?
3. What are some of the cultural challenges associated with aging, particularly in the workplace, and how can and should these challenges be met and overcome?
4. What are some of the "unearned" advantages and privileges of being "young" in the "American" culture, and how can they adversely affect the workplace?
5. How can age become a "daily indignity" in the workplace, and how can and should such an indignity be dealt with by management?
6. How does one balance and treat conflicting cultural perceptions of age and aging, and especially clashing views on older workers?

CHAPTER 4

LEGAL ANALYSIS OF AGE DISCRIMINAITON IN EMPLOYMENT

In the global business environment of the 21st century, effective management of personnel enhances internal business relationships, perceived career success, organizational commitment, overall job performance, and the reduction of turnover. The United States surely possesses the most extensive and comprehensive body of laws against discrimination of all types in employment. Other countries, however, perhaps because they are composed of more homogeneous peoples, may not have felt the need to develop anti-discrimination legal schemes. Yet, in certain other countries, the laws actually may require discrimination based on religion or national origin, if certain characteristics are synonymous with a particular religion, especially an official "state religion," or a dominant ethnic group which controls a country. The global business person must take into account all such laws that govern the employment relationship. This understanding must encompass not only the laws of his or her own country, but also the overseas application of his or her country's laws, as well as the laws of the host country. This chapter, therefore, provides a detailed explication of the U.S. Age Discrimination in Employment Act (ADEA) and other age discrimination laws. The chapter also discusses the nature and role of the Equal Employment Opportunity Commission in implementing and enforcing age discrimination laws in the United States. The substantive and procedural aspects of an age discrimination lawsuit are addressed as well as the defenses thereto. The extraterritorial reach of the ADEA and certain global legal perspectives on age discrimination are also presented in the chapter.

The Law of Age Discrimination in Employment – An Overview
The global workforce evidently is becoming older. In the United States, for example, in 2007, the Bureau of Labor Statistics reported that there were 76.9 million people in the workforce who were age 40 or older (Grossman, 2008). More people are living longer, and working longer – by either choice or, particularly in today's uncertain economic times, necessity. The increasing age of the workforce, the presence of age bias in society generally, together with the fact that the consequences

of unemployment fall more harshly on older people, make the topic of age discrimination in employment a very significant one - legally, ethically, and practically. Moreover, as "older" employees get even older, their pension and health care costs concomitantly increase for their employers, thereby making older employees attractive targets for workforce "downsizing." Furthermore, not only are older employees disadvantaged in their efforts to retain employment, but also to regain employment when they are discharged from their jobs. Weak economies today also adversely affect older workers more harshly, particularly since, when business is not good, employers may feel compelled to reduce the number of their most "expensive" employees, who are typically their oldest workers. Moreover, in a "tight" economy, older workers are the ones most likely to have a more difficult time to secure a job, let alone a comparable job, after they have been "downsized." Today, therefore, many older workers are remaining in the workforce; and the projections are that the percentage of older workers in the workforce will expand. In the United States, the *Miami Herald* (Sherman, 2008) reported on a study by the American Association of Retired Persons that the percentage of people 65 and older who continues to work has grown from 10.8% in 1985 to 16% in 2007. Moreover, for people aged 55 to 64, the numbers have increased from 54.2% in 1985 to 63.8% in 2007. The topic of dealing with older workers in the workforce, particularly as the workforce ages, therefore, emerges as a very important legal subject matter indeed.

In contrast to intentional age discrimination, covert discrimination exists against older employees, which seems to be subtler in nature; and human resource managers should be aware of such subtle forms of discrimination. Further research has revealed that unintentional "code words" often are used during the interview process, such as "we're looking for go-getters" and people who are "with-it" to describe desirable employees. Generally, "buzzwords" seem not to apply to people who are seasoned and experienced, just "old." However, as will be seen, the phase "over-qualified" may be a pretextual code word indicating age discrimination intent. According to a *U.S. News and World Report* article (Clark, 2003), titled "Judgment Day," about two thirds of all U.S. companies use performance as at least one factor when deciding whom to lay-off during "tough" economic times. Many firms use the "forced ranking" system since executives like this process because it seems to be the "fairest and easiest way to downsize." Unfortunately, "older workers" seem to get the "worst of it" as larger portions of them lose their jobs possibly due to biases and because they earn more income and earn more benefits compared to their younger counterparts. For example, in 1999, Ford wanted to increase diversity in its work environment and change Ford's culture to be more change oriented while embracing new technology, and new markets. As such, Ford created a new performance appraisal process for its 18,000 salaried, white-collar employees whereby supervisors were required to give a yearly grade to each of their subordinates of A, B, C (Jones et al, 2002). If an employee received a C, that employee could not receive a pay increase and if this happened two years in a row, the employee was either demoted or fired. In 2000, the management told the supervisors to give only 10% "A"s, 80% "B"s, and 10% "C"s in their overall performance appraisals. The following year it was the same except 5% was moved from C (5%) to B (85%). The new process supposedly negatively affected some older managers, since it has been a very negative experience with 42 employees filing two class action lawsuits against Ford claiming that the new process was used to terminate older managers. Their attorney had suggested that Ford stereotypically assumed that older workers were slow to change or learn "new" things, and consequently tried to diminish their numbers. In another situation, Schering-Plough, a New Jersey based firm, was ordered to pay one of its ex-employees the amount of $435,000 in punitive damages and $8 million in compensatory damages based on evidence that his managers engaged in age discrimination by firing him (Jones et al, 2002). This employee, named Maiorino who was a salesperson, had worked for the company about 35 years and had several times been commended for his sales performance. While in his 60s, Maiorino had repeatedly declined enticements of early retirements. Then, he reported that management had instituted unfair practices against him to make him look "bad" on paper, and to build a "paper trail" to justify firing him. These unfair practices included very difficult tasks, higher standards than others were held to, and being spied on (Jones et al, 2002). The company had his direct boss meet him at dinner, and gave him his termination letter. Some of the former customers who sided with the employees actually boycotted the company for such unfair labor practices.

Unfortunately, age discrimination in the workplace impacts people of all sizes, races, colors, religions, and ethnicities. Segrave (2001), in his textbook titled *Age Discrimination by Employers,* wrote that consistently from country to country, it is apparent that age discrimination in employment creates difficulties, and begins earlier for women. Such discrimination, which can be highly unethical and totally illegal in the United States, is causing many managers anxiety, and is forcing many of them to court. One of the greatest fears of company officials and individual managers is the likelihood of either being sued for something they have done intentionally or unintentionally, or for something they should have considered doing but did not. It is no secret that age-related lawsuits are proliferating, and more recently age related claims have been on the rise due to layoffs, which seem to be targeting older workers. Juries often side with aggrieved employees, even if the evidence is flimsy. Because of these trends, companies and their managers are realizing the need to protect themselves by periodically reviewing workforce diversity and analyzing the workplace for latent signs of discrimination (Administration on Aging, 2001). Facts show that it is imperative that older workers are kept in the workforce as long as possible since there will be a shortage of skilled labor starting as soon as the next few years when the economy improves and if eligible older workers decide to retire early (Harvey and Allard, 2002). The importance of protecting older workers, therefore, is a topic of enormous importance not only in the U.S. but also globally.

United States Anti-Discrimination Law

The Civil Right Act of 1964 is the most important civil rights law in the United States. This statute prohibits discrimination by employers, labor organizations, and employment agencies on the basis of race, color, sex, religion, and national origin. Regarding employment, the scope of the statute is very broad in scope, encompassing hiring, apprenticeships, promotion, training, transfer, compensation, and discharge, as well as any other "terms or conditions" and "privileges" of employment. The Act applies to both the private and public sectors, including state and local governments and their subdivisions, agencies, and departments. An employer subject to this Act is one who has 15 or more employees for each working day in each of 20 or more calendar weeks in the current or preceding calendar year. One of the principal purposes of the Act is to eliminate job discrimination in employment (Cavico and Mujtaba, 2008). The focal point of this work is Title VII of the Civil Rights Act, which deals with employment discrimination.

Discrimination, in employment or otherwise, can be direct and overt or indirect and inferential. Typically, there are two types or categories of employment discrimination claims against employers involving the hiring or promotion of employees. The first theory of recovery is called "disparate treatment," which involves an employer who intentionally treats applicants or employees less favorably than others based on one of the protected classes of color, race, sex, religion or national origin. The discrimination against the employee is intentional and purposeful, and thus the employee needs to show evidence of the employer's specific intent to discriminate. However, intent to discriminate can be inferred. So, for example, when the employee is a member of a protected class, such as a racial minority, and is qualified for a position or promotion, and is rejected by the employer while the position remains open, and the employer continues to seek applicants, then an initial or prima facie case of discrimination can be sustained (Cavico and Mujtaba, 2008). The "disparate treatment" analysis was articulated by the U.S. Supreme Court case of *McDonnel Douglas Corp. v. Green* (1973) and modified by *Community Affairs v. Burdine* (1981) and *St. Mary's Honor Center v. Hicks* (1993). The analysis for a "disparate treatment" claim involves a shifting burden of proof as follows: (1) first the complainant must put forth credible evidence to establish a *prima facie* case of discrimination; (2) then if such evidence is established, the defendant employer must then articulate, through admissible evidence, a legitimate, nondiscriminatory explanation reason for its actions; and finally, (3) the burden then shifts to the plaintiff to establish that the employer's proffered reason is a pretext to hide discrimination (HR Guide, 2009; Cavico and Mujtaba, 2008; *McDonnell Douglas*, 1973, pp. 802-04; *Burdine*, 1981, pp. 252-56).

The other legal avenue claimants may travel to prove their employment discrimination claims is called "disparate impact," or at times "adverse impact." This legal doctrine does not require proof of an employer's intent to discrimination. Rather, "a superficially neutral employment policy, practice or standard may violate the (Civil Rights Act) if it has a disproportionate discriminatory impact on a protected class of employees. Such a practice will be deemed illegal if it has a disproportionate discriminatory impact on a protected class and the employer cannot justify the practice out of business necessity" (Cavico and Mujtaba, 2008, p. 501).

Disparate impact as a legal doctrine was first solidified in case law by the U.S. Supreme Court case *Griggs v. Duke Power* (1971), where facially neutral but mostly irrelevant pre-employment tests administered by the employer had a disparate impact on African-American applicants. The court articulated the public purpose of the "disparate impact" doctrine, to wit, to correct past societal wrongs against minorities; and in ruling against the employer, the court stated: "It was to achieve equality of employment opportunities and remove barriers that have operated in the past to favor an identifiable group of white employees over other employees. Under the Act, practices, procedures, or tests neutral on their face, and even neutral in terms of intent, cannot be maintained if they operate to "freeze" the *status quo* of prior discriminatory employment practices" (*Griggs,* 1971, pp. 429-430). When explaining the justification for the "disparate impact" theory, the court stated "good intent or absence of discriminatory intent does not redeem employment procedures or testing mechanisms that operate as "built-in headwinds" for minority groups and are unrelated to measuring job capability" (*Griggs*, 1971, p. 433). Twenty years later, the Civil Rights Act of 1991 was enacted, and this law included a provision codifying the prohibition on disparate impact discrimination articulated in the *Griggs* case. The 1991 statute indicated that "an employee could prove his/her case by showing that an individual practice or group of practices resulted in a disparate impact on the basis of race, color, religion, sex, or national origin, and that the employer had failed to demonstrate that such a practice was required by business necessity" (Cavico and Mujtaba, 2008, p. 527).

The United States certainly has a very well developed corpus of law governing the employer-employee relationship, most notably the Civil Rights Act, which among other provisions prohibits discrimination in employment based on certain protected categories, such as race, color, gender, national origin, and religion. For years, however, there has been significant disagreement in the governmental, legal, and academic communities regarding whether U.S. employment discrimination laws apply abroad; and if so, which laws, and how so. These questions certainly are more than "academic" for U.S. business managers operating in an increasingly competitive global economy. For example, how can a U.S. firm conduct business in a country that actually may legally require discrimination in employment against women or people of a certain religion or national origin, if the U.S. firm is under legal enjoinment pursuant to U.S. civil rights laws to treat all its employees equally and thereby not to discriminate?

The United States today is only one of a small number of countries that afford comprehensive legal protection against discrimination in employment. Title VII of the Civil Rights Act of 1964 prohibits discrimination in employment on the basis of race, color, religion, sex, and national origin. The Age Discrimination in Employment Act of 1967 added age as a protected category. The Americans with Disabilities Act enacted in 1990 extended these protections to employees with disabilities. U.S. federal law and the Equal Employment Opportunity Commission are not the only "players" in the U.S. anti-discrimination scene. As a federal system, the states in the United States can have, and do in most cases, comparable bodies of anti-discrimination law as well as regulatory administrative agencies. Also note that in the United States most state anti-discrimination agencies work in conjunction with the Equal Employment Opportunity Commission so discrimination claims can be handled in an efficient and effective manner. Furthermore, the states may provide greater legal protections than the federal government and federal laws do (Labriola, 2009). In addition, there are significant sanctions that confront the foreign as well as the U.S.

firm that intentionally violates U.S. anti-discrimination laws, including the payment of monetary damages, the reinstatement of the adversely affected employee, and the payment of attorney's fees and costs. These legal protections safeguard the employees of "covered" U.S. firms in the U.S. as well as the employees of foreign multinational firms in the U.S. The crucial questions, of course, are whether these important U.S. legal protections extend overseas to safeguard U.S. citizens working abroad for U.S. firms as well as the foreign employees of the U.S. firms in the host country.

The U.S. Age Discrimination in Employment Act of 1967

The purposes of the U.S. Age Discrimination in Employment Act (ADEA) are to promote the employment of older persons based on their ability and not their age, to prohibit arbitrary age discrimination in employment, and to assist employers and employees to find methods to meet the problems arising from the impact of age on employment. The law recognizes the grave problems resulting from age discrimination against older workers, particularly long-term unemployment, as well as the burden that age discrimination places on commerce and the free flow of goods and services. One important objective for the promulgation of the ADEA was the elimination of age discrimination against older job applicants. It was believed that the elimination of age discrimination in employment would reduce long-term unemployment of older workers, thereby diminishing poverty among the elderly.

The ADEA is a federal law which prohibits an employer from failing or refusing to hire a protected individual, or discharging an employee within the protected age category, or otherwise discriminating against such individuals, because of their age regarding compensation and the other terms and conditions of employment. The ADEA specifically makes it an illegal employment practice for an employer to refuse or fail to hire a person, or to discharge an employee, or to otherwise discriminate against any person, with respect to compensation, terms, conditions, or privileges of employment, including hiring, firing, promotion, layoff, compensation, benefits, job assignments, and training, due to this person's age. Moreover, it is illegal for an employer to limit, segregate, or classify its employees in any way which would deprive a person of employment opportunities or otherwise adversely affect a person's status as an employee because of such person's age. The ADEA applies to employers that have twenty or more employees, including state and local governments and the federal government. The statute also applies to employment agencies and labor organizations. Job applicants are also protected by the statute. The ADEA covers hiring, termination, compensation, as well as other terms and conditions of employment. The term "employee" is defined very broadly under the statute. As one commentator noted, the statute "...does not...define the term 'employee' with specificity. The circular statutory definition – an 'individual employed by any employer' – is broad enough to be almost meaningless without interpretation by regulation or case law" (Labriola, 2009, p. 371). The statute extends protection to public as well as private sector employees; however, the employees or persons in order to be protected must be at least 40 years of age. There is no upper level age limit to the statute's coverage. In 1986, the U.S. Congress removed the upper age limit in the statute, which had been 70, almost entirely. Although the

ADEA offers protection only to workers 40 years or older, it must be noted that a number of states in the United States, including Florida, Maine, Alaska, Maryland, and Mississippi, have their own employment discrimination laws that do not specify any age limit. The ADEA defines "employer" as a "person" involved in an industry affecting commerce with twenty or more employees for each working day in each of twenty or more calendar weeks in the current or a preceding calendar year. A "person" is defined as one or more individuals, a partnership, an association, a corporation, or a labor organization, among other entities and relationships. Pursuant to the ADEA, when discrimination is found and there is evidence that the employer has acted in a willful and intentional manner, the aggrieved employee may be awarded "liquidated" damages of double the salary he or she was deprived of due to the discrimination. Moreover, in some states, such as California and Ohio, plaintiff employees who prevail may be awarded potentially much more lucrative "punitive" damages if the employer acted in a bad faith or malicious manner. The ADEA also applies to employment agencies and labor organizations. Note, however, that in 1996, the U.S. Congress amended the ADEA to permit public employers to discriminate on the basis of age in the hiring and mandatory retirement of law enforcement officers and firefighters. Originally the ADEA protected workers aged 40 to 65; then the upper limit was raised; and eventually it was removed; but with no changes to the lower age limit. However, there are many states that have a lower age limit, ranging from age 21 to specifying no age (that is, workers of all ages are protected). As noted by the American Association of Retired Persons it its 2008 report, "*Reassessing the Age Discrimination in Employment Act*," "these state laws parallel the current evolution of age discrimination legislation in Europe" (Neumark, 2008, p. 23).

It is important to note that the ADEA does not bar the termination of older employees; rather, the Act only bars discrimination against them. Accordingly, an employer can defend an ADEA lawsuit by establishing that an employment decision was based on reasonable and legitimate non-discriminatory reasons other than age, such as poor performance. Moreover, despite the connection between age and high salary, the ADEA does not automatically prohibit the discharge of a highly paid or compensated employee solely based on financial considerations. Employers thus are allowed to save money by eliminating highly paid positions; however, each employment decision must be handled on an individualized, reasonable, and fair basis; and consequently any "blanket" rules that would adversely affect older employees could trigger an ADEA lawsuit. Finally, an employer may involuntarily retire an employee who is at least 65 years old and who has been employed during a two year period in a legitimate executive or high level policy-making position, and who is immediately entitled to an enumerated employer-financed pension. As a result of such rules, U.S. firms, pursuant to the influence of U.S. civil rights laws, might move more in the European direction of an expectation of lump sum buyouts for older workers when their jobs end, typically called "early retirement buyouts."

The Equal Employment Opportunity Commission (EEOC) is a federal government regulatory agency empowered to make anti-discrimination laws in the form of administrative rules and regulations pursuant to civil rights laws enacted by the U.S. Congress as well as to enforce civil rights laws, including the ADEA. The

EEOC, in December of 2008, enunciated an important ruling regarding health benefits for retirees. The EEOC ruled that employers now can reduce or eliminate health benefits for retirees when they turn 65 years of age and thus become eligible for Medicare. The new policy permits employers to create two classes of retirees, one with more comprehensive health benefits for employees under 65 years, and another class with more limited benefits, or no benefits whatsoever. The rationale for the rule was to assist employers to provide and to continue to provide health benefits to employees. Of course, employers in the U.S. are not yet required by federal law to provide any health benefits to employees, either active or retired. This new EEOC policy thus establishes another explicit exemption from the ADEA for employers that now can scale back or eliminate benefits for workers over 65 years of age. Moreover, under the rule, employers can, if they choose, provide health benefits only to those retirees who are not yet eligible for Medicare; and retiree health benefits can be changed, reduced, or eliminated when a retiree, former employee, becomes eligible for Medicare. Also, employers now can reduce or eliminate health benefits provided to spouses and dependents of retired employees 65 years of age or older, regardless of whether the benefits for the retiree are changed. The rationale is that active employees and retirees under 65 have a greater need for health benefits since they typically are not eligible for Medicare; and that this new EEOC policy gives employers the flexibility they need to provide such coverage. In June of 2007, the United States Court of Appeals for the Third Circuit, in the case of *AARP v. EEOC*, ruled that the Equal Employment Opportunity Commission could implement the exemption to the Age Discrimination in Employment Act, thereby allowing employers to alter, decrease, or eliminate health benefits for retirees who reach the age of Medicare eligibility (Kaczorek, 2008). The EEOC had proposed this exemption after many employers began to eliminate retiree health benefits in order to avoid liability for age discrimination. Although employers are not required to provide retiree health benefits, many older persons in fact rely on this coverage in order to meet their health care needs. Consequently, according to one commentator, by allowing the EEOC to effectively repeal a portion of the ADEA, the court has undermined legislation that protects against age discrimination (Kaczorek, 2008).

Job Advertisements and Employment Applications
Although most ADEA claims are brought as wrongful discharge lawsuits, rather than in hiring situations, there are two age-related hiring problem areas for employers to be concerned with: 1) job notices and advertisements and 2) pre-employment inquiries during the job application process. Regarding the former, as a general rule, the ADEA makes it illegal for an employer to include age preferences, limitations, or specifications in job notices or advertisements. For example, a help-wanted notice that contains terms and phrases such as "age 25 to 35," "young," "college student," or "recent graduate" will be construed by the EEOC as violations of the ADEA unless an exception applies. The rationale is that the use of such "young" expressions will deter the employment of older persons. Regarding pre-employment inquiries during the application process, the ADEA does not specifically forbid an employer from asking about an applicant's age or date of birth. The

employer actually can state in an advertisement or application for the applicant to state his or her age or date of birth. However, any age-related pre-employment age inquiries will be very closely scrutinized to ensure that the question was made for a legitimate purpose, and not to improperly discriminate against an applicant based on his or her age. The concern with age questions is that they not only might indicate intent to discriminate based on age, but their mere asking may deter older workers from even seeking employment. The employer is also advised to tell the applicant the question regarding his or her age is for a permissible purpose and not one proscribed by the ADEA.

Finally, it is interesting to note the relationship between age claims and appearance-based discrimination claims. Regarding the latter, as noted, it is a general rule of law in the United States that there is not a discrimination claim for appearance discrimination since the appearance is not a protected category under federal civil rights laws. Thus, for a victim of appearance discrimination to prevail, he or she must somehow connect the appearance discrimination to another impermissible form of discrimination, such as race, color, gender, disability, and of course, especially for the purposes herein – age. There is, quite logically, a relationship between appearance and age since physical attributes change with age. Moreover, this relationship is strengthened due to the fact that most people make the assumption that advancing age correlates to a deterioration in physical appearance. Therefore, a claim that a person was not hired due to an aged appearance would not work as a "pure" appearance claim, but might be successful as an age discrimination case if the plaintiff could demonstrate that he or she was not hired because the employer felt that he or she looked "too old."

Non-Retaliation Provision

The ADEA also has a non-retaliation provision. The statute makes it unlawful for an employer to retaliate against an employee for opposing employment practices that discriminate based on age, or for instituting any age discrimination complaint, testifying, or participating in any manner in an investigation, proceeding, or legal action pursuant to the ADEA. Although the non-retaliation provision in the ADEA applies only to the private sector, the U.S. Supreme Court in 2008 ruled that non-retaliation protections in the statute apply also to federal government employees.

The Equal Employment Opportunity Commission

The ADEA, as noted, is enforced in the U.S. by the federal government regulatory agency – The Equal Employment Opportunity Commission (EEOC). The EEOC is permitted to bring a lawsuit on behalf of an aggrieved employee, or the aggrieved employee may bring a suit himself or herself for legal or equitable relief. In either case, the ADEA provides the right to a jury trial. The number of older workers has steadily increased in the United States over the past decade. Similarly, over the past decade, the number of age discrimination claims filed with the EEOC has been increasing too. It also again must be stressed the ADEA is a federal, that is, national law. Since the U.S. is a federal system, it accordingly must be noted that almost all states in the U.S. have some type of anti-discrimination age law – law, moreover, which may provide more protection to an aggrieved employee than the federal law does.

According to EEOC, for the fiscal year 2008, which ended September 30, the agency received the unprecedented number of 95,402 workplace discrimination claims, which represented a 15% increase from the previous year; and charges based on age discrimination and retaliation saw the largest annual increases (EEOC Press Release, 2009). To compare, for the 2004 fiscal year, the Commission received 17,837 charges of age discrimination; resolved 15,792 age discrimination charges; and recovered $60.0 million in monetary benefits for charging parties and other aggrieved individuals (not including monetary benefits obtained through litigation). The Equal Employment Opportunity Commission reports that age discrimination claims are still a major factor; however the percentage of such claims declined in the mid 1990s compared to previous data. However, it did increase again in the turn of the new century. One reason for this decline in the mid 90's is attributed to the over 40 population as being one of the fastest growing demographic segments in the United States. Age discrimination settlements and jury awards are substantially higher than those awarded for race, sex, or disability cases. Individuals claiming discrimination based on age were awarded an average of $219,000 compared to the low to mid $100,000 for race, sex, and disability (Mujtaba *et al*, 2003). An increasing number of corporations have been accused of age discrimination in the years 2001 to 2003 since there have been many layoffs due to the downturn of the economy. Even before the downturn of the economy, there were accusations of age discrimination by major corporations. For example, in 1997, First Union Corporation, a major banking institution agreed to pay $58.5 million to 239 former employees to settle an age discrimination suit, and Continental Airlines paid between $7 and $8 million to 207 employees (Steinhauser, 1998). Kelly (2003) states that many employers in the past few years have reduced their operating costs and the number of their employees by specifically targeting highly compensated employees that, more often, tend to be the "older workers." To illustrate a local example, the Ft. Lauderdale *Sun-Sentinel* newspaper reported in April of 2009 that in Broward County, Florida, for the fiscal year 2008, age discrimination claims filed with the EEOC increased by 21% from the previous year (Pounds, 2009).

The EEOC, which administers the ADEA, provides updated information on charges of age discrimination cases that have been filed with them. For example, Table 1 provides some of the data and these statistics that show a rise in age discrimination cases during the recent years. Further updated information and data can be retrieved from the Equal Employment Opportunity Commission's website (www.eeoc.gov/stats/charges.html) which is compiled for each year. While reviewing the EEOC data on July 25, 2005 for a longitudinal observation, it showed that the percentage of race related charges has decreased between 1992 (from 40.9%) and 2004 (to 34.9%). The percentage of charges filed on the basis of religious discrimination has increased from 1.9% in 1992 to 3.1% in 2004, showing a huge increase. Similarly, the number of complaints or charges related to Title VII has progressively and steadily increased from 14.5% in 1992 to 25.5% in 2004. At the same time period, the data revealed that the percentage of sex, national origin, and disability related charges had remained very similar from 1993 to 2004 with small changes in between the years. While age related charges have increased, many managers still may remain skeptical, and thus believe that age discrimination is not a major problem. Yet, the data shows that it really is, since such discrimination adversely impacts people of all races, ethnicities, body sizes, genders, and disabilities.

Table 1 – Age Discrimination Charges (EEOC Data, 2005)

Year	Charges of Age Discrimination Filed with EEOC	Percentage of Total EEOC Charges
1992	19,573	27.1%
1993	19,809	22.5%
1994	19,618	21.5%
1995	17,416	19.9%
1998	15,191	19.1%
1999	14,141	18.3%
2000	16,008	20.0%
2001	17,405	21.5%
2002	19,921	23.6%
2003	19,124	23.5%
2004	17,837	22.5%

Table 1.1 – Age Discrimination Charges (1999-2009)

	FY 1999	FY 2000	FY 2001	FY 2002	FY 2003	FY 2004	FY 2005	FY 2006	FY 2007	FY 2008	FY 2009
Receipts	14,141	16,008	17,405	19,921	19,124	17,837	16,585	16,548	19,103	24,582	22,778
Monetary Benefits (Millions)*	$38.6	$45.2	$53.7	$55.7	$48.9	$69.0	$77.7	$51.5	$66.8	$82.8	$72.1

Retrieved on January 12, 2010 from: http://www.eeoc.gov/eeoc/statistics/enforcement/adea.cfm

The Wall Street Journal (Levitz and Shishkin, 2009) reported the most recent discrimination data from the EEOC. The paper reported that age discrimination allegations by employees are at a "record-high," increasing 29% to 24,600 claims filed for the year ending in September 2008, which figure was an increase from the 19,103 claims filed in 2007 (Levitz and Shishkin, 2009, p. D1). The *Wall Street Journal* also noted that employment discrimination claims overall had increased, now also at a "record high," totaling 95,402, which represented a 15% increase (Levitz and Shishkin, 2009, p. D1). The paper underscored that the "most dramatic" increase in complaints to the EEOC was in the age discrimination category (Levitz and Shishkin, 2009, p. D1). Data also was provided by the EEOC in March of 2008. As reported by

HR Magazine, the agency's annual report of private sector discrimination charges "painted a disheartening picture" (Grossman, 2008, p. 63). There were 83,000 discrimination claims filed with the EEOC in 2007, which represented the largest one year increase since 1993; and age discrimination charges, which numbered 19,103, had, as characterized by *HR Magazine*, the "dubious distinction" of increasing the fastest, with a caseload 15% greater than the prior year (Grossman, 2008, p. 63). However, it should be noted that more than six times the number of people in 2007 complained of race discrimination than age discrimination. *HR Magazine* provided a list of factors contributing to the dramatic rise in age discrimination claims to the EEOC:

- Greater awareness of the law.
- An increase in the number of U.S. workers who in fact are protected by the ADEA (50% of the workforce according to the Bureau of Labor Statistics).
- The percentage of older workers continuing to rise as "baby-boomers" age through their work lives.
- A faltering economy which is compelling many employees who had intended to retire to extend their time in the workforce (Grossman, 2008).

However, despite the prominence and power of the EEOC, it is constrained by the large caseloads and limited resources, as all government agencies are, but also by delimited legal leverage. It is important to note that as of 2008 the EEOC only had 200 attorneys to service the whole country (Grossman, 2008). The agency, as will be seen in detail in the next section, has the power to investigate and to mediate and conciliate claims, as well as to make critical findings of "reasonable cause" for discrimination and to bring such a case to the courts. Yet the agency does not have the authority to render final legal judgments on the merits of a case or to impose financial or other sanctions on behalf of aggrieved employees. *HR Magazine* (Grossman, 2008) also provided data indicating the number of claims filed with the EEOC, the treatment, and the resolution thereof. In 2007, the EEOC found "reasonable cause" in 629 age discrimination cases; the agency's general counsel filed 32 lawsuits, with the majority alleging discriminatory discharge. Overall, in 2006, the EEOC filed 383 lawsuits for all types of discrimination claims. Of these, 339 ended in consent decrees or settlements and 11 were resolved by voluntary dismissal; and of the 33 cases actually resolved by court orders, the EEOC prevailed nine times. Regarding age discrimination charges resolved in 2007, 79% were resolved by a finding of no reasonable cause and administrative closure; and 21% resulted in merit resolutions for the complaining employee. Moreover, in 2007, the EEOC found reasonable cause in just 3.9% of the age discrimination cases investigated. In addition, in 2007, 46% of age discrimination claimants were layoff or discharge cases, 15% regarded the "terms and conditions" of employment, 11% were harassment cases, 8% hiring, 7% discipline, 6% promotion, 4% wages, and 3% were demotion. Finally, for all types of discrimination cases in 2007 which were resolved through settlement and conciliation, the EEOC collected $66.8 million, which represented an average of $4,140 for every claim filed. One illustration of a settlement of an age discrimination case mentioned by *HR Magazine* was the 2005 Sprint Nextel case, which involved

1,697 former employees who were subject to a lay-off, and which was settled for $57 million (which, as emphasized by *HR Magazine*, also resulted in the plaintiffs' attorneys "walking off with a cool $19.4 million in legal fees") (Grossman, 2008, p. 70.) On the state level in the United States, the Academy of Management published an article discussing an Ohio State University study of 12,000 age discrimination claims filed with the Ohio Civil Rights Commission from 1988-2003. The study indicated that termination was found to be the most frequent method to base an age discrimination claim (used in 66% of the cases), followed by age harassment (12%) and exclusion from hiring (10%) (Santora and Seaton, 2008, p. 104).

Equal Employment Opportunity Commission Procedures

The ADEA allows any person who is aggrieved by a violation of the statute to institute a civil action in any court of competent jurisdiction for any and all legal redress which will effectuate the purposes of the ADEA. *HR Magazine* related the EEOC's initial, and very practical, procedures regarding the very large number of discrimination claims the agency receives:

> EEOC officials learn to cherry-pick from among the charges, looking for obvious winners, especially those that will have an impact beyond the complainant and, perhaps most important, generate publicity, serving as a deterrent....As complaints flow in, they're assigned to three baskets: Basket A, which contains potentially high-profile claims and those where discrimination seems apparent; Basket B, which holds claims that could go either way; and Basket C, which contains claims that don't look promising. When employers receive a charge, they are not told what basket it falls in. For cases in Baskets B and C, the EEOC generally offers parties a chance to settle through mediation (Grossman, 2008, p.66).

However, the right of any person to bring such a legal action will be terminated upon the commencement of a legal proceeding by the EEOC to enforce the rights of the employee pursuant to the ADEA. The ADEA specifies that for a legal action brought pursuant to the statute, a party is entitled to a trial by jury on any issue of fact in any lawsuit for the recovery of amounts claimed owing as a result of the alleged violation of the statute. However, no civil action can be commenced by a person pursuant to the ADEA until 60 days after a charge asserting unlawful age discrimination has been filed with the EEOC. Such a charge, moreover, must be filed within 180 days after the alleged unlawful discrimination occurred. In an interesting U.S. Supreme Court case in 2008, the Court ruled that if the EEOC makes a mistake in investigating employees' allegations of age discrimination and notifying the employer, the employees nonetheless are still allowed to pursue an age discrimination lawsuit against their employer. In the case at issue, the EEOC failed to notify the accused employer that several of its employees had filed a complaint alleging age discrimination against the employer. When the 60 day period transpired, the employees wanted to sue, but the employer contended that it had not been notified of the charges by the EEOC. The EEOC is legally obligated to notify employers of age discrimination charges since, during the 60 day period before an employee can file a lawsuit, the EEOC is supposed to resolve the dispute informally. In the Supreme Court case, the employees, who were couriers at FedEx, contended that their employer was discriminating against them because of their age when it adopted performance benchmarks that they would find difficult to meet. They consequently asserted that this policy was an attempt to force older workers out of the company before they would be entitled to receive employment benefits, and therefore this policy was in violation of the ADEA. The problem arose when one of the employees filed an informal "questionnaire" with the EEOC together with an affidavit specifying the allegation. Was the questionnaire with the affidavit a technical "charge"? If so, the EEOC had to notify the employer. The company argued that the couriers had no right to bring the lawsuit since the company had not been notified of the legal action and consequently had been denied an opportunity to resolve the dispute by means of informal mediation. "Charge" is not precisely defined in the ADEA; and the employee did not file a formal EEOC "charge of discrimination"; yet the EEOC should have notified the employer of the filing of the questionnaire, and should have commenced an investigation. The Supreme Court, nevertheless, allowed the employees to bring a formal lawsuit against their employer. Actually, regarding the procedural aspects of EEOC, the Supreme Court has articulated that the ADEA has to be "interpreted in a way that reflects the realities of the individuals who file charges with the EEOC. Specifically, these individuals are, for the most part, (1) unrepresented; (2) lay individuals; (3) not highly educated; and (4) cannot be assumed to have detailed knowledge of the ADEA statutes and regulations" (Schwartz, 2009, p. 692).

The Age Discrimination Lawsuit – Procedural and Substantive Elements

Employee's Initial or Prima Facie Case

When the EEOC finds "reasonable cause," it grants the aggrieved party a "right-to-sue" letter which allows the employee to proceed to the federal courts. The agency itself actually may go to court on behalf of the complaining employee, or the employee may also choose to be represented by private legal counsel. Regardless, in either situation, the *prima facie* case is the required initial case that a plaintiff employee asserting discrimination must establish. Basically, *prima facie* means the presentment of evidence which if left unexplained or not contradicted would establish the facts alleged. Generally, in the context of age discrimination, the plaintiff employee must show that: 1) he or she is in an age class protected by the ADEA; 2) the plaintiff applied for and was qualified for a position or promotion for which the employer was seeking applicants; 3) the plaintiff suffered an adverse employment action, for example, the plaintiff was rejected or demoted despite being qualified, or despite the fact that the plaintiff was performing his or her job at a level that met the employer's legitimate expectations; 4) after the plaintiff's rejection or discharge or demotion, the position remained open and the employer continued to seek applicants from people with the plaintiff's qualifications. These elements if present give rise to an inference of discrimination. The burden of proof and persuasion is on the plaintiff employee to establish the *prima facie* case of discrimination by a preponderance of the evidence. However, based on a 1996 Supreme Court case, *O'Connor v. Consolidated Coin Caterers Corp.*, it is not a necessary element to the plaintiff's *prima facie* case for the plaintiff to show that he or she was replaced by a person under 40 years of age, the ADEA minimum age. That is, the fact that one person protected by the ADEA lost out on a job opportunity to another person also protected by the ADEA is irrelevant, so long as the aggrieved party lost out because of age. Of course, as a practical matter, the fact that a person's replacement is substantially younger in age than the person replaced should emerge as a far more reliable indicator of age discrimination.

The Disparate Treatment Theory

"Disparate treatment," in essence, means intentional discrimination. That is, the employer simply treats some employees less favorably than others because of their age (or other protected characteristic). Proof of a discriminatory intent on the part of the employer is critical to a disparate treatment case. The plaintiff employee can demonstrate this intent by means of direct or circumstantial evidence; but the employer's liability hinges on the presence of evidence that age actually motivated the employer's decision. A disparate treatment case will not succeed unless the employee's age actually formed a part to the decision-making process and had a determining affect on the outcome. Of course, if the motivating factor in the employer's decision was some criterion other than the employee's age, then there is no disparate treatment liability.

Direct Evidence

Direct evidence is evidence that clearly and directly indicates the employer's intent to discriminate; that is, such evidence is the proverbial "smoking gun" that directly discloses the employer's discriminatory intent. In building a case, one commentator noted that "offering direct proof of motive in the form of ageist slurs or other incriminating behavior is a more common approach, and one that is likely to be more effective. Such evidence must, however, be evaluated on a case-by-case..." (Labriola, 2009, p. 380). An example of such direct evidence would be a memo to terminate all older men since they are technologically less knowledgeable and capable and resistant to technological changes. Illustrations would be statements that the employee is too old for certain work, or too old to make "tough" decisions, that the employee should be spending more time with his or her family, or playing golf or fishing, as well as constant questioning of the employee as to his or her retirement date and/or plans. Concrete examples of actual "ageist" language of a demeaning and derogatory nature that can provide evidence of discriminatory intent include: "that old goat," "too long on the job," "old and tired," and "he had bags under the eyes" (Quirk, 2008). Also evidencing an intent to discriminate are such "young bloods" remarks, such as "We need young blood around here," "Let's bring in the young guns" (Quirk, 2008), and the employee "needs special treatment because she is getting old"

(Pounds, 2009). In another case, the Second Circuit Court of Appeals found that allegations that two waitresses were repeatedly assigned to less desirable work stations and work shifts than younger wait-staff were sufficient to make out a claim for age discrimination. In the case, the employer made comments to the waitresses to "drop dead," "retire early," "take off all that makeup," and "take off your wig,'" thereby giving rise to a claim of age discrimination as well as a hostile work environment (Laluk and Stiller, 2008). In another Second Circuit case, the appeals court further noted that the probative value of the age comments does not depend on how offensive they were. For example, the fact that the supervisor's assertion that the plaintiff employee "was well suited to work with seniors" was not offensive; yet it was indicative of the supervisor's discriminatory intent. The court found that considering the supervisor's remarks in the context of all the evidence, the remarks were legally sufficient to sustain a reasonable inference that the supervisor was motivated by age discrimination in discharging the plaintiff employee (Laluk and Stiller, 2008).

Nevertheless, not every type of age insult will be found actionable by the courts (Labriola, 2009). Consequently, the further the discriminatory memo, remark, or comment is made from the time of discharge, the greater the risk that a court will brand it as a "stray remark," and thus find it too remote to qualify as direct evidence of discrimination (Labriola, 2009). Similarly, the more ambiguous and general the comment is, or the more the statement can be subject to varying interpretations, there exists less likelihood that a court will declare it direct evidence of age discrimination (Labriola, 2009). Another important factor in determining the viability of a statement as direct evidence of age discrimination is whether the statement was made by a decision-maker or a person with supervisory, managerial, or executive authority in a company or organization.

Circumstantial Evidence

Age discrimination is an intentional legal wrong. Since proof of this wrongful intent– discriminatory or otherwise - is notoriously difficult for a plaintiff to obtain, the courts at times permit discriminatory motive to be inferred from the facts of the case. Age bias can thus take the form of broad assumptions about "older" workers that cannot be shown to be supported by the facts. Examples would be oral or written statements that infer age bias, such as comments that older workers are "over qualified" or "computer illiterate" or reflect other negative assumptions. Another example would be when an employer discharges a successful and experienced older worker, and replaces him or her with a person with no or less experience or with different and lesser academic credentials. Other problematic situations would arise from suspicious timing of or even from the fact of differences in treatment, such as better treatment of similarly situated employees not in the protected class. Regarding the differences in treatment, if it is systematic and thus rises to the level of a pattern, or as one court said, a "convincing mosaic," the inference of age bias and deliberate discrimination is naturally much stronger. Burden-shifting is an integral part to a circumstantial evidence case. That is, the plaintiff employee must still make out his or her initial or *prima facie* case, and thus raise an inference of discrimination, but one that can then be rebutted. Next, in order to rebut this inference, the defendant employer must show that its policy or practice was based on an appropriate, legitimate, and non-discriminatory business reason. Examples would be poor performance, resistance to management, and failure to report to new managers or supervisors, or the need to match employees with positions that require a certain knowledge and skill-set.

The U.S. Supreme Court in 2008 made it somewhat easier for plaintiff employees to present circumstantial evidence of age discrimination by ruling that the federal district courts have the authority to allow what is called "me, too" evidence of age discrimination. Such evidence basically consists of supporting evidence from other employees at a company that they had been discriminated against because of their age. A key factor for a judge to decide whether to admit such evidence is whether the evidence of discrimination by the same or other supervisors or managers is closely related to the plaintiff's circumstances.

Pretext

In a circumstantial case, when the defendant employer does contend that its rationale was an appropriate, legitimate, and non-discriminatory business one, the plaintiff employee is allowed to show that the proffered reason was really a pretext for discrimination. Pretext means that the employer's stated reason was fake, phony, a sham, a lie; and not that the employer made a mistake or error in judgment or made a "bad" decision. A pretexual reason is one designed to hide the employer's true motive, which is an unlawful act of age discrimination. The courts accordingly have allowed the employer's explanation to be foolish, trivial, or even baseless, so long as the employer honestly believed it. The genuineness of the reason, not its reasonableness, is the key. The plaintiff employee bears the burden of showing that the employer's proffered reason was merely a pretext. The plaintiff employee, however, need not show the pretext beyond all doubt; he or she need not totally discredit the employer's reasons for acting; rather, he or she must provide sufficient evidence to call into question and to cast doubt on the legitimacy of the employer's purported reasons for acting. Providing such evidence of pretext allows the plaintiff employee to contend that the reason given by the employer for the discharge or demotion or negative action was something other than the reason given by the employer. The following types of evidence have been used by the courts to enable the plaintiff employee to demonstrate pretext: 1) disparate treatment or prior poor treatment of the plaintiff employee; 2) disturbing procedural irregularities or the failure to follow company policy; 3) use of subjective criteria in making employment decisions; 4) the fact that an individual who was hired or promoted over the plaintiff was obviously not qualified; and 5) the fact that over time the employer has made substantial changes in its proffered reason for the employment decision (Tymkovichfn, 2008).

However, there are limits as to what a court will accept as evidence of pretext. To illustrate, for many years, attorneys have encouraged employers to publish and widely disseminate written policy statements of their commitment to non-discrimination. Attorneys have argued that the published policies were an important defense tool in any subsequent lawsuit (Corbin and Duvail, 2008). In the 2007 case of *Hoard v. CHU2A, Inc. Architecture Engineering Planning,* the United States Court of Appeals for the Eleventh Circuit addressed the legal relevance of an employer's failure to have a published anti-discrimination policy, and concluded that the failure did not demonstrate that the employer's stated reason for its adverse employment action was pretextual. In *Hoard,* the plaintiff was an employee who was a fifty-eight year old man. He brought a lawsuit against CHU2A, alleging age discrimination as prohibited by the Age Discrimination in Employment. After an adverse district court decision, the employee, Hoard, argued on appeal that the absence of a published policy by the employer constituted adequate evidence of pretext. The district court entered summary judgment in favor of CHU2A because the court decided that Hoard failed to establish any evidence of pretext to rebut the employer's stated, legitimate, non-discriminatory reason for the adverse employment action taken against him. The appeals court summarily rejected the employee's contention and thus affirmed the district court's decision (Corbin and Duvail, 2008). Nonetheless, it is still very prudent – legally, morally, and practically – for an employer to have a written and communicated anti-discrimination policy.

Once sufficient evidence of pretext is shown, a judge may allow a jury, as finder of fact, to infer that the true reason for the action was improper age discrimination. The failure of the employer to give any reason – foolish or not – for the discharge of an older worker at the time of termination has been construed as evidence that the employer's asserted business reason, for example, allegedly poor performance, which was given much later, was merely a pretext for discrimination. The prudent employer is well advised, therefore, despite a certain management "prevailing opinion" to the contrary, to provide in a direct and unambiguous manner to a terminated employee, even an employee at-will, at the time of discharge, an appropriate business-related reason for the discharge, and to have a written record of the transaction.

The Disparate Impact Theory

Disparate impact discrimination means unintentional discrimination on the part of the employer. In a disparate impact case, the employer's policies and practices are neutral "on their face" in their treatment of employees, yet they fall more harshly or disproportionately on a protected group of employees; and they cannot be justified by legitimate, reasonable, and non-discriminatory business reasons. The disparate impact theory has long been a widely used and accepted means of establishing illegal discrimination under Title VII of the Civil Rights Act.

The U.S. Supreme Court in 2005 enunciated a major decision regarding age discrimination in employment in the case of *Smith v. City of Jackson, Mississippi* (2005). The decision expands the protection afforded older workers pursuant to the Age Discrimination and Employment Act. The decision allows protected workers, over the age of 40 to institute age discrimination lawsuits even when evidence is lacking that their employers never purposefully intended to discriminate against the workers on the basis of age. As a result, the decision substantially lessens the legal burden for employees covered by the statute by allowing aggrieved employees to contend in court that a presumably neutral employment practice nonetheless had an adverse or disparate or disproportionately harmful impact on them. However, the Court also allowed the employer to defend such an age discrimination case by interposing that the employer had a legitimate, reasonable, and job-related explanation for the "neutral" employment policy. The Supreme Court case initially was brought by older police officers in Jackson, Mississippi, who argued that a pay-for-performance plan instituted by the city granted substantially larger raises to employees with five or fewer years of tenure, which policy, the officers contended, favored their younger colleagues. The lower courts had dismissed the lawsuit, ruling that these types of claims were barred by the statute. The U.S. Supreme Court, however, in a 5-3 decision, ruled that the officers were entitled to pursue the age discrimination lawsuit against the city. Justice John Paul Stevens, writing for the majority, stated that the Age Discrimination in Employment Act of 1967 was meant to allow the same type of "disparate impact" legal challenges for older workers that minorities and women can assert pursuant to the Civil Rights Act. Yet Justice Stevens also noted in the decision that the same law does allow employers the legal right to at times treat older workers differently. It is important to note that pursuant to the Civil Rights Act, employers can successfully defend a disparate impact case only by showing the "business necessity" for a neutral but harmful employment policy, which is, it seems, a much more difficult test to meet than the "reasonable" explanation standard of the ADEA. In the Supreme Court *Smith* case, the defendant, City of Jackson, successfully articulated a reasonable factor other than age underlying is pay plan, namely reliance on seniority and rank. The City's decision to award larger raises to lower level employees in order to bring salaries in line with that of neighboring police forces was found to be a decision based on a "reasonable factors other than age" (RFOA) that was motivated by the city's legitimate objective of attracting and retaining police officers. Moreover, under the RFOA standard, it was not necessary, the Court ruled, for the City to consider whether the method it adopted was the most reasonable method of achieving its goals.

The U.S. Supreme Court's age discrimination decision emerges as a victory for older workers covered by the ADEA. Such protected workers now do not have to have direct or "smoking gun" evidence of intentional age discrimination in order to file a civil rights lawsuit; rather, all that is required is evidence of disproportionate harmful impact stemming from a neutral age employment policy. Employers, whether U.S. employers or foreign employers doing business in the United States, now must be much more conscious of the consequences of their employment policies on older workers, particularly regarding the criteria used to determine hiring, termination, especially layoffs, as well as pay scales and retirement plan changes. Employers also must be prepared to provide and explain the "reasonable" factors other than age that would justify the employment policy causing the disparate harmful impact on older protected workers. The Court's *Smith v. City of Jackson* case thus extended the "disparate impact" Civil Rights Act theory of Title VII to cases instituted under the Age Discrimination in Employment Act of 1967. Now, employees can challenge their employers' employment practices that have an adverse impact on protected older workers without having to prove that their employers intentionally discriminated against them. As such, the Court thus "opened the door" to plaintiff employees who could not demonstrate that their employees intentionally treated them unfavorably because of their age.

It is very important to be aware that a disparate impact case is materially different from a disparate treatment case. In a disparate impact case, the plaintiff employee need not prove an intentional act of discrimination by his or her employer in order to recover. In essence, the plaintiff employee will first have to show that there is a statistical disparity, and that younger and older employees are affected differently by the policy or practice; and then he or she will have to demonstrate that the challenged practice was based on age In a disparate impact case, moreover, the plaintiff employee cannot establish his or her initial case by pointing to a general policy of the employer that produced the disparate impact; rather, the plaintiff employee must isolate and identify the employer's specific age-motivated policies or practices that are allegedly responsible for any perceived disparities, and then link them to the disparity. That is, a close "nexus," or connection, must be established between the specific practice and any observed statistical relationship in order to prove illegal discrimination. It is important to note that in 2009 the U.S. Supreme Court made it even more difficult for a claimant to prove age discrimination. The Court in *Gross v. FBL Financial Services* ruled that age must be the key factor in the employment determination, as opposed to being a reason for the improper decision. The Court used the old common law, tort, "but for" test as the legal standard in a modern day age discrimination context; that is, the employee must show by a preponderance of the evidence that "but for" the illegal age discrimination the negative employment determination would not have occurred (Legislation, 2009). One commentator (Fleischer, 2009) noted that "this is a higher standard than that imposed on other victims of discrimination who must show that discrimination was a 'motivating or substantial factor' in the decision" (p. 7G). Therefore, even if the motivating factor is correlated with age, for example, in making pension plan or health care plan changes or engaging in a reduction-in-force to eliminate high salaries or reduce health care costs, which have a greater adverse impact on older employees, the employer can still avoid liability under the ADEA if the discriminatory age motivation was not the key factor in the decision. The result, according to one commentator (Fleischer, 2009), is that "since many older workers are paid more, they are let go because of their salaries. Proving age was the 'but for' reason for termination will be impossible because the employer will be able to point to the salary savings as the real motive" (p. 7G). This Court ruling thus provides further support for the employer because the federal courts have ruled that age and years of service or rank can be deemed to be "analytically distinct"; and consequently the employer can take cognizance of one while ignoring or downplaying the other. In such a case, the plaintiff employee must identify the specific aspects of the plan which in fact caused the disparate impact. Similarly, even though an employee's deteriorating level of competence may be related to his or her advancing age, the poor performance factor can be deemed reasonable and legitimate. Of course, the employer in such situations then should be able to distinguish these motivating factors, and then to demonstrate that the motivating factor, such as rank or years of service, or a legitimate concern with perceived too high salaries, or poor performance, was in fact the non-age-connected motivating factor and thus a "reasonable" one.

In June of 2009, the U.S. Supreme Court enunciated another very important decision dealing with the discriminatory effects of the "disparate impact" legal doctrine. Although the case was a race-based affirmative action one and not an age case, the decision is still significant for age discrimination claimants. In the case of *Ricci v. DeStefano* (2009), the Court decided by a 5-4 determination that the city of New Haven, Connecticut had discriminated against white firefighters in violation of Title VII of the Civil Rights Act of 1964. The court, in essence, ruled that the municipal governmental employer, the city of New Haven, had "over-corrected" its promotional policies in their attempts to avoid liability under a "disparate impact" theory. This decision will necessitate the re-evaluation of employers' hiring and promotional policies across the United States and has ramifications for not "merely" for race-based claims. The crux to this important case centered on the operative fact that the city of New Haven, Connecticut discarded the promotion test results for firefighters on which minorities had scored poorly. City officials contended that if the city did not discard the results the minority applicants would have sued the city. In New Haven, in 2003, 58 white firefighters, 23 blacks, and 19 Hispanics took the promotion tests to determine who would qualify as lieutenants and captains. Nineteen qualified for the positions, and thus were eligible for promotion. However, no blacks and only two Hispanics qualified. There were 15 slots to fill. The city's civil service board refused to certify the results, thereby obviating them and denying the promotions to all who had earned them. The city explained that it feared a disparate impact lawsuit civil rights lawsuit from the minority candidates. As a result, 17 white candidates and one Hispanic sued, claiming violations of their statutory rights under Title VII of the Civil Rights Act as well as constitutional violations pursuant to the Equal Protection clause. The lead plaintiff was Frank Ricci, who is dyslexic, and who said he studied for 8 to 13 hours a day for the test, and who also said he hired an acquaintance to tape record the study materials. The firefighters lost their case at the federal district court level and in the U.S. Court of Appeals for the Second Circuit. They then appealed to the U.S. Supreme Court, which reversed the lower court decisions.

Justice Anthony Kennedy, writing for the majority, stated that mere fear of litigation alone cannot justify an employer's reliance on race to the detriment of individuals who passed the examinations and qualified for promotions. Specifically, Justice Kennedy stated that there must be "a strong basis in evidence to believe it [employer] will be subject to disparate-impact liability if it fails to take the race-conscious, discriminatory action" (*Ricci*, 2009, p. 47). He further restated the district court's comment that *"the city rejected the test results because too many whites and not enough minorities would be promoted"* (*Ricci*, 2009, p. 37). Justice Kennedy also wrote: "Without some other justification, this express, race-based decision-making violates Title VII's command that employers cannot take adverse employment actions because of an individual's race" (*Ricci*, 2009, p. 37). Justice Kennedy generally explained the purpose of Title VII was to promote hiring on the basis of job qualifications rather than on the basis of race or color and its goal was to create a workplace free of discrimination where race was not a barrier to promotion. In the New Haven case, Justice Kennedy criticized the municipality's practice by stating that "the city rejected the test results solely because the higher scoring candidates were white." (*Ricci*, 2009, p 38). Justice Kennedy noted in his decision a contradiction in Title VII of the Civil Rights Act, promulgated by Congress in 1964, which prohibits intentional discrimination on the basis of race and other protected characteristics, and its 1991 amendment codifying the *Griggs'* "disparate impact" theory of recovery. Justice Kennedy concluded the majority opinion by explaining:

> No individual should face workplace discrimination based on race. (The city) thought about promotion qualifications and relevant experience in neutral ways. They were careful to ensure broad racial participation in the design of the test itself and its administration....The process was open and fair. The problem, of course, is that after the tests were completed, the raw racial results became the predominant rationale for the City's refusal to certify the results. The injury arises in part from the high, and justified, expectations of the candidates who participated in the testing process on the terms the City had established for the promotional process. Many of the candidates had studied for months, at considerable personal and financial expenses, and thus the injury caused by the City's reliance on the raw racial statistics at the end of the process was all the more severe (*Ricci*, 2009, pp. 59-60).

To be clear, the U.S. Supreme Court in the New Haven firefighter decision did not strike down the disparate impact doctrine on statutory or constitutional grounds. The disparate impact doctrine is thus still the "law of the land." Rather, the court invalidated the New Haven employment decision of discarding the tests by saying the city had violated Title VII of the Civil Rights Act of 1964. For an employer to throw out a test that has a disparate impact, the employer must have, said the court, "a strong basis in evidence" that the employer will be sued and lose a disparate impact lawsuit before discarding test results solely based on race. However, an employer will still be allowed to bring in racial considerations and the potential racial impact into the testing process, but now the employer must do so "during the test-design stage," said Justice Kennedy. In offering some guidance to business managers, Justice Kennedy wrote: "Title VII does not prohibit an employer from considering, before administering a test or practice, how to design that test or practice in order to provide a fair opportunity for all individuals, regardless of their race. And when, during the test-design stage, an employer invites comments to ensure the test is fair, that process can provide a common ground for open discussions toward that end" (*Ricci*, 2009, p. 47.).

Employer Defenses - Generally
The ADEA affords the employer certain statutory defenses to age discrimination lawsuits. An employer is allowed to take an action otherwise prohibited to comply with the terms of a legitimate employee benefit plan or a *bona*

fide seniority system (though generally a seniority system cannot require the involuntary retirement of employees). An employer is also permitted to justify a disciplinary decision or a discharge on grounds of "good cause." Furthermore, similar to Title VII of the Civil Rights Act, an employer is allowed to discriminate on the basis of age where age is a *bona fide* occupational qualification reasonably necessary to the normal operation of the particular business. Finally, and most significantly, the ADEA provides the employer a defense to an age discrimination lawsuit when the employer can demonstrate that the differentiation is based on "reasonable factors other than age." Of course, what is a *bona fide* occupational qualification as well as a reasonable factor other than age are difficult exceptions to define, and thus are often determined by the federal courts on a case-by-case basis. The EEOC itself cautions that no precise and unequivocal determinations can be made as to the scope of these defensive provisions. Finally, it should be noted that there is some debate in the legal community as to whether the "reasonable factors other than age" provision in the ADEA is a "safe harbor" provision totally precluding employer liability if applicable, or "merely" an affirmative defense that is provided to employers and, significantly, one that must be affirmatively asserted or lost. To be safe, the employer is well advised to treat the "reasonable factor" defense as an affirmative one. The ADEA also contains defenses for *bona fide* seniority plans and employee benefit plans.

The Bona Fide Occupational Qualification (BFOQ) Exception

The employer can also defend an ADEA lawsuit by interposing the *bona fide* occupational qualification doctrine (BFOQ). Pursuant to the BFOQ doctrine, the employer will be obligated to show that the challenged age criteria is reasonably related to the normal operation of the employer's business, and that there is a factual basis for believing that only employees of a certain age would be able to do the particular job safely or effectively. That is, the employer must demonstrate that all or substantially all persons excluded from the job in question are in fact not qualified due to age. Age certainly can be a relevant factor in certain jobs, and thus rise to the level of a BFOQ, such as in professional sports (Savage, 2008).

A job notice or advertisement which specifies or limits age is illegal pursuant to the ADEA; however, the employer may do so when age is demonstrated to be a valid BFOQ reasonably necessary to the normal operations of the business. Examples of the BFOQ would include airline pilots, police, firefighters, and bus drivers, as well as others for whom certain physical requirements are a necessity for efficient job performance. It must be underscored that with the BFOQ defense, the employer admits that age was in fact a factor in the decision to fire or to not hire, but the employer possesses a legally justifiable excuse for the need to rely on age. The BFOQ defense is a limited one, however. To prevail, the employer must demonstrate that it had reasonable factual cause to believe that all or substantially all of the older persons would be unable to perform the duties of the job in a safe and efficient manner. If the employer's rationale in interposing the BFOQ is the objective of public safety, the EEOC will require that the employer demonstrate that the challenged age restriction does in fact effectuate that public policy goal, and that no reasonable alternative exists which would better or equally advance the goal with a less discriminatory effect.

Courts, moreover, have construed the BFOQ defense narrowly in all civil rights cases, though the mandatory retirement of airline pilots has been upheld. The EEOC itself counsels that the exception will have only limited scope and application.

The Reasonable Factor Other Than Age (RFOA) Defense

The ADEA's significant "reasonable factors other than age" provision allows the employer to defend an age discrimination claim by demonstrating that "reasonable factors other than age" were the reason for the adoption of the employment policy or practice in question. That is, the employer can argue that age did not motivate the decision to fire or to not fire, but that another non-discriminatory reason, such as poor job performance, was the true reason behind its action. When this defense is raised against an individual claiming discriminatory treatment, the burden is on the employer to demonstrate that the "reasonable factors other than age" exist factually. This RFOA test emerges as a much more efficacious defense than the "business necessity" test under the Civil Rights Act. In the latter, the employer must ascertain whether there are other alternative ways for the employer to achieve its objectives without resulting in an adverse impact on a protected class; whereas in the former, the "reasonableness" inquiry does not encompass such a search for alternatives. So long as the "factor" is not improperly age-connected, is reasonable, and advances the employer's goals, such as financial considerations, it will be sufficient as a defense. The employer under the ADEA does not have to search for a less discriminatory alternative or even the "most reasonable" approach; rather "merely" a "reasonable" one will suffice for a defense. Furthermore, "reasonableness" does not encompass the employer's decision being absolutely necessary, or wise, or even a well-considered one – merely reasonable and non-discriminatory. The employer is even allowed to have "mixed motives"; that is, once the employer presents evidence of the "reasonable factors other than age," the employer's policy or practice will be validated legally even if age played a part in the promulgation of the policy or the implementation of the practice. However, in discharge situations, especially in a reduction-in-force, employers nonetheless must be careful of the criteria that they employ to retain and to terminate workers. Reasons and ratings based on specific skills and knowledge will be easier to sustain as objective and fair, but criteria that are subjective such as "flexibility" and "creativity" could be problematic for the employer as such "loose" standards could provide, or could be so construed by a jury as, a pretext for age discrimination (Savage, 2008).

Based on a federal Court of Appeals decision, once the employer interposed this "reasonable factor," the burden of proof was shifted to the plaintiff employee to disprove the employer's "reasonable factor" contention. However, in June of 2008, the U.S. Supreme Court, in a 7-1 decision, *Meacham v. Knolls Atomic Power Laboratory*, reversed the appeals court (*Meacham*, 2009). In a technical, procedural, yet very significant, victory for older workers, the Supreme Court placed on employers the burden of proving that a lay-off, reduction-in-force, or other presumably "neutral" job action that adversely impacts older workers was based not on age but on some other "reasonable factor." The case can be deemed a "significant" one because "it will be costlier and more difficult for employers to defend against age discrimination disparate impact claims" (Schwartz, 2009, p. 691). Nevertheless, age very well can be related to compensation; but if the employer's focus is to reduce or adjust compensation to meet "market demands," and the employer relies on such non-age factors as rank or years of service of compensation level, the employer may be acting reasonably, and accordingly could prevail in sustaining its burden. Moreover, unlike a Title VII case, it will be insufficient for the plaintiff employee to demonstrate that there exists other more reasonable and less discriminatory ways for the employer to achieve the same results. All a court has to do is to decide whether or not the employer's asserted "factor other than age" is a "reasonable" one. Once reasonableness is determined, a court's legal inquiry under this aspect of the ADEA is ended. The RFOA test, therefore, is a considerably lesser legal standard than the "business necessity" test for Title VII of the Civil Rights Act. Consequently, although the *Smith v. City of Jackson* decision on its surface seemed to considerably help employees pursue their age discrimination disparate impact claims, the Supreme Court did so by enunciating a legal standard that makes the successful pursuit of such claims very difficult. Furthermore, the Supreme Court's decision in *Meacham* "does not diminish the significance of the plaintiff having the burden of identifying the specific employment practice that is alleged to create the disparate impact" (Schwartz, 2009, p. 691).

The Older Workers Benefit Protection Act

The Age Discrimination in Employment Act was amended in 1990 by the Older Workers Benefit Protection Act (OWBPA). In addition to providing additional protection for employees' benefits, the OWBPA also deals with waivers. First, regarding waivers, the ADEA contains specific provisions that enable employees to give up their right to sue pursuant to the statute. Any employee waiver, however, must follow the specific criteria set forth in the 1990 amendment to the ADEA - the Older Workers Benefit Protection Act. OWBPA requires waivers to be knowing and voluntary and thus valid. Several requirements must be present for an employee's waiver of ADEA rights is legal. The waiver must be: 1) in writing and be understandable, 2) specifically refer to ADEA rights or claims, 3) not waive rights or claims that may arise in the future, 4) be in exchange for valuable consideration, 5) advise the person in writing to consult with an attorney before signing the waiver, and 6) provide the person with at least 21 days to consider the agreement, and at least seven days to revoke the agreement after signing it. Even though an employee may have validly waived his or her rights under the ADEA, such a waiver will not adversely affect the EEOC's rights under the statute. Second, regarding benefits, the OWBPA amended the ADEA to specifically forbid employers from denying benefits to older employees. However, in limited situations, an employer may be allowed to reduce benefits based on its employees' age, so long as the cost of providing the reduced benefits to older employees is the same as the cost of furnishing benefits to younger persons.

The Extraterritorial Effect of U.S. Employment Law

The globalization of the world's economy has resulted in employers assigning increasingly larger numbers of employees to international assignments. One initial issue that results from such globalization is the responsibility of multinational companies that operate in the United States. The general rule of law in such a case is that U.S. civil rights laws apply to multinationals operating in the U.S. or its territories to the same extent as U.S. employers. Employees are covered regardless of their citizenship or work authorization. Employees who work in the U.S. are protected by U.S. law whether they work for a U.S or foreign employer. The exception arises when the foreign employer is covered by an international treaty, convention, or other agreement that limits the full applicability of U.S. anti-discrimination employment law, for example, by allowing the foreign company to prefer its nationals over others for certain positions. Another important, and more problematical, employment discrimination issue concerns the rights of workers who are employed by a U.S. employer or by a foreign employer in a workplace in a foreign country. The difficult issue is whether the extensive U.S. legal protections afforded to employees in the U.S. carry overseas. This legal question typically is regarded as an issue of the "extraterritoriality" of U.S. law. A U.S. company that is "going global" thus must be prepared to face the legal as well as practical implications of establishing operations overseas, in particular the challenging situation when a company finds itself torn between obeying U.S. law and complying with the law of the host country.

The early, leading Supreme Court case ruling on the extraterritoriality of U.S. law was not an employment discrimination case, but rather dealt with federal anti-trust law. In *American Banana Company v. United Fruit Company* (*American Banana Company v. United Fruit Company,* 1909), although both parties to the dispute were U.S. citizens, the alleged violation of the Sherman Anti-Trust Act occurred in Panama. The Court unanimously ruled at the time that the Sherman Act did not apply to acts occurring beyond the borders of the U.S. Moreover, a majority of the court expressed reservations concerning even extending a statute extraterritorially. Another concern, raised by Justice Holmes writing for the majority, was that extending a statute extraterritorially would contravene the fundamental sovereignty principle of international law. *American Banana Company* consequently set forth the general rule governing extraterritorial jurisdiction; that is, a very strong presumption exists against the extraterritorial application of U.S. law. This presumption, furthermore, can be overcome only in exceptional instances.

The leading employment discrimination extraterritoriality case was the Supreme Court's 1991 decision in *EEOC v. Arabian American Oil Company* (*EEOC v. Arabian American Oil Company,* 1991). In the so-termed *Aramco* case, the Supreme Court was called upon to decide whether Congress intended to apply Title VII of the Civil Rights Act of 1964 to United States citizens working for U.S. companies in foreign countries. The Supreme Court, in a 6-3 decision, which affirmed the lower court's decision, ruled that Title VII did not reflect the requisite clear expression of U.S. Congressional intent to overcome the presumption against extraterritoriality of statutes. Consequently, the Court held that the protections of Title VII did not extend to a U.S. citizen working for a U.S. company overseas. The Court compared Title VII of the Civil Rights Act to the Age Discrimination in Employment Act, which as will be seen, was amended in 1984 by Congress so as to add provisions that specifically addressed conflicts with foreign laws, thereby revealing Congress' extraterritorial intent, which was "ambiguous" in the language of Title VII. The judicial limitation thereby expressed on the extraterritorial scope of federal law, absent a clearly stated statutory intention to the contrary, underscores the deference the courts give to sovereignty concepts and international law comity concerns that might be contravened if U.S. courts attempted to extend too broadly and intrusively U.S. law, especially labor and employment laws, to other nations. As the Court noted in *Aramco,* it is a "longstanding principle of American law that 'legislation of Congress, unless a contrary intent appears, is meant to apply only within the territorial jurisdiction of the United States,'" (*EEOC v. Arabian American Oil Company,* 1991, (quoting *Foley Bros. Inc. v. Filardo,* 1949). Very soon after the Supreme Court had ruled in the *Aramco* case, Congress attempted to overrule the decision by at least partially extending U.S. employment discrimination law overseas. Accordingly, the Civil Rights Act of 1991, as amended by the Civil Rights Act of 1991, was promulgated to protect certain employees of U.S. firms overseas. Congress thereby expressly amended and enlarged the scope of Title VII (as well as the Americans with Disabilities Act) to provide a clear indication of Congress' extraterritorial intent to reach U.S. business firms that operate outside the U.S. as well as those under the "control" of a U.S. entity.

The 1991 amendments to the Civil Rights Act expanded the definition of the key term "employee" to include any U.S. citizen employed by a U.S. company in a foreign country or by a foreign company that is controlled by a U.S. firm. Foreign employees working within the U.S. are protected, whether working for U.S. or foreign multinational firms, as are U.S. citizen employees, of course. However, and most significantly, outside the U.S., only U.S. citizens working for U.S. firms or firms controlled by U.S. firms are protected, since foreign employees working outside the U.S. were expressly excluded from protection when employed in a foreign country, even by a U.S. firm. Therefore, Section 109 of the Civil Rights Act of 1991 amended both Title VII and the Americans with Disabilities Act to extend certain extraterritorial protection to employees.

When the U.S. Congress has legislated with an explicit intent to have extraterritorial impact for U.S. law, the courts will recognize that intent. However, if there is a "gray" area, the courts can determine the legal result by judicial interpretation. Yet, even where there has been an express Congressional intention to have extraterritorial effect, the courts can interpret the law in a manner that allows defenses and qualifications. Accordingly, the courts developed three main defenses to allegations of employment discrimination overseas. These defenses are as follows:

- Was the discriminatory employment decision made by a foreign person not "controlled" by a U.S. employer?
- Does either Title VII of the Civil Rights Act or the ADEA conflict with the host country's laws, so that the U.S. employer confronts "foreign compulsion"? That is, would compliance with U.S. law violate the host country's laws?

- Does the performance of the job reasonably necessitate a particular characteristic, such as age, gender, or religion, thereby permitting the employer to interpose the standard *"bona fide* occupational qualification" defense to employment discrimination?

Since the 1991 amendments to the Civil Rights Act have made Title VII and the ADEA co-extensive in their extraterritorial protection, the courts have interpreted these seminal employment protection statutes with reference to one another. These post-amendment cases provide guidance generally on the nature of extraterritoriality, and specifically when extraterritoriality will be applied in a particular case.

An initial important legal issue is to determine who exactly is a U.S. employer. An employer will be deemed to be U.S. employer if it is incorporated or based in the United States or it if has sufficient connections to the United States. This critical determination is made on a case-by-case basis based on the following criteria: 1) the employer's principal place of business, that is, the primary place where its facilities are located; 2) the nationality of the company's dominant shareholders and/or those possessing voting control of the company; and 3) the nationality and location of the management of the company, including directors and officers. Another essential extraterritoriality legal issue is whether the foreign company is sufficiently controlled by a U.S. "parent" company, so as to be subject to U.S. anti-discrimination employment statutes. Determining exactly, however, the nationality of a business' controlling person or entity is a difficult undertaking. The ADEA initially declares that when an employer "controls" a corporation whose place of incorporation is a foreign country, any prohibited employment practices engaged in by such a corporation shall be presumed to be engaged in by the employer. The ADEA also holds that the protections of the Act shall not apply to the foreign operations of an employer that is a foreign "person" not controlled by a U.S. employer. The Act, finally, articulates four factors to determine the crucial corporation "control" test, which is applied on a case-by-case basis: (1) the interrelationship of operations; (2) the existence of common management; (3) the centralized control of labor relations; and (4) the common ownership or financial control of the employer and the corporation.

The application of the "control" test, therefore, is critical to determining whether these seminal employment anti-discrimination statutes will be enforceable against a foreign subsidiary of a U.S. "parent" corporation. If the foreign firm is not controlled by a U.S. company, then U.S. citizens employed overseas by the foreign company will not be protected by U.S. anti-discrimination laws; and these employees rather will have to seek redress pursuant to the labor and employment laws of the nation where the foreign firm was incorporated or does business. Therefore, a foreign firm as well as its putative or assume U.S. "parent" must consider whether, applying the four "control" criteria, it is sufficiently controlled by a U.S. multinational corporation.

The ADEA also has an explicit "foreign laws" or "foreign compulsion" defense which allows U.S. firms the legal "license" to discriminate in employment when the enforcement of U.S. discrimination laws would result in a violation of foreign law. This defense, usually called the "foreign laws" defense, means that a U.S. employer will not be liable if compliance with Title VII would cause the U.S. firm to violate the laws of the country where the workplace is located (*ALPA v. TACA*, 1985). An example of this "compulsion" defense is provided by the EEOC in its Enforcement Guidance, which states that an employer will have a "foreign laws" defense "for requiring helicopter pilots if employed in Saudi Arabia to convert to Moslem religion where Saudi Arabian law provided for beheading of non-Moslems who entered holy area" (EEOC Compliance Manual, 1993). Another example would be a U.S. employer operating in a foreign country that has a mandatory retirement law for employees working in that country. Similarly, the foreign country may have a law that forbids women from supervising men, thereby precluding a U.S. firm from promoting the most qualified person – a woman – to a managerial position. The degree of flexibility provided by this defense is well illustrated by the federal appeals case of *Mahoney v. RFE/RL, Inc.* (*Mahoney v. RFE/RL*, 1995), where the court ruled that when U.S. law would cause a U.S. firm to violate a foreign collective bargaining agreement (which technically is not even a law), the foreign compulsion defense nonetheless applies. It is important to emphasize that the U.S. federal court rejected the EEOC's view of the matter. The decision is noteworthy because in many countries the demarcation between legalistic law and social customs and practices is not as distinct as it is in the United States. What constitutes a "law" is an uncertain legal issue. Informal guidance or informal communications from the foreign government will be inadequate. Basically, a law must be a precept that exists in the country of operation, is generally applicable, mandated by the government of that country, and most likely must be explicitly codified in statute, case law, or government regulation. At a minimum, the EEOC will require that the employer who intends to use this defense state the specific source of authority on which relies on to constitute a foreign law. Of course, if there is a penal or other severe sanction to violating this law, such punishment will bolster the employer's foreign law defense.

The aforementioned *bona fide* occupational qualification defense explicitly arises from Title VII of the Civil Rights Act. The BFOQ defense has been deemed by the courts to have extraterritorial application too. Thus, pursuant to the BFOQ doctrine, an employer may engage in discrimination if certain characteristics are reasonably necessary to the normal operations of the particular business or enterprise. For example, in *Kern v. Dynalectron Corporation* (*Kern v. Dynalectron Corporation*, 1984) the court held that conversion to Islam was a BFOQ for a pilot flying helicopters to Mecca since non-Moslems flying into Mecca would be, if caught, beheaded.

The Age Discrimination in Employment Act first was amended by Congress in 1984 to make it applicable extraterritorially. The term "employee" was amended to include any individual who is a citizen of the U.S. employed by a U.S. employer or its subsidiary in a workplace in a foreign country. Unless a person is a U.S. citizen, he or she is not included in the definition of the term "employee" if he or she works overseas. That is, nothing in the ADEA, or the amendments thereto, or the courts' interpretations thereof, regulating age discrimination by U.S. firms against foreign nationals in foreign countries in a foreign workplace. The ADEA also has been interpreted by the courts not to cover foreign nationals when they apply in foreign countries for jobs in the United States (*Reyes-Gaoan v. North Carolina Growers Association,* 2001). Furthermore, it does not cover determinations by foreign employers regarding jobs in foreign countries, even if the applicant is a U.S. national in the United States, since the nationality of the employer and the location of the future work are the controlling factors (*Denty v. SmithKline Beecham Corporation,* 1997).

The Age Discrimination in Employment Act also protects U.S. citizens working overseas for a U.S. controlled foreign employer (*Morelli v. Cedel,* 1998). The ADEA provides that the prohibitions of the Act shall not apply where the employer is a foreign person not controlled by an U.S. employer; *Morelli v. Cedel,* 1998). "At a minimum," declared one court, "...the ADEA does not apply to the foreign operations of foreign employers – unless there is an American employer behind the scenes" (*Morelli v. Cedel,* 1998). The ADEA, therefore, does not apply to a foreign corporation operating outside the U.S. even when the foreign firm employs U.S. citizens unless a U.S. company controls the foreign corporation. Regarding the important "control" issue, the aforementioned four critical factors are specified in the Act; and thus are used by the courts in ADEA cases to determine control: 1) interrelation of operations; 2) common management; 3) centralized control of labor relations; and 4) common ownership or financial control of the employer and the corporation. The purpose of the statutory "control" element, according to one court, is to protect the principle of sovereignty; that is, "no nation has the right to impose its labor standards on another country". The Act, however, does protect employees working in the U.S. for a domestic branch of a foreign company

An exception to extra-territoriality also exists if the application of the Age Discrimination in Employment Act would violate the law of the other country where the workplace is located. This principle, as noted, termed the "foreign laws" or "foreign compulsion" defense, means that a U.S. employer will not be legally liable if compliance with the ADEA would cause the employer to violate the laws of the nation where the workplace is located. In one aforementioned ADEA case, the U.S. Court of Appeals for the District of Columbia ruled that where the U.S. law would cause a U.S. company to violate a foreign collective bargaining agreement, which technically could be argued as not equating to a "law," the foreign compulsion defense applied (*Mahoney v. RFEIRL,* 1995).

An employer in the United States whether a domestic or an international one must be aware of U.S. anti-discrimination employment law, such the ADEA, as well as the extra-territorial application of U.S. civil rights laws. At some point, everyone is going to be protected by the ADEA since everyone gets older, regardless of race, national origin, or gender. The all-encompassing nature of the ADEA distinguishes that law from all other anti-discrimination statutes. The class of protected people is very broad (Sherman, 2008). Yet the global business person must also be concerned with other legal jurisdictions' anti-discrimination law. The next section, accordingly, will provide some selected "global legal perspectives" of age discrimination law.

Global Legal Perspectives

The United Kingdom in 2006 promulgated its first law prohibiting age discrimination (Brettle and Dowling, 2007). The law is known as the Employment Equality (Age) Regulations (EEAR); and the law implemented a European Union "directive" that requires all member states of the European Community to ban age discrimination pursuant to their "local" laws. As pointed out in a 2007 article in the *Legal Report* of the Society for Human Resource Professionals (Brettle and Dowling, 2007), in some significant aspects the British law provides greater protection that the U.S. ADEA. First, similar to the U.S. law, the EEAR encompasses recruitment, hiring, training, promotions, benefits, and discharges. Also, the EEAR similarly prohibits intentional/direct discrimination as well as adverse/disparate impact discrimination. The EEAR similarly bans retaliation, which the British call "victimization" (Bretttle and Dowling, 2007). The EEAR, however, has broader coverage than the ADEA as it protects partners in any partnership and independent contractors. It is interesting to note that before the passage of the EEAR, employers in Britain were allowed to advertise age ranges in help-wanted advertisements (Brettle and Dowling, 2007). The EEAR now not only prohibits this practice, but also deems job advertisements that specify minimum experience levels as mandatory or even preferred criteria as "suspect." The rationale for the "experience" ban is that such requirements may have an adverse impact against younger workers (Brettle and Dowling, 2007). The preceding illustration is significant since it indicates that the EEAR protects not only the "old" but also the "young" from discrimination in employment. A difficult legal and practical problem could thus emerge in the United Kingdom, since employer policies that reward seniority, especially with regard to compensation and benefits, very well could have an adverse impact on younger workers. Such preferential seniority-based policies are of course permitted by the ADEA in the United States. The EEAR does have a BFOQ defense which may be broader than the one in the ADEA since the former allows discrimination based on age so long as it is "objectively justifiable as a proportionate means of achieving a legitimate aim" (Brettle and Dowling, 2007). The EEAR, moreover, does allow the employer to offer different pay and benefit scales so long as they are consistently applied, serve a legitimate business purpose, and produce some business benefit (Brettle and Dowling, 2007). Finally, similar to other European Community laws, the EEAR permits an employer to engage in mandatory retirements, typically at age 65, but the statute nonetheless imposes an affirmative obligation on the employer to consider an employee's continued employment beyond age 65 (Brettle and Dowling, 2007).

Turkey presents a most interesting case of the difference between the law of employment discrimination and the actual practices of business. The main anti-discrimination statute is the Labor Act of 2003. This law guarantees workers the "fundamental right to equal treatment" (Sural, 2009). This Act prohibits discrimination on the basis of race, sex, language, religion, political opinion, political belief, disability, union membership and the fixed-term or part-time nature of the work (Sural, 2009). However, the Act does not explicitly protect against age discrimination (Sural, 2009). Age is implicitly covered by the aforementioned "fundamental right to equal treatment" language in the statute as well as Turkey's "transposition" of the European Union's Directives against discrimination in employment (Sural, 2009, p. 260). In Turkey, based on the Labor Act, there are requirements for "equal employment opportunity" for personnel hiring, selection, and screening, including job advertisements, interviews, and tests. Moreover, Turkish employers assert that they support equality of opportunity, evidenced by recurrent expressions that employers are "Equal Opportunity" employers and/or employers who welcome applicants regardless of race, color, religion, gender, age, national origin, marital status, disability, etc). Nevertheless, three commentators (Bassim, Sesen, and Sessen, 2007), in a comparative analysis of Turkish and English job announcements, found that in the English newspapers examined they found no age limitations for employment applications; but in the Turkish ones they found 149 ads that contained age limitations for positions, and, moreover, that contained different age limitations for male and female applicants. The commentators also reported that in not one of these advertisements did the employers explain the reasons for the age and/or gender requirements for the positions. Finally, another commentator writing in early 2009 noted that "so far, there has not been a court decision specifying a contested discrimination as one on the basis of age" (Sural, 2009, p. 260).

The European Community's Social Charter sets forth twelve fundamental employment law rights, to wit: free movement, fair pay, improved working conditions, social protection, collective bargaining, vocational training, worker consultation and participation in management, health and safety protection in the workplace, protection of children and adolescents, protection of the aged, and protection of those with disabilities (Dowling, 1996). However, "The Social Charter and the social documents it spawned are virtually silent on the employment doctrine which worries the U.S. most: anti-discrimination law. With the conspicuous exception of sex discrimination, the European social agenda omits anti-discrimination protections for racial minorities, religions, and, notwithstanding the Charter rights protection, for the aged and handicapped, these groups as well" (Dowling, 1996, p. 77). The European Union, however, has issued a Directive to its members, called the Equal Treatment in Employment Directive, which seeks to address age discrimination in employment; but one commentator has criticized the Directive as a "minimalist approach" and "defective" because it only covers access to employment and does not cover training, education, and health care issues (Sargeant, 2004). Yet another commentator related that instead of proposing a ban on age discrimination, certain European Community legislators have proposed that employees should possess a presumptive right to be free of age discrimination, but also that employees should be afforded the freedom contractually to relinquish voluntarily that right (Sunstein, 2002).

The European Council of the European Union also has adopted a Directive (2000/78) which mandates that member countries adopt age discrimination civil rights laws. The Directive, it is important to point out, prohibits age discrimination regardless of age, instead of specifying that people over a certain age are protected. Thus both younger as well as older workers are protected from age discrimination in employment. Indeed, as noted by the AARP in its 2008 report, Reassessing the Age

Discrimination in Employment Act, "the United States appears to be rather unique in protecting older workers only" (Neumark, 2008, p. 24). The AARP also notes that "ironically, in light of their aging populations, despite some ambiguity it appears that the directive allows European Union members to retain mandatory retirement ages" (Neumark, 2008, p. 24).

Summary

This chapter examined the laws of age discrimination in the United States and in a global context too. This chapter, therefore, provided a detailed explication of the U.S. Age Discrimination in Employment Act (ADEA) and other age discrimination law. The chapter also discussed the nature and role of the Equal Employment Opportunity Commission in implementing and enforcing age discrimination law. The substantive and procedural aspects of an age discrimination lawsuit were addressed as well as the defenses thereto. The extraterritorial reach of the ADEA and certain global legal perspectives on age discrimination were also presented in the chapter.

The U.S. Age Discrimination in Employment Act was the primary legal doctrine reviewed in this chapter. The purposes of this statute were to promote the employment of older persons predicated on their capabilities and not their age, to prohibit arbitrary age discrimination in employment, as well as to assist employers and employees to find approaches to solve problems stemming from the impact of age on employment. This chapter in particular disclosed that the plaintiff employee's legal burden in the U.S. for establishing a successful case of age discrimination against his or her employer is a very challenging one indeed. Moreover, if the employee is suing under a disparate impact theory, he or she will be faced with the reality that the employer defendant need only produce evidence of "reasonable factors other than age" to justify, and thereby to sustain legally its employment policy or practice. The chapter indicated that the recent Supreme Court *Smith v. City of Jackson* case, although creating an expansion of potential employer liability under the ADEA, nonetheless also provides employers with a defense when they base their policies and practices on "reasonable factors other than age." United States multinational business firms, as well as foreign firms operating in the U.S., first obviously must be aware of U.S. civil rights law when conducting business in the United States. These firms also must be keenly aware of the important and far-reaching legal extraterritorial rule that a U.S. company that employs U.S. citizens anywhere in the world generally will be subject to a civil rights lawsuit if these employees are discriminated against based on the protected categories. These employees, moreover, can maintain a lawsuit in the U.S. for discriminatory employment conduct that occurs overseas. The BFOQ doctrine, although theoretically a defense, may not work in practice as a viable strategic approach for U.S. operations or U.S. employers operating abroad. Ascertaining ahead of time what is "reasonably necessary" for "normal operations" of the business is at best a difficult challenge. The chapter indicated that perhaps the BFOQ doctrine could be useful as a tactical defensive tool to the firm when it is attempting to defend itself after the fact; but the doctrine is simply too nebulous, and its use too hazardous, to be useful in international business employment determinations. This chapter also stressed the extraterritoriality of U.S age discrimination and other civil rights laws; and indicated that as a general rule, U.S.-based companies that employ U.S. citizens outside the U.S. or its territories, as well as multi-national companies that operate in the U.S. or its territories, are covered by U.S. civil rights laws. Thus, U.S. citizens that are employed outside the United States by a U.S. employer or a foreign company controlled by a U.S. employer are protected; but employees who are not U.S. citizens are not protected by U.S. civil rights laws when employed outside the United States. Accordingly, one "theme" to this chapter is that the wise, ethically egoistic, global employer is well-advised to be cognizant of all these important civil rights anti-discrimination statutes.

Questions for Discussion

1. Why is the fact that the United States is a federal form of government a critical fact for anti-discrimination law analysis?
2. Why are the terms "employer" and "employee" critical to an analysis of the U.S. Age Discrimination in Employment Act?
3. Why is it critical pursuant to the ADEA to differentiate between the termination of older workers and the discrimination against them?
4. Why is there such a large increase in the number of age discrimination claims made to the Equal Employment Opportunity Commission? How does the EEOC handle such a large number of claims? Why is the EEOC's claim designation critical to a successful lawsuit?
5. What must the employee demonstrate to make an initial case of age discrimination? Provide an example.
6. What is the disparate treatment form of age discrimination? How is it proven from an evidentiary standpoint? Provide an example.
7. What is an employer "pretext," and how does it operate in an age discrimination in employment case? Provide an example.
8. What is the disparate impact theory of age discrimination? Provide an example. How does an "impact" case differ from a "treatment" case?
9. What is the employer's BFOQ defense? Provide an example.
10. What is the employer's RFOA defense? Provide an example. Does this defense give too much latitude to the employer? Why or why not?
11. How does U.S. age discrimination law operate extra-territorially? Provide an example.
12. What are some global legal perspectives on age discrimination law based on the material in this book or another country's legal system you are familiar with?

CHAPTER 5

ETHICAL ANALYSIS OF AGE DISCRIMINATION

In addition to ascertaining the legal aspects of doing business internationally, the moral implications of doing business must be examined. Since most international business decisions have both legal and moral implications, the prudent manager of a multinational firm must be sensitive to the ethical implications of decision-making, and be prepared to confront ethics in a philosophical as well as practical sense. Foreign business people must be aware of U.S. moral norms, particularly as they apply to employment. Moreover, U.S. business people must be able to address the differences between U.S. employment moral standards and the standards of the host country where one's firm is doing business. Such ethical awareness is critical in a human resources context. The legal "answer" to this issue is clear, at least initially, to the U.S. business person. That is, when the business activity of the firm takes place within the host country, the U.S. multinational firm need only comply with the legal precepts of the host county, if any exist, presuming, of course, there is no extraterritorial application of the U.S. multinational firm's home country law. The ethical "answer" to this question is much more perplexing, indeed. What if the host country has standards that are different, and arguably "lower," than those of the United States? How should the ethical U.S. multinational firm proceed? One, perhaps too simple, ethical solution is for the U.S. firm merely to comply with the moral standards of the host country. Yet what if compliance with these standards results in harm to the host country's society or to the firm's own employees? This chapter seeks to answer these perplexing questions by introducing the reader to ethics as a branch of philosophy. Two ethical theories are presented for analysis and comparison: ethical relativism and Kantian ethics.

Ethical Relativism

The multinational business enterprise clearly will be confronted with different ethical beliefs and moral standards in the various countries and societies in which it does business. Moreover, there may be a conflict between the moral norms of the U.S. compared to the moral norms of the home or host country. How should the multinational firm proceed? Should it merely adopt the conventional moral practices of the host country? That is, "When in Rome, do as the Romans"? Or rather should the firm apply the, perhaps "higher," moral standards of the U.S. to its operations in the host country? The existence of different, societal-based, ethical beliefs and moral standards perforce evokes the ethical theory of ethical relativism.

Basic Tenets of Ethical Relativism

Are there objective, universal, moral rules, upon which one can construct an absolute moral system? Are there moral rules applicable to all peoples, in all societies, and at all times? An ethical relativist firmly denies the existence of any universal truth in morality. There are no universal standards by which to judge an action's morality; morality is merely relative to, and only holds for, a particular society at a particular time. Morality is a societal-based phenomenon. Morality is nothing more than the morality of a certain group, people, or society at a certain time. What a society believes is right is in fact right for that society. The moral beliefs of a society determine what is right within that society; if the prevailing moral view says an action is "right," the action is right. Society consequently is the source of all morality (Cavico and Mujtaba, 2005, 2009).

In China, for example, reverence and respect for the aged have long been enshrined as moral norms. As a matter of fact, the Chinese moral precept of filial piety recently has been "translated" into a Chinese legal precept. The *Miami Herald* reported that there is now a law in China that requires Chinese people to provide for the care and well-being of their elderly parents, including, the paper noted, "comforting them and catering to their special needs" (Johnson, 2005, p. 17a). Respect for a person's family elders, especially one's parents, is ingrained in the Chinese tradition, culture, ethics, and values; and now this societal norm has been promulgated as an enforceable law. It is interesting to note that the Chinese law, called "Protecting the Rights and Interests of the Elderly," maintains that support for the elderly "shall be provided for mainly by their families," thereby shifting responsibility away from the government. The *Herald* also noted that the law requires spouses to "assist in meeting the obligation" for their in-laws. The law does not state the level of assistance grown children must give to their parents; but the law does allow parents to sue their children in court for a lack of support. Yet, the *Herald* also quoted a Chinese lawyer, who stated that such lawsuits "never happen"; rather, the situation usually is reconciled, thereby underscoring other important Chinese societal norms – avoidance of conflict and "loss of face," as well as cooperation, mediation, compromise, and peaceful resolution.

Different societies, of course, have different conceptions of right and wrong. What one society thinks is right, another society may conceive as wrong. The same act, in fact, may be morally right for one society and morally wrong for another. Since according to ethical relativism there are no moral standards that are universally true for all peoples, in all societies, and at all times, and since there is no way of objectively showing that one set of beliefs is to be preferred, the only way to determine an action's morality is to ascertain what the people in a particular society believe is morally right or wrong (Cavico and Mujtaba, 2005, 2009). So, if a society believes that discrimination in employment based on religion, national origin, or gender is morally appropriate, or even required, then such discrimination *is* moral, at least for that society. Of course, the following countries are part of this society analysis, and thus, as the research results for this book will show, have their own distinct cultural perspectives and policies, particularly regarding age and age discrimination moral norms:

- Afghanistan
- Turkey
- United States
- Jamaica
- Bahamas
- Thailand

These cultural perspectives and moral norms, particularly regarding older workers and age discrimination in employment, will be covered extensively in the next two chapters.

Effect of Ethical Relativism on Business People

Because different societies have different customs and beliefs, the relativism of morality is an important issue that the manager of a multinational business firm inevitably will encounter. Many employment issues, such as discrimination and sexual harassment, raise significant trans-societal and cultural concerns. U.S. and foreign opinions as to the morality of these practices might differ sharply, for example, as to what constitutes sexual harassment. An ethical relativist simply would advise the business manager who operates in different countries, and who thus confronts societies with different moral beliefs, simply to follow the moral standards prevalent in whatever society he or she finds himself or herself. Following the host country's morality is certainly a convenient approach to take; yet the doctrine of ethical relativism probably has persuaded more people, particularly business people, to be skeptical about ethics than any other line of thought.

Justification

There is some rational justification for respecting some set of conventional moral beliefs. Some moral prescriptions are necessary in the area of social as well as employment relationships; and people are, and should be, inclined to respect those prescriptions which have in fact survived and which have a history of respect. It is, moreover, well and proper to know something of the customs of other peoples, so as to more rationally judge one's own customs and to avoid thinking that everything contrary to one's own beliefs and conventions is wrong. Ethical relativism can appeal to tolerance of every kind of society; it militates against being "judgmental" toward other groups of persons. It also is advantageous, for eminently practical reasons, for the manager of a multinational firm to be cognizant of the culture and mores of the societies where the firm conducts its business operations.

Problems with Ethical Relativism

Defining "society": A fully realized and individualized society is at best a rare phenomenon. Even within relatively simple societies there are diverse cultures, subcultures, social classes, and kinship and work groups. These fragments constantly confront one another and interact; and in so doing exchange and modify conventions and beliefs. A united and distinct group, which one reasonably could term a society, might even tolerate a great diversity of practices and beliefs. Regardless of how small and socially homogeneous the group, there still will be some divergence in moral opinion. In large, complex, heterogeneous, social systems, the "society" will contain a myriad of smaller "sub-societies" that co-exist, yet that reflect different standards and attitudes. Definite moral beliefs also can be ascribed to many of these "sub-societies." An individual, moreover, can simultaneously belong to distinct sub-societies, cultures, and groups, all with different moral norms and beliefs (Cavico and Mujtaba, 2005, 2009). Regarding the societal view of age in the U.S., the Supreme Court of the United States in an age discrimination lawsuit related that "one commonplace conception of American society in recent decades is its character as a 'youth culture,' and in a world where younger is better, talk about discrimination because of age is naturally understood to refer to discrimination against the older" (*General Dynamics Land Systems, Inc. v. Cline*, 2004).

In a heterogeneous world, filled with heterogeneous societies, the presence of so much diversity offers a serious challenge to the ethical relativist. What constitutes a society for the purposes of ethical relativism? What are the boundaries of a society; how does one determine where one society ends and another begins; whose beliefs and practices form the core of values for the society; and what exactly are these beliefs and practices? Particularly in an age of multinational business firms and the increasing "globalization" of economic activity, the doctrine of ethical relativism raises many serious questions. In the context of employment discrimination overseas, for example, certainly a U.S. firm and its personnel, due to a very strong U.S. societal belief in individual human rights in employment and otherwise, will have difficulty in doing business in a society that straightforwardly upholds discrimination as the moral norm against women, older people, and minority groups in employment.

Comparative moral judgments: One obvious drawback to ethical relativism is that no comparative moral judgments are possible. Since there are no external, universal, objective, moral standards, there is no impartial way of evaluating and deciding among different practices and beliefs. One cannot say that any practice or belief is better or worse from a moral perspective than any other. No matter how seemingly reprehensible or praiseworthy a society's practices and beliefs, nothing correctly can be adjudged wrong or right because comparative judgments require absolute moral standards, which the ethical relativist denies (Cavico and Mujtaba, 2005, 2009). There may be some absolute "moralists" who argue that U.S. law, especially anti-discrimination law, should be even more extensively and forcefully applied abroad. Yet some foreign societies, particularly those dominated by a particular religion, may be offended morally by such U.S "cultural imperialism"; and thus may reject U.S. criticism of their practices, and may resent any attempt to expand

U.S. influence overseas. The attempt to "export" U.S. moral norms may result in international and political difficulties for U.S. firms as well as the U.S. itself. An ethical relativist, of course, would neither condemn nor praise any employment practice, but rather would merely adopt and adapt to the relevant society's moral norms.

Societal agreement: The norms in one society very well may differ from the norms in effect in another society. What is right and what is wrong will not always be the same in different societies; but under ethical relativism, what is right for a society is right for that society. As a consequence of taking this ethical relativistic perspective, two bizarre and contradictory results ensue: agreement on morals is, in principle, impossible; and no societal disagreements are possible (Cavico and Mujtaba, 2005, 2009). Since each society has its own true "right" view, no two societies, in principle, can disagree as to the morality of an action, such as discrimination in employment.

Criticizing a society: If one is an ethical relativist, it makes no sense, and it would in fact be wrong, to criticize the practice and beliefs of other societies, as long as they adhere to their own standards. One can no longer say that the customs or beliefs of other societies are morally inferior to one's own. One's own society has no special status; it is merely one among many. There is certainly no place for moral reformers. One must cease condemnation of other different societies, regardless of how "atrocious" their practices are. It would be arrogant to evaluate the practices of a society and attempt to persuade the other society to change its view. Rather, one should adopt an attitude of tolerance. All one can, and should, do is report what a society believes about an action, and conform accordingly (Cavico and Mujtaba, 2005, 2009). Thus, if discrimination in employment based on age, race, religion, gender, or national origin is morally acceptable in the host country, then all the ethically relativistic firm has to do is conform to the prevailing discriminatory norms in its employment practices. If one accepts ethical relativism, it is also wrong, and makes no sense, to criticize the practices and beliefs of one's own society. If right or wrong is relative to a society, it must be relative to one's own society too. Consequently, one's own established standards are correct and any attempt to reform them must be taken as "mistaken". Since right or wrong is determined by the standards of a society, one cannot propose changes for the "better" because there is no way to judge the reforms as better (Cavico and Mujtaba, 2005, 2009). Thus, the U.S. firm wanting to impose the presumably "higher" moral standards of its home country to its employment practices overseas might be accused of being overly righteous and perhaps even condemned as a "cultural imperialist".

Yet people do recognize that moral standards of their own society, as well as other societies, are wrong; and this judgment implies that the moral standards that a society accepts are not the exclusive criteria of right and wrong (Cavico and Mujtaba, 2005, 2010). The idea, for example, that the practice of slavery cannot be evaluated ethically across societies, cultures, and times by a common moral standard appears not only mistaken but also quite ridiculous. Similarly, the idea that because certain discriminatory employment practices are morally accepted in certain societies does not make them immune to "higher" and more absolute ethical judgment.

Illogical approach: Common sense informs one that conventions and beliefs do differ among societies, cultures, groups, and times. Yet, the culturally relativistic fact that societies have different beliefs, including moral beliefs, does not logically mean that all societal-based moral beliefs are equally acceptable and right (Cavico and Mujtaba, 2005, 2009). The ethical relativist's approach is a flawed one. He or she argues from the fact of societal diversity to a conclusion about the lack of any universal, objective, and true morality. The approach is not logically sound because the conclusion does not follow from the premise. Even if the premise is true, the conclusion may be false. To say that morality derives from societal norms and beliefs is not to say that whatever is customary is right and true. One cannot infer logically from the fact of societal diversity that there is no way, and can never be any way, to establish one view as absolutely correct. One should not be tempted to conclude from the fact of diversity that there are not any true moral standards to resolve differences in beliefs. When two societies have different moral beliefs, for example, regarding discrimination in employment, all that logically should follow is that one of them probably is wrong.

Universal moral standards: The fact that there are differences in moral positions among societies does not mean that there are no universal moral standards and rules. There are reasons to think that all societies actually do share the same basic moral norms. The underlying similarities of human beings the world over, the actual, well-established, normal habits of people, revealed in their conduct and language, and the similar conditions necessary for survival and advancement, are all evidence of common human needs, dispositions, and aspirations. Human beings share a belief in fundamental human rights that apply to all people, in all places, and at all times. People, moreover, speak out whenever and wherever universal human rights are denied or violated (Cavico and Mujtaba, 2005, 2009). There are moral standards that clearly are universal and that have been, and are, esteemed by the peoples of every society. There is agreement, commonalty, and invariability concerning a core of moral rules that forms a part of the ethical system of all societies. Standards, for example, that treat murder, stealing, lying, treachery, cruelty, uncontrolled aggressiveness, discrimination, self-indulgence, selfishness, and laziness as immoral vices are universally held. Standards that treat equality, fairness, honesty, integrity, promise-keeping, faithfulness, loyalty, kindness, self-control, and industry as moral virtues are accepted by all societies. These standards are constant and universal and do not depend on societal variation (Cavico and Mujtaba, 2005, 2009). It makes no sense to say that a rule against causing unnecessary suffering, or a rule respecting property rights, or a rule against discrimination in employment, may be held for one group of people and not for another. These universal norms recognize that people are social beings, that cooperation is necessary for survival, and that people need moral rules and prohibitions to lead a common life.

These moral norms are the minimally necessary pre-conditions for any society to exist at all. There are certain basic moral rules that must be followed in each society if a society is to survive and its members are to interact with each other effectively. Norms, for example, against killing or injuring the members of the society, taking their property, and using language untruthfully when communicating with them, form part of this moral minimum. If these norms are not complied with, if there is not some protection for persons, property, representations, and promises, then the social system will not survive and there will not be any society at all. One cannot avoid these minimal moral obligations, not to murder, steal, and lie, without removing oneself from society altogether (Cavico and Mujtaba, 2005, 2009). The same arguments can be asserted to support a universal moral norm against discrimination in employment. Societal moral norms, despite surface differences, do tend to converge on a common core; and thus may not be as diverse as the ethical relativists contend. One accordingly can recognize "different" moralities as being one universal morality through their common, invariable, and constant core.

Factual v. moral disagreement: Are moral disagreements among societies really disagreements about facts? That is, are disagreements based not on differing moral beliefs, but on nothing more than the attempt to apply universally recognized moral rules to specific factual situations? The apparent diversity of beliefs among societies may be only apparent. Societies do agree on certain fundamental moral standards. Different views on specific moral issues may not reflect deep differences in fundamental moral beliefs, but instead are reflections of differing factual circumstances and different experiences among people (Cavico and Mujtaba, 2005, 2009). One commentator accordingly has suggested that "tackling age discrimination is not just about removing measures that treat one age group less favorably than another. Not all differences between the young and the old are as a result of age. There is, for example, the idea of 'cohort phenomena.' These are the result of different experiences of people born at different times. Older people may, for example, have grown up in a very different cultural and educational system than young people and may have been taught how to learn in a different way. Failing to appreciate this may place older people at a disadvantage in training, as the approach used now will be the one which young people are more accustomed to. Perhaps, therefore, in order to remove any discriminatory treatment of older people in training there is a need to consider culturally appropriate techniques" (Sargeant, 2004).

Universal moral rules v. universal practice: Although people from different societies actually may not agree on all moral norms, this automatically does not mean that there are not ultimate, fundamental, moral norms which everyone ought to believe. Fundamental moral rules are universal, but they may be not universally practiced. Members of one society, for example, will agree that they should not kill, steal, lie to, and discriminate against, one another, but they may think it permissible to inflict these actions on members of other societies. Morality, therefore, is not relative; it simply is not practiced universally (Cavico and Mujtaba, 2005, 2009).

One important example of universal moral norms is the United Nation's *Universal Declaration of Human Rights*, adopted by the General Assembly of the United Nations on December 10, 1948. In the context herein of employment discrimination, the Declaration states that "everyone is entitled to certain rights and freedoms, without distinction of any kind, such as race, color, sex, language, religion, political or other opinion, national or social origin, property, birth, or other status" (United Nations, 1948, Art.2).This fundamental non-discrimination principle applies to the specific rights enumerated in the Declaration. For example, Article 23 states that "everyone has a right to work, to just and favorable working conditions, to a just remuneration ensuring for himself and his family an existence worthy of human dignity." Such rights are posited by the United Nations as "Universal," though in practice they may not yet be universally adhered to. The ethical firm, therefore, may have to apply higher, and more stringent, universal ethical principles in order to be a truly moral firm with respect to its overseas employment practices.

Experience: People's own experiences contradict ethical relativism. People do make comparative moral judgments; and people do marshal ethical arguments in support of their moral criticisms. There are conflicts in societal conceptions of morality and people do make moral judgments (Cavico and Mujtaba, 2005, 2009). The global business context, a practice in one's home country, such as employment discrimination based on race, national origin, religion, or gender, very well could be deemed an immoral practice, yet that very same practice could be construed as quite proper in the host country. How does the global business firm contend with such a conflict in societal moral norms? The answer is not to retreat to the too simple and easy confines of ethical relativism. Rather, trans-societal and trans-national moral judgments can be, are, and should be made. If ethical relativism is true, such judgments, criticism, and arguments are doomed to failure. Moral reformers, moreover, certainly would have no place in an ethically relativistic universe. For a U.S. multinational firm, for example, it would be problematic, to say the least, to engage in employment practices such as discrimination based on race, religion, gender, or national origin, because the vast majority of U.S. citizens, including the firm's own employees, would find such practices morally odious, and would vociferously condemn them as such. In the new global marketplace, moreover, the standards for appropriate conduct, both legally and morally, have been evolving so rapidly and extensively that they have blurred the concepts of nationality, society, and citizenship, which historically have been determined by applicable national law and distinct societal moral norms.

The fact that moral judgments are made, however, does not imply that there is a single and complete ethical theory to answer satisfactorily all moral issues, and that it is always easy to ascertain what is right and wrong. Ethical analysis does mean that societal rules, actions, and beliefs can be determined to be right or wrong based on reasoning from ethical principles. Ethical principles do allow one to dismiss certain societal "moral" rules as inadequate. One pernicious consequence of ethical relativism, with its emphasis on culture, custom, and convention, is to "short-circuit" the ideal of the universal-absolute-good out of human consciousness (Cavico and Mujtaba, 2005, 2009). The challenge for the multinational firm, rather, is to establish consistent ethical methods, to rationally raise, discuss, and resolve moral issues, to classify actions as right and wrong, and to make the classification universal and operational.

Conclusion to Ethical Relativism
Moral beliefs may be in part the internalized reflection of the views of one's society, transmitted by one's parents and other societal influences. The resulting moral norms can be prescribed, explained, and reinforced by the society's customs

and conventions. The norms, in addition, can function as instruments for maintaining social cohesion and stability. Following the customs of one's society, therefore, does provide an explanation for performing an action. The international business person, moreover, is well-advised to be keenly aware of the moral norms where he or she is contemplating doing business. Adherence to social convention, however, does not provide a complete justification for engaging in an activity. Acceptance of societal norms generally is not the product of logical ethical reasoning. Moral norms need further justification. Rational arguments are necessary to establish what a societal practice ought to be; and to determine whether a person should be guided by an essentially non-reasoned conformity to societal convention. A too ready disposition to conform to the practices of a society may not in fact be a virtue, but rather a weakness and vice. Fundamental moral rules are not relative. Not every moral rule varies from society to society. Societies may differ in some moral beliefs, but there is agreement on fundamental rules. It is a mistake, therefore, to overestimate the amount of differences among societies; and certainly to construct an ethical theory based on these differences. Several societies have believed in the morality of the practice of slavery throughout history; yet slavery was morally wrong then, as well as now, despite societal norms. The same absolute arguments can be made against discrimination, discrimination in employment, and age discrimination in employment.

Kantian Ethics

The Kantian approach to ethics, in contrast to ethical relativism, views morality from the perspective of universal rights and duties, thereby superseding any viewpoint of morality based on societal norms (Cavico and Mujtaba, 2005, 2009). Kant's Categorical Imperative, therefore, clearly will demand that the international firm do more than merely comply with the host country's moral norms or even legal regulations regarding discrimination in employment. The Categorical Imperative will demand that the moral person, regardless of the law and any prevailing ethically relativistic or cultural norms regarding discrimination against certain types of persons or people with certain characteristics, treat human beings as worthwhile and valuable "ends" deserving of dignity and respect, and never treat them as mere "means" or things or instruments and never subject them to disrespectful or demeaning behavior (Cavico and Mujtaba, 2005, 2009). In the context of the age discrimination, Kantian ethics would demand that one treat an older person, or for that matter a younger person, not solely on his or her age, but whether the person possesses the capability to do the particular job. Accordingly, as emphasized by Santora and Seaton, "...managers and the companies they work for need to change their attitudes toward older workers. Older workers are not just a commodity that can be tossed aside" (2008, p. 104).

Kantian ethics is fundamentally based on rationality; that is, the clear-thinking, objective, and intelligent person will be able to reason to the moral answer to the problem (Cavico and Mujtaba, 2009) The rational person surely would realize that discrimination based on age or other, especially immutable characteristics, such as race, color, national origin, and gender, may be the consequence of incorrect and impermissible stereotyping and prejudice, both individual and societal. The rational person certainly would want to be considered for a job or a promotion based on his or her ability, not age; and thus the rational person will reason that other people similarly situated want to be judged for what they can do, and not who they are or how old (or young) they are, and regardless of any contravening laws (or absence of laws), or ethical or societal norms. Accordingly, the rational person will reason to the logical ethical conclusion that it is immoral to discriminate against people based on their age.

Summary

This chapter introduced the reader to ethics as a branch of philosophy. Two ethical theories are presented for analysis and comparison: ethical relativism and Kantian ethics. Ethical relativism as a philosophic moral theory used to make judgments of "right" and "wrong" and "good and bad" based on societal and cultural beliefs and practices was explicated fully. Ethical relativism will emerge as a very important ethical theory as well as provide a philosophic and practical context for the material the reader will encounter in the cultural perspectives and aging discussion in Chapter 6 as well as the results of the authors' own age and cultural values surveys in Chapter 7.

The moral assessment of a business situation is naturally made more difficult by the presence of different national, societal, and cultural perspectives as to what it means to be moral. As this chapter emphasized, ethical relativism, of course, is an ethical theory that gives precedence to these societal cultural beliefs in determining moral conduct. Ultimately, however, the international business person morally may be required to act not only above and beyond the law, but also above and beyond relativism in ethics; and thus may be required to apply universal ethical principles and moral standards to employment practices wherever and whenever business is conducted. Just as the law differs from one country to another country, so does the definition of moral behavior and the delineation of appropriate cultural norms. The law, of course, can be viewed as a foundational "value" prescribing one's behavior; yet ethical codes, moral rules, and cultural norms may impel one to exceed the "moral minimum" required by the law. The United States possesses a highly developed legal system proscribing discrimination based on race, religion, national origin, gender, and age. Other nations, however, do not possess such comprehensive legal prohibitions. When an "American" manager or employee is called upon to evaluate the propriety of an action, such as employment discrimination, one must consider not only the whole legal context, including U.S. employment discrimination law as well as the host country's law, but also the ethical, moral, and cultural context. Because the laws of the host country are frequently different from those encountered in the U.S., managers must review them carefully, not only for legalistic reasons, but also for the ethical attitudes the laws may reflect. A nation's laws historically have been shaped in part by its social traditions and conventions and beliefs, including its moral standards and mores. The authors, therefore, in this chapter spent a great deal of time in explicating the ethical theory of ethical relativism since that ethical chapter will emerge as a very important variable when establishing cultural perceptions of age, aging, older workers, and age discrimination in employment, which will occur in the following two chapters.

Questions for Discussion

1. What is the ethical theory of ethical relativism? Do you agree or disagree with its major tenets? Why?

2. How are the theory of ethical relativism and the concept of culture inextricably intertwined? Provide examples. What are some of the advantages and disadvantages of this "connection"?

3. How can ethical relativism be used to make moral judgments regarding age, aging, older workers, and age discrimination in the workplace?

4. How does the theory of ethical relativism differ from Kantian ethics? How are moral determinations made pursuant to both theories? Which theory do you believe is the superior ethical theory? Why?

CHAPTER 6

VIEWS OF AGING IN DIFFERENT CULTURES

The purposes of this chapter are to provide perspectives of aging, an aging workforce, and age discrimination in the workplace in selected countries where the authors and their colleagues and contributors have been able to obtain information and data. The following countries will be offered as illustrations to provide perspectives of aging: Jamaica, Turkey, Afghanistan, Thailand, the Bahamas, and the United States.

Aging and Culture

Jamaica

Jamaica is one of the many islands of the Caribbean with strong historical and cultural ties to both West Africa and Great Britain. The population, almost three million, is a diverse blend of many different races with the majority being of African descent. Over the centuries, there has been a variety of marriages of both different races and cultures, inevitably resulting in a fair tolerance of diversity. However, there are issues of discrimination arising out of what has been loosely called the *"classis model"* or more formally, *"class discrimination."* This, of course, is a legacy of the Island's history of slavery and colonialism, where the slave owners and colonizers were the "haves" and the working class members were the "have-nots." During slavery, and later colonization, Jamaicans were identified not only based on skin color, but also based on wealth and status.

The advent of the information age, aided by the Worldwide Web and Cable Television, has exposed Jamaicans to various other cultures. One could assume that with the majority of Jamaicans being of African descent, as well as the British influence on their culture, that Jamaicans would have very distinct ideas on social issues such as age discrimination; and, ostensibly they do, but in reality Jamaicans seem to take their cues from the outside world - the "first world." In this regard, no single culture has impacted the Jamaican people as much as that of North America. Jamaican attitudes tend to mirror American norms, beliefs, and values more and more as the years progress. As has been the case in North America, there has been a trend towards age discrimination in Jamaica. While there are no specific laws governing this issue locally, and accordingly, very little public reflection on the matter, an informal review of several typical Jamaican companies reveals that persons between the ages of forty five (45) and sixty five (65) are more likely to be "downsized" or laid-off, and less likely to be hired. There is also a noticeable trend towards encouraging early retirement. As a matter-of-fact, a colleague of one of the authors at Nova Southeastern University stated that during early 2003, her brother was forced into early retirement from his long-term employment in Jamaica because he was 55 years of age and he was bluntly told the reason was because of his age.

Over the past decade, many Jamaican organizations have engaged in some form of restructuring, leading to changes in their workforce. Quite often, restructuring that involves automation or reengineering results in redundancies of supposedly "less qualified persons" and the recruitment of more *"technologically savvy"* personnel. These new recruits somehow mostly seem to fall within the ambit of the age group defined as *"Generation X,"* and more recently, *"Generation Y."* In discussions with various local (Jamaican) managers involved in the recruitment process revealed an interesting trend (Mujtaba, Hinds, and Oskal, 2004). While most managers are willing to admit to a preference for hiring from the Generation X pool of knowledge workers, hardly anyone is willing to call that preference "age discrimination." When prodded for a classification of this type of behavior, managers cite other factors as their motivation. One manager indicated that he assesses recruits for *"a bias towards particular mindsets."* He indicated that it has been his experience that job seekers from the Baby Boomer Generation are more likely to suffer from *paradigm paralysis,* and consequently are less likely to be open to new perspectives, especially from younger colleagues. Accordingly, he said, he would be willing to admit to *mindset* discrimination, but not age discrimination. Another factor cited was the knowledge level of the younger workforce compared with that of the older generation. Although the older recruits inevitably have more experience, this is not always a requirement for the job. Recruitment Managers indicate that they would prefer to hire younger, "brighter" workers, who presumably are open-minded and trainable, rather than older workers who are *"set in their ways."* It is believed that the younger generations are more "teachable" because they pursue higher levels of academic learning, which better prepares them for experiential learning. Supposedly, they are also more in tune with and thus open to new technologies compared to their older counterparts. Conversely, Jamaica is a Third-World country, which had only one major university during the 1960s to 1980s, and as a result only a small percentage of the local "baby-boomers" were afforded tertiary level education. Therefore, the Jamaican people may have less appreciation of the need for continuous learning, which is a feature of the new "learning organization."

Managers also cited a third "honorable and justified" reason for their preference of younger workers: this being the *"economic reality of diminishing returns."* It is believed that older workers cost more to maintain, and are less energetic than younger workers. One manager actually cited his views based on *"personal experience"* that *"a person's performance tends to peak after a number of years (roughly eight years) and after that the rule of diminishing returns sets in."* The authors consider these views expressed in support of this preference for a younger workforce to be very disturbing, especially in light of the fact that many of these views are not supported by factual research, but merely on perception. It is also disturbing that managers do not see their behavior as being discriminatory.

Jamaica, like many other third world countries, is just beginning to view human resources management as a multi-dimensional field and, as such, many sensitive issues, including age discrimination, are not routinely addressed. However, as a member of The International Labour Organization (ILO), and also based on Jamaican's habit of mirroring "American" norms, Jamaicans will no doubt become sensitized to, and take appropriate actions against, such issues as age discrimination in the workplace in the foreseeable future. Despite the fact that age discrimination in employment is may be regarded as wrong by some in Jamaica, nonetheless it is practiced by employers. For example, in that nation's leading newspaper appeared an ad by a employment staffing company requesting candidates for certain business and management positions, and specifying among other requirements that the applicants "Must be between the ages of 26-40 years" (The Sunday Gleaner, 2005, p. 16). Such an ad in the U.S. would subject the employer and the recruiting company to a Civil Rights age discrimination lawsuit, at least by the candidates who met the requirements and who were over forty years of age. The ADEA specifically makes it illegal for an employer or an employment agency to print or publish any employment ad that indicates any preference, limitation, or specification based on age.

During the 1990s, "the Jamaican economy performed poorly as shown by the macroeconomic indicators" as stated by Dastoor, Roofe, and Mujtaba (2005). There were high levels of unemployment and negative, or very low, economic growth rates (Downes, 2003). The government, along with other major political leaders, agreed to the gradual liberalization of the economy and the implementation of a system similar to that in the United States. Problems during this period led the Jamaican government to use economic liberalization to try to achieve low inflation, but the huge debt burden caused the exchange rate to depreciate and concomitantly the interest rate to continue to rise. This resulted in increased imports and decreased exports (Dastoor, Roofe, and Mujtaba, 2005). Jamaica's pursuit of the policy of neoliberalism in the 1980s under Prime Minister Edward Seaga followed a period of democratic socialism that left a battered economy (Dastoor, Roofe & Mujtaba, 2005). Dastoor, Roofe, and Mujtaba (2005) stated that "This policy called for a coalition between the state and the private sector. This was successful in some sectors but the general picture of the Jamaican economy still looked grim" (Henke, 1999.). Liberalization is a move in which the state opens up a predominantly free economy and relinquishes control over key industries. This U.S. style economy was adopted to encourage prosperity through a low inflation model, following the continued deterioration of the economy and the inability of the government to stabilize the economy (Dastoor, Roofe & Mujtaba, 2005). There is no current consensus on the extent to which Jamaicans and Americans are the same or different in terms of cultural value orientation. Some research indicates there are no differences (Cavico & Mujtaba, 2004), while others, for example Hofstede (2001), report there are differences. According to Cavico and

Mujtaba, Jamaican students tend to be very competitive and often attempt to earn the highest score within their teams and classes. This is, perhaps, partly a consequence of the rigid British orientation. Cavico and Mujtaba report that Jamaicans are similar to Americans in terms of Machiavellian thinking. Machiavelli's name is often used in business and leadership literature to symbolize a sinister "real-world," "moral jungle" view. Cavico and Mujtaba's results, based on Jamaican and American students' Mach (Machiavellian) V Attitude Inventory scores, showed that there is no difference between the two groups (t=0.0929, p=0.9264). Even though the students were raised in two different cultures (countries), there are no significant differences between Jamaicans and Americans (Mujtaba and Hinds, 2004). It thus appears that both the Jamaican and "American" cultures encourage similar attitudes with regard to management styles and strategies in the corporate environment to get ahead and secure resources for one's personal or professional objectives. A large percentage of men (approximately 54%) were "high Machs" compared to only 28% of women who scored high in this study. Therefore, Cavico and Mujtaba's research indicates that Jamaicans and Americans have similar views and attitudes toward the Machiavellian style of management.

With respect to national culture, Hofstede (1980) initially identified four cultural dimensions to explain work-related cultural differences among societies. Later Hofstede (1993) added another dimension to individualism, masculinity, power distance and uncertainty avoidance, when he put forward the long-term/short-term orientation dimension. *Collectivism* (COLL) characterizes a culture in which people from birth onwards are integrated into strong, cohesive in-groups that, throughout their life, protect them in exchange for unquestioning loyalty (Hofstede, 2001). Collectivist cultures value group loyalty over efficiency. *Individualism* (IND) denotes a cultural value that stands for a society in which the ties between individuals are loose, and "everyone is expected to look after himself or herself and his or her immediate family (Hofstede, 1997, p. 51). Dastoor et al's (2005) research followed Hofstede in viewing collectivism and individualism as end points of a single dimension. The average world score on IND is 43 and US has the highest score (99). Jamaica's lower than average score shows that the members of the society are far more concerned about the welfare of the other members of the society than are those in the US culture (Dastoor, Roofe, and Mujtaba, 2005). *Femininity (sex roles)* describes a society in which social gender roles overlap (Dastoor, Roofe, and Mujtaba, 2005). Both men and women are supposed to be modest and concerned with the quality of life. There is no strict distinction between the work roles of men and women. *Masculinity* (MAS) describes a society in which gender roles are clearly distinct: Men must be assertive, tough, and focused on material success; women are supposed to be modest, tender, and concerned with the quality of life. Masculinity versus femininity differentiates countries that value economic growth and the acquisition of material goods over social and sometimes family relationships (Dastoor *et al*, 2005). *Paternalism* (PAT) describes managers who take a personal interest in the private lives of workers (Dorfman and Howell, 1988) and who assume the role of parents because they consider it an obligation to support and protect their subordinates (Redding, Norman, and Schlander, 1994). A Western perspective of

PAT appears in Dworkin's (2002) description: the interference by an individual or a state in one's life justified by a claim that the person will be better off or protected from harm (Dastoor *et al*, 2005). *Power Distance* (PD) denotes "the extent to which the less powerful members of institutions and organizations within a country expect and accept that power is distributed unequally" (Hofstede, 1997, p. 28). When PD is high, hierarchical differences are respected and organizations are highly centralized. Where it is relatively low, decentralization is popular and subordinates expect to be consulted. Hofstede calculated the world average score for PD as 55. The score for both the U.S. and Jamaica (40) is lower than the world average and indicates that there is moderate equality between the various levels within the society including families and government. This, Hofstede (2003) states, makes for a more stable cultural environment (Dastoor *et al*, 2005). *Uncertainty Avoidance* (UA) is "the extent to which members of a culture feel threatened by uncertain or unknown situations" (Hofstede 1990, p. 113). Low UA describes a culture that is tolerant of ambiguity and futures unknowns. High UA fosters career stability, formal rules and long job tenure and views innovation and change as potentially dangerous. The U.S. score of 46 is below the world average of 64; Jamaica's very low UA score points to a society that is open to taking risks and willing to undertake changes and innovations. This may relate to long periods of political and economic instability in Jamaica. The higher U.S. score indicates less tolerance of risk, and accordingly shows a preference for more defined set of rules and regulation governing its citizens (Dastoor *et al*, 2005).

Soeters and Recht (2001) posit that education prepares people for future roles in society, and also serves to create commitment to the implementation of societal values. The U.S. classroom is multinational; and one role of teaching in this atmosphere is to "bridge" differences in values and thus reduce prejudices and stereotypes (Hambrick, Davidson, Snell, and Snow 1998). Although Hofstede (1993) stated that one's basic value orientation is not easy to change, there is no evidence that after a prolonged exposure to the "American" culture, the value system of the Jamaican student would not be affected. Examining the value orientation of Jamaicans, as well as assessing their willingness to adapt to the "American" culture, is a way to test divergence, convergence, and cross-vergence theories. Convergence speaks to the merging of different cultures by such factors as technology, globalization, economic growth, and industrialization (Connor et al., 1993). Divergence, on the other hand, is a state in which there is a marked strength exhibited by individual cultures despite globalization. Cross-vergence occurs as cultures are exposed to each other, and new cultural characteristics are formed that are distinct from other cultures (Holt, Ralston & Terpstra 1994). Certain research supports the three. Dastoor *et al's* (2005) empirical study compared value orientation for adult learners of two nationalities (Jamaican and US) and also Jamaican students in the US. Results indicated that there was only one significant difference among 10 possibilities: Uncertainty avoidance (UA). Jamaican students in the United States (U.S.) were higher on UA than U.S. students. Dastoor *et al*, further concluded that the theory of divergence can explain the finding that Jamaican students in Jamaica and in the U.S. are significantly different on Uncertainty Avoidance (UA) than United States

(U.S.) students because Jamaican students in the U.S. maintain their distinctiveness (on UA) despite their interaction with the U.S. culture. The findings of no differences on the other four dimensions lends support to Convergence theory which proposes that different cultures become similar due to the influence of globalization and other processes that bring cultures into close contact with others. Over the last five centuries, there has been some convergence and cross-vergence within the U.S. As immigrants come to the U.S. from a greater diversity of cultures than previously (for example, more Afghan and Turkish immigrants), and as globalization and the internet continue to bring more nations together to interact in the marketplace, one can expect to see more changes. Awareness of possible societal transformations can assist workers, managers and leaders to empower themselves and others to contribute the demands and challenges of globalization in the twenty-first century work environment.

In earlier years, many older workers seemed to have been less aware of the increasing trend towards the recruitment of a younger work force by some Jamaican companies. Many were in denial, and some assumed that those from their age group who were being "sent home" prematurely were either poor performers or were having difficulty adapting to changes. As these Baby Boomers become more aware of their vulnerability to a similar fate, based mainly on their age, many have become more thoughtful of this phenomenon, and some now are very outspoken on the issue. For example, one bank manager, who believes he can see his early departure from his lifetime career looming just around the proverbial "corner" (in this case the corner may be a matter of months at worst or one to two years at best), was quite passionate in expressing his views on the issue. In a discussion about the issue he said, "I believe that organizations that are embracing this trend are making a big mistake. Take for example the West Indies Cricket Team; they are currently suffering from a lack of experience on the team (Personal communication with Rosemarie Edwards, August 2005). The managers and selectors threw out all the experience without any clear vision for succession planning or continuity through knowledge management. Of course, the fresh ideas and energies that the younger workforce brings to the table are good for growth and innovation. However, companies need to employ a "blended" approach in order to maintain balance, as a failure to manage the transition from one generation to the next will result in failure for the organization." He also noted that while North America, which had been among the "trendsetters" in this age discrimination phenomenon, has changed its approach, Jamaican companies nevertheless continue the practice. Another manager in the same organization had even more thought provoking views on the issue. He believes that many of the aging workforce members do not even realize that they are "aging" because they still feel so relevant, energetic, and enthusiastic. They know they have much to offer, and so they often do not realize that management feels otherwise. This older "Generation Xer" feels that the plight of the Baby Boomers will soon be impacting his own generation and this he believes, is creating an unsustainable trend. He suggests that organizations should make themselves aware of those aging workers that have retooled, and then seek to leverage *their* fresh ideas and invaluable experience. Younger workers often have very innovative ideas, but they lack the benefit of past experiences and the wisdom of age. This can lead to costly mistakes for the organization. "As a matter of fact", he said, "organizations will eventually realize that this practice is costing them more than just good experience, it will eventually impact the bottom line negatively." He posits the view that having a larger workforce of younger employees, especially at higher levels where labor is more costly, is not financially prudent. "Younger persons," he explains, "require more time off during their child bearing years (Jamaican women are entitled to three months paid maternity leave for up to three children); demand more expensive benefits, such as housing subsidies and educational assistance; and, are more likely to move on to another organization, which will increase recruitment and training costs." The other major factor cited by the persons interviewed is the psychological impact of being delineated by age. Often, such persons respond to this phenomenon as a type of prejudice that alienates them from their younger counterparts. There is a perception of superiority assumed by the younger recruits who feel that they are replacing others by virtue of the ineptitude of those being replaced. This fact breeds disrespect towards the older workers still on the job and negatively impacts morale and team spirit. As a result, older workers sometimes become unwilling to share their wisdom and experience; and younger workers form cliques. The younger workers also develop a mentality of wanting to amass as much as they can in the shortest possible time because they are mindful that the same fate may one day reach them. This consequence sometimes results in the worst kind of individualistic and Machiavellian behaviors.

Dorothy Leonard, co-author of *Deep Smarts: How to Cultivate and Transfer Enduring Business Wisdom,* had this to say in a recent article: "…people with deep smarts can be indispensable. Why? Because their particular brand of expertise is based on long, hard-won experience." Leonard further stated that "… deep smarts are experienced based and often context specific, they can't be produced overnight or readily imported into an organization." The focus of this work and other literature on the value of experience has been effecting new approaches to the retention of a more experienced workforce. Even so, many organizations are slow to adapt to changes in their environment; and thus many are still practicing age discrimination; yet in some cases without even realizing that they are doing it.

Turkey

Turkey is a Middle Eastern country with a population of about 70 million people. About 90% of the total population consists of moderate Muslims, mostly struggling to become economically stable society with the morals that comes from a religious, but still laicized, background. It has been a secular country since 1923, when the founder of Turkish republic called Ataturk established the democratic and secular Turkey. About half of the population is in the range of 20-40 years of age. As such, Turkey may be the one of the largest countries that has a high percentage of young population in the Middle East, and maybe in Europe as well. Nevertheless, the government has not devised a feasible long-term strategy to benefit this generation. There are two kinds of corporations and businesses in Turkey: private companies that belong to the individuals and families; and government-owned and government-managed companies. The difference in performances of those two sectors is quite remarkable. Because of the fact that the private sector is purely profit-oriented, the private sector tends to be more open to new ideas from the young/dynamic employees. Eventually, this openness to new ideas and resultant innovation makes the private sector more competitive and up-to-date. The reason for the Turkish government to be involved with business life was mainly because of the fact that when Turkish Republic was established almost 80 years ago, after the collapse of one of the biggest empires in history, called the Ottoman Empire, almost none of the Turkish people and Turkish families were financially able to invest or establish any businesses or corporations. That is why the new government of the new-born Turkish Republic decided to establish the frontier of a new industry for almost 80 years ago. Ataturk's original idea was to establish corporations that are necessary for survival in the industries that play an important role in country's future; and then to sell them to the interested individuals and families that wanted to run them. Since then, it has been a continuous project for the government to leave the management of government-owned incorporations to the private sector. Presently, the Turkish government mainly runs the corporations that deal with water management, power plants management, heavy metal industry (steel, etc.), and so on. The challenge for an older employee in the private sector is more difficult than that of the government-owned sector. Moreover, the perception in the private sector is that the government-owned companies suffer from a lack of dynamism and innovation.

The common view of the Turkish culture is that the older a person is, the more maturely he or she will react to a crisis, not only in the business, but also in one's personal life. Moreover, there are plenty of common sayings that emphasize the importance of being older and experienced. For example, one's words do not count, unless one is able to grow facial hair (that is, the sign of getting old). In comparison to the Western countries, despite the fact that the percentage of young generation is higher in Turkey, the average ages of employees in the corporations tend to range close to 40's. In other words, the percentage is still remarkably higher in Turkey than that of other countries in Europe, and the young generation still suffers from not being able to find enough opportunities to start their professional business life. In terms of job security, Turkey is a country that mostly views the experience of an employee that comes with age as superior to the perceived advantages of youth. The common perception is that unless the company is going bankrupt or one commits a shameful crime, most companies tend to keep the employees until they retire. In the government-owned sector, one has the opportunity to continue working even after the retirement age. On the negative side, too much security for an employee sometimes causes a lack of motivation for productivity and a decrease in performance that usually lead to loss of profit.

In Turkey, moreover, almost all of government-owned companies suffer from the fact that there are too many employees working for a few available positions. This situation eventually affects the overall performance, and causes the Turkish government plenty of problems, particularly the millions of dollars in deficit. In addition, most of the young generation, who are getting ready to start building their professional careers, end up losing hope in finding a decent position to start with, and after spending remarkable amount of time searching for a job. Because of the security of the existing jobs for current employees, mostly the older employees, the younger ones do not tend to have enough opportunity to prove themselves as young and dynamic members of the workforce. Even if they do get an opportunity to start working, they usually find themselves in the middle of conflicts or disputes with older and more experienced employees in order to apply their "young" and fresh ideas to their organizations. This fact is also considered to be one of the reasons for the migration of young Turkish workforce to other countries, such as the United States, Canada, Australia, and Europe, where the youth seem to be more appreciated. Research conducted by different universities in Turkey, such as the Middle Eastern Technical University, shows that the young workforce wants to explore the possibilities in other countries that prefer employing young individuals. As indicated, sometimes a country's cultural preferences and conditioning for older workers can cause difficulty for the younger generation. The young generation in Turkey is trying to find alternative solutions to the existing challenge (especially age discrimination toward younger employees), so they can become a dominant force into the business world and in the government sector. Unfortunately, because of the fact that bringing a lawsuit is almost impossible against the Turkish government and its integrated system in professional business life, the young generation continues exploring other possible solutions to be able to step into the professional business life by traveling to other countries. Turkey is now seeking to join the European Community; and when and if Turkey becomes a member, it will have to adjust its laws accordingly.

Afghanistan

The word "*Afghan*" represents all people born in Afghanistan, descendants of Afghans, and those who were official citizens of the country, as agreed upon by the ten-day deliberation of *Loya Jirgah*, the General Assembly, in the 1964 constitution. Symbolically, the term Afghan stands for love, courage, devotion, dignity, commitment, loyalty, and the desire to make sacrifices for one's country and people. The word further symbolizes loyalty to local norms, patriotism, and dedication to the Afghan customs. Afghans are known to be people of honor, great hospitality, and are committed to being masters of their own destiny. Many Afghans are also known for their stubbornness and loyalty to the traditional norms of behaviors transferred on from one generation to the next via actions, words, and cultural infrastructures. Such stubbornness and loyalty, beneficial or costly to one's well-being, come from centuries, generations, and many years of being conditioned to the local values of the Afghan culture.

Afghanistan is about the size of the state of Texas in United States, and with an approximate population of 31,000,000 people. There are people of different ethnic backgrounds in Afghanistan, and some of the common ethnic are Pushtuns, Tajiks, Baluchis, Nuristanis, Uzbeks, Khirghiz, Hazaras, and Turkmans. Pushtuns and Tajiks make up the largest groups of Afghans; and the majority of the laws and rules have been set by them or their ancestors which may amount to unearned privileges for those who of these majority backgrounds. There are more than twenty different languages being spoken in Afghanistan, with the main ones being Persian (Dari or Farsi) spoken by at least 60% of Afghans and Pushtu spoken by about 38% of

Afghans. Afghanistan also has about 2.5 million Kuchis (nomads) who travel, sometimes thousands of miles, to different parts of the country as the seasons change. Historically, the nomads used to bring and pass information from one place to another; however, with the advent of technology their information transfer role has diminished. The dominant religion is Islam, practiced by about 99% of the population, with the other one percent making up the minority religions such as Hinduism, Christianity, and Judaism. As such, over many centuries, Afghans have integrated Islam into their way of life both at home and in the workplace. Spiritual beliefs have also been integrated into their politics, thereby leading to strong nationalism. As a matter-of-fact, Afghanistan's flag has three distinct colors of black, red, and green. *Black* color represents the occupation of foreigners, the *Red* portion represents the blood of freedom fighters, and the *Green* part represents freedom and faith. Therefore, their perceptions of age and aging are heavily influenced by their spiritual beliefs and nationalistic ideals which are passed on from the older generation to the younger ones in the community. While age discrimination toward older workers currently does not seem to be a huge challenge in Afghanistan, as the people can use all the work experience that they can get, Afghans have their share of other ethnic and war animosities, which they must overcome. Those who are familiar with the Afghan history know group conflict has existed in Afghanistan for many centuries; and the ethnic animosities are deep rooted.

Thailand

The foundation of the Thai customs and mores lies in the structure of the family. The managers and leaders in the workplace can be paternalistic or, at times, authoritative, and this might conflict with some of the values of the new generation of Thais that openly express their values as is traditionally the norm in most Western societies. To have a harmonious working relationship between employees and managers, it is best that both come from a homogeneous cultural background or at least understand each other's values. It should be understood by all Thai citizens and expatriates living in Kingdom of Thailand that following the local traditions and respecting cultural norms are very important.

The Kingdom of Thailand is known as The Land of Smiles and it is situated in South-East Asia. Thailand shares land borders with Myanmar (Burma), the Andaman Sea, Laos, Cambodia, the Gulf of Thailand, and Malaysia. While Thailand might have some cultural, economical or religious commonalities with their neighbors, they also have conflicts. Even among themselves, there are about 64,800,000 people in Thailand that share different languages, customs, religious backgrounds, and even cultural patterns which can cause conflict among people in the workplace as well as in society. The ethnic groups in Thailand are composed of Thais (75%), Chinese (14%), and others (11%). Meanwhile, the common religions in Thailand are Buddhism (95%), Islam (3.8%), Christianity (0.5%), and Hinduism (0.1%). While the country has been slowly moving toward industrialization over the past two decades, the Thai society is agrarian since 80% of people are involved in some form of farming. Thus, at times people can also be in conflict with nature when they rely on natural rain to produce water for their crops. The agriculture system brings the Kor-Fon culture (begging the goddess for rain) and Long-Caek culture (to help others in a village to harvest the rice). Thais value nature; and they value harmony since most people believe that good deeds bring about more good deeds. Values and the way people behave are patterns that create a culture. For Thais, enjoying freedom and independence are at the core of the culture as they have an identity which expresses freedom and independence.

The one commonality in the values of most Thais is their religious beliefs, especially Buddhism. Thai culture is heavily influenced by Buddhism and Hinduism beliefs. Buddhism has had the most influence on Thai culture. Different spiritual beliefs could be cause for major personal and societal conflicts as witnessed by historical events around the world. Furthermore, the extension and spread of Western culture from globalization and information technology can cause conflict with the way things are and where the future of the Thai people is headed: from farming and calmness to populated cities that are noisy, polluted and full of traffic jams. Examples of Western traditions that extend in Thai society are clothing, greetings and sports which might not be preferred by all generations of Thais. People learn about the Thai culture and the Buddhist principles from a young age and Thais consider the concepts of sin (*bab*) and merit (*boon*) in their actions which directly impacts their values. The Buddhist principles are an important part of the Thai people and their culture. The Buddha emphasized three characteristics of existence: *Dukkha, Anicca,* and *Anatta. Dukkha* is suffering. Dukkha tends to refer to anxieties experienced in the course of living. If you set a goal and are experiencing difficulty attaining it, this can be dukkha. If you love someone and that person does not reciprocate, that may amount to dukkha. The gap is not the problem; it is how you perceive it and how you deal with it that matters most. *Anicca* is impermanence. All things are subject to the forces of nature. Even the rock is gradually worn down by incessant rain drops. *Anatta* means no-self and it relates to the non-substantiality of self or personality since the self or soul that we believe is ours does not really exist. According to Buddhism, we are very lucky to have been born in a form that tends to maintain its shape as we move from task to task. Our compounded form comes into contact with nature and must fight disease, discomfort, and changing conditions. Since there is no essence, no constant state of being, we are subject to many different (impermanent) conditions. These thoughts, beliefs and perceptions might prepare and condition Thais to effectively deal with the conflicts that they face on a day-to-day basis. In conflicting situations, Thais are likely to meet others and the changing conditions around them with a balance of cooperation, compromise and harmony. Thai people use the terms *dukkha* (thuk) and *anicca* (anichang) often in daily speech as they tend to be relatively open to change and more accepting of loss. The *dhamma*, or "Buddhist life," encourages the Eightfold Path, to put to an end or control the existence of *Dukkha* (suffering). The Eightfold Path includes proper understanding, thought, speech, action, livelihood, effort, mindfulness, and proper concentration in life's daily activities. Thai people consider the *dhamma* or Buddhist life pattern when they make major decisions. Due to their socialization and long history, as part of their culture, Thais tend to value their elders and older age.

The Bahamas

The Bahamas is an archipelago of more than 700 islands and 2,400 cays that stretches 50 miles southeast from the tip of Florida to the southwestern coasts of Cuba and Hispaniola (Haiti and Dominican Republic). It is said to be the "playground" of the "rich and famous," and it is alleged that between the months of November to April of any given year, the Bahamas has one of the highest concentration of wealth and celebrity in the world.

The proximity to the United States, the institution of slavery, and British colonialism were the "fuels" that propelled the development of the Bahamas. The system of slavery, which became very important economically to the colonizers of the Caribbean, was also established in the Bahamas, although it differed somewhat from U.S. and Caribbean slavery. The poor soil of the Bahamas only allowed for small farming. Plantations were small with the largest one comprising about 380 slaves. These slaves suffered with limitations to their freedom and customs, and were severely punished when there were infractions; but since many of them were trusted "house slaves" of the Loyalists, they generally lived fairly well. The interaction of master to slave was a benevolent one, with many masters trying to convert their slaves to Christianity, and also secretly engaging in sexual intercourse. Male slaves were encouraged to copulate with as many females as possible to ensure an increased slave population. Strong family ties were discouraged among the slaves, and so was the sense of mutual responsibility between husband and wife, father and son. Because of the limited agricultural system and the limited crops that thrived in the poor Bahamian soil, after emancipation there was not a great demand for slave labor, as was the situation in most Caribbean countries, where indentured labor was needed, and filled primarily by Chinese and East Indian people. It is this progression of cultures and world events that have shaped the political and economic decisions that have placed the country in an enviable position today.

The Bahamas is a diverse country that is made of people with different belief systems. Since the country is a very religious society, they tend to value older age. The following are some of the common religious beliefs and the percentage of people affiliated with each:

- Baptist – 35%
- Anglican - 15%
- Roman Catholic – 14%
- Pentecostal/ Evangelist - 8%
- Church of God - 5%
- Methodist - 4%
- Others - 15% (e.g. Greek Orthodox, Mormons, Jehovah Witness, 7th Day Adventists, Jewish, Rastafarians, Voodoo)

The Bahamas plays host to more than 41/2 million visitors each year, largely U.S. citizens since the Bahamas is very close geographically to the U.S., and Bahamians are very comfortable with U.S. culture and customs. The Bahamas is the leading Caribbean tourist destination, which generates about 50% of the gross domestic product (GDP), and directly or indirectly employs about 60,000 people which is roughly half of the total workforce. The Banking and Finance sector is the second pillar of the Bahamian economy, accounting for about 16% of the GDP and employ more than 5,000 persons.

The Bahamas has strong bilateral relationships with the United States and the United Kingdom, represented by an ambassador in Washington and High Commissioner in London. The Bahamas also associates closely with other nations of the Caribbean Community (CARICOM). The Bahamas has an ambassador to Haiti and works closely with the United States and CARICOM on political and migration issues related to Haiti. The Bahamas has diplomatic relations with Cuba, hosting a Cuban Ambassador and recently opening a Bahamian Consulate in Cuba. A repatriation agreement was signed with Cuba in 1996, and there are commercial and cultural contacts between the two countries. The Bahamas also enjoys a strengthening relationship with China. The Commonwealth of The Bahamas became a member of the United Nations in 1973 and the Organization of American States in 1982.

The United States historically has had close economic and commercial relations with the Bahamas. The U.S. shares ethnic, cultural, and historical ties with Bahamians. The Bahamas is home to more than 30,000 American residents. In addition, there are about 110 U.S. related businesses in the Bahamas. In 2004, about 87% of the 5 million tourists visiting the country were Americans. As a neighbor, the Bahamas and its political stability are especially important to the United States. The U.S. and the Bahamian governments have worked together on reducing crime and reforming the judiciary. With the closest island only 45 miles from the coast of Florida, the Bahamas often is used as a gateway for drugs and illegal aliens bound for the United States.

The United States

Perspectives of aging can be found in the scholarly as well as "popular" literature in the United States – and from the perspectives of younger as well as older workers. To, illustrate, *HR Magazine* in June of 2008 declared that "the scourge of age discrimination continues to be endemic" (Grossman, 2008, p. 64). *HR Magazine* provided two examples. The first was a survey of 5000 workers age 50 and over conducted for Retirement.Jobs.com in Waltham, Massachusetts, in which 77% of the respondents have either experienced or have observed age discrimination and bias in the workplace. In a companion survey of 165 employees, 78% indicated that discrimination based on age was a "a fact of life" in the workplace (Grossman, 2008). Secondly, all these findings, related *HR Magazine*, paralleled a survey conducted by the Roper polling organization for the American Association of Retired Persons where two-thirds of the workers aged 45 to 74 indicated that they had experienced or observed age discrimination in the workplace, and, even more disturbingly, 80% of job seekers stated that they were facing age discrimination (Grossman, 2008). The Academy of Management article reported on an Ohio State University Study of more than 12,000 cases on age discrimination in employment filed with the Ohio Civil Rights Commission from 1988 to 2003 (Santora and Seaton, 2008). The results of the study indicated that "in the cases examined workers around the age of 50 – people who ordinarily have many productive years left to contribute to the workplace –

experienced considerable age discrimination" (Santora and Seaton, 2008, p. 104). The Academy of Management article concluded by asserting "…the findings of this study do show that age discrimination is unfortunately alive and well in the workplace" (Santora and Seaton, 2008, p. 104). Similarly, *Newsweek* magazine reported in June of 2008 that "there is still enormous resistance and unwillingness to consider older workers for job hires" (Gross, 2008, p. 18). *Newsweek* quoted a corporate executive recruiter who stated that corporate boards look askance at older candidates because "somebody in their mid-60s isn't going to take an 18 hour-a-day job" (Gross, 2008, p. 18).

The "Younger Workers" Perspective
Another perspective – from the vantage point of younger workers - of age discrimination in the United States can be seen from an article published in the *Journal of Applied Management and Entrepreneurship* by Courtney L. Bibby, based on her research study, "Should I Stay or Should I Leave? Perceptions of Age Discrimination, Organizational Justice, and Employee Attitudes on Intentions to Leave" (Bibby, 2008). The study tested the relationship among certain demographic and work characteristics and a variety of variables, to wit: age discrimination, organizational justice, job satisfaction, organizational commitment, and turnover intention. The research was based on a survey of 251 engineers associated with the Florida Engineering Society. The study encompassed both organizational factors, such as perceived age discrimination and organizational justice, and individual work-related factors, such as employee attitudes including job satisfaction and organizational commitment) that may contribute to turnover intentions among employees. For the purposes of this book, the age variable will be primarily addressed. Bibby's findings indicated that age was a significant predictor of age discrimination, and that there was a significant relationship between age and the perception of age discrimination. Specifically, and perhaps surprisingly, younger engineers perceived significantly ore age discrimination than their older employees.
Bibby stated that "perceived age discrimination occurs when preferential decisions are based on age, rather than on an individual's merit, credentials, or job performance" (Bibby, 2008, p. 64). Bibby also pointed that out that "…limited research has been conducted in the area of age discrimination in employment against young adults when young adults are defined as individuals between the ages of 19 and 40" (Bibby, 2008, p. 64). Bibby noted that "socio-psychological and physiological differences are noticeable within age discrimination. For example, the ageing process may lead to physical and mental deterioration, which oftentimes leads to stereotypical judgments on a grouping of people based on age" (Bibby, 2008, p. 65). Bibby's three age-related research premises in her study are as follows:

- Young adult engineers perceive more age discrimination and have greater intentions to leave than other age groups of engineers.
- There are significant relationships between age and perceived age discrimination and perceived organizational justice.
- Age perceived age discrimination and perceived organizational justice are significant explanatory variables of intentions to leave among engineers.

Bibby used an online survey to test the validity of these premises. Members of the Florida Engineering Society were sent an email message asking for their participation in a 10 minute on-line survey. Out of a sample size of 4300 engineers, the final producing sample of 251 was a self-selected one. Bibby related that perceived age discrimination was measured by a scale adapted from Foley's (Foley et al., 2005.) Perceived Gender Discrimination scale, which was in turn adapted from Sanchez and Brock's ten-item scale created to measure perceived ethnic discrimination among Hispanic employees (Sanchez and Brock, 1996). The response format for the Perceived Age Discrimination scale was a five point Likert scale, which is one dimensional, and where the high scores are associated with higher perceived age discrimination (Bibby, 2008). The majority of the sample consisted of white (95.2%), male (85.3%), non-Hispanic (93.2%) engineers. The average age of the engineers was 47.1 years, and the average job tenure of the engineers was 9.29 years. A majority of engineers completing the study were also business managers who had either completed some type of graduate level program (42.6%) or obtained at least a college degree (57.4%). The majority of engineers (74.1%) classified themselves as Civil Engineers (Bibby, 2008).

Bibby found that younger engineers (below the age of 40) perceived significantly more age discrimination than their older counterparts, which Bibby related was consistent with past-literature. The findings also indicated that a relationship existed between age and age discrimination, which Bibby suggested reveals that "various age points may play a critical role in the amounts of age discrimination that occurs" (Bibby, 2008, p. 78). Bibby also found that perceived age discrimination was also a significant predictor of intention to leave an organization. Perceived age discrimination, in fact, was found to be the best explanation of intentions to leave. Bibby concluded with the thought-provoking comment that the U.S. Age Discrimination in Employment Act only protects employees over the age of 40, yet the "results from this study indicate that eliminating discrimination may lie in continuing changes to public policy" (Bibby, 2008, p. 79).

Age, Moral Cognizance, and Morality: The Defining Issues Test

Does the age of a person relate to that person's moral cognizance or moral maturity; that is, does the ability to make moral determinations based on reasoning from ethical theories and principles relate to one's age?

This section of the book is based on the survey results of researchers examining the relationship of age to moral maturity. All the studies, of course, have encompassed research beyond the variable of age; but naturally the focus of this part to the authors' book is to make the reader aware of the age research and, most importantly, to see whether the reserachers observed a relationship between age and morality. Specifically, the researchers sought to discern their participants' moral cognizance/maturity on Lawrence Kohlberg's moral cognizance scale pursuant to James Rest's Defining Issues Test (DIT), which assigns a "P" morality score ("P" for "principled") indicating the level on Kohlberg's scale. At the highest level of the Kohlberg scale is the "principled" person who makes moral decisions based on reasoning from ethical theories and principles (Cavico and Mujtaba, 2009). The authors of this book for presentation and analytical purposes have divided their findings from DIT dissertations into three general categories: 1) those examining the age variable with a student population, 2) those examining the age variable with a private sector employee population, and 3) those examining the age variable with a public sector employee population.

Age and Moral Maturity Research

The following studies sought to ascertain whether a relationship existed between the age of the student and his or her level of moral maturity.

Melissa Hickman (2008) examined the ethical reasoning levels of business and accounting students at religiously-affiliated colleges and universities using the Defining Issues Test-2. The age of the students was one of the variables that she sought to determine its influence on the ethical reasoning abilities of the students. Her primary research question dealt with whether accounting students at religiously-affiliated colleges exhibited greater ethical reasoning abilities than accounting students at secular colleges (Hickman, 2008, p. 6). She did have two secondary variables dealing with age in her hypotheses: "Does age influence the level of ethical reasoning abilities of accounting students"? "Is the relationship between age and ethical reasoning abilities moderated by religious affiliation in colleges'? As to the first variable, Hickman found that there was a relationship between age and the ethical reasoning abilities of accounting students. As to the second hypothesis, however, she found no moderating affect on the age variable by attendance at religious affiliated schools (Hickman, 2008, pp. 6-8). Hickman also noted that according to Kohlberg's model of stages of moral maturity, the development of moral reasoning should increase with age. Hickman also pointed to two studies that did find a relationship between age and morality: "By issuing a survey to business students ranging in age from 21-40+ years old, Ruegger and King (1992) sought to determine if age is a factor in determining an acceptable ethical behavior of an individual. These students evaluated the ethical acceptability of 10 questions….(I)t was found that as age increases so does ethical reasoning. Jones and Hiltebeitel (1995) specifically focused on accountants when determining if variables, such as age, play a role in ethical reasoning skills. It was concluded in this study that age does impact ethical reasoning skills. However, Hickman also pointed to another study conducted by Ducat on doctoral students which determined that increases in age did not result in increases in ethical reasoning skills (Hickman, 2008, p. 68). She concluded that the prior literature, as well as her own work, showed "mixed results" (Hickman, 2008, p. 68).

Donna Galla (2006) examined the moral maturity level of adult working students who worked in the finance and accounting fields. Her age research questions (Galla, 2006, p. 36) were as follows: "Is there a relationship between the moral maturity level of finance and accounting professionals and the variable of age? In other words, is there a difference in moral maturity level, as measured by the Defining Issues Test, between finance and accounting professionals who are 35 years of age and older and finance and accounting professionals who are under 35 years of age"?

Although the older group of professionals had higher moral maturity scores, "the main effect for the subject's age was not significant...(Galla, 2006, p.52)." Accordingly, Galla concluded that the age of the participants did not have any "significant effect" on their moral maturity scores (Galla, 2006, p. 52).

   Chiulien Chuang Venezia (2004) focused on determining the level of ethical reasoning abilities of accounting students in Taiwan and the United States. One of the variables that she tested was the age of the students. Her age research question (Venezia, 2004, p. 63) was as follows: "Is there a difference in the level of ethical reasoning by age of accounting students"? Her results indicated that there was "no significant difference in the level of ethical reasoning between accounting students who are under 23 years of age and accounting students who are 23 years of age and older" (Venezia, 2004, p. 87). Yet, Venezia did point to several studies in which age and moral maturity showed a relationship: "(A)ge is positively associated with (DIT) P scores. Researchers (Hau & Lew, 1989; Iceman et al., 1991; Jones & Hiltebeitel, 1995; Grasso & Kaplan, 1998) have found that age is positively associated to moral reasoning ability. She noted the following age studies in particular: "Hau and Lew (1989) used a Chinese version 6-story DIT to examine 242 secondary school and university students in Hong Kong. Their findings showed that older university students were morally more mature than younger school students in their P (moral maturity) score. They concluded that educational level and age are positively associated with moral reasoning....Jones and Hiltebeitel (1995) investigated members of the Institute of Management Accountants. The surveys were mailed to 1,000 members of whom 250 were usable for research. The results indicated that age is a significant variable in the full sample....However, some researchers (Ponemon & Gabhart, 1990; Elm & Nichols, 1993; Eynon et al., 1997) found that age has no effect (Venezia, 2004, p. 44)." Again, as with the aforementioned Hickman student study, the overall results presented were mixed.

   Carol Cannon (2001) examined the moral reasoning abilities of 226 adult working learners at a private university in the southwestern part of the United States. Age was one of the variables that she tested. Her age premise was as follows: "Higher levels of moral development, as measured by the DIT, are significantly related to higher levels of chronological age for working adult learners (Cannon, 2001, p. 166)." Furthermore, she posited: "If age is related to differences in moral development, with adults evidencing continuing development, then it is anticipated that the work adult learners in the present study, aged 36 or greater, will exhibit a higher moral development level than working adults younger than 36 (Cannon, 2001, p. 195)." Cannon's results "...revealed that DIT scores for working adults, equal to or over the age of 36, were significantly higher... than DIT mean scores of working adults younger than 36 years" (Cannon, 2001, p. 195). Cannon's review of the age and moral cognizance literature overall corroborated her findings and conclusion. She related that "in a ten-year, interdisciplinary, longitudinal study examining factors of moral development, Rest (1986) discovered consistent gains in moral judgment with increasing chronological age. Thoma (1985) found further empirical support for age as a predictor or moral development in a meta-analysis of multidisciplinary ethics studies. Ford and Richardson (1994) reviewed eight moral development studies of which five found no significant relationship between age and moral development, and three reported significant, but contradictory results. Borkowski and Ugras (1998) further observed a positive relationship between chronological age and moral development in a meta-analysis of empirical studies ranging from 1985 through 1994. Studies specifically in accounting, on the other hand, tend to provide conflicting evidence to the relation of chronological age and moral development (Enyon, Throley, Hill, & Stevens, 1997; Ponemon, 1990; Shaub, 1994). Overall, however, these studies suggest that attitudes/behavior appear to become more ethical with age, thereby providing empirical support for Kohlberg's CMD theory that individuals will increase in moral development as they mature (Cannon, 2001, p. 166)."

Private Sector Employees

William J. Freeman (2007) studied the cognitive moral development of managers in "knowledge management" firms with those in non-"knowledge management" firms using the DIT-1 survey instrument. One of his research variables was designed to ascertain if there was a relationship between the age of the managers and moral maturity. Freeman's age variable (Freeman, 2007, p. 61) was succinctly posited as the following research question: "Is there a relationship between age and moral maturity"? The DIT was administered to two distinct groups: one group consisted of managers in firms successfully utilizing "knowledge management" as a key performance of success; and the second group consisted of managers in a company not using "knowledge management." The "knowledge management" firm was designated by one attaining the Malcolm Baldrige National Quality Award. The demographics regarding age for both groups were basically the same. Freeman's age results revealed a correlation between age and moral maturity, but not a significant one. His ultimate finding, therefore, was that there was not a significant relationship between age and moral maturity in either "knowledge management" or non-"knowledge management" firms (Freeman, 2007, p. 92). However, Freeman noted that his results on age were "at variance with substantial research that found age as a significant influence in moral maturity (Dahl et al., 1988; McCabe et al., 1991; McNeel, 1994; Rest 1986; Rueeger & King, 1992; Weber & Wasieleski, 2001) (Freeman, 2007, p. 107)."

Chunlong Huang (2006) conducted a cross-cultural examination of the moral maturity levels of U.S. and Japanese expatriate managers in Taiwan as well as Taiwanese managers who worked for Taiwanese based multinational corporations. His research questions (Huang, 2006, p. 7) encompassing the age of his participants were as follows: "What are the variables influencing the ethical reasoning of these managers? For example, do demographic variables (i.e. Age, Gender, and Education)...relate to moral reasoning"? His specific age hypothesis, stated in the Null form, was: "There is no relationship between age and level of ethical reasoning for managers" (Huang, 2006, p. 73). His results indicated that there was no relationship between the age and the level of ethical reasoning of the managers he surveyed (Huang, 2006). Huang, however, did discuss in his literature review several studies that found a relationship between age and morality: "In their study, McCabe et al (1991) concluded that 'age correlated positively with ethical decision-making;

suggesting that maturity enhances ethical decision making' (p. 958). It is generally agreed that older individuals tend to be more ethical or possess a more strict views of moral issues than younger ones. As individuals progress through the experience of life, Kohlberg (1984a) contends, they should develop higher stages of moral cognition. A survey conducted by Ruegger and King (1992) suggested that students in the 40-plus age group were the most ethical. The findings are consistent with Allmon et al (2000) research that older students exhibit more ethical inclinations (Allmon et al., 2000; Borkowski & Ugras, 1998). Accordingly, younger people tend to be less ethical than older people (Mellahi & Guermat, 2004; Miesing & Preble, 1985) or more tolerant over a wide range of issues (Longenecker, McKinney, & Moore, 1988), as older workers had stricter interpretations of ethical standards" (Serwinek, 1992) (Huang, 2006, p. 55). Yet Huang (2006) also pointed to a study by Lynon et al. in 1997 that found that age had no effect on the level of moral reasoning (p. 55).

W. Thomas Heron (2006) examined the moral development and ethical decision-making of information technology professionals. Participants were selected from multiple companies in Pennsylvania whose principal business involved the production and delivery of IT products and services. The IT sample consisted of programmers, analysts, product and service support staff, project managers, and database administrators. Heron's age research questions (Heron, 2006, p. 94) were as follows: "Is there a difference in ethical maturity level between different age groups of IT professionals? Is there a difference in the ethical maturity level, as measured by the DIT-2, between IT professionals who are less than or equal to 35 years of age and IT professionals who are over 35 years of age?? Heron's age results indicated that there was "no difference in ethical maturity level between different age groups of IT professionals (Heron, 2006, p. 143)."

Donald L. Ariail (2005) examined the values and moral development of certified public accountants in Georgia. His age research question (Ariail, 2005, p. 138) was as follows: 'Is there a difference in the moral development of CPAs of different age groups"? He divided the CPA age groups into the following categories: under 30, 30-39, 40-49, 50-59, and 60 and over. Ariail (2005) found that the age groups 40-49 and 50-59 had higher DIT moral maturity scores than the other categories, but the scores were not statistically significant, and thus he answered his age research question in the negative (pp. 198-204). Arial in his literature review pointed to studies that showed a relationship between age and morality, but conversely he related that prior studies with accountants showed no relationship between age and moral development or a negative relationship (Ariail, 2005).

Pamela K. Smith Evans (2004) investigated the ethical maturity of African-American business professionals who worked as managers and employees in the private sector as well as entrepreneurs, and who were members of the National Black Master of Business Administration organization. Among other variables, she sought to determine if age influences their ethical maturity levels. Her age research questions (Smith Evans, 2004, pp. 48-49) were as follows: "Is there a difference in ethical maturity level between different age groups of African-American business professionals? That is, is there a difference in ethical maturity, as measured by the Defining Issues Test, between African-American business professionals who are under 35 years of age and African-American business professionals who are over 35 years of age"? Smith Evans' results showed that "there is no difference in ethical maturity level between different age groups of African-American business professionals (Smith Evans, 2004, p. 74).

Maisie E. Reid (2004) examined the cognitive moral development of health care executives working in a managed care organizational environment. Her age related research questions (Reid, 2004, p. 53) were as follows: "Is there a relationship between ethical maturity level and health care professionals' age? Specifically, is there a difference in ethical maturity level between health care professionals who are 40 years of age and over, and health care professionals below 40 years of age"? Reid distributed 550 DIT surveys to health care professionals at a large county health care hospital district in southeast Florida. Within age groups, 56% of her respondents were under 40 years of age, and 44% were 40 years of age and older. The data that Reid obtained did not show any significant difference between ethical maturity level of health care executives and their age (Reid, 2004, p.72). Reid, however, did observe that her age findings were "...inconsistent with findings of most prior DIT studies, which indicate that (moral maturity) scores advance in age and education" (Brockett, Geddes, Westmoreland, & Salvatori, 1997; Elm & Nicholas, 1993; White, 1999; Wimalasiri, Pavri & Jalil, 1996) (Reid, 2004, p. 76).

Joseph Chavez (2003) examined the moral maturity scores on Kohlberg's scale as measured by the Defining Issues Test of banking employees in southeast Florida. His survey sample consisted of 300 participants working in the banking industry. The age of the employees was one of the factors that he tested. His age research questions (Chavez, 2003, p. 44) were as follows: "Is there a relationship between moral maturity and age of banking employees? In other words, is there a difference in moral maturity level, as measured by the Defining Issues Test, between banking employees who are over 30 years of age and older and banking employees who are not yet 30 years of age"? His results indicated that "the data shows that the banking employees that are not yet 30 years and younger tend to have lower (moral maturity) P scores than banking employees who are 30 years of age and older (Chavez, 2003, p. 58). Regarding his age variable, Chavez concluded: "The common perception of being 'older and wiser' may prove correct since the results of this study show that participants older than 30 years of age made moral and ethical decisions closer to those moral philosophers with the highest degree of moral maturity" (Chavez, 2003, pp. 58-59).

Age and Ethics Research

Mujtaba conducted a study of the ethics of Supermarket managers and employees using Professor John W. Clark's Personal Business Ethics Scores (PBES) instrument (Mujtaba *et al.*, 2009; Mujtaba, 1996). Clark created scenarios which reflected common, every day business issues, and then asked respondents to approve or disapprove each decision made in the scenario. The survey respondents would answer "somewhat approve" or "approve" if they approved of the decision; and if they did not approve, they would answer "somewhat disapprove" or "disapprove." The responses were based on a Likert scale of 1 (approve) to 5 (disapprove) with 3 being a mid-range option or no opinion. He explained that "this type of questioning, according to Clark and Baumhart, does not put a person in the position of approving or not approving an immoral act. People, in general, do not want to provide answers that might make them look immoral. So approving or not approving the decision made in the case would allow them to support either a personal gain, a corporate gain, or a wider social pattern" (Mujtaba, p. 110). The Clark instrument used by Mujtaba had 11 scenarios dealing with specific moral situations arising in business, for example, price conspiracy, insider information, "sharp selling," expense account padding, promotions based on "connections," bribery, and pirating employees (Mujtaba, p. 126). The responses to the scenarios result in a personal business ethics score, thereby "…measure(ing) one's commitment to personal integrity and honesty in the given business situation. These scenarios also measure one's level of commitment to the observance of the laws governing business" (Mujtaba, 1996, p. 132).

Mujtaba targeted managers and employees of a Fortune 500 Supermarket chain with more than 110,000 employees at the time. The company had been voted one of the hundred best companies to work for in the United States. The surveys were distributed to Supermarket managers and employees in the central Florida region. Twelve hundred surveys were sent; six hundred were sent to managers and six hundred to employees. A total of 635 surveys, comprising a response rate of 53% were returned; 632 of them were usable. The male and female respondents were just about evenly divided.

Mujtaba compared the business ethics results of Supermarket managers who had at least five years of management experience with Supermarket employees who were 25 years of age or younger and who had no formal management experience. One of the comparisons in his study was based on age; and one research question to be answered was whether age affected the ethics of the individual. Mujtaba's age-related hypotheses were as follows: "Null Hypothesis I – Individuals who are 25 years old or younger will have Personal Business Ethics Scores (PBES) that are equivalent to or greater than those individuals who are 26 years of age or older. Alternative Hypothesis I - Individuals who are 25 years old or younger will have Personal Business Ethics Scores that are lower than those individuals who are 26 years of age or older" (Mujtaba, 1996, pp. 7, 119). He thus posited that Supermarket employees who are under the age necessary for moral maturity and who possess no Supermarket management experience will have lower PBES scores than Supermarket managers and executives. Mujtaba's results revealed that "the PBES mean value for individuals 26 years of age or older is significantly higher than the PBES value for individuals 25 years of age or younger" (Mujtaba, 1996, p. 135). Therefore, his Null Hypothesis I was rejected; and thus the Alternative Hypothesis was supported; that is, respondents 25 years of age and younger had lower PBES scores than respondents who were 26 years of age and older. Based on his study, Mujtaba concluded that age was indeed a factor in moral development. He further concluded that "as individuals grow older and/or gain more management experience, their moral maturity and sophistication grows stronger, and their understanding increases. One possible explanation is that as individuals grow older an gain experience, their understanding of moral issues increases through the daily reinforcement of moral actions in the company or society in general" (Mujtaba, 1996, p.163).

Mujtaba also discussed the scholarly literature examining the relationship between age and moral decision-making. He related: "Age...can account in moral decision-making of individuals, because people gain more experience and develop a more sophisticated view of the worlds as they grow older (Piaget, 1975; Kohlberg, 1984; Gilligan, 1982). There seems to be a clear consensus between researcher findings that older managers are more ethical than younger managers (Carroll, 1975); and younger workers feel as though they are under pressure to compromise their ethical standards (Posner & Schmidt, 1987; Baumhart, 1961)" (Mujtaba, 1996, p. 79). Thus, his review of the literature was corroborated by his findings.

Public Sector Employees

Franck Aurel Hyppolite (2003) examined the ethical maturity level of public sector employees at the local government level. His sample consisted of 400 managerial, supervisory, and non-managerial employees employed by Broward County, Florida, municipalities therein, and local government agencies. Age was one of the variables he tested. His age research question (Hyppolite, 2003, p. 128) was as follows: "Is there a relationship between the ethical maturity level and the age of public sector employees"? His specific age hypothesis, stated in the Null form, was as follows: "There is no relationship between the ethical maturity level and the age of public sector employees" (Hyppolite, 2003, p. 81). This null hypothesis, however, was rejected, meaning that he in fact did find a positive relationship between age and morality in his study (Hyppolite, 2003, p. 128). Hyppolite (2003) discussed his age finding: "The fourth research question focused on relationship between the ethical maturity level and the age of public sector employees and confirmed this research analysis. This study's findings exposed that there was a significant correlation between the two variables. Hence, this research observation generated important conclusions for the study of both age and Cognitive Moral Development (CMD). The average P-score (for moral maturity) of older participants was higher than the one of younger respondents. As one matures with age, one's average P-score increases....Indeed this current research indicated age was a predictor of individual maturity level" (p. 139).

Lexine V. Arthur (2003) examined the cognitive moral development level of contracting professionals at the federal administrative agency – the General Services Administration (GSA). She sought to see if a relationship existed between age, among other variables, and the cognitive moral development of her survey population at the GSA. Arthur's age related research questions (Arthur, 2003, p. 39) were as follows: "Is there a relationship between ethical maturity and age of the contracting professional? As measured by the Defining Issues Test, is there a difference in ethical maturity between contracting professionals and the age of the contracting professionals."? She found that there was a relationship but not a statistically "significant" one; and thus she concluded that there was no significant relationship between the age of the contracting professionals and their level of moral maturity (Arthur, 2003, pp. 68-69).

Sandra E. Ford Mobley (2002) examined the moral development level of managerial employees of the state of Virginia. Age was one of her variables. Her age research questions (Mobley, 2002, pp. 51-52) were as follows: "Is there a relationship between the ethical maturity level and public sector managers' age? In other words, as measured by Rest's DIT, is there a difference in ethical maturity level between public sector managers who are 45 years of age and over and public sector managers below 45 years of age." Although her data indicated that the 45 and older category had higher moral maturity scores, the difference was not statistically significant, and thus she answered the age research question in the negative (Mobley, 2002).

Rosalind Osgood (2002) examined the moral judgment of elected municipal government officials in the state of Florida. Age was one of her variables to be tested. Her age research questions (Osgood, 2002, p. 29) were as follows: "Is there a relationship between ethical maturity level and age of municipal elected officials? In other words, is there a difference in ethical maturity as measured by the Defining Issues Test, between municipal elected who are over 35 years of age and municipal elected officials who are not over 35 years of age"? Her results showed that there was not a difference in the ethical maturity level of municipal elected officials based on their age (Osgood, 2002, pp. 49-50).

Karelia Martinez-Carbonell (2002) examined the cognitive moral maturity levels of school administrators in a large metropolitan school district in southeast Florida. The sample consisted of administrators, specifically principals of elementary, secondary, adult education, and special needs schools. One of her objectives was to ascertain if a relationship existed between the age of the principals and their level of moral maturity. Her age research questions (Martinez-Carbonell, 2002, p. 14) were as follows: "Is there a difference in ethical maturity level by age of school administrators? That is, is there a difference in ethical maturity level, as measured by the Defining Issues Test, between school administrators who are over 35 years of age and school administrators who are 35 years of age and under"? Her results indicated that there was no significant difference in the moral maturity levels of school administrators based on their age. However, she noted: "Longitudinal studies consistently demonstrate a significant positive trend between a person's age and moral maturity" (Rest, 1986; Rest, Davidson, & Robbins, 1978) (Martinez-Carbonell, 2002, p. 54).

Summary on age research. Kohlberg's Cognitive Moral Development theory posits that as a person increases in age, his or her capability and level of moral reasoning should concomitantly and progressively increase too. Furthermore, as a person increases in age, so does the complexity of the moral questions that a person will confront; and accordingly moral reasoning *should* increase with age. So, does age in fact relate to morality in the sense of moral cognizance or moral maturity? The evidence obtained by researchers, as well as their review of the age and morality literature, is plainly mixed. Eight studies found that there was a relationship between age and moral maturity, though not necessarily a statistically significant one; whereas eight studies found there was no relationship between age and moral maturity. Perhaps age in combination with education would demonstrate a stronger link to moral maturity than between "mere" age and moral maturity (Mobley, 2002, p. 74;

Mujtaba, 1996, p. 24). In fact, Heron (2006) pointed to one study that reported that 38% of the variance in the DIT (moral cognizance) scores can be explained by the variables of age *and* education (p. 87).

Summary

The purposes of this chapter were to provide perspectives of aging, an aging workforce, and age discrimination in the workplace in selected countries where the authors and their colleagues and contributors have been able to obtain information and data. The following countries were offered as illustrations to provide perspectives of aging: Jamaica, Turkey, Afghanistan, Bahamas, Thailand, and the United States.

This chapter provided a brief background on some of the governmental, legal, and cultural expectations surrounding employment practices in the United States, which has the most complex and detailed legal system, and other selected countries. Besides providing a brief country background, the chapter presented the cultural norms and expectations of individuals in Jamaica, Turkey, Afghanistan, the Bahamas, Thailand, and the United States. There are both extensive as well as explicit policies and rules regarding employment practices related to older workers and aging in the United States. However, there seems to be very little legal policies regarding older workers and aging in the countries of Jamaica, Turkey, Bahamas, Thailand, and Afghanistan where cultural practices are guiding many employment decisions in the workplace. This chapter also presented scholarly research on the relationship between age and morality.

Questions for Discussion

1) Is there age discrimination in Asia – in employment and otherwise? Why or why not? Provide examples with explanations thereof.
2) How are the values of the people in Asia similar to and different from the values of the people of the United States? Provide examples with explanations thereof.
3) How are the values of the people in Asia different from and similar to the values of the people in Jamaica, Turkey, Afghanistan, Bahamas, or Thailand? Provide examples with explanations thereof.
4) How do the people of any of the countries examined in this chapter, or any country or culture you are familiar with, regard age, aging, older workers, and age discrimination in employment?
5) In the U.S. engineering study discussed in this chapter, do you, based on your own experience and knowledge, agree with the key finding that younger engineers perceived more age discrimination than older ones? Why or why not?
6) Do you think that there is a positive relationship between age and morality? Are older people more ethical? Are older workers more ethical? Why or why not?

CHAPTER 7

CROSS CULTURAL COMPARISON AND EMPLOYMENT PRACTICES

Effective leadership in employment practices and decision-making is an essential element of business in the twenty-first century's global environment. International business practices vary from country to country; therefore, global leaders should be aware of the culture and social standards of foreign nations where they operate. Global leaders and managers should be prepared to make decisions that are efficient, effective, and aligned with both local and international norms and policies. These leaders thus need to ensure processes throughout the global organization are accurate and that all the subsidiaries and employees are treated fairly and are regarded as an equal to the parent company. Before international managers and leaders of multinational corporations are asked to make global employment decisions, they should be given factual information, training, and awareness about the local laws, norms, perceptions, and expectations of people in each country in order to make fair hiring and retention decisions. In order to effectuate these objectives, actual data on cultural perceptions is necessary. Accordingly, the authors created a survey instrument, an *Age and Cultural Values Questionnaire* and conducted a cross-cultural survey focusing on attitudes to older workers in the workplace and the presence of age discrimination. This chapter provides the survey purpose, methodology, results of the qualitative research, the analysis thereof, and the actual comments about age discrimination practices provided by respondents from the countries of Afghanistan, Turkey, Jamaica, Bahamas, Thailand, and the United States. These comments represent the qualitative aspect of what people think with regard to age in their cultures and how they perceive age discrimination practices in their workplace.

Purpose of Study, Background, and Methodology

There seems to be cultural convergence in many human resources practices among various countries as a result of technological advancements and commonalities. However, oftentimes, employee hiring and retention practices are heavily influenced by cultural norms and mores; and consequently international managers should be aware of different practices at various localities. The purpose of the study, particularly the qualitative component, was to ascertain the cultural views of aging and employment practices regarding older workers from the people of the United States of America, Jamaica, Turkey, and Afghanistan. The research question was: "*Is age viewed differently among the people of Afghanistan, Turkey, Jamaica, and the United States of America?*" The authors proposed that there are some cultural differences in how people view age in each country surveyed; and such cultural views regarding older workers do impact employment practices and hiring decisions. Gathering data thus could provide a clearer understanding of differences from the view of people in these presumably four different cultures. This factual information can be used by global employees, managers, and human resource professionals working in multinational corporations, as they design procedures and policies for attracting, hiring, developing, promoting, and retaining an experienced workforce within each country. The four countries chosen for this study were selected because the authors had access to workers, managers, and professional organizations in them that would cooperate in the information gathering and research process. Furthermore, these are cultures that the authors have the most experience with as they have lived in them, worked in them, or with people from them, and have completed studies about them in previous projects. It is expected that such studies will be duplicated in other countries to further provide factual and practical information that can be used by global managers and multinational corporations as they design and practice fair employment policies.

Several years ago, the authors set out to have discussions with employees, managers and researchers from various countries around the world regarding age and older workers. As a result, in early 2005, it was decided that a structured qualitative survey could be used to formally gather information on how the people of Afghanistan, Jamaica, Turkey, and the United States view age as per their cultural conditioning and the current employment practices related to older workers in their country. A simple and straight-forward survey was designed so it could be distributed to a "convenient" sample of individuals from each country that can speak, read and understand English. As such, the survey questions were worded so the survey could be easily understood by individuals whose first language is something other than English. Initially, in a pilot study, the surveys were handed out face-to-face to a sample of about 30 diverse individuals in Fort Lauderdale to see how they interpreted each question on the survey. As a result, a few of the questions were separated into several questions and some words were changed to further clarify what was being asked. This process led to the final version of the survey which was used for this study.

The individuals who received the surveys were colleagues, friends, professional educators, trainers, staff, students, government employees, contractors, or simply members of various newsgroups that facilitate or distribute up-to-date information to subscribers. Participants were provided sufficient information about the study and its purpose on a cover letter within the electronic communication (email). To minimize confusion and simplify the data gathering process, separate links for surveys in each country were created and sent to the people of those countries. The directions provided each person a link for the survey. On the average, the survey took about ten minutes to complete. The response rate could not be determined mathematically since the number of subscribers to some of the newsgroups was not known to the researchers. However, a response rate of 20% was estimated as per the known number of colleagues and possible number of subscribers to various newsgroups that may have received the survey information. Participants in each country were given a period of three weeks to asynchronously complete the survey as per their availability, and they were encouraged to respond within the allotted time since it would only take about ten minutes. However, participants were able to complete the survey even months after the allotted time since the survey was available to them. During a given month, only individuals from one country were sent the survey for completion. During a four-month period, the surveys were sent to people of four different countries and the responses were received electronically within this four-month period (February to May 2005). Surveys were sent first to Afghans, then to Jamaicans, Turkish, and finally to Americans in the United States. The survey was first distributed electronically through the Internet to a group of professional Afghans living in Afghanistan, the United States, and many other countries throughout the Middle East, Europe, and Asia in the early months of 2005. The participants were encouraged to complete the survey within a three-week period. A month later, the survey directions and link were sent to people in Jamaica, and they too were asked to respond within a three-week period. In the following two months, similar procedures were followed with Turkish and American populations. The demographics of respondent populations and their views on age related questions from the questionnaire are shared in the next section.

Initial Survey Results and Implications

For the primary data, there was an estimated 20% response rate (a total of 677 individuals) to the survey from the countries studied. Parts of this research were originally published in the January issue of *Journal of Applied Management and Entrepreneurship* (Mujtaba, et al., 2006). As can be seen from Table 2, there were 57 respondents from Afghanistan, 42 from Jamaica, 36 from Turkey, 92 from the Bahamas, 379 from Thailand, and 71 respondents from the United States of America for a total of 206 respondents. There also was an equal distribution of both genders responding to the survey and presenting their views on aging and employment practices regarding older workers.

It was very interesting to note that the preponderance of respondents from the U.S. and Jamaica are female. Given the later "scores" and comments regarding the prevalence of age discrimination, it is possible that older females may feel, perceive, or observe the presence of such discrimination more keenly than males. Perhaps this is an avenue for future research in order to see if there is a relationship between gender and the perception of age discrimination.

It was interesting to note that the representation among the age groups is more or less evenly balanced between "young" (the first two categories) and "old" (the second two), except for Turkey, where the "young" clearly outweigh the "old." Yet this disparity does show up in the Turkish scores, except perhaps for the category of "evidence of age discrimination against 'younger workers,'" where half the respondents reported seeing evidence of such discrimination.

Also, for United States, the bulk of the respondents are "White" with only one Hispanic, which seems surprising. Thus, the age discrimination reported for the U.S. is by predominantly white respondents, which means perhaps that the age discrimination is not "colored" by race, skin color, or ethnicity discrimination. So, age discrimination impacts people of all backgrounds regardless of each individual's unique characteristics.

Table 2 - Number of Respondents	
Country	*Total*
Afghanistan	57
Turkey	36
USA	71
Jamaica	42
Bahamas	92
Thailand	379
Total	677

The education level was very high for all categories, but nonetheless sizable numbers of respondents reported that they did not know whether age discrimination against older workers was illegal in their country. As a matter of fact, out of 206 respondents from the four countries, 48 "did not know" or were not sure if age discrimination was legally wrong in their country. Clearly, something may be lacking in all this advanced education with regard to hiring practices and awareness of rules. Of course, many of these so called "well educated" individuals are more likely to become managers and leaders because of their education and, thus, should receive training on age-related employment practices.

For the United States, 63 out of 71 respondents chose "education" as their employment industry which makes the fact that the USA category reported in Age Perceptions that "older workers" by a 42-29 majority do NOT get more respect than younger workers, which cast doubt on being an "older" and "respected" academic.

The United States category reported by a "vote" of 42-29 that it had diversity training, and the other categories had significant minorities reporting such training, all of which makes the fact that so much age discrimination in employment was reported even more disturbing. Perhaps the diversity training should have a much stronger age component, which could be another avenue for future research.

All categories of respondents reported that older workers get more respect than younger ones, except notably for the United States, which reported that older workers do NOT get more respect from managers and employers. This result, again, is disturbing considering the educational levels and educational setting of the U.S. respondents.

Once again, the U.S. figures are disturbing, as more than half the respondents reported that it is more difficult for U.S. older workers to get jobs in their country. Moreover, this result occurs despite the facts of U.S. age discrimination law, the awareness of such law, as well as the respondents' thoughts and moral norm regarding age discrimination as morally wrong, and the prevalence of diversity training.

With regard to evidence of age discrimination, the scores were close for Turkey and Afghanistan in reporting "no," and also close for Jamaica in reporting "yes"; but yet again the U.S. scores were disturbing, as by a "vote" of 45-26, the U.S. respondents reported seeing evidence of age discrimination against older workers.

With regard to age discrimination against older workers being legally wrong, respondents from Turkey and Jamaica reported "no" by sizable margins, but there was a very big "do not know" "vote." Afghanistan reported "yes" by a material margin, but also with a fair "do not know" "vote." What is very clear is the U.S reporting, where an overwhelming number of respondents (63) stated that such discrimination was legally wrong, with only three reporting "no" and only five reporting "do not know." Yet the fact that U.S. law prohibiting age discrimination exists, and that people are overwhelmingly aware of this law, apparently does not prevent, as reported by the respondents, age discrimination against older workers from occurring in the United States. This provides further support for the notion of cultural conditioning being a very strong "driver" of human behavior.

In all the countries except Turkey, which had a "tie vote," the respondents reported that such discrimination was morally wrong, but with material "do not know" "votes"; but for the U.S., by a 58-7 vote, with seven "do not know" "votes," the respondents reported that age discrimination was morally wrong in the United States. Once again this presumably prevailing moral belief in the U.S. that age discrimination is morally wrong apparently does not prevent such discrimination from happening in employment. The conclusion also provides further support that cultural conditioning can be a strong influence on the behavior of individuals regarding employment practices.

All country categories reported by wide majorities that they regard age discrimination against older workers as personally morally wrong. The U.S. figures are especially evident, as 69 said "yes," and no one reported "no," and only two respondents said they did not know.

All country categories by wide majorities reported that such discrimination was wrong. Thus, for both young and old workers the respondents believe that discrimination against them based on their age is morally wrong. People of all countries seem to believe that an employee should be hired based on qualifications for the job's requirements rather than his or her age category.

Bahamas and the United Sates Comparison[1]

For comparative study, using statistical analysis, the authors studied the responses of Bahamians with those the respondents from the United States. This

---

[1] *Coauthored with Albert Williams and Marissa Samuels, Nova Southeastern University.*

specific study tested 15 multiple regression models to see the relationship between age discrimination and the variables, including gender, age, race, country where you live the most, country were you presently live, education, years with your current employers, industry, and diversity training. The constant term was significant for all 15 multiple regressions, implying that there were other variables that could have been included in the analyses. Gender was significant for 2 of the 15 models. Males felt that it was easier for younger workers to find employment. Females were more inclined to work with both younger and older workers. Race and age were not significant factors in this study. Country where you live the most was significant in 5 models. Those participants living in the U.S. tended to not engage in age discrimination as compared with those living in the Bahamas. Education was significant in 1 model. More educated participants tended to not have ethical and moral issues with age discrimination. The variable, Years with your current employers, was significant in 1 model. Those with longer periods with their current employers did not see evidence of age discrimination by managers. Industry was significant in 3 models. Those employed in education and government did not perceive age discrimination as compared with those in the private sector. Diversity training was significant in 1 model. Those who had diversity training were aware of age discrimination towards both younger and older workers. The diversity training and education findings emerge as significant in that an organization that is committed to enhancing the education levels of its employees as a well as providing them with diversity training should expect to see beneficial results in a more legal and moral workforce, particularly regarding discrimination in the workplace.

Using statistical analysis, the authors also compared the responses of Americans with respondents from Thailand. The authors, once again, tested 15 multiple regression models to see the relationship between age discrimination and the variables, including gender, age, race, country where you live the most, country were you presently live, education, years with your current employers, industry, and diversity training. The results demonstrated that gender was significant for 2 of the 15 models. Males tended to discriminate based on age towards older workers. Females were more inclined to work with both younger and older workers. Age was significant once, since younger respondents experienced age discrimination towards younger workers by managers. Race was significant in 3 models. White and Black Americans were more inclined to not discriminate based on age, Asians were more inclined to discriminate in favor of older workers. Country where you live the most was significant in 3 models. Those participants living in the U.S. tended to not discriminate based on age as compared with those living in Thailand. Education was significant in 5 models. More educated participants tended to not have ethical and moral issues with age discrimination. The variable, Years with your current employers, was significant in 4 models. Those working for longer periods with their current employers did not see evidence of age discrimination by managers. Industry was significant in 3 models. Those employed in education and government did not witness age discrimination as compared with those in the private sector. Diversity training was significant in 5 models. Those who had diversity training were more aware of the prevalence of age discrimination towards both younger and older workers. Moreover, those respondents with diversity training were more fully aware of the legal and ethical ramifications of age discrimination.

The main implication of this research is that diversity training and awareness make a difference in the perceptions of people regarding discrimination based on age. Therefore, companies that are concerned about the proper and fair treatment of their older workers and prospective employment candidates should provide relevant diversity workshops and programs. These workshops and training should have a very strong foundation in the law, particularly anti-discrimination law, as well as an emphasis on ethics, especially the absolute necessity of treating employees and applicants in a respectful, dignified, worthwhile, and moral manner. By instituting such diversity training, employers will be able to achieve and maintain high morals as well as morale in the workplace, to recruit qualified diverse applicants, and to make sure they are obeying legal laws when operating in the United States.

Thailand and the United Sates Comparison[2]

This study was conducted similar to the Bahamian and U.S. comparison. For the first dependent variable, representing "Do "older workers" get more respect than "younger workers" in your country?", significant beta coefficients were found for the constant term (b=1.151 with p-value= 0.000) and the independent variable, Education (b = -0.039 with a p-value = 0.001). The significant constant term implies that there are other factors that can explain this dependent variable that were not included in the model. The results for education implied that more educated respondents from the both countries felt that more respect was given to older workers than younger workers. For the second dependent variable, representing, "Do "older workers" get more respect than "younger workers" from managers and employers in your country?", significant beta coefficients were found for the constant (b = 1.431 with a p-value<0.0001). For the third dependent variable, representing "Do you prefer to work with older workers, younger workers or both?", significant beta coefficients were found for the constant term (b = 2.519 with a p-value of 0.000) and Gender (b = 0.102 with a p-value = 0.055). Gender was marginally significant, and implied that males had a slight preference to work with older employees than females. Females tended to prefer to work with younger employees or both. The fourth dependent variable, representing "Do most managers in your culture prefer to work with older, younger or all workers?" had significant beta coefficients for the constant term (b = 2.337 with a p-value = 0.000), Race (b = 0.093 with a p-value = 0.002), and Country where you lived the most (b = -0.051 and a p-value = 0.002). The same explanation is given for the constant term. The significant result for Race implied that White and Black respondents stated that managers preferred to work with older workers, while Asians respondents stated that managers preferred to work with younger workers or both. For the independent variable, Country where you live the most, respondents from the U.S. stated that managers preferred to work with both older and younger employees while respondents from Thailand stated that managers preferred to work

---

[2] *Coauthored with Albert Williams, Nova Southeastern University, and Jatuporn Sungkhawan, Southeast Bangkok College.*

with older employees. These two independent variables produced different results. In regards to gender, the sixth dependent variable, representing "Is it more difficult for "older workers" to find jobs in your country?" had significant beta coefficients for the constant term (b = 1.704 with a p-value = 0.000), Gender (b = -0.078 with a p-value = 0.034), Industry (b = -0.027 with a p-value = 0.006), and Diversity Training (b = -0.072 with a p-value = 0.049). This result implied that male respondent from both countries felt that it was not more difficult for older employees to find jobs. Females from both countries felt that it was more difficult for older employees to find jobs. Respondents in education and government felt that is was not more difficult for older workers to find jobs. Respondents in the private sector felt that it was more difficult for older workers to find jobs. This finding reinforces the belief that the private sector prefers younger workers. Those with diversity training felt that it was more difficult for older workers to find jobs. Diversity training exposed the participants to many dimensions of discrimination and thus impacts their understanding of the workplace.

Overall, this study also tested 15 multiple regression models to see the relationship between age discrimination and the variables, including gender, age, race, country where you live the most, country were you presently live, education, years with your current employers, industry, and diversity training. Gender was significant for 2 of the 15 models. Males tended to discriminate based on age towards older workers. Females were more inclined to work with both younger and older workers. Age was significant once since younger respondents experienced age discrimination towards younger workers by managers. Race was significant in 3 models. White and Black Americans were more inclined to not discriminate based on age, Asians were more inclined to discriminate in favor of older workers. Country where you live the most was significant in 3 models. Those participants living in the U.S. tended to not discriminate based on age as compared with those living in Thailand. Education was significant in 5 models. More educated participants tended to not have ethical and moral issues with age discrimination. The variable, Years with your current employers, was significant in 4 models. Those working for longer periods with their current employers did not see evidence of age discrimination by managers. Industry was significant in 3 models. Those employed in education and government did not witness age discrimination as compared with those in the private sector. Diversity training was significant in 5 models. Those who had diversity training were more aware of the prevalence of age discrimination towards both younger and older workers. Moreover, those respondents with diversity training were more fully aware of the legal and ethical ramifications of age discrimination. The main implication of this research is also that diversity training and awareness make a difference in the perceptions of age discrimination.

Observations from the Study

As a result of the overall review of the data from each country and the respondents' verbatim comments (included later in this chapter), one could make some observations regarding cultural views about aging and its behavioral implications in the workplace of each culture. At a general level, one can make some conclusions with regard to "unearned privileges" or "unearned advantages" to various categories of workers in different cultures. Previously, *unearned privilege* was defined as advantages given to some individuals and withheld from others, without regard to their efforts or abilities, because of their perceived difference. What is interesting to think about is that such privileges often come to one group or category of individuals at a cost to other individuals or category of workers. From a qualitative analysis of the data, one can conclude that younger workers in the United States and in Jamaica tend to receive unearned privileges simply because of their age. Such privileges to young workers mean stereotypes, biases, and discrimination to those individuals who fall in the category of older workers. So, older workers in the United States and in Jamaica are at a disadvantage when they are competing for jobs against younger individuals in the marketplace. One must reflect on the fact that all younger workers will eventually become older workers, thus losing the unearned privileges to those who are seen as young.

Similarly, because of tradition and thousands of years of cultural conditioning, older workers in Turkey and Afghanistan seem to enjoy unearned privileges. It is important to emphasize that these are simply assumptions about older workers being wise and mature until they prove themselves otherwise. It is also assumed that younger workers are not at the same level of maturity as older workers until they prove themselves otherwise. Therefore, younger workers with extremely high levels of knowledge and maturity when compared to many older workers are only given the opportunity after they have proven themselves. So, young workers might be at a disadvantage in such cultures when they are competing for jobs against older workers.

It is striking to see that the U.S. respondents, principally from the education sector, reported such a prevalence of age discrimination, and especially so considering that the U.S. has such an extensive anti-discrimination legal network, which the vast number of the U.S. respondents were aware of, and also that the U.S. respondents reported their beliefs as well as the prevailing norms that age discrimination was legally wrong, ethically and morally wrong, and, moreover, they reported that they had diversity training. So, what does the data reveal? Despite all the legal and moral norms as well as the training, the respondents still report significant age discrimination in the United States. It is clear that national and international managers, leaders, and twenty-first century professionals need to effectively prepare and deal with age discrimination issues in their workplace.

The current data supported previous data and the conclusions of other researchers with regard to the widespread presence of age discrimination in the United States. Raymond Gregory (2001) pointed out that "I can still state, without fear of contradiction, that age discrimination continues to be a common practice in the American business firms." Gregory ends with an optimistic view by stating that "isolated instance of enlightened thinking on the subject of age discrimination might very well be a harbinger of fairer days for older workers in the future." Gregory also stated that "Discrimination against middle-aged and older workers has long been a common practice of American business firms. Nearly all middle-aged and older workers, at some time during their work careers, will suffer the consequences of an age-biased employment-related action." While the law prohibits age discrimination in the American workplace, workers over the age of 40 are "nevertheless subjected to adverse employment decisions motivated by false, stereotypical notions concerning the physical and mental abilities of older workers" (Gregory, 2001). As such, older workers in the U.S. workplace are often encouraged into premature retirements, denied developmental opportunities that can lead to promotions, denied deserved transfers or job promotions, terminated for causes that have little to nothing with their performance, and are excluded from long-term decision-making due to biases and assumptions. Gregory (2001) mentions that "America will be an even better country once age discrimination in the workplace is eliminated." The authors of this book also hope that the elimination of age discrimination in the workplace comes faster; and, of course, you (the reader) can be a huge factor in this process by doing your part to become aware of such biases and not letting inaccurate stereotypes and myths about older workers negatively impact your hiring decisions.

Respondent Comments from Afghanistan
1. Although in Afghanistan respect comes with age but discrimination against poor and people with no ties to rich and famous is common. Even the educated Afghan-Americans who were suppose to help stabilize and reconstruct the country, when in power, offered their relatives and friends the high paying positions and other favors such as distribution of land, gas stations, all sorts of permits. As an Islamic country, youth should respect their elders for they receive God's reward for doing so and vice versa. Older people are considered blessing at home contrary to U.S. where they are deposited to the nursing homes. Even when older people make mistakes, the youngsters would not voice to humiliate them, which sometimes is not such a good thing. At the work environment, since Afghanistan is not fully computerized yet like many developed nations, experience is preferred. It is believed that by practice one omits making errors or perfection is achieved. Finally, elders reserve special rights over younger individuals – one should restrain from abusing them or cause any harm to them or even ignore them. The elders speak first, start eating the food first, lead the way and walk first, and set first at the top while others are standing poise. When setting, they make sure their back is not towards them. Most young co-workers respect their elder colleagues by calling them "uncle" or "aunt" to avoid calling them by their real names (surely, we are talking about decent people and decent behaviors of the majority).
2. The public sector, NGOs, UN Agencies, Donor Offices all in a row are replacing 90% of their older workers with young workers. However, in the private sector the older workers with good experience are still getting the jobs. However, the private sector has very limited job opportunities. And that is due to the fact that these experienced public servants are used to work at lower salaries. Whereas, the younger workers not only avoid working at low wages but are also ambitious to replace the managers above 40 years old.
3. In Afghanistan, people are stepping in a new world and the new world starts with new technology. The older workers are not always familiar or are less familiar with them, which delays the process of accepting new system with new

technology. This is one of the main reasons for age discrimination. The other reason is that older workers have communist systems in mind and this issue makes them to be discriminated from young generation.

4.   Afghanistan's government officials are now restructuring their laws and should make sure that "older workers" and "younger workers" are welcomed to all jobs.

5.   The older you are the lesser you are "worth" in the corporate American culture.

6.   There was no age discrimination in Afghanistan against older workers, but there is age discrimination against older workers in the USA, particularly in the industrial and manufacturing sectors of economy.

7.   In Afghanistan, age is not yet a big issue because life expectancy continues to be very low. The retirement age is set at 55 years, which I think is not fair.

8.   I think it is wrong to discriminate against older workers, because they have knowledge, they have learned through experience. They are more laid back due to the fact that they do not need to be as aggressive in doing things as they were young, but one should not hold that against them. As for young worker, they also need to be given a chance to prove themselves. You cannot discriminate against them simply because they are young or inexperienced. You have to let them apply themselves and show what they can do. We all have to start somewhere.

9.   I believe that the level of age discrimination depends in the industry or the specific organization where one works. The two different categories of work field that I have experience in are sales/business and pharmaceutical/health. In these two fields I have noticed that sales/business favors youngsters with more energy and enthusiasm where pharmaceutical/health favors older workers with more experience.

10.   I think I like to work with older people and the reason is that they want to work (at least most of them), and the second thing is that they listen. But of course sometimes you see they are useless in their job or in today's language they are not computerized. We had a few people (older guys) in our office and they were very intelligent but they were really slow which sometimes makes you crazy. But at the same time. I learned myself how to be quick or what does it mean to be quick. I like to work with younger people as well... because I can teach them how they can work and work efficiently.

11.   It is difficult to for older workers in my country to update their knowledge about the modern way of management. They are hard to change and adopt.

12.   I think they should give the work to someone who is able to do it best, where I work we have old coworkers who are over 60 years of age and just don't want to retire. They are paid the highest salary while us young worker do their work for them. I think just having few grey hair doesn't really make you the expert in your field of work. I do agree that experience is important but in today's society most young people are educated and much more aware of the environment around them than the old generation. I have heard of cases where a young intelligent person applied for a job and the person was told that he can't get the job because HE IS NOT OLD ENOUGH, not because he is not qualified but because he does not have those few grey hair to look smart and qualified in the eye of the employer. It is sad.

13. In my country, old age people get more respect or attention everywhere, they are listened, their ideas accepted and everyone thinks they know everything, even if they don't. I am not against respect for elders but I want younger people to be heard as well. Their ideas be accepted if they are right.

14. Personal ambition and drive is what equates to success with one's career, not age.. Discrimination is present everywhere, including with a variety of age groups.

15. It's upsetting to see that even in today's society, age and personal looks DOES play a role in getting a job. I have seen my former employer throwing away applications after seeing someone dropping off an application. The media is a good example showing women having cosmetic surgery before going for a job interview because they think it will give them a better chance. Regardless of their race, ethnicity, age, and gender. I believe if a person meets the requirements/criteria and can perform the tasks then they should get the job.

16. In my opinion, older people are an asset to the organization.

17. Discrimination of any kind, age, place and ethnicity is totally wrong.

Respondent Comments from Turkey

1. I have noticed the difference in treating younger workers between USA and Turkey. This difference is mostly in terms of Job security. Older employees in Turkey tend to keep their jobs longer than they should, and by doing that they not only play a negative role in terms of feasibility, but also they close the doors to young people to start up with no experience. Older people with experience tend to find jobs easier than younger new starters.

2. The company at which I work is trying to back everything- no matter right or wrong – that they do. I have been working at the current company for a year now and continuously disturbed by the two women with whom I am sharing the room. I have talked about the issue with my director many times; however although he knows that I am right, he does not support me at all since the others have been working at the company more than seven years now and he just does not want to deteriorate his relationship with them.

3. As long as demand and supply is not in balance younger people will be preferred due to less cost and their ability to adjust themselves to new developments. The increase of efficiency due to technical innovations will never balance and for this specific reason age discrimination cannot be avoided because of wild competition in world.

4. In Turkey, it is not pronounced but people over 35 are considered as older workers. Due to the size of the younger population, you can often see statements such as "applicants should be younger than the age of 30" in job listings. People respect older workers in terms of their experience but some older workers are not that open to change either.

5. I do not support any kind of discrimination. But in reality companies must have a choice between younger and older ones. I am not sure what should be considered to make a choice.

Respondent Comments from United States of America

1. Age discrimination against "older workers" is rampant in this country (United States). It is criminal!
2. Younger workers want to get to the top much more quickly than before. I believe they have a high sense of entitlement. Generally, the older workers that I see feel stuck in their positions and don't like change. Younger workers have little patience for this and dismiss their experience and intelligence.
3. North America is somewhat culturally diverse. See "Nine Nations of North America" or related literature. I wonder just how much diversity there is within and among the regions discussed in geographical terms. So living in the USA may not identify anything like a homogeneous population. I expect there will be more age-related conflicts as we get a substantially large older population. This conflict will become more visible toward the end of this decade when major parts of the baby-boomer generation try to retire. Both public and private pension plans will not be able to cover them. Then I expect political forces will emerge to tax the young to support the old; and contrary-wise to avoid taxes on the young.
4. Each individual should be evaluated based on their own merit and current and potential contribution to their organization, NOT age or any other improperly prejudicial criterion.
5. Age should be at the end of one's hiring criteria. Capability and getting along with others should be at the top of the list.
6. In our place of work, they hire the very young, who in turn stay to finish their education and leave. This is not good. The position they held keeps getting passed around and in the process it loses some of knowledge about that position. They need more mature people who could stay longer and give value to their job.
7. Currently, I live in the Bahamas where younger workers feel that the older workers should quite active employment and give them a chance on the social mobility ladder.
8. Several older workers perceive that they will not be hired for new employment because they are too old. I've heard several people over 50 say that they can't leave this organization because they are too old to obtain employment elsewhere. On the opposing side, I've heard opinions from younger workers dismissed because "they don't know what they're talking about." Usually followed by a comment on the lack of experience. My sense is that this is a perception problem on both sides.
9. It seems that a lot of 50-year old men lose their jobs and are the unemployable. A lot of people under 25 don't seem to be treated as though their opinion matters. Women seem to experience it more than men
10. Directors, managers and supervisors should feel good about having older workers: they are experienced, reliable, and are more loyal.
11. Female workers experience more discrimination than male workers and older female workers experience far more discrimination that their male counterparts.
12. Older workers are still "respected" in my country as is in Jamaica and most of the Caribbean. However, the situation is changing as Governments especially, are insisting that older workers SHOULD RETIRE when they have reached

'retirement' age. Also, the 'respect' for older workers appears to be "changing" as young people have different 'mind sets' with regards to "age."

13. The older worker brings maturity, experience, a sense of responsibility, and usually a stronger work ethic than younger workers. It seems like it's harder for an older worker to change jobs as the potential employer prefers a younger worker.

14. While the public philosophy in the US is that age discrimination is both illegal and immoral, when individuals are asked to submit CVs with past work history (generally for more than the last 5 years), approximate age becomes apparent to the prospective employer, making the possibility of age discrimination "easy."

15. Seniority prevails as is "paying one's dues." Younger workers, especially those without work experience have a difficult time "breaking" into corporate arena. Top jobs are opportunities for those highly educated and with connections.

16. I think that "over 40"---is too young to be considered an older worker–"over 50" would be more appropriate.

17. An employee's worth and candidacy for consideration in a new job should be based upon competence, knowledge, and experience – regardless of age.

18. I think in general, older workers are discriminated against, particularly when seeking a position. In the education field there is probably less of this going on because more experience is looked upon as something good and the pay will reflect that. In other businesses, two young people could be hired (at the salary of the one older individual) to do the work that one older person was doing and who was let go because "their position was no longer needed."

19. I certainly have heard of issues that older workers have had with employers who replace them with younger, less expensive workers, then wonder what happened to all of the quality and customer service that they had before. Older workers bring stability to the organization (as Wal-Mart knows), while young workers take time off to go to the beach, to party, and do not have the dedication that the older worker brings to the workplace.

20. Discrimination in any form is ethically and morally wrong. We must hold to the Golden Rule. We must learn to look beyond the physical person and accept and appreciate those who are different.

21. I feel that older workers should have a set age to retire and adhere to it, instead of 'clogging up' the system and hindering younger employees from entering to higher positions. I feel that companies need to have policies in place so people would know beforehand what their retirement age is. I feel it is inhumane to abruptly force retirement on anyone. Employees deserve to leave with their dignity intact.

22. When it comes to age discrimination of the younger workers, I think the younger they are, the better to gain experience. The older when you reach a certain age of about 65, I think it's time for you to retire. You have worked all your life, so it's time to enjoy life.

23. In my opinion, in the Bahamas, we have challenge with the work ethic of the younger worker, as they are eager to get the job, however that zeal seems to die as though they do not want to work.

24. I find that older workers are stuck in the past and not open for change. On the other hand younger workers are more interested in the amount of money they make versus the type of job. The younger workers do not want to do manual labour, they prefer to work behind a desk in an office.
25. Old and young can make positive contributions to any company.
26. Older workers may perhaps give less productivity but their attendance and punctuality are much better than younger people. They are more dedicated to the organization.
27. Yes, I do not think anyone should be discriminated no matter what age the (person) might be. As long as they meet the requirements for the job and are capable of performing, why turn them down? Everybody (has) to work. Unless they are a minor or way beyond the retirement, I think they should be given a chance.
28. When it comes to the older workers, I think that when they reach age 55 years, they should consider retirement.
29. Age issue in our country is morally wrong because when you reach a certain age, government and private firms do not want to hire you. Also if you are too young and inexperienced for the position. Most older workers are not in the forefront of business such as the receptionist because people tend to want to see a young face.
30. As statistics show, we are living longer because we are learning how to care for our bodies more. Therefore, although they may be old they still have a lot of job experience that organizations can still tap into to train younger employees. Therefore, even though the older workers may reach retirement age, perhaps organizations can look at hiring older workers as consultants or trainers. This may be prove to be an asset for organizational growth.
31. I feel that older workers are valuable to organizations. Most of them have a wealth of knowledge that should be passed on to younger generations. As long as they are performing at an acceptable level they should be considered. Older workers are wiser, mature, and they have a great sense of loyalty to the organization.
32. Yes, we have such a dilemma. People at both ends of the age continuum are either workers or slackers. So we have to do a whole lot of sifting to ensure we get the best workers/performers/non-slackers at any age....Some diversity is always welcomed from the work/job standpoint even though it is not always welcomed on other "fronts."
33. In some cases, individuals may be old, but well within the retirement age, however they are forced to retire or take a package because the institution favors younger people for the job positions.
34. I feel that as long as one contributes to the development and growth of their company and themselves, then age should not be a factor. I fortunately have not been faced with discriminatory actions against myself or anyone I know since I have been employed.

Respondent Comments from Thailand

1. I don't really feel that there is discrimination in school and workplace in my country, Thailand, but sex and age discrimination (are) very extreme in my family. It is probably a part of Chinese culture (my grandparents were from China). In my family, whatever older people said (is) always right and (the) male is always the first priority.
2. I think that the individual should be viewed instead of the age. There are older people who are mentally sharp and able to perform. And some young people are very bright and capable of achieving great things.
3. I believe many promotions are filled based on ethnic background or relationship (friends) with hiring manager. Companies are putting managers in place just to fill affirmative action and are afraid of lawsuits. I believe young workers don't have same work ethics as older generation, perhaps because of age or today's society which is more dependent on TV and video games.

Respondent Comments from Jamaica

1. Age discrimination is not an issue that is prevalent in Jamaica at this time. The issue is the shortage or lack of jobs for both young and old people. There has not been a public incident that relates to age discrimination because employees need persons with the requisite education and skills to fill positions of the few available jobs.
2. I have never heard of age discrimination until I came to this country, the USA.
3. Throughout my years of employment in Jamaica I noticed that older workers without college degrees were made redundant and younger workers (college grads and high school grads) were employed to replace the older (more established) workers. The younger workers were paid less than their older counterparts.
4. Discrimination is totally wrong. However it is human nature to have perceptions. Older workers are normally viewed as being more responsible and experienced. This normally implied that older workers would be more productive. Young workers are very productive. Many younger workers are more goal oriented and focused on being successful, therefore they put in the effort to achieve that success. Everyone should be given a chance to improve themselves. Some younger workers are lazy and irresponsible but there are others who like responsibility and work well under pressure. On the other hand older workers are at times lazy and try to use their age as a way of manipulating young workers and have the young workers doing their jobs.
5. I find that older workers do sometimes display certain mindsets that cause them to respond slowly to changes and to be less open to the ideas posited by younger workers. However, older workers are usually more thoughtful in decision making and have the experience to aid them in considering a greater number of variables and possible adverse externalities. Younger workers usually have more fresh ideas. I believe both sides have their strengths and place in the workplace and should be treated equally and with respect and fairness.

6. Each prospective employee should be treated based on their attitude, aptitude, qualification and in some instances experience.
7. It is sometimes difficult for "older workers" to be employed especially if they are not qualified. However, if they are highly qualified, the younger workers do get some form of preference because they can be paid at the minimum of the scale.
8. The job market is very competitive. Depending on the type of jobs available and the income employers are willing to pay, they may make a decision to go for a younger person if the budget is tight. Where the funds permit qualification and experience which favors the older person takes precedence.
9. While I am unsure of the official legal position on age discrimination in Jamaica, most organizations have adopted a set of guidelines for business conduct which expressly forbids age discrimination. As such, the issue – if it exists – is not widely known or debated.
10. While older workers can offer experience not available from younger workers, younger workers are frequently more receptive to training and other opportunities that older workers disdain.
11. The views of the performance of younger workers have changed over the past 5 years or so with many "young" persons now in managerial roles.
12. Ability to perform at the required level should be one of the main criteria in determining who is employed. Far too often wisdom and experience is lost because someone has to retire as the age for retirement has arrived. This relates mainly to government employees and is felt in the area of education in particular.
13. In Jamaica, unemployment among young people is a very worrying problem. Employers all want workers with experience, which is, of course, the one thing, young people don't have.
14. Employment laws in Jamaica are not stringently upheld / enforced, therefore the issues of age and discrimination, while being felt to be morally wrong are not addressed and in some cases are not recognized for what they really are. Therefore, organizations by and large operate in whatever way suits them as they know that actions will not be brought against them, and should that happen, the burden of proof may result in rulings in their favor.
15. It is not really discrimination but older people feel threatened that employers would PREFER to employ some younger workers with degrees, because they may be more willing to accept less salary than they would. Younger workers are frustrated because they feel that although they may have the required qualifications they lack experience and most employers request this.
16. In many cases employers are of the opinion that "older workers" are somewhat set in their work habits; which if they are not good habits, it is more difficult for them to break out of than a "younger workers". On the other hand, I some employers who regard the experience of "older workers" as of a far greater value than the youthfulness and academic superiority of the "younger workers."
17. I believe that age should not matter, as long as the individual is qualified (training, experience and aptitude and has the right attitude to learn); then age should never be any issue. It is natural that the older worker is likely to have more experience and knowledge/ training since age will allow (that though it is

not necessarily always the case). And younger workers may not have enough time to gain the training and experience that may be required for a task. Though I believe that given equal opportunity in all respect age should not be an issue. The age will go along way with the right attitude whether as a cooperative follower or exemplary leader. Consequently, there should be no discrimination based on age as the only factor. Personal case of discrimination: when I just graduated from Teachers college, though I was told that I was qualified for certain jobs, I was also told that I was too young, this hurts then and it was not fair. Later the very persons required my service when I was older. Naturally I would have lost interest and zeal for such place.

18. What is regarded as discrimination? I consider mandatory retirement age of 62 or 65, as is the case in many institutions, age discrimination. The preference for older workers vs. younger workers depends on the job to be filled. In some cases, there is a preference for younger workers vs. older ones, and vice versa

19. Selection for a job is based on the capability of the person to perform in the position. This could be based on experience or education/training or a combination. Definitely some jobs will have requirements for expertise, which not many young persons have, although they have the educational background. Younger persons will therefore have to act perhaps in an 'apprentice' role until the requisite skills/expertise has been attained. On the job training is not a new concept in any culture. On the other hand, experience alone by older workers may at times not be sufficient. It would be advantageous to the older worker that job related qualifications be attained, whether he/she intends to retain present position, or change jobs/workplace.

20. Discrimination occurs in both categories of workers identified. The nature of the job will determine the level of discrimination. Some jobs prefer younger and attractive persons while others have a preference for older persons. Equally there is discrimination relating to sex and the survey did not capture that information. Age discrimination primarily occurs as younger persons are preferred for some jobs and older employees are preferred for others. Newer companies appear to have a preference for younger employees. With established companies as well as new companies management positions may more readily be offered to older persons as companies usually ask for experience covering a certain period of time.

21. In Jamaica older people get better jobs and higher salaries than younger persons performing the same jobs. As a younger person every interview that I go on for a job which I am qualified for and have the experience and expertise to perform the interviewer questions my capabilities because of my age (or perception of youth because I don't put it on my resume and I look young). Age is revered in Jamaica because people think that older persons possess greater wisdom, "stick-tuitiveness," and bring status to their establishments.

22. It is imperative that we treat each worker, regardless of age, as an equal. In addition my country should ensure that benefits that accrue in your activity years are protected legally and that you are still able to access vital financial assistance despite age.

23. Now that I am one of the older workers I worry that the time will come when I will be perceived as too old for certain jobs. I know that in some jobs being older is an advantage. Some companies prefer the work ethic of the older generation, while others will not hire you because you are perceived as being too expensive from a health insurance perspective. There are advantages and disadvantages on both sides of the issue and I think smart companies recognize this and make it work for them.

Other Respondent Comments by Country

1. *Brazil* – Managers in my country respect more "older workers," but prefer to work with "younger workers" because they are seen as more productive and more "coachable."
2. *Columbia* – Older workers have high levels of productivity due to their experience over the years and are very valuable to companies. Unfortunately, most companies don't value that. Younger workers are looking for opportunities to (grow) professionally based on their knowledge and studies, but need that chance or opportunity to get hands on business to start having working experience at young ages. Employees expect to hire "younger workers" with experience of "older workers," but they don't open (the) doors of opportunities frequently for younger people.
3. *Haiti* – In my country age discrimination is not an issue. The problem is many young graduates are unable to obtain employment because some of the older employees are reluctant to leave their positions....Most businesses favor older workers because they are considered more experienced.
4. *Haiti* – In Haiti, this a major issue because the person in charge prefers to hire a mature candidate. They prefer the older candidate, (since) the more he will be motivated. All in all, choosing a candidate based on age is considered as discrimination in certain countries.
5. *Pakistan* – Yes, I think that although discrimination depends on the type of work, it is younger workers (that) have more discrimination than older ones.
6. *Peru* – Everyone deserves the same opportunities, respect and (to) be treated with dignity.

General Evaluation of Comments

It is quite revealing to see the actual verbatim comments by the survey respondents, as these comments clearly indicate the challenge global managers will confront in managing a diverse workforce.

One respondent from Afghanistan stressed that respect for elders is based on the fact that the country is very religious, and thus requires that youth respect their elders. Any religious based moral norms against age discrimination would be very important to note. Another respondent stated that older workers with "good experience" can still get jobs in the private sector, but another said the main impediment was that older workers are not familiar with the "new technology." Other respondents also mentioned the technology factor as well as some older workers not being familiar with "modern" management. Another offered the very practical, and ethically egoistic, advice that it is wrong to discriminate against older workers because they have knowledge gained through experience. One respondent related that the retirement age is "set" at 55, but by whom, the private sector or the government? Most disturbing were the two comments by two different respondents. One was that "the older you are, the lesser you are 'worth' in the corporate American culture." The other comment was that there was no age discrimination against older workers in Afghanistan, but there was in the U.S., particularly in the industrial and manufacturing sectors of the U.S. economy.

Again, the technology factor was mentioned by respondents as an impediment to older workers, as well as their perceived inability to adjust and to be open to change. However, similar to the country of Afghanistan, the people of Turkey are heavily influenced by thousands of years of cultural conditioning and history that respect the elderly and their experience.

Once again, it was disturbing to read several comments regarding the prevalence of age discrimination against older workers from the U.S. respondents. One said that age discrimination against older workers was "rampant" in the United States. Another stressed that such discrimination was even more prevalent against older female workers. One comment revealed a particularly "Machiavellian" practice; that is, an employer using an applicant's past work history and resume (or curriculum vitae) so that his or her approximate age becomes "apparent," thus leading to the possibility of age discrimination, and even making such discrimination "easy," according to the respondent. Perhaps that comment revealed how the extensive U.S. anti-discrimination law could be circumvented. One other comment by another respondent was also provocative and thought-provoking, as the respondent stated that due to the older population growing substantially, there likely will be more "age-related conflicts" in the United States. The comments reflected a consensus that although there are positive aspects of obtaining older workers, such as their experience, the negatives of so doing, such as their perceived inability to change or adapt and the lack of technological skills, outweigh the positives.

One comment was troubling, and that was that the respondent did not know the "official legal position" on age discrimination in the country, but "the issue, if it exists, is not widely known or debated." This comment was echoed by another respondent that said that whatever employment laws exist in Jamaica, they are "not stringently upheld/enforced." One comment indicated that the mandatory retirement age at "many institutions" was 62 or 65, which the respondent felt was age discrimination. Finally, the same negative "theme" regarding older workers was reflected from the comments. That is, the benefits of hiring experienced and mature older workers were counterbalanced and outweighed by their lack of modern skills, and as one respondent said, being too "set" in their ways and their habits, which according to the respondent may be "bad habits."

Analysis of Comments

What is the purpose of having such an extensive body of anti-discrimination law, as well as prevailing moral beliefs – individual and societal and even religious-based norms – against age discrimination, and what is the purpose of having "diversity" and sensitivity training, which presumably include an age component, when so much age discrimination in employment is reported by the data and the comments, especially in the United States. Perhaps the law, ethics, religion, and the training are superseded by perceived negative picture of older workers in the culture. Thus, more specific laws or perhaps more stringent laws, or more diversity and sensitivity training are necessary for managers, who recruit, hire, develop, and promote workers, Yet, based on the survey results obtained by the authors, what may really help older workers the most is more technology training and relevant training regarding modern techniques of business management. Resolving these workplace issues - legally, morally, and practically - thus emerges as a critical task for modern day, global, business leaders.

Limitations of the Study and Future Directions

Understanding cultural norms and local practices related to hiring and developing the "older worker" is important for international managers and researchers. While this qualitative study focused on determining the perceptions of people about aging in Afghanistan, Jamaica, Turkey, and the United States, the resources were limited. Furthermore, the survey distribution was limited to those who could speak and read the questions in the English language since the survey was not translated to local languages. Besides having a relatively small sample size, it should be noted that the populations completing the survey were not necessarily representative of the general population in each culture. It is recommended that future researchers translate the questionnaire to the local languages and distribute to more individuals in order to secure a higher percentage of respondents that are a better representative of the local population than the current study. It is also recommended that future studies track the results of some questions using a Likert Scale, while collecting more demographic information from the respondents than included in the current survey. Such changes to the survey also will allow for quantitative analysis of the data and it will make it easier for researchers to duplicate the study with different segments of individuals and industries in the same culture. Future studies also can perhaps analyze the perceptions of male and female respondents using quantitative analysis. Other variables such as education, citizenship, education, and management experiences can also be used to determine the awareness of age discrimination practices in each culture regarding "older workers." Another interesting study might be to provide training to managers of each culture regarding "best" hiring practices in the hiring and retention of "older workers' and then conduct a longitudinal study to determine whether such education or training sessions actually make a difference in their hiring practices. The research question could be related to whether such training sessions result in behavioral changes when it comes to recruitment, hiring, retention, and development of older workers in the workforce.

Summary

In order to effectuate one of the major purposes of this book, actual data on cultural perceptions was necessary. Accordingly, the authors created the survey instrument, an *Age and Cultural Values Questionnaire*; and the authors conducted a cross-cultural study focusing on attitudes to older workers in the workplace and the presence of age discrimination. This chapter provided the survey purpose, methodology, results of the qualitative research, the analysis thereof, and the actual comments about age discrimination practices provided by respondents from the countries of Afghanistan, Turkey, Jamaica, Bahamas, Thailand, and the United States. These comments represented the qualitative aspect of what people think and believe with regard to age in their cultures and how they perceive age discrimination practices in their workplace.

Questions for Discussion
1. Based on your own observations, is there age discrimination in employment practices in the United States or other countries you are familiar with? Provide examples with brief explanations. Is such discrimination illegal in this country? Is it regarded as unethical? Why or why not?
2. From the data obtained from the authors' first survey, despite the fact that the U.S. has explicit and specific laws against age discrimination in employment, many respondents reported that that periodically observed age discrimination in employment against older workers. Why? What is the cause of this illegal discrimination based on age?
3. From the data obtained from the authors' first survey, despite the fact that many U.S. respondents reported that they personally believe age discrimination is morally wrong, and that their society regards it as morally wrong, nonetheless reported material evidence of age discrimination in employment against older workers. Why? What is the cause of such unethical discrimination based on age?
4. From the data obtained from the authors' first survey, Afghanistan and Turkey were two countries where the respondents reported the least amount of age discrimination against older workers, even though little anti-discrimination law exists and employers do little in the way of diversity or ethics training and education. What do you think are some of the reasons for these differences when compared to the United States?

CHAPTER 8

RECRUITING, RETAINING AND DEVELOPING OLDER WORKERS

In today's diverse workplace, managers in an organization must learn how to deal with employees of all ages. It is important to understand that just like any other applicant an older person must meet the employer's required qualifications for the job. Some examples include education, training, skills, or licenses. The older candidate must be able to perform the essential job tasks. In today's work environment, social responsibility of managers and corporations goes beyond ensuring that older people are not discriminated against in the job application process, hiring, discharge, promotion, as well as training opportunities. An organization that creates an inclusive environment for individuals of all ages, genders, races, sizes, and ethnicities will benefit in many ways from having diverse employees and diverse customers. Accordingly, this chapter will discuss the very valuable role that older workers can play as coaches and mentors, particularly in regard to dispelling rumors and resolving conflicts in the workplace. The chapter, moreover, will present some of the "myths and realities" of "mature workers" based on recent articles. The chapter also will discuss the training of older workers, the goal of introducing older workers to the latest technology, involving older workers with technology, and developing the technological knowledge and skills of older workers. The benefits of technology for the older worker and his or her employer are explained and underscored. The chapter also presents the challenges as well as opportunities for older persons in the workplace; and relates what the older person himself or herself can to do to secure employment and to achieve success in the workplace.

Mature Workers: Myths and Realities

How are "older workers" perceived? What are the stereotypes affecting older workers? It seems that older workers have always found it more difficult than others to find jobs, and particularly new jobs after a layoff, and especially in difficult economic times. Why is this so? In part because many employers assume they are more expensive or will not stay long in jobs that pay less than they have earned previously (Rugabar, 2009). Richard A. Posthuma and Russell Campion, in an article in the *Journal of Management*, reviewed the academic literature on these workplace age stereotypes and studied the following negative stereotypes: 1) poor performance, 2) resistance to change, 3) lower ability to learn, and 4) more costly. The first negative stereotype is that older workers are expected to have lower job performance than younger workers. Explanations for the existence of this stereotype are that "people often think that older workers have lower ability (mental or physical), are less able to handle stress, or are less competent, and, therefore, their job performance is lower" (Posthuma and Campion, 2009, p. 165). However, Posthuma and Campion (2009) found that "despite the prevalence of the stereotype about older worker poor performance, extensive research shows very little evidence that job performance declines as employees age....In fact, performance often improves with age, and when declines are found, they tend to be small" (p. 166). They also pointed to a study that demonstrated that job performance actually increases with age when measured by productivity and peer evaluation, as well as other studies which indicated that job tenure is a better predictor of job performance than age (Posthuma and Campion, 2009).

The second stereotype is that older workers are "set in their ways," more resistant to change, and more difficult to train. The concern for employers, therefore, is that their return on training investments will be lower for older workers than younger workers who can be more easily trained. Yet according to Posthuma and Campion, commenting on the academic literature, "There is virtually no research that examines the validity of this stereotype" (2009, p. 168). They also raise a most interesting "change" question, that is, "when and why resistance to change may be functional or dysfunctional to the organization" (2009, p. 168).

The third stereotype is that older workers have lower ability to learn; and thus have less potential for development than do younger workers; and consequently older workers receive fewer training and development opportunities. As to the validity of this stereotype, Posthuma and Campion state that the research evidence is "mixed" (2009, p. 168); and they point out that "although one study of employee training in a retail setting found that older workers do not need more training than younger employees..., another found that older workers have less mastery of training materials and complete the training more slowly" (2009, p. 168). In addition, Posthuma and Campion relate that "there is also evidence that some training methods such as active participation, modeling, and self-paced learning may be more effective for older workers" (2009, p. 169). As such, they recommend that future research should examine why certain methods of training, such as lecture, online, self-paced, video interactive, role-playing, may be better for either older or younger workers.

The fourth stereotype is that older workers are more costly since they are paid higher compensation, use more benefits, and are closer to retirement. Posthuma and Campion state that several studies have revealed that this negative stereotype can engender a perception, especially by managers, that older workers have less economic value (2009, p. 169). However, Posthuma and Campion found that "there is comparatively little evidence on the validity of this cost stereotype" (2009, p. 170). Yet there is evidence, they note, that the salaries of older workers may be higher than those of younger workers (2009, p. 170). "However, there are other potential factors that may offset these salary differentials....for example, there is evidence that older workers have lower rates of absenteeism" (Posthuma and Campion, 2009, p. 170). Posthuma and Campion also emphasize that more research is needed to determine the validity of this stereotype and also to ascertain if other factors, such as the quality of work performance and diligence, may counterbalance higher salaries and benefits (2009, p. 170).

Posthuma and Campion (2009) conclude their article on a "high note" for older workers by discussing positive stereotypes of older workers, specifically that they are more dependable, honest, trustworthy, loyal, and committed to the job, and thus less likely to quit or miss work, and also that older workers are more stable as well as more social, sincere, nurturing, and sociable. Posthuma and Campion (2009) point out, moreover, that studies exist that show that older workers are less likely to steal from their employers, have lower rates of absenteeism, and are less likely to quit (p. 170).

Commenting on perceptions of older workers, Deborah Russell, the American Association of Retired Persons' (AARP) Director of Workforce Issues, admits: "Despite their strengths, older workers often are perceived to resist training, dislike answering to younger bosses or have poor computer training" (Carpenter, 2008, p. 4D). *Business Week*, in a 2008 article about formerly retired workers, called "The Unretired," now seeking to reenter the workforce due to their deteriorating economic condition, noted that "their job search is complicated by what some feel is a general reluctance to hire seniors, who may need extra training or health care" (Green, 2008, p. 48). *HR Magazine* (Grossman, 2008) presented some similarly disturbing findings regarding the perceptions, as well as "misperceptions," of older workers, in an article section titled "Mature Workers: Myths and Realities." The magazine listed six perceptions regarding older workers, and then discussed whether these perceptions were accurate. The six were:

- Older workers cost more.
- Older workers are absent more.
- The health care costs of older workers are greater.
- Older workers are harder to train.
- Older workers are "coasting," that is, waiting for retirement.
- Older workers require "special treatment," which causes intergenerational clashes.

First, regarding the cost factor, the "reality" according to *HR Magazine* is that older workers do cost more, "but not by much." Citing an Urban Institute study of compensation and health care costs, *HR Magazine* indicated that the "financial divide" is only about 10%. Specifically concerning the productivity factor, the "answer" depends on one's perspective. Thus if one is "...an economist, older workers are less productive because they may have higher salaries. If you're a psychologist, they're equally productive because they may have more experience" (Grossman, 2008, p. 40). *Business Week* noted that senior executives add value to the organization by contributing the intangible values of "gut, patience, and perspective" (Lowry, 2008, p. 50). *Business Week* also noted that older workers possess "institutional knowledge," which many, frequently "job-hopping" younger workers, especially managers, may lack (Lowry, 2008, p. 48). The authors of this book would also point out that based on their own experiences and knowledge, older workers may actually cost less if they possess retirement and health care benefits from either previous employment or the government than younger workers who may need all these benefits fully. Also, there is an enhanced productivity factor that inures to older workers who are more committed and loyal and who bring years of knowledge, experience, and wisdom to the job. Older workers thus "work smarter" as well as longer.

Second, regarding the absenteeism issue, *HR Magazine* reported U.S. Bureau of Labor Statistics figures: In 2007, full-time employees ages 25-54 were absent at a ratio of 3.2 per 100; whereas employees ages 55 and over were absent with greater frequency, but not by much, at a ratio of 3.6 per 100. The conclusion was that the data does not exist that older workers are sick more. Moreover, the magazine quoted an executive from Borders who stated that older workers "are more loyal and are less likely to call in sick with false reasons" (Grossman, 2008, p. 40). The authors of this book would also like to relate that based on their knowledge and experiences, older workers appear to take fewer sick and "personal" days than younger workers.

Concerning the third factor, health care costs, *HR Magazine* indicated that there is a gradual increase in health care spending for workers age 40 and beyond. However, any "significant differentials" do not occur until age 65. The magazine reported the findings of two studies: One was an Urban Institute 2004 study that found that the difference in health care claims filed by workers aged 55-64 compared to employees aged 25-34 was about $900. The other study was by the AARP in 2005 which found that the employees aged 55-64 cost on average 1.4 to 2.2 times as much in health care costs than workers aged 30-40.

The fourth factor involved training. *HR Magazine* related that older workers do in fact as a general rule require more assistance and "hands-on practice." The magazine reported a survey conducted by the Center on Aging and Work at Boston College which disclosed that 44% of human resource managers indicated that older workers are "reluctant to try new technology," and that "some workers have been slow coming around" (Grossman, 2008, p. 41). Nevertheless, the magazine quoted a company executive who said that older workers do "come around when given more time" to technology (Grossman, 2008, p. 41), as well as related that a 2006 survey of more than 400 organizations revealed that only 15% viewed the technology gap as a "potential downside" to hiring older persons (Grossman, 2008, p. 41). The authors of this book also would add that, yes, it may take longer to train older workers to enable them to acquire new skills and knowledge, but older workers do in fact change jobs less frequently; and accordingly it actually may be more cost effective to train older rather than younger employees.

The fifth factor raised the "coasting" question; that is, that older workers are merely waiting for retirement. This *HR Magazine* declared was a "myth," citing a national study of 600 organizations wherein the human resource managers reported no significant drop-off of productivity for older workers. The study also found that older workers were "more committed" to their careers than younger employees.

Perhaps distressingly, the study in addition found that significant percentages of workers in all age categories were "coasting" (Grossman, 2008, p. 41).

Finally, the "special treatment" and concomitant "intergenerational clashes" assertions were addressed by *HR Magazine.* The magazine reported an intergenerational, worker, "roundtable" discussion regarding these issues in 2007. The discussion revealed that "baby-boomers" criticized their younger colleagues for inappropriate dress, for being "ill-mannered," and for spending too much time on cell phones; whereas younger workers criticized their older colleagues for their unwillingness to see the "value of energy and fresh thinking young people bring to collaboration," as well as for the failure of many older workers to learn to use technology (Grossman, 2008, p. 41). Nonetheless, *HR Magazine* opined that the "fear of intergenerational dissonance may be hype" (Grossman, 2008, p. 41). The magazine quoted a Borders executive who trained and coached employees for many years. This executive stated that actually a firm will have more conflict if it has employees predominantly in the 20-25 years category; rather, what is better for the organization is a "good mix" of employees, and particularly employees that will respect one another. The executive also noted that older employees tend to have a "calming influence" in the workplace (Grossman, 2008, p. 41). *HR Magazine* also raised the issue of conflict occurring in the workplace due to employers accommodating older workers with part-time and flexible schedules. Yet one common sense solution to this "special treatment" or equity problem is for the employer to offer to all its employees "flextime," compressed and reduced scheduling, part-time, and telecommuting work options. In addition to concerns about increased health care costs, there is another related impediment to the hiring of older workers – fear by employers of worker disabilities and disability-related lawsuits. As noted by the AARP:

Another potential problem posed by population aging is that as people age, the incidence of work-limiting disabilities rises. One consequence of the overlap between age and disability is that many aggrieved older workers may have the option of pursuing discrimination claims under either the ADEA or the Americans with Disabilities Act....In particular, the increased likelihood of an ADA claim, coupled with the possibility of greater success under the ADA than under the ADEA, may deter employers from hiring older workers even if they are not disabled at the time of hire, out of a fear that they will subsequently become disabled and impose firing costs (Neumark, 2008, p. ix).

The AARP, in its 2008 report, Reassessing the Age Discrimination in Employment Act, also commented on the contentious issue of the productivity of older workers (Neumark, 2008). The AARP first indicated that "research in the industrial gerontology literature illustrates how productivity changes with age, with some evidence pointing to either flat or slightly declining productivity in certain jobs as workers age, and other evidence pointing to declines in acuteness of vision or hearing, memorization, finger dexterity, and computational speed" (Neumark, 2008, p. 6). However, the AARP noted that "there may be offsetting increases in skills based on accumulated knowledge, and in communication skills, leadership ability, maturity, and loyalty" (Neumark, 2008, p. 6). Most interestingly, the AARP also noted that "at the same time, there is far more variation within than between age groups, so blanket statements about declines in age will, of course, often be inapplicable to individuals" (Neumark, 2008, p. 6).

Another challenge of retirees returning to the workforce is the potentially awkward situation of older workers being supervised by managers and supervisors who are young enough to be their children. A company must be sure that both the older workers and younger supervisors are comfortable with that situation. Actually, some companies have retained outside consultants to train younger managers on how to supervise older workers (Lee, 2008).

So, are U.S. companies prepared to attract, hire, retain, and accommodate older workers? Can they accommodate older workers? Can companies effectuate the transfer of knowledge from older to younger workers? According to one 2007 survey reported in Yahoo Finance, only 18% of employers surveyed stated they had a plan or policy to recruit older workers, and only 28% had a strategy to retain older workers (MacDonald, 2009). Such a report is particularly unsettling when it is clearly in the interest of organizations to recruit, hire, and retain older workers.

Training and Older Workers

In an article in *HR Magazine,* Grossman (2008) made the surprising assertion that "older workers may not receive a proportionate share of training dollars" (p. 46). One reason for the disparity may be that employers may believe that it is more difficult to teach older people new knowledge and skills, especially of a technological nature, and concomitantly that the employer's training budget can be more efficaciously spent on younger workers. *HR Magazine* pointed to a survey conducted by the American Association of Retired Persons where only 51% of workers over 55 years of age received formal training from employers within a 12 month period; whereas 79% of workers aged 25-34 received such training. Yet studies showed that the performance of older workers remained comparable to their younger colleagues. So, asked *HR Magazine*, how do older workers acquire, maintain, and advance knowledge and skills? One possible answer is that the training may be "informal"; that is, the "training" is accomplished by reading an instruction manual, talking to and learning from colleagues, or simply figuring out the solution oneself (Grossman, 2008).

Yet older workers, particularly in jobs that require them to change and adapt, may require more formal types of training. Unless new job knowledge and skills are tied to the experiences of older workers, more formal training and more time in training most likely will be required. *HR Magazine* notes that "adults in their 60s take roughly 50% to 100% longer than those in their 20s to learn and perform any new task" (Grossman, 2008, p. 43). One sensible approach, as recommended by the magazine, is firstly to be cognizant of the fact that older and younger workers do not respond to training in the same way, and then secondly to use "segmented" training approaches, as opposed to a "one-size-fits-all" approach, in order to improve results. For example, "hands-on" training as opposed to lectures emerges as a more effective training method for older workers since they tend to learn visually and experientially at the same time. Moreover, the training pace for older workers must be kept at a moderate pace, since if the training is conducted too rapidly, which can occur in mixed age groups, the older workers may be impeded in their learning by feelings of pressure and competition from their younger colleagues. However, it is also important to note that older workers may have difficulties with self-paced online learning, especially if they are having troubles or concerns with technology. Younger workers may be used to interacting solely with computers; but that is not how some older workers interact and learn. The "comfort level" with technology may not be present with older workers, who, in addition, may have vision challenges from continually reading from a computer screen. Thus, one solution will be for an organization to offer many types of training geared to different learning styles, ranging from traditional classroom experiences to online learning to small group discussions and practice (Grossman, 2008).

Older Workers as Coaches

Due to the changing demographics of the business world, such as more global competition and the introduction of new technologies, organizations are discovering that traditional strategies and tactics of management are no longer sufficient to remain competitive. As such, coaching is becoming to be recognized and practiced as an effective tool to increase morale, performance, and the "bottom-line" through the success of each individual associate. For example, about 90% of employees who received coaching in their jobs say that it improved their job performance and professional success. In organizations where coaching is effectively practiced as a management style, the bottom-line performance is two to three times better than the traditional "command-and-control" type of organizations. Furthermore, it has been proven that employee commitment increases when there is a strong, positive relationship between the manager and his/her employees. These types of relationships are developed best as a result of effective coaching. Since older workers are the ones with most experience, skill, management, and leadership experience, they can make great coaches and mentors to younger employees. Consequently, they should receive training, education, and proper development to effectively serve in such value-maximizing capacities.

Effective relationship-oriented coaching creates more knowledgeable and competent employees, reduces errors and rework, and greatly assists in bringing new changes to the culture. Both effective and even ineffective managers tend to know what makes a good coach. The difference lies in being able to transfer this knowledge into successful actions with employees to increase their performance and success. Effective coaching skills make a manager's job easier, as such skill enables greater delegation leaving him/her time to take on bigger projects. It builds the manager's reputation as a developer of people, while also increasing productivity, since everyone will know the expectations as well as the critical fact that what they do matters. Coaching also can develop trust and produce a good relationship between managers and employees. Last but not least, good coaching skills can increase creativity, innovation, morale, and teamwork since everyone will feel safe working in an inclusive environment.

So, what is coaching? Simply stated, *coaching* is about developing a trusting relationship with your people, so one can jointly clarify expectations and departmental goals, thereby leading to specific action plans for their achievement. Accordingly, there are many situations where coaching skills will be very effective, and the following list presents some important ones:

1. Reinforcing good performance.
2. Motivating employees to new heights and peak performance levels.
3. Orienting a new employee into the department or organization.
4. Providing new knowledge to individuals about changes and tactics.
5. Training a new skill for a new task that needs performing.
6. Following up on competencies passed on during a training session.
7. Explaining the current or new standards and how they can be achieved.
8. Setting priorities for effective time management with those employees who need it.
9. Introducing someone into the cliques and groups which may exist within the "political circles" in the organization.
10. Clarifying expectations and correcting poor performance.
11. Increasing the self confidence of an employee about the task or new responsibilities and challenges.
12. Conducting a performance review.

Coaching is not an innate skill; but rather it is learned. It occurs through one's life - personally and professionally. Effective coaching is the process of letting people know that what they do matters to you and to the organization. Furthermore, it is about letting them know that you are there to help them to be the best they can be as their success is important because it matters to you. It also is about being sincere, specific, direct, and to-the-point about both good and poor performance so they can take personal responsibility for their achievements. From this perspective, coaching is, and it can be, one of the most important functions managers perform because it communicates performance levels, expectations, importance of the tasks and responsibilities, and also it communicates a caring attitude. The following list summarizes some of the main elements involved in coaching:

1. Before beginning the coaching session, be sure to plan exactly what you want to achieve, and the potential benefits for the other person.
2. Start on a positive note and establish a common ground by having a supportive environment.
3. Communicate clearly, listen effectively, show that you care, and do not "beat around the bush." Clearly and caringly state the challenge, opportunity, and/or expectations.
4. Be respectful of the other person's feelings, honor and dignity. Create a non-threatening environment for the interaction, dialogue and discussion.
5. Be culturally sensitive by getting to know the other person's background, values, and anticipate his/her reactions.

6. Avoid value judgments, stereotyping, and labeling the behavior of others.
7. Use empathic listening skills to clarify your understanding and the other person's perspective.
8. Stay with the point and do not get side-tracked with other issues. Restate the purpose of the session and ask what specific things can be done to increase or improve performance. You can offer assistance, but avoid providing solutions–let the individual come up with the solutions. Your job is to lead them in the right direction.
9. Document and clarify the specific plan suggested by the employee, the expected level of performance, and how the plan will improve performance. Seek agreement and summarize the conversation.
10. End on a "positive note" and thank the person for coming up with the specific plan.

Older Workers as Mentors

Mentoring can be seen as an "art" since it requires experience and leadership traits. Mentoring can also be seen as a science since it can be formalized, structured, and taught. *Mentoring* is a continuous process of sharing relevant information with selected others in the organization that can maximize the success of the institution, while guiding and supporting each person toward individual and collective achievement opportunities. *Mentoring* is a developmental, caring, sharing, and helping relationship where the mentor helps the mentee. A mentor can be a person who offers knowledge, insight, perspective, or wisdom that is helpful to another person in a relationship which goes beyond duty or obligation. A mentor also creates opportunities for exposure, provides challenging and educational assignments, and serves as a role model and advisor to the mentee. Such relationships often evolve informally, but managers can encourage and formalize them. Effective mentoring requires listening, caring, and other forms of involvement between mentors and mentees. According to experts, mentoring is often used to achieve the interests of special groups and populations, conserve and transfer special know-how, encourage mentee contributions, bring employees together in a new social environment, help people reach their full potential, enhance competitive position of a person or department, and develop better relationships around the globe. Mentoring is a collaborative effort on the part of the mentor and the mentee. Effective mentoring is a relationship built on trust, where the mentee confides personal information and characteristics to the mentor, and the mentor guides the mentee toward growth and learning opportunities. A good mentoring program usually is focused on specific learning objectives where both the mentor and mentee receive training. There are many "deliverables" from a mentoring program, which can encompass easier recruitment of the best talent, more rapid induction of the new recruits, improved staff retention, improved equal opportunities, performance and diversity management, increased effectiveness of formal training, reinforcement of cultural change, improved networking and communication, and reinforcement of other learning initiatives.

Successful organizations recognize the value of mentoring and mentoring programs as an effective way to address diversity, manage organizational knowledge, retain stellar performers, gain valuable experience, cope with crises, and prepare for succession. *Newsweek* magazine in 2008 provided several examples of very successful entrepreneurs, executives, managers, and leaders in business who are now serving in mentoring roles: Karl Ichan, 72, former "corporate raider" and hedge fund manager, George Soros, 77, stock trader and oil analyst, Warren Buffet, 77, and Kirk Kerkorian, 91, both legendary stock traders and legendary capitalists, Jack Welch, 72, former head of General Electric, Rupert Murdoch, 77, media mogul and now owner of the *Wall Street Journal*, and T. Boone Pickens, 80, former oilman and hedge fund manager (Gross, Daniel, 2008). As *Newsweek* underscored, these men have been very successful, have a vast amount of experience, especially in dealing with past economic crises; and now they are actively engaged in mentoring. *Business Week* did a similar survey, titled "Extreme Experience," which chronicled the success of older business executives and entrepreneurs and the vast amount of experience that they accumulated and are sharing (Lowry, 2008). The magazine compiled a list, called "Twenty-Five Over Seventy-Five," of such "seniors" ranging from age 75 to 100 who "wield real influence" in global business. Actually, *Business Week* found so many older "extreme experience" executives that they compiled another such list for their online site (Lowry, 2008). The magazine list included such business people, also as noted in *Newsweek*, Kerkorian, Pickens, and Murdoch, and also included such other notable business people as Sumner Redstone, 85, chairman of Viacom and CBS, Hugh Hefner, 82, Playboy editor-in-chief, as well as many other business senior "success stories." *Business Week* emphasized that these "extreme experience" executives possess not just great experience, but also "historical perspective, as well as impressive contacts built up over a lifetime. They can be adept at weighing risks and spotting opportunity. These are useful attributes at a time of epic upheaval (when) in industry after industry, rapid-fire change is putting executives to the test" (Lowry, 2008, p. 48).

These aforementioned business leaders, executives, and entrepreneurs are, of course, very well known. Yet there are many people and organizations with very good experiences in mentoring and coaching people and acting as leaders, and who are willing to share their knowledge and experience. There are also individuals from under-represented groups, and not only older people, but also women, Asians, Hispanics, Native Americans, and African-Americans in the fields of business, the public sector, and education. Great mentors are great leaders as they share similar characteristics. Just like leaders, mentors are not limited to influencing others "merely" professionally at work, since mentors can guide people at home, in the community, at places of worship, at the soccer field, in the Tae Kwon Do classes, and other such interactions. According to experts, there are many roles that professional mentors play including: teacher or tutor, coach, "be-friender," counselor, information source, nurturer, advisor, net-worker, advocate, and role model. Regardless of the mentoring location, some specific elements of highly effective mentors and leaders are that such individuals:

1. Are experienced, and respected in the field.
2. Have current knowledge and are professionally confident.
3. Are trustworthy, confident and show high self-efficacy.

4. Use transformational leadership skills.
5. Willingly share their knowledge and guide others.
6. Remain approachable.
7. Have great passion for their work.
8. Know what to communicate, how to communicate, when to communicate, and how to help improve the mentee.
9. Excel at creating exciting learning environments for mentees.
10. Connect exceptionally well with others.
11. Challenge mentees to reach their full potential.
12. Get extraordinary results using a variety of skills to get their points across and to bring about the needed behavioral changes in their mentees.

The goal of a mentoring program should be to help leaders, managers, coaches, and senior employees in the firm to be highly skilled, self-aware, inclusive, energetic, and creative, and to carry a zest for mentoring into the organization every day. Mentoring is not an easy task, but such is the obligation bestowed on the fortunate ones. Highly effective mentors and leaders understand that developing others requires self-reflection, sensitivity, risk taking, interdependency, and teamwork among all parties (mentors, mentees, managers, peers, and senior officers). They also understand that such a synergy requires forging a partnership, inspiring commitment, growing both the mentor and mentee's skills, promoting persistency, and shaping the environment so all parties can achieve their goals. Often mentors (managers, leaders, and coaches) cannot influence the working environment for the entire organization. However they can control the area in which they are responsible for by applying the following tactics:
- Build visibility as a role model.
- Strengthen the learning climate in the department.
- Leverage organizational culture and systems.

Mentoring programs, using older workers, can help companies share knowledge, success, network, and build strong relationships with peers around the globe. Mentoring is a work-related partnership for the purpose of professional development between two or more individuals that allows an individual with more experience (the mentor) to share his or her skills, knowledge and experience with the mentee who has less experience. Mentoring is also an effective strategy that can contribute significantly to overall professional development of all employees. The use of mentors should also be considered and strongly encouraged when designing an effective repatriation program for international employees. Mentoring is a growing strategy used today for developing the talent of employees in professional positions. Mentoring programs in large organizations tend to be formal, while allowing a great deal of flexibility and informality in the relationships. Effective mentoring programs should benefit the mentee, the mentor, and the organization. A mentoring program can develop the leadership, management, and coaching skills of managers to create a productive culture. Effective mentoring in the twenty-first century organization requires the skills of management, leadership, and coaching, which are critical to the new employee's development. Mentoring relationships are helpful for most new and veteran employees, and they are especially helpful for employees working in different cities and cultures. One best way to reduce the negative impact of a strong culture in a new organization can be to have one or more experienced mentors who help one understand and effectively assimilate into the organization.

Coaches and Mentors Resolving Conflicts and Dispelling Rumors

Older workers, as coaches and mentors, can be great "change agents" and catalysts for effectively handling conflict in the workplace. Because of their experience and earned respect, older workers that are educated in the art of handling conflict and effectively settling rumors can serve in the capacity of conflict resolution agents. Also, as noted in *Business Week*, "age confers on its wearer a certain immunity to internal politics" (Lowry, 2008, p. 50). Furthermore, philosopher Blaise Pascal once said, "never speak well of yourself." It is better to let one's actions, as a leader, do the talking. Philosophers encourage leaders to "Live a life that will earn you the kind of reputation you desire. People will notice; be humble and you will be lifted up; demanding respect and admiration is like chasing an elusive butterfly; chase it, and you'll probably never catch it; sit still, be quiet, be confident, and it may land right on your shoulder." Actions speak louder than words and a leader's overall behavior will certainly communicate much about his/her character to others than anything s/he says.

Sharing information with others is a fact of life, and spreading misinformation with others is also a reality, especially when there seems to be years of animosity and distrust of corporate leaders due to job insecurity, layoffs, bribery, and other such actions caused by selfishness or corporate greed. Accordingly, it is necessary that educated individuals not spread misinformation about leaders, politicians, or one's colleagues in the workforce. Effective leaders can benefit from the facilitation skills and wisdom of Socrates about why rumors or certain messages should not be shared with others, especially when the message has not been verified to see if it is true, important, or even useful. Perhaps one can use this story to take a stand and hopefully influence others to "stop" and think about "the spoken words" and its impact on the person. People often wonder why some people have such great friends and manage to keep them. If one successfully applies the "Triple Filter Test" in one's conversations, the same could work for everyone. The following is the story behind the "Triple Filter Test" coming from Socrates, as he saw an appropriate opportunity to teach a great lesson in the given situation.

In ancient Greece, Socrates was reputed to hold knowledge in high esteem. One day an acquaintance met the great philosopher, and said, "Do you know what I just heard about your friend?" "Hold on a minute," Socrates, the great situational leader, replied. "Before telling me anything I'd like you to pass a little test. It's called the "Triple Filter Test." "Triple filter?" said the acquaintance. "That's right," Socrates continued. "Before you talk to me about my friend, it might be a good idea to take a moment and filter what you're going to say. That's why I call it the triple filter test."

1. *"The first filter is Truth.* Have you made absolutely sure that what you are about to tell me is true?" "No," the man said, "actually I just heard about it

and..." "All right," said Socrates. "So you don't really know if it's true or not."

2. *"The second filter is the filter of Goodness.* Is what you are about to tell me about my friend something good?" "No, on the contrary..." "So," Socrates continued, "you want to tell me something bad about him, but you're not certain it's true. You may still pass the test though, because there's one more filter left."

3. *"The third one is the filter of Usefulness.* Is what you want to tell me about my friend going to be useful to me?" "No, not really."

"Well," concluded Socrates, "if what you want to tell me is neither true, nor good, nor even useful, then why tell it to me at all?" This is why Socrates was a great philosopher and held in such high esteem. Rumors, which seem to flow often among people, should be stopped and corrected instead of being spread when they have no reality but can damage an individual's reputation or harm morale in the department. So, one should always remember the application of the "Triple Filter Test" by passing one's messages through the filters of "truth," "goodness," and "usefulness." It is, therefore, a moral imperative for leaders to always make sure what is said is true, good, and useful before it is passed on to others. Leaders can certainly use similar strategies to influence their followers, and thus hopefully stop people from passing on damaging rumors and misinformation in their workforce.

During an interpersonal conflict with a team member or colleague, one can remain focused on stating the facts, one's feelings, and future expectations, rather attacking the other person. For example, when hearing an offensive comment or joke about older people, minorities, or women in the workplace, one can immediately use the 3-F model (facts, feelings, and future expectations) by calmly saying: "When you make comments like that about women..., I feel angry and disappointed because...they are false and inappropriate in the workplace. Please don't make comments like that again." In most cases, repeating the facts of what was said by the person, one's feelings as a result of hearing what was said, and future expectations would take care of the situation as this approach brings this concern to the attention of the person making the comment. The person is likely to either clarify the misunderstanding, if that was the case, or change his or her behavior as a result of this awareness. As such, there may not be a need to place an official complaint with the human resources department or the company's lawyers since the goal is to have a healthy work environment. This is a very effective method used by skilled individuals to bring about positive changes in their departments one person at a time, thereby eliminating the existence of a hostile work environment. Of course, if the candid discussion, based on the 3-F model, does not work, and there is a repetition of inappropriate comments, then one must take appropriate actions to inform the organization. After all, the best way to resolve conflict is to seek cooperation from all parties involved and to create a "win-win" solution for everyone. Of course, with training and development, most "older workers" can be perfect candidates for the creation of "win-win" situations.

Developing and Involving Older Workers in Technology

In the technological sector, *Business Week* reported the findings of Professor Norm Maloff at the University of California whose research indicated that age discrimination was "rampant" in the technological industry (Wadhwa, 2008). To make matters worse for older workers, they may feel alone in the struggle to keep up with the world of technology, since most people in the United States as well as globally apparently assume that older workers are not interested in new knowledge and skills, particularly technological ones. It may seem like a difficult concept to accept the myth that older workers will never "learn computers" or get involved with technologies such as the Internet. Elderly people, in general, may be at a lack of knowledge when it comes to technology because it is so new and different to many of them. Since people are all creatures of habit, it is true that as individuals age they get comfortable doing things a certain way. When new and more effective ways are presented to them, they may feel as though they do not need to learn. They may wish to do things as they always have. This is a valid belief; yet not understanding that technology can really benefit older workers is a mistake. There is extensive information available to older workers who wish to learn; but it is incumbent on them and their employers to tap into the resources to find and acquire these new methods. Luckily, there are many resources available to elderly at their fingertips. Some of the resources available are supported by the American Society on Aging (ASA), American Association of Retired People (AARP), Gerontological Society of America, and the Silver Surfers from the United Kingdom. These organizations strive to help the elderly population learn and especially be able to effectively use technology to their benefit. They use tools such as extensive libraries of information, how-to guides, and assistive technology that are specially tailored to the needs and desires of older people. Of course, older workers are not alone in this struggle to integrate technology into their changing lives. There are many organizations that assist older people in learning about not only technology but also continuing in any education that they desire.

American Society on Aging

The American Society on Aging (ASA), founded in 1954, is an association of diverse individuals bound by a common goal: to support the commitment and enhance the knowledge and skills of those who seek to improve the quality of life of older adults and their families (ASAging.org, 2004). The ASA offers services of professional education, publications, resources, educational products, and award programs that aid in the advancement of elderly education. A section in the professional education is the ASA's Web-Enhanced Seminars where, via the internet, people can view recorded and live seminars on various topics concerning aging. Web Seminars are a cost-effective, high-quality training option for professionals working with aging issues and older adults (ASAging.org, 2004).

In addition to the Web-Seminars, the publications that ASA offers are far more extensive. The ASA's mission states "Insightful, timely and widely respected, ASA's print and electronic publications are a premier resource for thousands of professionals in the field of aging," for its publications section. Let us focus on a particular publication that relates to older people and technology in the *Generations Journal* of the ASA. The article is named "Aging and Information Technology: The Promise and the Challenge," and discusses some of the advancement technology has made and its conformity to elder needs. The article talks about the increase of web sites and resources available and useful to older people. Jeffery Finn, the author of the article states, "Unquestionably, the Internet and the World Wide Web are the driving forces prompting professionals in aging to reexamine their delivery of services and prompting consumers to rethink the relationships with these professionals...By mid 1998, more than 2,000 aging-related Web sites are expected to exist, up from 25 in mid 1995" (Finn, 2004, ASAaging.org). This article shows the dramatic increase in support for getting the elderly to work more closely with technology. Older people frequently are captivated by the promise of information technology as a means to keep them connected to their past, their present, and their future. They realize the wealth of knowledge that the Internet has to offer including endless medical information and studies, news reports, history information, and many other things that may be of interest to the elderly. Another point that they can relate to is that much of the new technologies today are directly related to them. In hospitals and care centers, new technologies assist in maintaining and improving the health of human beings. An example of this is health monitoring systems that do not require someone to be present for the monitoring to occur. It can be done remotely from a central location. "ASA is a valuable resource to anyone interested in aging issues...Through our constituent groups and numerous special projects ASA carries out its commitment to education, diversity, and quality of life for older adults" (ASAging.org, 2004). They also provide specialized educational products that customers can order from their "E-Store." These products include books, journal issues, videos, and multimedia packages geared towards the education of the elderly.

The ASA, in an effort to promote involvement the elderly community, offers award programs that recognize elderly achievement, such as Best Practices in Human Resources and Aging, Business and Aging awards, Graduate Student Research awards and Healthcare and Aging awards. The Best Practices in Human Resources and Aging is described as, "For model staff recruitment, training and/or management" (ASAging.org, 2004). This award encompasses success in an organization's diversity training programs as well as how the company performs its staffing. The Business and Aging awards program is described as, "For exemplary programs and services in the private, for-profit sector, in two award categories: large company; and small company" (ASAging.org, 2004). This award is for for-profit companies that show outstanding performance in accommodating older people and their families. The Graduate Student Research award is presented annually to a graduate student for research relevant to aging and applicable to practice. A review panel judges the research on the quality of its conceptual framework, methodology, presentation, and analysis of findings, as well as its significance to practice in the field of aging. The Healthcare and Aging award is given to organizations that have demonstrated high-quality, innovative programs that enhance the health-related quality of life in older adults (ASAging.org, 2004). The ASA annually presents these awards to recognize excellence in the studying in the field of aging. The ASA gives offers broad services that help elderly people.

American Association of Retired Persons

The American Association of Retired Persons, also referred to as the American Association of Retired Persons (AARP), also provides great resources for the elderly interested in advancing their technological skill levels. The AARP website under the Computer and Technology section offers news updates concerning technology tailored to the older generation. It introduces concepts that have been proven difficult to learn by older generation in an easy-to-learn format. One example is their "Gadgets and how to Guides" section of Computers and Technology which has reviews of new products on the market that have the possibility of benefiting older people through step-by-step instructions on commonly accepted principles such as getting started on email and how to find files on your computer. In the how-to-find files article it starts off easy such as, "Here's a common scenario. You know you saved a file, but it isn't where you thought it would be. How can you find your errant file? It's fairly easy if you use a simple feature that is built into Windows" (Berger, AARP.com, 2004). Among the younger generations, this knowledge is "a given"; but since the older generations are just starting to use computers this is an excellent starting guide that is not belittling. A separate section is how to use the Internet in the favor of older people. In this section, AARP presents several options for learners of different skill levels. For beginners, it starts the learning by saying, "Congratulations! You're on the Internet! Now you will probably want to learn a little more. You've come to the right place. By working through this Learn the Internet program, you will find out how to do many useful things. You will learn how to create and organize Favorites, how to make text larger, how to customize your browser, how to capture Internet information, and much, much more" (AARP.com, 2004). Over time, the factor that affects older people from learning technology related things is due to the diminishing of their motor skills due to advancing age. The product review shows how products can assist elderly people in everyday functions. For instance, a product review is on the Bose QuiteComfort 2 Headphones is described as: "The first QuietComfort headphones were comfortable, produced excellent sound and greatly reduced outside noise making them extremely useful for air travelers and those who frequent noisy environments. Bose kept all these great features in the QuietComfort 2. Bose then tweaked the headphones with small changes that turned them into an all-around excellent product" (Berger, AARP.com, 2004). Although this product was not necessarily geared toward older people, it can greatly help them. The AARP thus is a great resource for older people who want to learn technology. The organization proves it is an excellent resource that is specifically geared to the elderly.

Gerontological Society of America

The Gerontological Society of America (GSA) does not offer such a wide range of services; however, it does offer some interest groups that educate older people. The "*Technology and Aging*" forum is an area discussing training issues in communication and information technology (particularly the Internet) by senior citizens. This forum provides information on using the Internet in the interest of senior citizens, including areas of focus such as searching for trustworthy health information on the internet, which is an important concern that involves age-specific, well-planned curriculum development. Also, this group discusses how generations relate in their understanding of technology and the trends that relate.

Silver Surfers

The Silver Surfers is a charity organization whose mission is to promote internet usage with elderly people in the United Kingdom. Currently 62% of British people have tried the internet and only 15% of British people aged 65 or over have been online. This was an area that needed to be improved. However, because of many of their efforts the number of British people age 55 and over that use the internet increased 90% in 2001. Studies also show that older surfers are keen to keep their finances in order over the net, which accounts for more than 40% of online banking in the U.K. There are various events to promote Silver Surfers, including Silver Surfers Day. Silver Surfers' Day is managed by Hairnet, the company that makes learning technology simple and effective—whether involving a large organization or a private individual. Monthly and annually a Silver Surfer is nominated to be the "silver surfer" of the month/year where eligible individuals are to submit a picture of an "elder" of the age of 50 or above using and enjoying the Internet.

Technology Benefits for the Elderly and Older Workers

Assistive technology is a key feature in empowering the elderly, especially pertaining to employment opportunities. Many of these assistive technologies require little intervention or knowledge of technology by the operator, but they help a great deal. Assistive Technology is defined as technology that supports, bolsters, or helps a person do something. Assistive Technology has helped work with the elderly. One example is the volume control technology found on common things such as phones, TVs, and stereos, so someone with a hearing loss can keep up with the information he or she needs to be part of the community (ILTech.org, 2004). For those with vision impairment, Assistive Technology has helped with devices like magnifiers on computers. Also for magazine, journals, and subscriptions people can call the publisher to see if they have versions available to suit one's needs. Assistive Technology can be expensive, but there may be government assistance available to those who need, and qualify, for it.

The reason that the elderly have a more difficult time with technology is because most of the technology created is made for young people and by young people. However, the American Association of Retired People's website helps elder people connect with one another and explains how to do this in its guide to meeting people on the Internet. It starts by saying, "The approach of Valentine's Day may make you feel lonely. No mate? Not a soul to talk to? No valentines coming your way? Don't feel bad. You're not alone" (Berger, AARP.com, 2004). This indicates that there are many elderly people who are alone and at a lack of resources in meeting people. Using the method of the Internet to come together with people with similar interests has endless possibilities. Some of the interests that AARP supports on their message boards are described as the AARP Computers & Technology message boards, which have many "regulars" who ask and answer questions and interact with each other. Other popular AARP message boards are Grief & Loss, Health & Wellness, and Travel. If one is a movie fan, one should look into message boards and chats at movie-related Web sites. No matter what one's hobbies or interests, there are sure to be others on the Web who share one's enthusiasm (AARP.com, 2004). These message boards are of great benefits to the mental health of elderly people.

There are many other resources available to use towards assisting elderly people in learning and using technology effectively. The ASA, AARP, GSA, and the Silver Surfers present endless options to older people who have the desire to learn technology. Many of these technologies, as older people learn about them, show to be of great benefit. The ASA offers products such as professional publications and educational opportunities. The AARP provides a "Gadgets and how to Guides" section in their website which can help the elderly in learning and understanding technology. The GSA provides special interest groups that help elderly people come together to talk about their interests. The Silver Surfers is a charity organization in the United Kingdom for the purpose of promoting the use of the Internet by older people. Significantly, the research conducted for this book indicates that learning technology skills may be just as important to older workers in securing and maintaining jobs as the presence and enforcement of age anti-discrimination laws.

Many of the best firms in the world are in search of wisdom, more specifically the type of wisdom that comes with age and experience, which makes companies and organizations successful. Jamrog and McCann (2003) mentioned that about 43 percent of the civilian labor force will be eligible for retirement within the next ten years (by 2013). Therefore, there will be a shortage of talented and skilled professionals that accompany top leadership. So, companies will have to implement effective strategies for attracting, hiring, developing, and retaining an experienced workforce. There are many excellent practices in attracting and hiring "senior citizens"; and the process often starts with the elimination of behaviors stemming from one of the most common barriers which are traditional biases and stereotypes toward older workers.

Hiring Practices for Older Workers

Many organizations and individuals believe that the education system in the United States has failed to deliver graduates who are fully qualified to enter into, and to meet, the demands of today's labor market. Consequently, more and more organizations are trying to retain, recruit, and hire older workers because of their skill, professional expertise, and accumulated knowledge. John Lavelle (2007), writing in *Public Personnel Management*, explains:

> In traditional corporate careers, retirement marked the end of the employment relationship in both a symbolic and absolute sense. Now the end of the employment relationship may be the precursor of a new relationship with the same employer, whether it be immediate, virtual, or deferred...Three post-employment possibilities are included:

experience/contingent (former staff or retirees returning immediately to work under contract arrangements, marking the shift from employee to independent service provider); *alumni*, who assist in corporate business development...; and *rehires* (former staff who plan to return at a later career juncture and whose return would be welcome) (p. 378).

Plato, the philosopher, said 2000 years ago that: "It gives me great pleasure to converse with the aged. They have been over the road that all of us must travel and know where it is rough and difficult and where it is level and easy." The demand for the aged and the wise with corporate management and leadership is clearly on the rise. While there seems to be a global decrease in the professional labor supply, there is a rise in demand for experienced professional workers. According to the Bureau of Labor Statistics (2002), about 50 percent of the workforce in the United States will be made up of individuals forty-five years or older, and the same workforce age trends are occurring in most developed nations. The increase of older workers in the workforce is caused from the aging baby boomer generation, low birthrates in the last third of the twentieth century, and discouragement of early retirement caused by economic conditions (Kanfer and Ackerman, 2004). Kanfer and Ackerman (2004) state: in the United States and other Western countries, aging is usually associated with general decline, particularly in cognitive, physical, and intellectual capabilities of a person. However, researchers in a number of domains have shown that the assumption of general decline with age is simplistic and can be misleading. Age is one dimension of diversity; and diversity is a complex and, at times, challenging reality for most managers and employees in today's diverse world (Jones et al, 2002). The best way to use this diversity toward organizational objective is to learn about it, make sure everyone is treated fairly, and appreciate the increasing diversity of the workforce. Unfortunately, as Jones et al. (2003) state: "We are the land of diversity and yet we are seemingly without the conceptual ability to take that reality in, accept it and work effectively with it. Of course there are many historical reasons for bias and deeply seeded reasons of prejudice that we don't even understand, but even so, we must manage them." According to the 2000 Census, the median age of a person in the United States is the highest it has ever been (35.3 years), and this fact has certain implications for the workers and managers. Furthermore, those who fall between the ages of 45-54 years old had the greatest population growth.

The elderly professionals are often in the position of being fairly healthy, wealthy, and selective in terms of what they would like to do in their later years. As a result of their years of productive work in society, they tend to live in better neighborhoods and often have hobbies and/or community roles. As such, one barrier for attracting the elderly is that they can be selective in determining where they would like to work. Oftentimes, they would like flexible hours with options to come and go to pursue their avocations and personal community obligations. So, the fact that they do not apply to all organizations is one barrier. Another barrier is the fact that they want flexible hours with jobs that offer the opportunity to fulfill their socialization and other higher order needs for self-actualization. Some of them may also want to work in positions that do not require too much new learning or physical activity since they have been through all this before and would rather not deal with it again. So, wanting selective jobs is yet another barrier in entering the workforce. However, the most common barrier for those older workers who do apply for specific jobs in the workplace is probably the widespread stereotypes and biases on the part of interviewers which result in not hiring the elderly. Increasingly, older workers are claiming that opportunities have been limited for them due to stereotypes, biases, and structures that are designed to discourage them from the work environment.

When such age discrimination becomes an "unseen" part of the culture, it can hinder the organization's morale, productivity, and may possibly cause many legal problems for the firm. Creating an effective organizational culture that avoids age discrimination requires long-term commitment and resources since there are no panaceas. Organizational leaders and managers must be concerned about age discrimination, since an increasingly larger percentage of the workforce is coming, and will continue to come, from the older population as "baby-boomers" continue to age. According to the United States Census Bureau and the Administration on Aging, the number of Americans who are 65 years of age or older has increased by a factor of 12 since the early 1900s.

Table 3 – Statistics on Older Workers

Year	Americans 65 Years of Age or Older
1900	3 million (4%) older workers.
2000	35 million (13%) older workers.
2011	First baby boomers will turn 65 years of age!
2030	Estimated at 70 million people (20%)

It is critical that employers exercise extreme caution within their corporate culture to minimize any inferences that older workers are being mistreated. How can this happen, one might ask? It actually starts at the top. Corporate culture is shaped at the top of the corporate "ladder" by the senior executives and managers who determine how human resources are to be utilized. If key executives are entrenched in a culture that views younger people as being more successful and aggressive and older people as being more complacent, then those beliefs will create a negative climate that will permeate throughout the organization, thereby, causing subordinates to "buy into" the same type of behavior. Given this, senior executives and managers, as well as the entire workforce within organizations, should make every effort to ensure their corporate culture is positive and free of illegal and unethical discrimination, thereby avoiding any instances that may make older workers feel uncomfortable, disrespected, or victimized

Changing Paradigms of Aging

The United States has a diverse population of over 303 million people. The perspective on aging in the U.S. can be seen from the high level of discrimination against older workers due to biases and stereotypes against older workers. An American by the name of William Osler in 1905 said: "Take the sum of human achievements...subtract the work of men above 40...we would practically be where we are today" (Segrave, 2001). Segrave mentions that an anonymous personnel executive in 1910 stated that: "A man who has failed to make good at 45 is not wanted today; he will never make good." Daniel Motley, in 1915, is quoted as having said: "It is more delightful to be surrounded by the young, with hopefulness, gladness, and outlook in their eyes." Yet, a statement appearing in the New York Times' editorial page in 1916 read as follows: "That disinclination to hire old workers is actually a decent thing, proportional to the employer's kindness of heart." Such views, expressed today by citizens and "American" comedians, associated with aging are common in the United States. They are representative of how the "American" society feels about aging, and, as such, youthfulness is valued and "older age" is not. These mindsets are causing an increasing number of the aging "baby-boomers" to constantly search for the "fountain of youth," when in reality there is no such panacea. Nonetheless, such societal views tend to impact the workplace since executives and managers that make hiring decisions do come from the society.

The "American" culture seems to be obsessed with youth (Kelly, 2003), as can be seen from the increasing number of cosmetic surgeries while members of the media are fully capitalizing on such obsessions in their ads and selling efforts. Such youth-mindedness is also accompanied by a negative perception of aging in society, which is inclusive of the workplace. While many of the Asian and Middle Eastern cultures value and respect older individuals (both in their personal and professional lives), Americans view aging from a negative perspective as if it was a "bad thing." These negative perceptions tend to convey the message that older workers are not able to keep up with new technology or new ways of doing things because they are not open-minded. These negative perceptions regarding older workers and technology also were clearly revealed in the research results and participant comments in the survey study conducted by the authors for this book. Besides the perception of not being up-to-date on technology, older workers in "American" society are seen as: "deadwood, incompetent, closed minded, un-trainable, and less productive" (Kelly, 2003). Of course, as mentioned before, these are stereotypes and myths that are not factual; and individuals disproving these myths are ubiquitous in today's workplace. Nonetheless, such views tend to put older individuals at a disadvantage as they attempt to compete in the job market with their younger counterparts. On the other hand, young Americans tend to have this "unearned privilege" or "unearned advantage" that comes to them at a cost to "older workers." Older workers tend to possess the following positive qualities: functioning well in crisis; possessing basic skills in writing, reading, and arithmetic; being loyal; functioning as solid performers; and having good interpersonal skills. Older workers, therefore, have various talents that are vital to multinational businesses in today's organizations.

The presence of more "older workers" being active in the workforce presents many challenges and opportunities for organizations. The challenges are stereotypes and age discrimination that are widespread in the U.S. workforce. Organizations must effectively transcend such challenges, and proactively take advantage of the experienced workforce as they attempt to be globally competitive. There are many proactive firms such as Publix, based in Lakeland, Florida which employed more than 140,000 employees in 2010, that need to be congratulated for their efforts to reduce/eliminate age discrimination in the workplace. As a matter-of-fact, Publix leaders and executives need to also be congratulated for their national award as one of the country's Top Employers of older workers, which was presented to them in September (2002) in Washington D.C. through the Experience Works Prime Time Awards Program. Of course, there are many other such proactive organizations that value employee loyalty and experience, which eventually either reduces age discrimination in the workplace or, in ideal scenarios, eliminates it.

Personal Responsibility of Older Workers

Tiffany Hsu (2009), citing Bureau of Labor statistics, reports that over the last two years, the number of people in the United States aged 55 and older who are working has risen to almost 1.5 million, so as to total more than 26 million in March of 2009. However, Hsu (2009) also reports that the number of people in the United States who want a job but who cannot find one has more than doubled in the same time period to almost 1.8 million people. The Bureau of Labor Statistics indicated that it takes an older worker over the age of 55 six weeks longer to secure a new job than it does for younger workers (Krome, 2008). In July of 2009, the *Sun-Sentinel* newspaper of Ft. Lauderdale, Florida (Rugabar, 2009) reported the latest Labor Department statistics indicating that workers aged 55 years and older were jobless an average of 30 weeks compared with about 21 weeks for workers under 55 years of age. Furthermore, the jobless rate for people over 55 years of age rose to 7% in June of 2009, which represented the highest percentage for that age group since records were kept dating back to 1948 (Rugabar, 2009).

Older persons seeking work need to demonstrate to prospective employers that they can contribute and add value to the organization, that their past accomplishments are a good indication of their future performance and thus their value-adding potential, and concomitantly that the value they add is commensurate with the salary they seek (Fein, 2008). Older workers bear the burden of demonstrating to prospective employers that they are productive and can remain productive. Older workers also must convince employers that their loyalty, sound judgment, even temperament, and respect for others can make them good role models for younger workers (Moos, 2008).

Individuals who are considered to be "older workers" may not always be able to reduce or eliminate the presence of age discrimination during the hiring and recruitment process; yet they should and can take certain steps to make sure they are not victims of such stereotypes and biases. One challenge many older workers, especially senior citizens, face is finding interesting jobs that pay well after retirement (Jamaican Handbook, 2001). Yes, good jobs are still "out there" and, with some searching, they can be found. There are many helpful suggestions which can be used by everyone at a personal level to increase one's chances for a successful job hunt. The *Jamaican Handbook* (2001) and other researchers offer many tips for being prepared and getting a suitable job; and the following are a few of them for consideration:

1. What is more valuable to a company, someone with the skills and education, or someone that has the skills, education, and experience? Market your skill, education, and experience with pride.
2. What if you only have the experience but lack the skills and education? Could you still be hired? The answer is "yes." Show them that you can learn the new skills and you are willing to get the required education.
3. At the personal level, one should always have an updated resume, get the new skills needed to effectively compete in the job market, continue one's professional development, network with professionals in the field, stay current on organizational changes, and use one's experience not only to assist the organization, but also the community to the furthest extent possible.
4. Take an inventory of yourself. Assess your physical, mental and emotional conditions and determine what you would like to do while earning the kind of income you would want for your services. Take personal initiative to update your skills. Keep current and marketable in your field. Things change quickly, you can change with them or you can get left behind complaining that life is not fair.
5. Realize that you might need help. Job hunting is not easy and many of the rules may have changed since the last time you looked for a position. It is fairly common to get assistance from support groups and employment offices.
6. Be prepared to take "no" for an answer. While you may see the job as a perfect position for you, the boss and the culture of the organization might not be for you and they might need someone with a different skill set or personality based on their needs (and not necessarily always because you are not qualified).
7. Learn to read the signs. When someone says "we will call you," often times this can mean that we don't have anything open for you. As such, there is no reason to wait by the phone for their call. Instead, keep on moving to the next organization or company to see who else might be able to use your skills and service.
8. Do not take rejections personally. People hire individuals based on many reasons and qualifications might not always be the only determining factor. So, no need to worry about why people did not select you for the job. Let it go and move on. It is always a good practice to send "thank you notes" for all interviews.
9. Search for the right jobs in the right places. Once you know the kind of job you would like to perform, then searching through the classifieds might not always be the best resort. As a matter of fact, newspaper ads are probably the

least effective for professional jobs (unless they are in the trade magazines and journals). It is fairly normal to call the company of your choice, visit their website or even visit the human resources department to see what possibilities exist and if they have a need for the type of service you can offer to them.

Overall, the suggestion is to keep learning, stay current, and you will always have a place in the job market. If an employer is biased in respect to age, point it out to them so they can learn, and it will be their loss not to have you working with them. Take an interest in the success of your company (regardless of your age) because their success is your success.

U.S. News and World Report provided some very practical "strategic" advice to older workers who are seeking jobs in an article aptly titled "How an Older Worker Can Get the Interview" (Wolgemuth, 2008). The article first noted the "tough reality" confronting older workers who may face employers who feel that they are "overqualified," or too expensive, or simply too old. However, *U.S. News and World Report* offered the following advice on how to secure an interview:

1. Keep it short. That is, keep your resume succinct. Even if the older worker has a vast amount of work experience, be concise but also make sure that your resume accurately reflects your experience and achievements. The idea is to generate interest about your employment potential. About one to two pages should suffice. No one is going to read your "life history."

2. Don't ignore your age. That is, raise the issue of your age immediately, just in case the employer may have an objection to your age. Of course, raise the age issue not directly, but by noting that you have had a great deal of experience and that you are a very mature person, and thus will be a very valuable employee.

3. Be strategic. That is, you should particularly focus on "networking." Accordingly, contact former coworkers and colleagues, family members, former fellow students, colleagues in professional and other associations. Use the local chamber of commerce as well as any online job or social networking sites for job leads.

4. Show off online. That is, supplement your traditional "hard copy" resume with an online one, such as with Visual CV, and make it a "multi-media" presentation that will highlight your technological skills. Again, keep the online version of your CV succinct but allow viewers to scroll down your CV and click on names, former employers, references, and degrees and colleges for further details.

5. Don't go "overboard." That is, be very careful about using video in your online CV. A short introduction of oneself lasting about a minute would be appropriate but lengthy videos of your work related speeches and work presentations could be "awkward and potentially self-destructive." The objective is to communicate your availability as well as your communication and technological skills (Wolgemuth, 2008).

Deborah Russell, the AARP's Director of Workforce Issues, emphasizes that "seniors need to assess their skills and seek out job-searching tips, particularly if they have not gone through the process in recent years" (Carpenter, 2008, p. 4D). She underscores to older workers that the job market has now changed; employers are accepting job applications online; and accordingly potential employees are expected to submit their resumes online (Carpenter, 2008).

The *Wall Street Journal* also had some very practical advice to older workers who are seeking to reenter the workforce. The title to the *Wall Street Journal* article (Greene, 2009), appearing in 2009, aptly and sadly summed up the deteriorating economic conditions: "There goes retirement." As the *Wall Street Journal* related: "Across the country, retirees who never imagined themselves returning to the workplace are polishing resumes and knocking on employers' doors. The problem: Most are running smack into the worst job market in almost three decades" (Greene, 2009, p. R1). Nevertheless, the *Wall Street Journal* noted that despite formidable challenges some retirees are finding work. Based on interviews with several retirees who had returned to the workforce, the *Wall Street Journal* offered the following advice:

1. Getting Over "the Sulk" – Do something to avoid depression. For example, one retiree took a job as a movie extra. The job just lasted a few days, but the work was rewarding and the retiree met a famous movie start. Now the retiree looks regularly online for work as an "extra," and recommends that other retirees do the same. Another took a job a local Starbucks as a barista. The goal was to "do something," to "get back into something," even if it was not what one wanted to do. Meanwhile, one can still look for other employment.
2. Scaling Back – Make a conscious decision to downsize. Be realistic in your job prospects. Do not expect the same salary as one did before one retired.
3. Staying in Touch – Stay in touch with your former co-workers after you retire. For example, regularly invite some of the key people that you used to work with to have lunch with you. When you do retire, do not completely detach yourself from your former work colleagues. Also, if possible, do not relocate year-round to a retirement haven.
4. Starting From Scratch – Do not always try to go back to the work that you did before retiring and that you know well. The job market may not afford you that "luxury." The key is to focus on what employers need; thus, "retool" oneself accordingly, if necessary.
5. Playing Geography – If a retiree is fortunate to have a second home in a retirement locale, that area may provide some additional employment opportunities, even if seasonal. Perhaps a retiree would not want to relocate permanently due to family connections at a primary residence, but do not overlook the employment opportunities that a second home could provide.
6. RetirementJobs.com – The *Wall Street Journal* article mentioned that retirees have had success using this online job-search tool for people fifty years of age or older (Greene, 2009).

The *Wall Street Journal* concluded its "There Goes Retirement" article by imparting some very practical and realistic advice to retirees seeking to reenter the job market: "simply try...to make the best of a bad situation" (Greene, 2009, p. R4).

Marcia Heroux Pounds, the business writer for the *Sun-Sentinel* newspaper of Ft. Lauderdale, Florida, offered the following advice to older workers on how to become and stay "ageless" in today's workforce (Pounds, 2009):

1. Stay Flexible – Evolve with your company; determine what you can do to support your company now, particularly if your firm is contemplating "cuts."
2. Remove Dates from Your Resume – If you have 15 years of experience or more, eliminate the high school and college graduation dates from your resume; and focus on work you did in the last decade that is relevant to the job.
3. Update Your Computer Skills – Make sure you can list basic computer skills on your resume. If necessary, take a computer course, even if your company does not pay for it.
4. Learn Social Media – Build a professional profile on such sites as LinkedIn, and include recommendations from colleagues and clients.
5. Do Not Brag About Your Experience – Do not appear as a person whose attitude is: "This is how we did it way back when." Employers, managers, and coworkers, especially younger ones, may not want to hear such declarations. Do not sound like there is only one way to do things – your way!
6. Have a "Success Book" of Your Work – This book should include letters of appreciation from customers and former employers, managers, and co-workers. The book should show how you successfully completed projects as well as other evidence of your achievements.

Overall, Pounds emphasizes the "flexibility" component to being "ageless," in particular by counseling older works to be flexible about the work they will accept as well as the salary, and not to expect the same salary they had at previous jobs, especially if those jobs were in large "expensive" metropolitan areas (Pounds, 2009, pp. 1D, 2D).

Furthermore, Tiffany Hsu (2009), writing for the Tribune Newspapers, and emphasizing that "the recession has not been kind to older workers," offered the following "tips for older job seekers":

1. "Update and rejuvenate: Spruce up your resume by keeping it short and emphasizing skills and achievements instead of the length of your experience. Be aware of your health and appearance. Recruiters can sense depression and illness. And a look that is too stylish or too dowdy can ruin a first impression."
2. "Your age is not the focus: Don't distract yourself with suspicions of age discrimination; keep a positive, confident attitude. Keep your college graduation dates off your resume and avoid discussing activities that might date you. If you seem overqualified, recruiters might make assumptions

about how much you want to be paid. If a company wants 15 years of experience, trim descriptions of your 40-year career."

3.   "Use age to your advantage: Stress your loyalty and dedication to a company. Recruiters will contrast that with younger workers who tend to hop between jobs and prioritize personal time over work. Seek out age-friendly employers with older employees and executives. AARP ha a good list."

4.   "Get connected: Stay wired by investing in a computer and a cell phone. Learn core computer skills such as word processing, spreadsheet design and internet searching. Sign up for an e-mail address and join networking sites such as Facebook and Linkedin" (Hsu, 2009, p. 5D).

Good Morning America, in a lengthy segment aired July 13, 2009, hosted by Andrew Cuomo and reported by Tory Johnston (Highlights from Good Morning America, 2009), first pointed out that it takes "older workers" nine weeks longer to find a job than younger workers, and also that for the year 2008, based on Labor Department statistics, age discrimination job claims had increased 28%. *Good Morning America* then provided extensive advice to older workers in the following areas: Job Saving Tactics, Talking About the Unemployment Interview, Covering Gaps in Your Experience, Job Search Tactics While You're Still Employed, But I Hate My Job, and Your Reentry After Time Off (Highlights from Good Morning America, 2009).

Life is not always "fair," and the "right" thing is not always done; yet, one needs to keep a positive outlook toward being fairly treated while expecting and hoping for the best. The job market and pay scales may vary greatly from place to place. Innocent individuals may even at times be victims of "politics" since some of the hiring practices are a result of political initiatives. For example, one should make every attempt not to play the victim of age discrimination. Sometimes people get "lucky" and secure the jobs they want with a salary that is generous. Sometimes one has to work extra-hard to earn it. This may require additional education, relocation, and starting at a lower salary to "get into the door." One may not get the desired job right away, but once one gets into an organization and "networks" with the right people, and that position becomes available, one will have a good "shot" at it. There are opportunities; one just has to look hard enough, long enough, see the right individuals; and one needs to be in the "right place at the right time" for the jobs one wants. So, if one is an older worker, then one should do the required "homework" about the company and go to the interviews with the attitude of "here is what I can bring to the organization and this is how I can help the department be more competitive." Avoid the tendency of "give me any job and I'll do it to the best of my abilities." Know your competencies and what you can offer; then go after getting the job you want with total dedication and commitment. Persistence "pays off," and one should also use his/her age and experience to determine the best way to move forward in serving a specific market with one's accumulated competencies.

Managers must remember that older workers are one of the valued categories of employees because they are stable, experienced, and consistent. Companies have recognized that older workers value stability and quality in their work. "We are now targeting and hiring alternate profiles. This industry is customer service–driven and older people are sensitive to customer needs," said Khan (2003). It is clear that some companies are tapping into the advantages of having highly skilled older workers within their organizations. Another example of a company that has utilized older employers while still exploring better ways of managing older employees is McDonald's. Michael O'Shaughnessy, employee relations director, McDonald's Australia, said that "fast-food" chains regularly target older employees. He went on to say that a program aiming at recruiting more "older workers" was "in the works" (Comtex, 2003) in their area. Other more detailed examples of moral as well as smart companies who recruit and retain older workers will be provided in the recommendations chapter to this book.

Job Opportunities for Older Workers

How can older workers enhance their employment chances in very difficult economic times? *Forbes* magazine in 2008 provided some very valuable online resources for older workers to secure employment (Ebeling, 2008):

- RetirementJobs.com – This career site is an online job board for workers aged 50 years old and more. There are more than 30,000 job postings available – from administrative to professional – as well as a data base of more than 150 "certified age-friendly employers," which, for example, offer health care benefits for part-time employees. *Business Week* reported in December of 2008, that the online "traffic" on the site increased from 250,000 visitors in July 2008 to 600,000 in November 2008 (Green, 2008, p. 48). The fact that the traffic more than doubled is yet another indication that many older people, including presumably many former retirees, are now looking for work.
- AARP Website (www.aarp.org/employerteam) - This AARP site lists companies, including AT&T to Walgreens, which the organization deems to be committed to the recruiting, hiring, and retaining of older workers. The site also includes federal government agencies as potential employers. There is a link on the site to current employment opportunities. The AARP program is called the National Employment Team, and it assists workers age 50 and over to find job opportunities
- Bridgestar Website (www.bridgestar.org) – The Bridgestone Group, a non-profit organization, offers a free online jobs board as well as advice for "bridgers," that is, people looking for jobs in the not-for-profit sector after retiring from jobs in the for-profit sector. There are openings, for example, for people in the finance, accounting, fundraising, marketing, and communications fields.

Older persons as well as "senior" employees looking for jobs also can visit the website "Seniors4hire.org" (www.Seniors4Hire.org) which provides a list of companies that recruits and hires older workers. This is an online career center geared to promote businesses that value a diverse workforce, and actively recruit and hire those who fall in the category of "older workers." In most cases, the jobs offered to older workers are of the nature that usually requires mature, experienced, and knowledgeable individuals, says Renee Ward-founder of www.Seniors4Hire.org (Senior Journal, 2004). According to the Senior Journal, there are at least 70 small businesses that are good places for older workers to be employed and some of the firms recently added to list are Regal Entertainment Group, Mayo Clinic-Jacksonville, General Nutrition Centers, New York Presbyterian Hospitals, Cost Plus World Market, Allina Hospitals and Clinics, RadioShack Corp, UCLA Healthcare, News America Marketing, FleetBoston Financial, Ryder System, Inc., and Providence Health System. Job seekers can become members with this center through their website, and membership is free. Another employment source for older workers is Retireeworkforce.com which is a company that conducts an online job board for retirees as well as the companies that would like to hire older persons (Lee, 2008).

Hiring seniors for project assignments or on a part-time basis saves on healthcare costs (Recruiting Seniors, 2004). According to a survey conducted by Thomas Regional, of the nearly 2,500 industrial small businesses owners surveyed nationwide, 63% stated that healthcare coverage is their biggest challenge. Hiring seniors to work part-time or on temporary assignments in most cases saves health care benefits costs (Recruiting Seniors, 2004). Furthermore, a 2003 survey from the Society for Human Resource Managers (SHRM) indicated that 68 percent of organizations employ older workers; however only 41 percent specifically target older workers in their recruitment efforts. The survey also indicated that reasons for hiring older workers included their willingness to work a flexible schedule, their ability to serve as mentors, and their invaluable experience. Of course, other important reasons included the reliability and strong work ethic which often comes with older workers. Generally, firms recruit and hire older or retired workers because they offer:

- Leadership and coaching skills for younger or new employees.
- Superior customer service experience.
- Stability.
- Ability to initiate sales and transaction dependability.
- Eagerness to provide support and guidance.
- Superior communication skills.
- Varied work experience.
- Better ability to work with mature clientele.
- An "old-fashioned" work ethic.

Overall, a mature employee's greatest assets (compared to younger demographics) are likely to be lower absenteeism, punctuality, less likelihood to change jobs, commitment to quality, superior customer service skills, enhanced personal skills, more eagerness to learn new skills, positive attitude, and the willingness to speak their minds and to point out the flaws of the organization. The former Secretary of Labor, Elaine L. Chao, said, "Nowhere is the case stronger for tapping the strengths of older workers than with employers facing the skills gap. Everywhere I go, employers tell me they are having difficulty finding workers with the right skill sets for the jobs they have to offer." This provides a golden opportunity to turn a challenge—the approaching retirement of an unprecedented number of Americans—into a "win-win" scenario for the economy and one's workforce.

According to various writers and articles, part of the problem for older job seekers today lies in a number of persistent myths that prejudice some employers against them. Some employers feel that older workers use medical benefits more than other groups and consequently raise the cost of medical insurance premiums for everyone. This is false because, in reality, seniors often use medical benefits less than some other age groups. Parents of younger children are the most frequent users, and as a result contribute more directly to increased premium rates. Some employers feel that older workers miss a lot of work. The fact is that senior workers have excellent attendance records, because they seldom miss work for personal reasons other than legitimate illness. Yet, others may feel that older learners cannot learn new techniques and new technologies. Again, the reality is that the capacity to learn is not a function of age. If one is skeptical, ascertain the growing number of senior citizens going back to college and getting advanced degrees every year. Companies hire older workers because they have certain characteristics that other generations of employees may not always have and the following are some elements cited by authors:

1. Older workers thrive on quality and hard work. They believe in putting in a full day's work for a full day's pay.
2. Older workers are loyal. They appreciate the opportunity to work and stick with those who give them a chance to perform and produce.
3. Older workers take great pride in their accomplishments. They care about doing a good job.
4. Older workers are dependable. They show up on time all the time. They take orders seriously, keep their promises and do what they say they will do.
5. Older workers do not always get involved in politics. They don't play political games, have hidden agendas or harbor secret ambitions. They are not interested in climbing the corporate ladder, so they don't have to resort to manipulation, dirty tricks or one-upmanship.
6. Older workers have more than their share of "emotional maturity" and common sense.

Statistics show that about 10,000 Americans turn 55 years of age every day. As such, tapping into the strengths of these older workers is an excellent way to save on training and benefits costs. According to the U.S. Bureau of Labor Statistics, since January 2001, the biggest job growth has been among those 55 and older, with 3.2 million new workers from this group. Table 4 presents the percentages of change in the U.S. older population, by age group as reported by the U.S. Bureau of the Census.

Figure 1 provides estimates and projections of the older population, by age group from 1995 – 2010 as gleaned from U. S. Bureau of the Census in 1996.

Table 4 – Changes in the Population of on Older Population

Time Period	Under 60	50+	55+	60+	65+	75+	85+	100+
1995-2000	4.6	11.1	7.3	4.1	3.5	12.1	17.2	33.3
2000-2010	5.6	27.0	27.3	22.6	13.5	10.7	33.2	81.9

In terms of gender, the labor force participation for ages 55 to 64 in 2002 consisted of 69% males and 55% females. These numbers are expected to be 75% males and 64% for females in 2012. So, an increasing number of older males and females will be working after their retirement years; and thus firms wanting to recruit, hire, and retain them must have specific strategies geared toward the older generation in order to get them. Experts state that older workers are likely not to apply for positions open to the general population because they fear they will not be considered for the job because of their age and biases toward them. Some of them also may wrongly feel that their experiences, skills, and abilities do not qualify them for the twenty first century employment opportunities. So, employers wishing to take advantage of the experience and reliability that seniors provide must communicate to this group that they are specifically targeting them for employment. Furthermore, these employers must go where they can find such experienced older workers in their communities and educate them about the available benefits.

Figure 1 – Projections of Older Workers

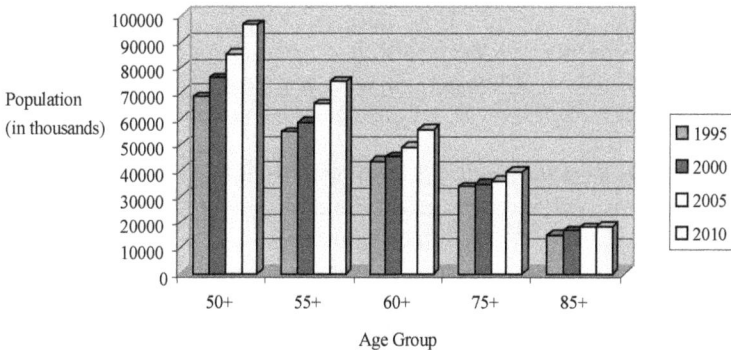

Moreover, according to researchers, 60% of workers between the ages of 50 and 70 plans, to work during their retirement or never retire at all. Thus, for companies, it is "simply" a business decision. With a worker shortage predicted in healthcare and technology-driven industries, companies need to do more to attract skilled older workers and retain current employees as they age. Many companies are finding themselves in the same position of needing more skilled employees; and accordingly among the benefits offered by employers to recruit older workers are:

- *Financial Services* - Most companies offer some sort of retirement plan, but the best ones provide workshops, seminars, and counseling. First Tennessee National Corp., a financial services firm in Memphis, assigns advisers to help employees devise retirement plans, and retirees have their own dedicated financial specialist.
- *Health Benefits* – Most employers offer not only basic benefits-prescription drugs and health, vision, and dental care but long term care insurance and short and long term disability insurance. Some even offer wellness programs. Roche Inc., a New Jersey-based pharmaceutical company, offers a program that includes free health screenings and customized fitness programs.
- *Training Opportunities* – This includes everything from skill development to career counseling. The Massachusetts Institute of Technology offers career training to all employees and courses specifically for workers over 50.
- *Mentoring* – Ideally it works two ways: 1) Experienced employees help train younger workers and 2) Older workers return to the company and receive a mentor to help re-train them. At Baptist Health, older employees receive bonuses for mentoring new employees.
- *Flexible Schedules* – Forget the "punch clock": 28.8% of American workers now have a flexible schedule, nearly twice as many as 10 years ago. SSM Health Care in St. Louis, Missouri, offers time off for dependent care, and spouses of retirees can take summers off to travel.
- *Phased Retirement* – Rather than "quit cold turkey," many employees prefer to ease into retirement. Bon Secours Richmond Health Systems in Richmond, Virginia, lets workers shift to part-time or on-call status and they have to work only 16 hours per two week pay period to retain benefits.
- *Welcome Back Policies* – Some companies allow retirees to return to work after they have left the job. The MITRE Corporation, a not-for-profit systems engineering and information technology company based in Massachusetts and Virginia, offers Reserves at the Ready, a program that allows retirees to be on call for part-time work.

One obstacle to the employment of older workers may the very mundane, though critical, problem of a lack of transportation. The National Institute of Aging reports that each year 600,000 people who are 70 or older cease driving, which can cut them off from employment opportunities and also necessary goods and services, especially medical care (Palmquist, 2008). The problem is exacerbated if older persons do not live in an area served by a reliable and efficient mass transportation system, such as rural and small town dwellers. Regarding public transportation, a 2004 report from the Surface Transportation Policy Partnership and the American Association of Retired Persons found that in areas where adequate transportation is available, older persons will use it, making 310 million trips in 2001. However, the report also found that one-half of non-drivers over the age of 65, 3.6 million people in the United States, remain at home at any given day, presumably in part due to a lack of transportation (Palmquist, 2008). One partial solution is a 2005 law, called the Safety, Accountability, Flexible, Efficient Transportation Equity Act. The law requires all communities receiving federal transit funds to create a local Coordinated Human Services Transportation Plan in order to determine what local transportation agencies as well as health-care providers, non-profit organizations, and volunteer organizations are responsible for specific transportation services. One problem, though, it is that the statute is only funded to 2009. Another solution to enhancing the mobility of older persons is by the use of volunteers. For example, in Eugene, Oregon, there is a Bus Buddy Program, and in Appleton, Wisconsin, there is a Making the Ride Happen program. Most interestingly, the Beverly Foundation in Pasadena, California, did a study in 2006 based on a survey of volunteers which found that of 500 drivers in 288 cities, more than one-half were 65 years of age or older (Palmquist, 2008).

In many cases, a company's attitude towards older workers has a lot to do with the industry. Age bias is especially pronounced in youth-oriented sectors, such as advertising, technology, and securities. The entertainment industry is notorious for its youth obsession. In a company like a "dot-com" with predominantly younger workers and very little training on cultural competency and diversity issues, one tends to find more age bias. Inexperienced young managers often have a difficult time supervising older workers due to their own inexperience and lack of effective management and leadership skills. There are many firms that attempt to differentiate themselves from their competitors through quality service by treating customers with respect and dignity. These firms are finding that an older workforce has the experience to treat customers like "kings and queens," while taking care of them with enthusiasm. As such, firms like Wal-Mart, Publix, Target, Wegmans, Stu Leonard, McDonald's, and many others do target older workers to help them create a culture of satisfying and delighting customers. One example of such a company is the Borders Group. *HR Magazine* (Grossman, 2008) related that Dan Smith, Borders' senior vice president of human resources, became very concerned when he joined the company in 1995 since the majority of the company's workforce was under 30 years of age, and the company was facing increasing labor shortages. The Borders executive, however, noted that the company's stores with older workers had much lower turnover rates, that these workers were more content, and the stores did better financially. Smith noted that the comparison of the company's workers under 30 versus over 30 years of age was "startling as to loyalty and stability" (Grossman, 2008, p. 40). Smith emphasized: "Older workers were more satisfied, were staying longer, and customer service seemed to be better in their stores. It became clear that we had to make these guys a bigger segment of our population" (Grossman, 2008, p. 40). Accordingly, Borders began to target people 50 and over for recruitment. Now, *HR Magazine* reports that the number of older workers in its stores has tripled. Eighteen percent of the company's employees are over 50 years of age; and two-thirds are between ages 50 and 60 years of age. One result, said Smith, is that turnover has considerably improved at Borders. Smith noted that in the retail book business, turnover is 100 to

200%; but in Borders the turnover rate is now half that and trending down. Furthermore, turnover at Borders is six times less for employees over fifty than for those under 50 years of age (Grossman, 2008). Yet just as important as formally recruiting older workers is the organizational culture of these firms as they focus on serving quality products, offering excellent service, providing flexible hours and benefits to part-time employees (mothers, fathers, older workers, individuals with disability, etc.), being involved in the community, and making charitable contributions. This type of an organizational culture makes employees proud of their firms and tends to not only attract, but also retain older workers since they too would like to be involved in such activities in the community. As such, the firms mentioned here for illustrations are successful, at least partly, because they have created such an organizational culture that attracts and retains competent and experienced workers.

Summary

Over the decades that the U.S. Congress enacted the Age Discrimination in Employment Act, some employers may feel as though they have justifiable economic reasons for not wanting to hire and train employees who may soon be retiring or who may stay and "eat up" health care monies. Furthermore, others rationalize that people do "slip" with age. Some writers have stated that reasoning skills may decline with age. While some of these myths/opinions might have been based on a few factual occurrences with some individuals, they are not representative of an individual's ability to successfully complete a task based on his/her age. For example, older workers are one of the desired categories of employees in New Delhi, India. Some of the reasons why older workers are among the sought after workers in India include: job stability, experience, and consistency of work. Companies have recognized older workers value stability and quality in their work, so they are taking advantage of it. There is a mutual benefit here because the companies offer older workers the stability that they desire, and in return, the older workers utilize their expertise and stability to the benefit of the organization (Khan, 2003). As more and more companies downsize, merge, and are bought out because of economic reasons, layoffs and cutbacks are inevitable. This fact concerns all managers because with these cutbacks, one cannot help but to think that the employment of older workers will be impacted significantly. The general feeling is that many more employers are going to focus on a more youthful workforce, rather than one that is mature and more experienced because of the stereotypes, myths, and costs associated with "older workers." It has been witnessed that individuals have lost their jobs over the past several years because of layoffs; and they have always wondered why certain employees with similar characteristics (such as being over the age of 40) were selected rather than others. Many of these people have had a number of years invested in their organizations, but were dismissed regardless of their seniority. It has also been witnessed that younger workers have consistently been brought into organizations, and this consistency of the age characteristic makes one wonder "why"? For these reasons, among many others, managers should consciously decide to increase their knowledge in human resources and age discrimination issues in order to become more aware of the laws governing unfair employment practices, in hopes of making a positive difference in the lives of many experienced, honest, loyal, able, knowledgeable, and willing workers in order to recruit and retain them.

This chapter provided examples of best practices and suggestions for finding, hiring, retaining an experienced workforce were explored. The chapter, moreover, presented some of the "myths and realities" of "mature workers" based on a recent article. The chapter also discussed the very valuable role that older workers can play as coaches and mentors, particularly in regard to dispelling rumors and resolving conflicts in the workplace. The chapter also discussed the training of older workers, the challenge of introducing older workers to the latest technology, involving older workers with technology, and to developing the technological knowledge and skills of older workers. The benefits of technology for the older worker and his or her employer were explained and underscored. The chapter also presented the challenges as well as opportunities for older persons in the workplace, and related what the older person himself or herself can to do to secure employment and to achieve success in the workplace.

Questions for Discussion

1. What are the benefits of recruiting, retaining, developing, and empowering older workers? Provide examples with explanations thereof.
2. What are some of the challenges of training older workers, and how can these challenges be overcome?
3. How can older people and older workers empower themselves?
4. What are some of the "myths and realities" regarding older workers? Do you agree with them? Why or why not?
5. How can older workers function as coaches and mentors and how can such roles produce value for the organization?
6. How can employers involve older workers in technology and develop the technological knowledge and skills of older workers?

CHAPTER 9

THE PHILOSOPHY AND SCIENCE OF AGING[3]

Twenty-first century human beings are living in a society where youth and youthfulness are highly prized. Today's modern technological society desires youthfulness more than anything, as people are driven by the "bright lights" of Hollywood and the idea that success is predicated on staying young as long as is possible. The advances in cosmetic medicine and surgery have acted as balancing evidence to this highly desirable culture of youthfulness in which nip-and-tucks, Botox, face-lifts, and other cosmetically devised jargons, have become part of the daily language of life. Furthermore, there are famous worshipful icons that have perpetuated the interest in an anti-aging revolution through a combination of fame, cosmetic surgery, and drugs. Such individuals have altered the effects of time, and consequently defied our ideas and concepts of age and aging as they seem to grow younger with time's passing. However, knowing that society is baffled by mundane surface reality, one should consider aging from a biological viewpoint; and then it becomes clear that aging is a highly internal process, despite the illusionary aspects of outward or external appearances which will inevitably vanish to give way to time's indelible prints, wrinkles, and old age!

This chapter first presents various definitions and concepts of age and aging, then defines and differentiates chronological versus mental aging, and describes the nature of the aging process. The chapter next discusses various cultural and religious factors that affect the age, the aging process, and the perceptions of the "old." The chapter examines "young" versus "old" age, with particular attention being paid to age and privileges and age and aging hierarchies. The relationship between age and business is presented in the chapter, particularly pertaining to the marketing and advertising of goods and services. Finally, a discussion of a spiritual affirmation of age and aging is provided with an emphasis on aging in a healthful and harmonious manner.

2- This chapter was co-authored with Donovan A. McFarlane, City College- Fort Lauderdale, Florida.

Concepts of Age and Aging

Aging from a medical point of view is the process of growing old or maturing, and also describes the gradual changes in the structure of a mature organism that occur normally over time and increase the probability of death. The fear of aging is the fear of death which typifies the process across all cultures and societies. "Man" is ever searching for ways to escape his mortality and aging gives no comfort to him, for as one ages naturally, provided no other defects lead to death, then aging eventually leads to death as the definition above communicates.

Aging from a biological viewpoint refers to the cumulative changes in an organism, organ, tissue, or cell leading to a decrease in functional capacity. This is one valid reason why age and aging are stigmatized as weakness, that is, physical weakness. When most young people think of the elderly, for example, they think of weakness and the associated degenerative aspects which the process brings along to human body and functionality. In humans, aging is associated with degenerative changes in the skin, bones, heart, blood vessels, lungs, nerves, and other organs and tissues. These degenerative changes increase the likelihood of death and diseases; and thus it is valid to associate age and aging with certain diseases and functional weaknesses. In fact, there are diseases and functional imbalances in human beings and other creatures which are age-specific.

Hayflick (1994) posits that biologists have proposed a variety of theories to explain aging, but most of them agree that this process is largely determined by genes. Aging is a very highly studied phenomenon; and the branch of medicine that deals with the disorders associated with aging in humans is called Geriatrics. Gerontology on the other hand is the discipline which studies aging in all its scope. It can be called the "Philosophy of Aging" since it takes on numerous avenues and perspectives across cultures, academics, and other fields. The human species has long been fascinated, or rather more concerned, with the aging process, which eventually culminates with death. The so-called "anti-aging revolution" has been long in its battle to conquer the "aging gene" in man. This battle is still ongoing; and the results of delayed aging have only been successful in laboratories and in non-human creatures. According to Hayflick (1994), scientists have learned how to double the life-spans of such laboratory organisms as roundworms and fruit flies through genetic manipulation; and mutant genes in mice have also been observed to have a comparable effect in postponing aging. However, there is still much research and knowledge to be obtained on aging in the human body as far as causes and "preventions" are concerned. The human body is complex, more so than any laboratory animal; and consequently the process of aging seems to be cumulative on both the mental-psychological and physical.

Aging is a process deeply embedded in human genetics, and as such takes place at the cellular level. According to Hayflick (1994), life-spans of cells in the human body are determined by strings of DNA (genetic material) called telomeres, which are located at the ends of the chromosomes. Each time a cell divides, the telomere becomes shorter; the senescence and death of the cell is triggered when the telomere is reduced to a certain critical length. Telomerase, an enzyme that can intervene in this process, is being closely studied in relation to cancer as well as aging

(Answers.com™, 2005). Aging is a biological process, and thus phrases such as one's "biological clock ticking" do have validity. "Man's" life is a "race against time" and biology in essence; and thus aging is the result of both simultaneously acting in unison.

Chronological and Mental Aging

Human beings age mentally as well as chronologically or physically. Mental aging reflects itself in our abilities to remember, understand, and perform mental functions and operations with increased or decreased dexterity. Mental aging is both a negative and positive process, as it can reflect itself in the decrease capacity of the brain or mind to perform regular mental functions such as memory tasks and logical operations. Old age mental diseases, such as Alzheimer's, Parkinson's, and others are dysfunctional processes closely associated with aging; they can be uniquely called aging disorders. The quest of an individual therefore, should be to age healthily in both mind and body. Another aspect to mental aging is intelligence quotient or component; one's mental age usually reflects increased acuity in mental functioning, abilities and operations regardless of their unequivocal physical or chronological age. For example, a twelve year old child with high social, psychological, and other aspects of intelligence would have a mental age which is far above that of an average twelve years old. In this case, mental aging has a positive side. Yet chronological or physical age is our true age reflective of time as well as the degenerative physical breakdown of body and bodily organs, tissues, etc as a result of the aging process; that is, the medical or biological aging process which eventually expresses itself in the form of external wrinkles and postural imbalances or changes. It is a natural process that every living creature experiences over time, and can only be affected minimally given our knowledge of the aging process and the interaction of nature and nurture in effectuating this process.

Specifically regarding aging in the workplace, *HR Magazine* succinctly noted "people gain some, lose some" (Grossman, 2008, p. 43). That is, even "as physical and mental abilities decline, experience and determination help older workers compensate" (Grossman, 2008, p. 43). Moreover, the magazine underscored that employers can help their older employees "tip the scales in the right way." *HR Magazine* discussed *three* main practical areas where employers can assist older workers, especially those aged 50-64, and thus make them more productive and also make the organization more successful. The three areas deal with 1) vision, 2) hearing, and 3) dexterity and flexibility. First, concerning vision, as people age, their vision deteriorates. That is, regrettably, a "fact of life." One's ability to see, and to read, especially from a computer screen, becomes much more difficult. *HR Magazine* emphasized that "the contrast between what someone over 55 sees compared to younger workers is startling" (Grossman, 2008, p. 44). The magazine referred to an expert, a biomedical and engineering professor at Cornell University, who said that in order to get the same visibility, older people "…will need 10 times more light" (Grossman, 2008, p. 44). Accordingly, lighting can make the difference! *HR Magazine* referred to a Canadian Research Council study which showed "…that with properly adjusted light, people do 24% more work and are 42% more alert at the end of the day" (Grossman, 2008, p. 44). *HR Magazine* also pointed to a "lighting visibility calculator" provided by Cornell University which measures the light a person requires in 10 year increments (Grossman, 2008, p. 44). Yet how does an employer determine the amount of light its employees require. *HR Magazine* offered two suggestions: One is from Deutsche Bank that has installed "task lighting" that allows each employee to select the amount of light that he or she requires. The other is for the employer to use illuminated keyboards, which make it easier for workers to set their sight-line from the monitor to the keyboard (Grossman, 2008). Second, concerning hearing, age-related hearing loss generally begins in the 40s, but there are a variety of factors, including genetics, of course, as well as whether one worked in a noisy environment, whether one used headphones, or regularly listened to loud music, that will determine the extent of hearing loss. *HR Magazine* indicated that when people reach their 50s and 60s, an estimated 50% of people experience some type of hearing loss (Grossman, 2008). Obviously, such hearing loss adversely can affect the older person's work performance. Speech will become less intelligible; he or she will be removed from the "flow" of conversation in the office; and the older worker will have to strain to hear sounds and voices which younger colleagues clearly can hear. *HR Magazine* suggests two things that employers can do to ameliorate this deleterious situation. First, employers can compensate for hearing loss by providing phones and other products with higher volume controls. Second, employers can remove unnecessary loud, noisy, and annoying noise distractions from the workplace. Finally, the third factor pertains to the dexterity and flexibility of older workers. *HR Magazine* initially notes that "thirty-one percent of jobs are primarily physical and require little cognitive ability" (Grossman, 2008, p. 44). Plainly, these are the types of jobs that older workers may have problems doing. The magazine also notes that people start to lose speed, strength, and dexterity as they age, with the loss beginning at age forty. Also, they tend to put on weight, gaining on average a pound a year beginning in their 50s. Naturally, such weight gain further slows them down. However, when one reaches 60, weight generally tends to go down as one loses body cells. What can one do? Stay active, stand, walk, swim, exercise, join a health club and get a personal trainer, practice various physical activities, engage in wellness activities, such as the Silver Sneakers exercise program offered by Bally's Health Club, and, most importantly, do not sit around and "vegetate." What can employers do? *HR Magazine* recommends that employers not only encourage and sponsor some of the aforementioned activities, but also that employers redesign job functions, adjust technological approaches, and commit to ergonomics to help workers compensate for the loss of strength and dexterity as well as to reduce worker discomfort. For example, have machinery and/or teams available to assist employees lift heavy objects or people, such as hospital patients (Grossman, 2008).

Nature and Nurture in the Aging Process

Aging is affected by both natural biological and environmental factors. While people are still studying the biological processes and functions responsible for aging, environmental factors have been observed to affect aging as well. Accordingly, scientists have discovered that they can significantly delay aging in mice by providing them with very low-calorie diets (Hayflick, 1994). In addition, recent studies of rhesus monkeys on low-calorie diets appear to be having the same results, and it is believed that these diets slow the aging process by lowering the rate at which tissue-damaging substances called "free radicals" are produced in the body (Answers.com™, 2005). With these successful studies scientist aim to develop antioxidant drugs that could slow the aging process in humans by protecting against free radicals. If this becomes an achievement, however, the environmental factors which affect aging in humans will need forms of studies and control as well. Scientists need to study the pattern and rates of aging across different terrains, cultures and people in order to uniquely understand how significantly physical environmental factors, as well as social lifestyles affect the aging process.

Aging in a human being is a combination of environmental, natural, biological, and social factors interacting with each other to produce the effects and signs of this progress and transition through time. Age and aging shape the contexts in which one lives one life as one becomes more and more aware of our mortality approaching old age. "Man" fears aging because s/he fears mortality and age more than any other natural process typifies human mortality as an intelligent species. Therefore, the quest of a person to arrest the aging process or eliminate its causes is a natural inclination towards perpetuating this life. The views one holds on aging will affect this inclination greatly; and thus a mark difference in the attitudes of individuals, nations, and cultures regarding the phenomena of age and aging have greatly impacted the anti-aging revolution and the fields of geriatrics and gerontology. Gerontology is the study of the physiological and pathological phenomena associated with aging, while geriatrics is the medical study of the physiology and pathology of age. Geriatric medicine has much to do before one can even consider arresting the aging process. The biomedical knowledge required to modify the processes of aging that lead to age-associated pathologies confronted by geriatricians does not currently exist. They argue that until we better understand the aging processes and discover how to manipulate them, these intrinsic and currently immutable forces will continue to lead to increasing losses in physiological capacity and death, even if age-associated diseases could be totally eliminated (Olshansky, Hayflick, and Cranes, 2004; Hayflick, 1994; Medina, 1996; Gosden, 1996; Bailey, 2001; Bailey, Sims, Ebbesen, Mansell, Thomsen, and Moskilde, 1999; Wick, Jansen-Durr, Berger, Blasko, Grubeck-Loebenstein, 2000).

Though the anti-aging revolution has made progress, most of the progress have been relegated to lifestyle practices designed for healthy living rather than a direct elimination of the aging process. According to Olshanksy, Hayflick, and Carnes (2004), optimum lifestyles, including exercise and a balanced diet, along with other proven methods for maintaining good health, contribute to increases in life expectancy by delaying or preventing the occurrence of age-related diseases. They further argue that there is no scientific evidence, however, to support the claim that these practices increase longevity by modifying the processes of aging. This is quite true, since scientists have yet to arrive at the direct causes of aging in humans, much less to provide an aging antidote to arrest the process.

Aging: Cultural and Religious Factors

Western cultures are more preoccupied than any others with age and the aging process. Old age has a decisively negative view in Western societies, where the elderly or being old is associated with weaknesses, diseases, waste, the "once a man twice a child philosophy," and other negative conceptions, views, and jargons. In Western societies such as the United States, being old or being referred to as "old" is extremely abominable. Most persons would rather be called "elderly" than old. In some smaller traditional nations, where the extended family is the norm and traditional practices have remained intact, nations such as Afghanistan, Turkey, Jamaica, and some other small Caribbean nations, being called "old" is not taken as disrespectful, but taken with reverence and pride, since it is considered a privileged blessing to live to see old age. In such smaller traditional nations with a more collectivist social culture, the old and elderly are an integral part of the society and the family, and are regarded as wise, noble, virtuous, and right. In "American" society, this is uniquely the opposite and thus explains the attitudes of young people towards age and the elderly. In fact, A colleague of one of the authors recently had a conversation with a nurse in her 50's after 35 years of practice in the field. She lamented on the attitude of young people towards age in the United States, and seems to express a concern that the young generation, teenagers in particular, seem to think of any one above 30 years of age as "old." This was quite a fascinating and interesting consideration given the trend in society to posit things and self towards the young and non-conforming. "American" and European societies are far too conscious of age distinction in shaping social attitudes, relationships, and climates.

Eastern cultures have rigid lines between the young and old. However, the old are seen in a noble light and regarded with great reverence and respect. For example, in Chinese and Japanese, as well as Indian cultures, the old person or an elderly one is the sage who is well-enlightened and knows the seasons, the past, present, and future. The old person or elderly is treated as the head of the family; that is, treated as a grand matriarch or grand patriarch who never loses that post regardless of functional capacity or physical debilitation. This fact may stem from the phenomenon known as "ancestral homage or worship" that prevails in some Eastern cultures. Regardless, the differences in attitudes towards age, aging, and the old are markedly different. Not all Western cultures treat age, aging, and the elderly with negative regards. The attitude towards age and aging will depend on a combination of factors, mainly on the particular culture and social make-up of that society, though it can be predicted that the more collectivist nations or cultures would have greater reverence and more positive views concerning age and aging.

Religion and religious beliefs and practices also have impacted the attitudes towards age and aging. A religion that holds old age in high esteem will influence a society to be more mindful of the elderly and less concerned with age as a distinctive factor separating people. Throughout the Bible and Quran, for example, many of the leaders or patriarchs were aged people; and this fact seems to have influenced a tradition of the elderly or the old being succinctly privileged in positions of religious leaderships or authorities on matters concerning life. For example, the Roman Catholic Papacy has been a great reflection of this, as well as the hierarchy of spiritual leadership. Age is seen from a religious point of view as part of God's plan for "man" in his/her current life; people grow old and die, but with the possibility of being reborn into a new light and life.

Old Age versus Young Age: The Age and Aging Hierarchy

The distinction between young and old is highly emphasized in all societies and cultures, especially through a society's social expressions, values, and social practices and lifestyles. This distinction has resulted in what can uniquely be called age discrimination or an "age divide," which is more pronounced in "American" society than any other. The age divide represents a battle of viewpoints and attitudes between young and old, which affects their interactions and the opportunities available to each in numerous settings and institutions. One area in which the age divide becomes very evident is the job market; and this situation usually reflects itself in the disparity of experiences between young and old when it comes to job requirements and pay. Decisively, age acts as a discriminating factor in the job market, as indicated by the authors' research results, as well as in various institutional settings and social environments. For example, there are positions and ranks in various institutions and society, which through tradition or law, possess age barrier requirements; and a unique example of this is the Presidency of the United States, and another is the office of the Pope. Other examples can be drawn from "corporate American" companies in which the CEOs or Board of Directors of companies seem to be from only within a specific age group. Age divide becomes an issue only when it deprives individuals of positive growth opportunities and advantages that would be open to them otherwise.

Age is normally divided according to lifespan; and as such, over a human being's lifespan, he or she passes through different age stages: infancy, toddler, childhood, adolescence, young adult, adulthood, middle age, and finally, old age, which culminates in death. Life span is defined as the observed age at death of an individual; maximum lifespan is the highest documented age at death for a species (Olshansky, Hayflick, and Carnes, 2004). In most countries, including the United States, adulthood legally begins at the age of eighteen or nineteen, and old age is considered to begin at age sixty-five. (Note: This age category should not be confused with the definition of "older worker" which begins at the age of forty pursuant to U.S. anti-discrimination law.) However, this view has been changing over the years, as countries like New Zealand seem to have a lower chronological base age for the declaration of adulthood. This circumstance is also typical of many African nations, as well as subcultures as influenced by their social, cultural and religious practices. The division of the aging stages of man has long been around, and Shakespeare's "*As You Like It*" memorably demonstrated it as follows:

- All the world's a stage,
- And all the men and women merely players,
- They have their exits and entrances,
- And one man in his time plays many parts,
- His acts being seven ages.

According to Shakespeare, these are infancy, childhood, lover, soldier, adult, old age, and senility and death. Over the past the aging of man has been grouped according to decades, and this seems to confirm the idea of "old age" beginning much earlier in the minds of those not in the decade divisions of age. Age division according to decade is shown in Table 5.

Table 5 – Aging Division for Older Workers

1. Quadragenarian: someone between 40 and 49 years of age
2. Quinquagenarian: someone between 50 and 59 years of age
3. Sexagenarian: someone between 60 and 69 years of age
4. Septuagenarian: someone between 70 and 79 years of age
5. Octogenarian: someone between 80 and 89 years of age
6. Nonagenarian: someone between 90 and 99 years of age
7. Centenarian: someone between 100 and 109 years of age
8. Supercentenarian: someone over 110 years of age

Aging is simply the process of getting older, and all human beings must pass through this process. In modern societies, especially in "American" society there is considerable social pressure to hide signs of aging, especially among women. This has been one central factor fueling the anti-aging revolution and the "booming" market for anti-aging products. One of the consequences of the pressure to hide signs of aging has also been the shift in relationship patterns and dynamics among the aging and elderly, as most people within specific age groups tend to gravitate towards having younger partners, and which even may result in unhealthy social relationships. This consequence often shows itself in the form of many older persons taking up with much younger ones, thereby breaking a kind of age-relationship norm which society reacts to, and sometimes very harshly too.

Figure 2: The Aging Process

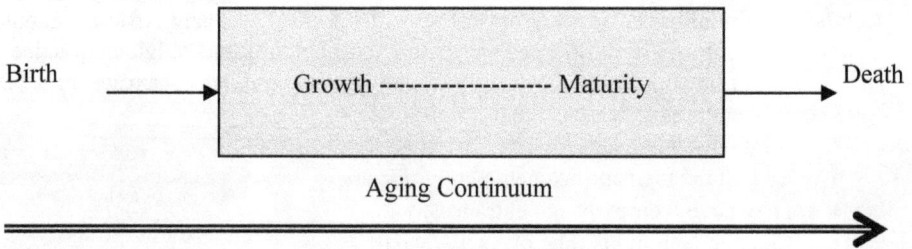

Birth → Growth ------------------- Maturity → Death

Aging Continuum

The aging process begins as early as birth and inevitably ends in death. Therefore, aging is a part of the growth and maturation processes of all creatures. As one grows and matures, old age will naturally set in, and eventually death arrests the processes of growth and maturation. The concept of old age and aging spells the mortality of "man," and this sets a person racing against time to accomplish his or her goals and dreams. Old age and death have become synonymous in languages and cultures, and thus one plainly understands that aging and old age in particular increase the probability of dying. Aging is a natural gravitation towards death, and as such slowing the process of aging should have the same result on death, slowing one's inevitable demise. See Figure 2.

Age and Privileges

There is no doubt that age and privileges are closely tied together. This relationship was illustrated in the earlier chapters with the discussion of "unearned advantages and privileges" that tend to come with the natural progression of aging at various times depending on the cultures' views regarding age. Sometimes, these unearned privileges are provided for younger workers, and at other times, they are given to older workers depending on the culture or sub-culture. In today's society, there are many institutions and situations in which one's age will act as a barrier towards some form of social or other physical activities. For example, persons under the age of 21 years are deprived of the ability to purchase alcoholic beverages in some places, and are also prohibited from entering certain entertainment establishments, such as adult entertainment centers and night-clubs. On the other hand, there are also exclusive social clubs based on age group requirements. This includes clubs which are designed for the purpose of entertaining teenagers only or senior citizens clubs. Age has become an issue which reflects the gender divide in "corporate America" as described by McFarlane and Mujtaba (2005). According to these authors, the differences between the genders are fundamentally at the heart of the gender debate, since each gender possesses unique qualities and attributes serving as foundation for distinction. This also becomes quite true when it comes to the young and the old; accordingly, the differences between young and old will naturally perpetuate any existing barriers of opportunities and privileges exclusive to either group.

Certain institutions in society have come to exemplify the privilege distinctions and barriers associated with age and aging. The most notable among these are political and religious institutions in which the old will naturally hold positions of authority and leadership above the young. There seems to be a tendency for presidents of the United States as well as senators and representatives in Congress to be decisively quinquagenarians or sexagenarians. In fact, these particular age divisions based on decade factoring seem to be the most popular groups from which positions of authority and leadership naturally derive in the beginning in our institutional settings. This seems to be more of tradition than an age divide. However, it still results in discrimination since it deprives younger persons of the opportunities to hold such offices and posts based on age contingent factor. Whatever the case, the young and the old both have certain privileges and opportunities, which naturally seem to derive from age rather than abilities and other factors.

Aging and Business: Age Distribution Effects

Within the field of marketing, researchers have seen how age and age characteristics have been used as instruments for marketers in reaching and meeting consumer needs and wants. Business and economics have made great use of age by dividing consumers into various cohorts. The area of marketing, known as marketing segmentation, refers to a demographic segmenting type which focuses on age and other integrally related people characteristics. Age classifications thus become central to businesses and marketing companies in attempting to "capture" the support of consumers. One of the most valuable business and marketing cohorts is that age group known as "young adults" because of their spending stemming from possession of an income and few other responsibilities demanding their income. Children and teenagers are also valuable cohorts, and their abilities to influence the spending patterns of their parents make them even significant to marketers and economists. The "young" are the central target of marketers (Answers.com™, 2005). Furthermore, it is stated that there is a popular belief that the middle-aged and the old are less likely to buy things, and as a result are traditionally viewed as being "set" in their buying habits and not nearly as "open" to marketing. Older people tend to be much wealthier and to save a much higher percentage of their income.

Global aging trends, therefore, hold significance for marketers, businesses, economists, and governmental planning agencies. Age distribution affects the availability and use of resources and the provision of services. An increase in the number of elderly, for example, means that a society or business will have to devote more effort, resources and time in providing for a larger senior population. According to Shackman, Liu, and Wang (2003), there have been small changes in age distribution between 1990 and 2000. Accordingly, the percent of population that is older increased slightly between 1990 and 2000 from 9% to almost 10% and this growth trend is expected to continue. Shackman, Liu, and Wang (2003) believe that this increase was larger within more developed countries, from 17.7% to 19.4%. The percent of population that is older is almost three times as high in more developed countries (19.4%) as it is in less developed countries (7.7%). There are numerous factors operating to effect the aforementioned changes in age distribution, and foremost among these factors is the HIV/AIDS epidemic, especially on the continent of Africa, where in some areas there is no longer a typical population-age-pyramid as the young adults and parents have been decreased rapidly in numbers leaving children and older folks behind. McGeary (2001) supports this viewpoint by stating: "AIDS in Africa bears little resemblance to the American epidemic, limited to specific high-risk groups and brought under control through intensive education, vigorous political action and expensive drug therapy. Here the disease has bred a Darwinian perversion. Society's fittest, not its frailest, are the ones who die — adults spirited away, leaving the old and the children behind."

Unfortunately, life expectancy in most African nations currently stands at 47 years (UNAIDS). According to Olshansky, Hayflick, and Carnes (2004), life expectancy in humans is the average number of years of life remaining for people of a given age, assuming that everyone will experience, for the remainder of their lives, the risk of death based on a current life table. For newborns in the U.S. today, life expectancy is about 77 years. According to these authors, this high expectancy which the U.S and many other developed nations not being ravaged by epidemics experiences stems from the rapid declines in infant, child, maternal, and late-life mortality during the 20th century that led to an unprecedented 30-year increase in human life expectancy at birth from the 47 years that it was in developed countries in 1900.

It is revealing to compare the United States to the world's other "great powers" when concerning the aging of the population. The U.S. Census Bureau estimated in 2000 that 40 million U.S. citizens were 65 or older, representing 12% of the total population. Moreover, the Census Bureau predicts that by the year 2030, the number will grow to 71.4 million, approximately one in five Americans (Palmquist, 2008). Due to steep declines in birthrates as well as significant increases in life expectancies, many other nations have also experienced a substantial aging of the population. Examples of such nations include Great Britain, France, Germany, China, Japan, and Russia. In the case of Russia, the country's population is not only aging but also shrinking, approximately to the extent of 700,000 a year (Haas, 2008). By 2050, at least 20% of the people in these countries, including the United States, will be over the age of 65, according to United Nations projections. Actually, the U.S. is growing older at a lesser rate than all the aforementioned countries (Haas, 2008). In Japan, more than one in three people will be 65 or older by 2050; China will have more than 329 million people over the age of 65 (Haas, 2008). Such an increase in older workers results in more people retiring and thus fewer people in the workplace. For example, the working age population (ages 15 to 35) of Japan and Russia is expected to shrink by 34% by 2050; and the decrease for Germany is expected to be 20%, France is 6%, and China is 3% (Haas, 2008). Fewer workers mean less work, and thus less economic activity. Unless there are commensurate gains in the productivity of the remaining workers, a nation's economic health will decline. For example, it is predicted that in China, the shrinkage in the working age population will result in an overall loss of 1% of Gross Domestic Product growth per year by 2020 (Haas, 2008). Labor shortages consequently will threaten economic growth, and not only in China. Therefore, as a matter of sound public policy, it is incumbent on nations to adopt policies and to promulgate laws that encourage older workers to continue working and to protect them from age bias in employment.

The Ideological Dichotomies of Aging: Theoretical Conceptions

There seems to be two extreme dichotomies when it comes to society's perspectives on age and aging; aging as progressive and aging as dysfunctional (See Figure 3).

The progressive view of aging can mostly be ascribed to Eastern cultures and societies that are typically collectivist and highly traditional, while the dysfunctional view of aging is very reflective of Western societies where youthfulness and non-conformist ideologies are more rampant. The dysfunctional view of aging views aging with a stigma of negativity; and thus age and aging, particularly old age, are equated with developmental and progressive weaknesses, decrease in mental and physical capacities, illnesses, diseases, lack of mobility, and all the "down-sides" of degeneration that occurs naturally in the aging process. These defects of aging and the aged are too well-emphasized in "American" society where youthfulness is equivalent to fortune and beauty, especially where the entertainment industry weighs in heavily on the "American" mind. The dysfunctional view of aging mainly focuses on the idea of aging as it culminates in death as a degenerative physical and biological mental process affecting human species. The old person then is regarded and treated by the young with a conscious awareness of death impending. The dysfunctional view of aging is highly operative in "American" society where "elderly" is associated with nursing homes, social security, disability, and age-specific diseases, such as Alzheimer, and loneliness. The dysfunctional view of aging is logical despite its negativity. After all, aging is a degenerative process in which organs, tissues, limbs, and bodily and mental processes are affected adversely with increased age. The process seems to be varied however across cultures and individuals, and this situation needs specific attention if scientists and those preoccupied with aging are to make any significant discoveries in the anti-aging revolution.

Figure 3 – Progress and Dysfunctional Perspectives of Aging

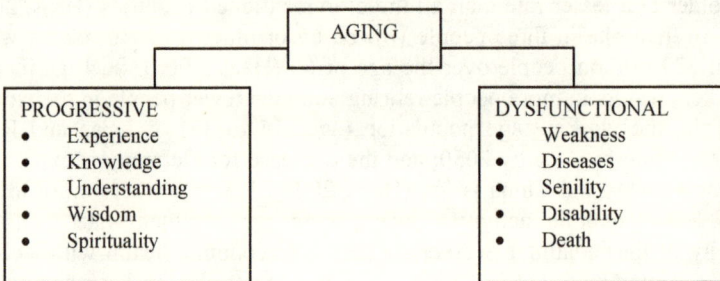

The progressive view of aging is a highly adaptive perspective for the human species. With one's inevitable mortality a person must come to view aging as part of one's natural transcendence. One must come to understand that aging eventually leads to death, and such a death is not the end of conscious spiritual development. This is a less popular view because it entails deep metaphysical and religious convictions which our scientific and technological societies have not fully grasped. Though the advent and ideology of life after death are part of most religious theologies, the idea has not become fully entrenched in one's daily life, and this causes one to have the fear people do of death and one's own mortality. Therefore, the dysfunctional view of aging prevails, stemming from the fear of death which is synonymous with old age.

The progressive view of death is highly entrenched in traditional practices, thoughts, legends, cultures, and ideals. The old or aging is seen as the birth and possession of wisdom, wide and far-reaching knowledge, superior understanding, indispensable experiences, virtues, and compassion; and in fact to grow old is a "blessing" since one could naturally die young. Many Eastern and Caribbean cultures have this progressive view of aging, and this explains the differences in treatment of old age and the elderly when it comes to reverence and respect from the younger generations within society. In Japan and China, for example, the elderly or "old folks" are treated with utter reverence and their opinions and experiences, knowledge and wisdom are highly prized, and they are looked upon for guidance throughout all areas of life. These two cultures are predicated on the idea of the "sage becoming" through old age and years of knowledge and experience developed through decades of life and learning. This ideology is typical of many Asian, Middle Eastern, African, and Caribbean cultures, and relegated to many societies in which tradition and ceremonies prevail with a close tie to nature and the past. In the United States, such practices have been replaced by the non-conforming ideas of young generations detached from the past; that is, separated from the old and wise. Yet the dysfunctional and progressive views of aging represent more of an interaction than an opposition, since both are valid within their constructs and assumptions regarding the aging process. In aging, one degenerates towards weakness and death, illnesses, and diseases, and simultaneously grows in wisdom and understanding, experience and knowledge, spirituality and love. Therefore, the balance is an eclectic view of the aging process, reflecting its "pros" and its "cons," which are all relevant parts of the transcending process of human conscious spiritual growth, but also clearly demonstrative of limitations and time.

Spiritual Affirmations for Aging Healthfully and Harmoniously

The aging process is a very beautiful one and brings experiences and knowledge despite the associated degenerative aspects. A child yearns to grow and become an adult; a teenager yearns to become an adult for the freedom and experiences which adulthood brings. Aging is a process of growth, maturity, and change which brings us closer to our human, individual, spiritual purposes, and destiny. One ages to become better individuals as one grows wiser and more beautiful in being. One must recognize aging as part of metaphysical spiritual growth, and accordingly cherish every stage of the process. One must strive to age healthfully and harmoniously while going through this reality. The aging process must guide one's ways and values while striving to accomplish goals and living happily. Below are some metaphysical spiritual affirmations for growing healthfully and harmoniously:

- I believe that to grow old is to grow wise and beautiful, fulfilling my destiny and the Creator's will.
- I will age healthily and harmoniously, growing in love, wisdom, knowledge, and understanding.
- I know that old age is a divine gift from the Creator, and he or she who grows to be old is blessed.
- I acknowledge that aging is a natural process that attunes one to the flow and rhythm of life and nature.
- I will age in happiness and prosperity, appreciating each and every day with joy.

- I will grow beautiful with each day's passing and shine bright with each rising sun.
- I value the belief that to age is to become love, truth and virtue.
- I will age with strength, vigor and vitality, knowing only laughter and gladness.
- I age not towards death, but towards eternal life and eternal youth.
- I will age without sorrow and grow old without sickness.

Insightful spiritual affirmations, therefore, can help one develop a positive and progressive view of aging. He or she will come to recognize aging as part of the Creator's plan for humanity, as a natural process which brings wisdom and understanding, and brings along the path towards our purpose and destiny. One should look forward to aging and aging beautifully and happily. Aging is a human reality, yet occurring with good will and love; and this is what the authors wish each man, woman, child, and living creature.

Summary

This chapter first presented various definitions and concepts of age and aging, then defined and differentiated chronological versus mental aging. The chapter next described the nature of the aging process. The chapter, moreover, discussed various cultural and religious factors that affect the age, the aging process, and the perceptions of the "old." The chapter examined "young" versus "old" age, with particular attention being paid to age and privileges and age and aging hierarchies. The relationship between age and business was presented in the chapter, particularly pertaining to the marketing and advertising of goods and services. Finally, a discussion of a spiritual affirmation of age and aging was offered with an emphasis on aging in a healthful and harmonious manner. By understanding aging and the aging process, employers can recruit, keep, and motivate older workers, and make older workers, and thus the organization, more productive and successful.

Questions for Discussion
1. How do different societies and cultures perceive aging, and how do these perceptions affect the workplace?
2. How do various societies and cultures perceive the "age divide" and "young v. old," and how do these perceptions affect the workplace?
3. How can, and should, an employer cope with an aging workforce?
4. Is it disrespectful to call a person "old"? What about a colleague at work? Why or why not?

CHAPTER 10

MANAGEMENT STRATEGIES - AGE DISCRIMINATION AND AN AGING WORKFORCE

The purposes of this chapter are to provide to leaders and managers practical strategies, tactics, and recommendations to comply with the law and also to maintain fair employment practices. First, detailed recommendations are supplied to managers on how to deal with the U.S. Age Discrimination in Employment Act and especially how to avoid legal liability pursuant to this important anti-discrimination statute. Recommendations are also provided on how to deal with and to defend age discrimination lawsuits pursuant to the ADEA. Next, recommendations are offered to managers on how to avoid discriminatory practices – based on age and otherwise – in the workplace. The chapter then furnishes recommendations to managers on how to deal with the challenges of an aging workforce as well as how to cope with older workers in the workforce. These recommendations are illustrated by U.S. domestic as well as global business examples.

Age Discrimination Laws–Strategies and Recommendations

Due to the aging of the workforce, U.S. law, particularly the ADEA, must be increasingly concerned with inducing the greater employment of older workers. This point was forcefully made in an American Association of Retired Persons report, called Reassessing the Age Discrimination in Employment Act (Neumark, 2008). The AARP first noted that the focus of the Equal Employment Opportunity Commission's (EEOC) enforcement efforts has been placed on terminations, and concomitantly there has been a "lack of activity related to hiring" (Neumark, 2008, p. viii). The AARP cited the EEOC data from 2006 which indicated that 40% of ADEA discrimination charges received by the Commission dealt with termination or lay-off determinations, but only 8.4% concerned hiring. Moreover, regarding age discrimination cases actually brought to court by the EEOC, termination and lay-off cases were 65% of the total compared to 23% for hiring cases (Neumark, 2008, p. viii). The AARP believes that for workers aged 65 and older, "a sizeable share of the higher employment among these individuals is likely to come not from continued employment in long-term careers, but rather from part-time or shorter-term jobs, perhaps with subsequent employers, in the form of what sometimes has been labeled 'partial retirement' or 'bridge jobs'' (Neumark, 2008, p. viii). Accordingly, as more workers over the age of 65 look for work, particularly "bridge jobs," after leaving their full-time careers, "then the focus of ADEA enforcement efforts on terminations might not serve the nation as well as going forward. Instead, it might become relatively more important to figure out how to ensure that age discrimination also does not deter the hiring of older individuals after leaving long-term, full-time work" (Neumark, 2008, p. viii). Any hindrances to hiring as well as impediments to filing hiring discrimination claims thus emerge as important legal and practical issues. Therefore, concludes the AARP, "policymakers may want to think about how the ADEA might be modified to provide more protection against age discrimination in hiring" (Neumark, 2008, p. viii).

An "older worker," as noted, according to the laws in the United States, is a worker that is 40 years of age or older. Unfortunately, there have been many firms that have shown patterns of discrimination against "older workers" in the United States' work environment, especially when it comes to hiring. The AARP in its 2008 report, Reassessing the Age Discrimination in Employment Act, commented on the disparity of ADEA hiring cases compared to termination ones: "The relative paucity of hiring cases compared to discharge or layoff cases could reflect the actual nature of the types of discrimination being experienced. But it also may reflect consequences of the legal framework set up to pursue age discrimination claims. First, hiring cases are more difficult to prove because it is more difficult to identify a class of affected workers. In contrast, in discharge or layoff cases the class typically consists of a group of workers employed (or previously employed) at a firm. Second, damages may be considerably higher in discharge or layoff cases, since workers lost jobs (and for older workers the job may have been relatively high paying) and there is evidence of difficulties in finding a new job....In addition, there can be substantial lost pension wealth accruals. In contrast, damages in a hiring case may be quite small, because an individual not hired by one employer has a reasonable expectation of being hired later by another employer" (Neumark, 2008, pp. 9-10).

The Age Discrimination in Employment Act in the United States presents leaders and managers with many challenges. Although the U.S. Supreme Court has ruled that the disparate impact theory now extends to age discrimination lawsuits, it is very important for the employer to realize that the theory is much narrower under the ADEA than pursuant to Title VII of the Civil Rights Act. The narrowness of the disparate impact theory in the age context means that the coverage of the statute – and the employer's potential liability therein – is much more limited in age discrimination employment cases. In particular, the "reasonable factor other than age" (RFOA) provision in the law means that certain employment criteria and practices that are legitimate and routinely used by employers very well could be legal despite their adverse impact on older employees as a group. The RFOA test, moreover, further narrows the application of the ADEA. For other civil rights lawsuits, the employer must ascertain whether there were other alternative ways for the employer to achieve its objectives without resulting in an adverse impact on a protected class. Yet due to the RFOA doctrine, the required "reasonableness" inquiry does not obligate the employer to under such a search for alternatives.

An employer confronted with an ADEA disparate impact age discrimination lawsuit, in order to sustain a defense, must produce credible and relevant evidence that the challenged employment policy or practice was based on reasonable factor(s) other than age. Moreover, this "factor," so long as it is reasonable and not age-related and advances the employer's goals, need not be absolutely necessary. The ADEA's RFOA test is not the "business necessity" test of Title VII of the Civil Rights Act. Furthermore, the employer does not have to search for the "most reasonable" approach. All that is required is a "reasonable" rationale for the action; and evidence that the employer relied on this non-age-related reasonable factor; and accordingly only "unreasonableness" will engender the employer's liability. Relying in some circumstances on rank, seniority, or years of service when making decisions may be in fact reasonable regardless of their relationship to age. Actually, there are many factors – age-related but arguably sufficiently distinct – that an employer could utilize as reasonable ones. Examples encompass: recruiting concerns, such as attracting or keeping technically and computer knowledgeable and capable employees; reputation concerns, such as honoring commitments to hire recent graduates or to recruit and hire at particular schools; budgeting concerns, such as reducing payroll costs by eliminating higher salary positions or off-shoring and outsourcing; performance concerns, such as making decisions based on performance or review ratings, evaluations, or needed useful skills; and dealing with the ramifications of mergers and other fundamental corporate change and restructuring, such as workforce reductions, lay-offs, reductions-in-force, and downsizing. What the employer cannot do is to use these rationales as a subterfuge to pull off the wholesale elimination of its older workers. Such a ploy would make the factor age-related and unreasonable and consequently illegal. Yet once the separation from age is achieved and reasonableness is determined, the employer prevails. The Supreme Court in the *Smith v. City of Jackson* case recognized that there may exist in employment certain quite necessary and legitimate job requirements and classifications that may have a greater adverse impact on older employees than younger ones. Such a "reasonableness" standard emerges as a very "employer friendly" one.

In an ADEA pretext case, the employer should be well aware that the plaintiff employee can bolster his or her case by demonstrating that the employer did not reveal the reason for the discharge, demotion, or negative job action to the employee until after the age discrimination claim was filed. Similarly, the plaintiff employee may be able to show that the reason for his or her discharge changed between the time of discharge and the filing of the age discrimination claim. In the aforementioned situations, the plaintiff employee's attorney surely will argue that the employer's reasons are fake and merely an afterthought to justify the illegal discriminatory treatment of the employee. As a result, a judge may permit the jury, as fact-finder, to determine whether the employer's belated reasons were true or false. In order to avoid such a legally untenable consequence, the employer should directly tell the employee at the time it takes the adverse action of the true, and appropriate, reason for it. If an employer is dissatisfied with an employee's work performance, it should expressly specify the sub-par performance as well as the problems it is causing; and do so in a clear and direct communication to the employee and "for the record." Once the criticism of the employee's performance is placed in the official company record, the employer will have a document in its favor to use to in the investigation and pre-trial stage of a lawsuit as well as to argue in court later as evidence of "reasonable factors other than age" for the adverse personnel decision. The employer must be aware that discrimination lawsuits often arise because an aggrieved employee does not feel that the employer possessed the relevant business factual justification to support the adverse action against the employee.

Establishing employment factors, therefore, which are legitimate and reasonable as well as analytically distinct from age, is the key management strategy to avoid legal liability pursuant to the ADEA. Thus, as with so much of the law – common law and statutory – the employer must strive for reasonableness in its actions. Even if an employee is an employee at-will and thus can be discharged for any reason (except an illegal reason, of course, such as age discrimination), and without any notice or explanation necessary, the wise employer is well counseled to first give, in a direct, clear, and unequivocal manner, to the employee the reasons for his or her discharge or job sanction; second, to make sure that the employer has the "hard" evidence to support the reasons, and third to give the employee an opportunity to be heard and to present any defense or excuse he or she may have. Even though it is not legally necessary to afford contractual or collective bargaining agreement "just cause" or "good cause" to a terminated or sanctioned employee, such fair treatment may be construed as morally and ethically mandated "due process" by the employee, his or her fellow workers, and perhaps later by a jury. Employers must realize that the typical employment law case is a factually intensive one. Accordingly, regardless of the legal "technicalities" involved, perhaps in the employer's favor, the astute employer surely must realize that the plaintiff employee's attorney will always attempt to claim that the employee was factually treated in an unfair and unethical matter; and such an accusation of immoral conduct by the employer can be very persuasive to a lay jury. Take the example of a long-term, older employee who was not properly monitored, not given warnings of poor performance, not coached or mentored to improve his or her performance, not even communicated with, who then was terminated for poor performance and replaced by a much younger employee, and who was then not given a fair chance to defend himself or herself. In such a scenario, if the employee's performance was in fact inadequate, the employer very well may have a technical legal defense, but the equities of the case very well could rest in the employee's favor, and ultimately before a perhaps sympathetic jury. A jury may be so offended by the employer's legal, but unethical, conduct toward the employee that the jury may disregard the judge's instructions to focus on the "legalities" of the case and rather concentrate on the morality of the employer's actions. A jury will respect the fact that the employer communicated with the employer, tried to mentor and coach the employee, allowed the employee to defend him or herself, and gave the employee a "second chance." And not only does an unethical employer have to worry about a sympathetic jury; judges are also human too; and may not like the "ethics" of the employer regardless of the legalities. Judges, regardless of their political persuasion or personal predilections, will not tolerate, and be very skeptical of, an employer who cannot or will not justify its actions, or does not even have records of personnel activity. As such, there is enough suppleness in the rules of procedure and evidence for a judge to undermine the employer's defense, perhaps by excluding exculpatory evidence on inadmissibility grounds.

Statistical analysis can be employed as a tool to avoid age discrimination lawsuits, especially disparate impact claims based on age. Attorney Mary Birk, in a 2008 article for the *Legal Report* of the Society of Human Resource Professionals, provides detailed guidance and recommendations on the use of statistical analysis to avoid disparate impact lawsuits based on age in the context of a reduction-in-force (RIF) (Birk, 2008). When an employer is contemplating the lay-off of workers due to business reasons, the employer must be aware of the potential of disparate impact claims based on age by employees who are over the age of forty. The *Wall Street Journal* in March of 2009 noted that it is possible that companies may be "targeting" older employees in certain lay-offs since older workers are generally the highest paid and have the most expensive benefits (Levitz and Shishkin, 2009, p. D1). Birk accordingly urges employers to use statistical analysis, not after litigation has begun, but before the RIF in order to ascertain the risk of age discrimination claims. Says Birk, "If the employer's statistical self-analysis uncovers disparities between the proposed impact of the RIF on protected older workers versus that of younger workers, the company is able to proactively make changes in its RIF decision to avoid such an impact" (Birk, 2008, p. 5). As discussed extensively in the legal chapter to this book, in order to establish an initial disparate impact case, the plaintiff employee must demonstrate an employment policy or practice that has a disparate, that is, negative or adverse, impact on employees protected by the ADEA than on younger workers.

A statistical analysis will test the statistical significance of any disparity in the lay-off or termination of younger v. older workers. Then, "if the observed number of terminations is statistically significant from what would have been expected randomly, statistical evidence of disparate impact discrimination may be established" (Birk, 2008, p. 5). A critical question to be answered is exactly what is a "statistically significant finding"? According to Birk, in such an employment disparate impact age case, "…experts will generally require either a statistical significance measure of 1 percent to 5 percent in order to show a correlation with age. These numbers, while not hard-and-fast, have generally been accepted by courts in disparate impact cases. When dealing with large samples, many courts have found that if the difference between the expected value and the observed number is greater than two or three standard deviations, most experts would find the results not likely to have been random. Theoretically, the higher the number of standard deviations associated with a particular result, the less likely that a random and nonbiased selection process would have generated the result in the absence of discrimination" (Birk, 2008, p. 5). Birk recommends that the statistical analysis be conducted by experts, because even though the comparison of younger v. older workers appears simple, "the calculations and factors to be considered are complex" and also "the failure to do a proper analysis will negate the value of the analysis as a legal challenge" (Birk, 2008, p. 6). She also recommends that "regression analysis" be used. Regression analysis is "a method of statistical analysis in which the relationship between two or more variables is examined to determine if there is an association between the variables" (Birk, 2008, p. 6). The objective of such an analysis is to ascertain "the possibility of disparate impact based on age in a RIF situation (by) determining if there was a correlation between the employees being laid off and their age" (Birk, 2008, p. 6). It is important to point out, asserts Birk, that such an analysis "does not determine if employees were actually laid off because of their age, but rather whether it is likely that such a result would have happened by chance" (Birk, 2008, p. 7). The underlying data, declares Birk, will be the "key" to analyzing the RIF and its consequences. As such, data for each employee to be laid-off and considered to be laid-off must be carefully collected, collated, and analyzed. Concomitantly, the criteria for choosing the employees to be laid-off must be clearly ascertained. In order to develop these criteria, the employer must have a "clear understanding" of the business and economic rationales for the RIF, for example, restructuring or reorganizing, centralizing or outsourcing functions or services, upgrading services thereby requiring a more educated and skilled workforce, or closing certain plants or locations completely (Birk, 2008). The proper grouping of employees emerges as another important element to the analysis, for example, comparing blue-collar employees to be laid-off to the blue-collar labor pool, and similarly comparing white-collar workers (Birk, 2008). Geographic boundaries as well as time periods for the RIF must also be considered (Birk, 2008). Prior to the RIF, after grouping the employees in an appropriate manner, the employees must be evaluated on objective, age neutral, criteria to determine which employees will be subject to the RIF. Assuming that age neutral criteria were used, and nonetheless there is still a disparate impact based on age produced by the RIF, then, as discussed extensively in the legal chapter to this book, the employer must be prepared to show to a court that "reasonable factors other than age" were used, and carefully, objectively, and fairly used, in order to effectuate the RIF. Such use of statistical analysis, counsels Birk, is "a proactive and valuable preventative step to limit an employer's risk of age-related litigation as a result of that RIF" and thus a "wise decision economically" and "an important human resource management tool" too (Birk, 2008, p. 8).

Labriola (2009), writing in the *Albany Law Review*, provided the following "general common-sense guidelines that can minimize a firm's risk of litigation" (p. 383):

1. Put Everything in Writing – "Your defense against an age-discrimination claim will be bolstered by your ability to back up your assertions in black-and-white. Document everything you do during potentially litigious actions and be able to demonstrate in your writing that your corporate culture does not foster an attitude of discrimination. Implement formal anti-discrimination policies and take steps to ensure that they are enforced in accordance with state and federal law" (Labriola, 2009, p. 384).

2. Educate Your People – "Mandate sensitivity training for managers and supervisors, and schedule sessions for new hires as soon as possible. Don't merely try to avoid litigation. Strive to create an educated atmosphere of

reasonable accommodation to the special needs of older workers where supervisors are comfortable offering employees options like flexible scheduling, part-time workloads..." (Labriola, 2009, pp. 383-84).

3. Terminate with Skill – "Don't simply fire an aging employee on pretext the first time she makes a mistake. If you concoct a phony reason for a discharge..., you'll pay a steep price when the truth comes out at trial. Harassing a worker into quitting does not improve your position; it merely changes the cause of action to unlawful constructive notice" (Labriola, 2009, pp. 384-85).

4. Think Strategically – "Justify a decision to demote or discharge with a paper trail of escalating disciplinary responses to earlier infractions. Craft non-discriminatory performance standards and retirement guidelines that show your actions to be fair and objective" (Labriola, 2009, p. 385).

5. Respond with Grace – "Pay attention when a worker accuses you or one of your employees of discrimination. Respond promptly and let the aggrieved employee know that you take the charge seriously and plan to right the situation before it winds up in court....Most importantly, do not even think about retaliating. If the worker has no case, a jury will figure that out. But no matter how solid your position, if you try to strong-arm an employee, you will wind up on the wrong side of the gavel" (Labriola, 2009, pp. 385-86).

HR Magazine (Grossman, 2008) offered the following practical points and suggestions to deal with potential and actual age discrimination lawsuits pursuant to U.S. law:
1. Employers should be practical and compassionate. Employers should offer "face-serving" severances tied to attorney approved releases that "ease non-performing workers out the door." Be aware that most people are willing to sign a release if they get some type of financial "package" as an incentive.
2. Bind employees, especially "high-powered" executives and "star performers," to binding arbitration clauses in their employment contracts.
3. Note that complaints of age discrimination typically involve hiring, treatment at work, or termination. Discharge cases account for more than one-half of the cases brought to the EEOC; and they are the cases most likely to move beyond the agency into the court system.
4. To preclude a lawsuit for discriminatory hiring, the employer must be able to show that a more qualified person was hired.
5. In a disparate or adverse impact discrimination lawsuit, the employer must be able to show that the reason for its job action was a reasonable and legitimate business one and was not discriminatory (Grossman, 2008).

HR Magazine (Grossman, 2009) provided additional general, practical advice on how to "defuse" discrimination legal claims, to wit:
1. Protect your information, for example, by conducting your own investigation pursuant to the direction of an attorney.

2. Gather facts quickly, particularly since as time moves on, employees can leave the company and documents can get lost or mislaid; and collect everything such as personnel files, disciplinary records, and pay records.
3. Do not "cut corners," that is, make sure you secure all documents and review them thoroughly, and also interview all relevant personnel; and do not make a conclusion after only talking to one or two people or reviewing one or two documents. The goal is to conduct a very thorough investigation, one which perhaps will reveal any weaknesses in your case
4. Document interviews, keep record of them, and retain them in the investigative file. Also ask employees to write up what they saw or heard regarding the situation, and ask them to sign or initial their statements (but do not "ask to hard" and if they refuse to sign or initial merely make a note of that on the file).
5. Do not "demonize" the discrimination claimant, as resentment may impair one's judgment in analyzing and fairly resolving the case.
6. Check out mediation, which the EEOC typically encourages, and which may save the employer time and money in the long-run; yet only seek to mediate if one is truly open to settling.
7. Respond fully to EEOC charges, which is required by the EEOC within 60 days; and, although the EEOC only requires a position statement, it is better, as well as expected by the agency, to provide a fuller explanation with supporting documentation. Such a course of conduct also indicates to the federal agency that you are cooperating fully.
8. Do not treat the EEOC like the "enemy"; that is, do not argue with or contest the claim at the investigative stage when the agency is "merely" requesting information.
9. Put the company's interests first; that is, determine your chances of prevailing, ascertain the costs of proceeding if the case is not settled, determine the impact on the company's reputation if the case continues, and ascertain what the effect on the other employees will be if the case continues. Accordingly, "the answers may yield a business decision that opts for fighting to the finish. Or they may point to the practicality of cutting your losses" (Grossman, 2009, p. 51).

The Academy of Management also provided some good "common sense" advice to managers; that is, "managers must realize that older workers will not just sit idly by and accept age discrimination; they will file age discrimination lawsuits; and they will win" (Santora and Seaton, 2008, p. 104). All the aforementioned advice can substantially reduce a company's or organization's risk of age discrimination litigation.

Finally, the very recent *Ricci v. DeStefano* disparate impact case, although a race-based one, presents challenges to managers, especially in the area of testing. Testing as well as educational and performance requirements can certainly cause legal problems for employers. Generally, "it is not unlawful for the employer to hire or promote employees on the basis of results of professionally developed ability tests provided that the tests are not designed to be used in a discriminatory fashion" (Cavico and Mujtaba, 2008, p. 503). However, it is essential for the employer to demonstrate that "the tests or educational requirements are predictors of, or significantly related to, important elements of work behavior and successful job performance" (Cavico and Mujtaba, 2008, pp. 503-04). Moreover, "...even if there is a showing that the tests are job-related, the courts will require that the employer use other different tests that have less of a discriminatory impact" (Cavico and Mujtaba, 2008, p. 504). The *Ricci* decision has surely complicated matters. The response to the court's ruling from employment law attorneys and human resources managers has been varied and contradictory. The decision will certainly have an impact. Yet what impact will it have? The *Wall Street Journal* stated that "uncertainty" has now been produced in the area of tests for employment and promotion (Tuna, *et al*, 2009, p. B1). The *New York Times* stated that the decision puts employers in a "damned if they do, and damned if they don't situation" (Greenhouse, 2009, p. A13)! Plainly, the new tests enunciated by the court will it much more difficult for employers to discard test results once they are administered, even if the tests have a disparate impact, and, as such, produce a disproportionately negative impact on members of a given racial group or protected category, such as older workers. Employers should carefully review their tests to be sure they are free of bias and are job-related. However, if tests or hiring, promotion, or layoff criteria are revised, especially after the fact if there is a disparate impact, to favor of or to protect minorities or other protected groups, then employers risk being sued for reverse discrimination as the city of New Haven was. Consequently, employers may abandon testing altogether. Or, conversely, they may use them more broadly.

Moreover, although the case dealt with a public sector employer, particularly those who use civil service exams, the legal standards announced by the court apply to all employers, including private sector employers; and the decision also applies not just to tests but to any type of policies, procedures, and standards used to evaluate, rank, and sort current and potential employees. Furthermore, the decision stands as a precedent not just for race-based cases but any type of disparate action claim. In the private sector tests for hiring and promotion are most commonly used by retailers, manufacturers, telecommunication firms, and businesses with large sales forces (Tuna, *et al*, 2009, p. B1). Employers, if they are concerned about the makeup of their supervisory ranks, then they must think very carefully about what type of test they are going to use at the "front end" (Doyle, 2009, p. 3A). They also must make sure that the tests, and for that matter their whole employment selection process, are neutral, objective, and fair. The goal is for employers to make their selection criteria "bulletproof" (Greenhouse, 2009, p. A13). Of course, this might make employers very cautious in using tests, which could include personality tests, honesty tests, computer skills, and physical fitness and co-ordination tests.

On the other extreme, some employers in order to avoid litigation may abandon tests completely in favor of other methods of selection and promotion, such as assessment centers, where applicants are evaluated in simulated real-life situations to see how they would handle them. Supporters of these assessment centers say they are better vehicles to measure communication and leadership skills as well as to ascertain an applicant's ability to handle emergencies. The Supreme Court decision, at the least, should motivate employers to re-evaluate what additional tools and processes are available to them in selecting and promoting employees. Outside experts and agencies should also see an increase in business as employers seek to independently validate tests. Consequently, the employment situation after this Supreme Court decision is "unsettling" and "muddled" (Bravin and Sataline, 2009, p. A1). Yet some things seem evident; that is, the Supreme Court decision will lead to more worry, work, and difficulty for employers, engender more litigation, and consequently cause more expense and costs for employers. It now appears that the already "fine line" that human resource professionals must traverse in the hiring and promotion of employees has just become narrower due to the New Haven decision. Therefore, it may be prudent for management to enlist the participation of all possible stakeholders in creating any contemplated written test so as to fall under the "safe harbor" announced by Justice Kennedy when he suggested that such racial preferences be addressed "during the test-design stage." Thus, by empowering the various stakeholders in this "test-design" stage, and by soliciting all participants' views during the "test-design" stage, management may be able to craft a written exam that is sensitive to minority, women, and older applicants and candidates as well as one that is acceptable to all parties. Trying to parcel the written test results after the fact, in a perhaps well-meaning attempt to avoid liability under the old *Griggs* and the Civil Rights Act of 1991 "disparate impact" standard, will only hasten the fall down the "slippery slope" into a legal liability quagmire and a concomitant public relations fiasco. That is the seminal meaning of the *Ricci v. DeStefano* decision.

Management Legal Strategies in an International Legal Context

Legal complexity naturally results from the globalization of business – in the employment field and otherwise. Foreign firms as well as U.S. ones consequently must be keenly aware of U.S. law; and also U.S. firms must be aware of not only foreign law, but also the extraterritoriality of U.S. laws. The employer's fundamental objectives, of course, are to obey the law, avoid getting sued and going to court, but if sued in court to prevail.

U.S. anti-discrimination employment laws clearly protect U.S. citizens working for U.S. employers, no matter where the workplace is located. The Civil Rights Act, the ADA, and the ADEA now have been amended to include protection for U.S. employees working overseas for U.S. firms. Thus Title VII, the Americans with Disabilities Act, and the ADEA currently are coextensive in their extraterritorial effect. These Acts accordingly have a very broad extraterritorial reach, encompassing not only U.S. firms doing business in the U.S. and overseas, but also U.S. controlled firms. A crucial issue, therefore, is whether a foreign firm is sufficiently controlled by a U.S. firm. Yet it is essential to emphasize that the courts consistently have held that only U.S. citizens are protected; and thus only a U.S. citizen may properly institute a discrimination lawsuit under Title VII of the Civil Rights Act and the ADEA based on employment decisions made at a foreign workplace by a U.S. employer or by a foreign employer controlled by a U.S. multi-national firm. Therefore, resident aliens and foreign nationals working overseas for U.S. companies are excluded from the protections of the Civil Rights Act as well as the ADEA. A "simple" solution to the extraterritoriality problem examined herein might be to apply U.S. employment discrimination laws to any company incorporated in the U.S., regardless of where its employment operations take place. Yet, this "answer" is not feasible due to the very strong presumption in U.S. law against the extraterritorial application of U.S. law, which typically is predicated on concerns about sovereignty, comity, and jurisdiction. This presumption is overcome only in exceptional instances. Legally, and most significantly, the distinct possibility exists of different global business practices and employment standards, as well as different degrees of legal protection, for U.S. employees and non-U.S. employees working for the same international business firm and in the same workplace. Failure to be cognizant of U.S. employment discrimination law, including its extra-territorial aspects, as well as the labor law of the host country, will result in increased exposure to legal liability for the multinational firm. Consequently, the manager of the multinational firm must ensure to the extent possible that the firm complies with both U.S. anti-discrimination employment law as well as the employment law of the host country.

Preventive Management Measures in To Avoid Age Discrimination

How and at what point does one step in to eliminate biased strategies that drive older people out of the company? One solution is to audit diversity ratios of the organization carefully and on a regular basis. It is essential to ensure there are non-discriminatory reasons for whatever decisions managers make. When there is a reduction in the workforce, it is necessary for management to do a careful analysis prior to implementing decisions about who will be laid-off. This act can be done through scenarios planning in order to see the impact of decisions before they are implemented. Before implementation of significant changes, managers should perform statistical analysis and review demographics; and then compare this information to what the expected results would be if implemented. Occasionally, indications of an effect on certain age groups will surface. When that happens, managers have to begin asking some "tough" questions, such as why is that happening. If the people one retains require certain skill sets, what are those skills? In addition, why is it that these people over 40 years of age do not meet the requirements? It could just be "the way the chips fall", but one would have to look carefully at planned separations. First and foremost, one must make sure to use non-discriminatory criteria for the decisions and that older workers are not disproportionately affected. Once determined, ensure that performance issues of affected employees are carefully documented and communicated prior to separation (Bennett, 1988).

There are several other ideas that might prove helpful in dealing effectively with age bias and discrimination in order to recruit, hire, and retain an experienced workforce. The following are a few helpful suggestions used by various consultants and organizations (Steinhauser, 1998; Mujtaba *et al*, 2003):

- Periodic Research - Conducting periodic research on how employees feel about older workers and how those feelings manifest themselves in the workplace;

- Educational Programs - Formulating educational programs designed to dispel myths and providing the facts concerning retirement, healthcare, and retraining;
- Support Mechanisms - Reexamining what it takes for individuals to progress within the organization and providing whatever support mechanisms are needed in order for them to progress;
- Benefits - Developing a friendly environment for older adults as part of work-family benefits;
- Appreciation - Building morale and higher productivity by demonstrating to older workers that they are valued and appreciated; and
- Management Commitment - Making sure senior managers and human resources staff are committed to the success of these efforts.

So, how can managers avoid the "nightmare" of being on the "wrong end" of a deposition or even worse a lawsuit? In most organizations, human resources professionals are unable to stay abreast of all staffing details. This is where managers' everyday decisions come into play, and especially where they are most likely to carry out decisions that leave them legally vulnerable. Not all instances of discrimination and harassment are easy to detect; and the laws are not always easy to interpret. In addition to the aforementioned preventative measures, there are, of course, common sense and good judgment solutions that must be considered as well, such as:

- First, avoid both blatant and subtle forms of age discrimination as well as inappropriate comments.
- Second, maintain candid one-on-one conversations with older workers regarding how they perceive the situation.
- Third, managers should ensure training opportunities are available to everyone and encourage older workers to keep their skills current.
- Fourth, provide good benefits suitable for the needs of older workers.
- Fifth, consciously recruit older workers from their places of socialization and invite them to the organization.
- Finally, avoid unexpected lawsuits. This result might be the most common category of "everyday management"; that is, managers must remain cognizant of common cultural and socioeconomic misunderstandings as well as important developments regarding older workers and age discrimination.

Furthermore, in order to create awareness and a culture of fair employment practices, global leaders and managers should institute relevant policies and procedures to bring about appropriate cultural changes in the organization. As presented in Figure 4, human resource professionals can apply the following steps to better manage various organizational-relevant cultural diversity dimensions and, thus to avoid, eliminate, and end age discrimination:

- Understand the culture and cultural attitudes towards age discrimination.
- Clarify cultural, national, and international laws applicable to employment practices in the organization.

- Ascertain and measure current organizational practices.
- Develop policies and implement procedures appropriate to the organizational values.
- Elicit support from senior management.
- Disseminate organizational policies and communicate expectations to all managers and employers.
- Educate and train all managers in fair hiring, developing, promoting, disciplining, and retaining of experienced employees.
- Consistently monitor program and enforce policies.
- Improve the program, policies, and procedures with regard fair employment practices.

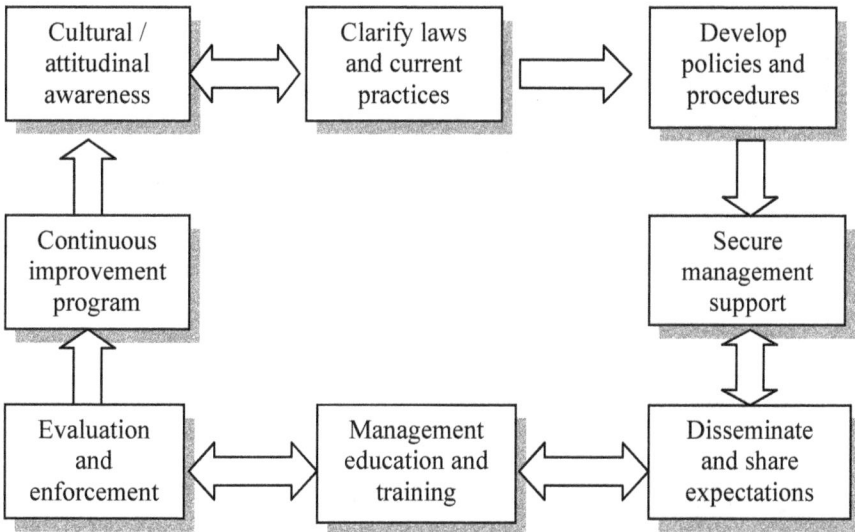

Figure 4 – Cultural Diversity Management Steps

Practical Management Strategies to Cope with an Aging Workforce

Research shows that the number of individuals aged 40 and above in the United States, and certain other developed nations, is growing at a much faster rate than the overall population (Schramm, 2005). Jennifer Schramm (2005) indicates that this trend will have a significant impact on the number of retirees compared to workers, which is estimated to reach one retiree for every four workers by 2050. Consequently, the decrease in labor pool in proportion to the number of retirees will have a huge impact on retirement, the experience level of the workforce, training and development strategies, and the recruitment efforts of most large, global organizations. While many countries will soon be dealing with the challenges of an aging workforce, the United States, Japan, and many of the European countries are already dealing with the effects of an aging population. Jennifer Schramm (2005) states that "Eventually, even countries that currently enjoy relatively large populations of young workers are likely to face this trend because even in these countries—usually developing nations—women are having fewer children and life expectancy rates are increasing." Schramm also states that the growing "older worker" population means a "major increase in government spending and budget outlays." As a result of this aging workforce, human resource professionals are strategizing to make sure they have the experienced workers needed to be successful in the competitive global environment of twenty-first century. Some of the actions the human resource professionals are taking in response to the aging workforce, according to Schramm (2005), are:

- Making more investments in training and development to boost employee skill levels.
- Engaging in succession planning and development.
- Training line managers to recognize and respond to generational differences.
- Bringing retirees back into the workforce.
- Offering customized benefits packages to employees.
- Conducting studies to determine projected demographic makeup of organization's workforce.
- Conducting studies to determine projected retirement rates in the organization.
- Changing employment practices to address the issue of discrimination against individuals with disabilities.
- Offering employment options designed to attract and retain semi-retired workers.
- Offering employment options designed to attract and retain Generation X and Y workers.
- Changing employment practices to address the issue of age discrimination.
- Changing health and safety policies to reflect the aging of the workforce. And,
- Using retirees as mentors.

Of course, the actions taken by human resource professionals to retain a competent and experienced workforce might be inclusive of many more strategies that are not listed above. However, the above list does provide a comprehensive category of "best practices" that can assist employers in the retention of an experienced workforce.

The fact that the age of the workforce is steadily increasing is consequently a challenge that most certainly will confront global business in the near future. Demographics show the workforce is aging rapidly. The *Miami Herald* in 2007 (Kelley, 2007) noted that a flat growth rate of under 0.5% was projected for the U.S. labor force for the next 60 years, which could engender a serious shortage of skilled workers. One result for business will be the reality of a very "tight" and competitive labor market. The astute employer will realize that older workers (those 62 and older, according to *Miami Herald*, and often called "mature" workers) not only will present a potential applicant pool of experienced, knowledgeable, and skilled workers, but also one that will afford an employer a competitive advantage. However, in order to tap this pool, employers must be cognizant of one key fact – that older workers will need and will demand flexibility – in work shifts, assignments, and in phrased retirements. Older workers will also need health insurance, not only until Medicare is available, but also assistance to pay for the increasing expensive Medicare supplemental health care policies. Employers, therefore, should now be considering strategies and tactics to retain and to attract older workers, to determine how to engage and stimulate them, and to ascertain how their knowledge and skills can be imparted to younger workers. Such strategies are particularly important in labor fields where there are already labor shortages and where a large percentage of the present workers are over 45, such as the nursing profession. Similarly, the *Wall Street Journal* reported in 2008 (White, 2008) that several U.S. companies, confronting worker shortages, are no longer overlooking the pool of older workers; rather, firms are attempting to convince older workers to remain employed longer as well as to recruit them for employment. The *Wall Street Journal* noted that by 2012 nearly one-third of U.S. workers will be over the age of 50. The *Wall Street Journal* recommended that employers adopt certain tactics to attract and to retain older workers: 1) offer flexible schedules, 2) provide training opportunities, 3) feature older people in recruiting materials, 4) offer competitive health care benefits, and 5) train managers and supervisors to manage employees of all ages. Yet the *Wall Street Journal* reported that only 18% of U.S. employers have any strategy to recruit older employees; and only 28% had a program to retain older workers at their own firms. Perhaps three main reasons for such reticence were reported in a survey mentioned in the *Wall Street Journal*: concerns about the high salary expectations of older employees, concerns about rising health care costs, and concerns that older employees would have to be taught new skills. Nevertheless, the *Wall Street Journal* article reported on several companies that now are adopting strategies and implementing tactics to retain and to recruit older workers. One company is Schneider International, Inc., a Wisconsin transportation and logistics firm. The company faced a serious problem: its workforce of truck drivers, typically aged 35 to 44, was shrinking due to a change in demographics. Consequently, the company decided to aggressively recruit workers over the age of 50. One tactic was to allow older workers to switch to, or to work on, a three-weeks-on, three-weeks-off program. The new schedule will result in a 25% decrease in salary, but the additional free time is an attractive feature for older workers. The *Wall Street Journal* also noted that Home Depot is seeking to utilize older workers especially when it opens new stores. One company tactic to recruit older workers has been to use the services of the American Association of Retired Persons (AARP) which has a link on its Website for its members to search for jobs. The AARP also has created the National Employer Team which features companies that the AARP deems "friendly" to older workers. The *Wall Street Journal* reported that 30 companies, including Borders Group, Inc. and MetLife, Inc., are now members of the "Team."

There are many illustrations of how ethically egoistic companies work to retain older workers. For example, Boeing has commenced a program, called 787 Dreamliner to retain older workers and to transfer older workers' knowledge to the next generation. When an older worker states that he or she wishes to retire, the worker is first asked "why." The company discovered that in many cases the older worker would like to keep on working, but not 40 hours per week. So, on a case-by-case basis the employers and managers explore employment options, such as phased retirement, telecommuting, contract work, and job sharing. The health care organization, Group Health, after discovering that 42% of its registered nurses were 55 and older, decided to implement a program for nurses who were five years from retirement that included opportunities to mentor and to teach as well as to work part-time after retirement. The Weyerhauser company has instituted a program for older workers, based on its own research that found that the vast majority of its employees aged 55 and older wanted to work longer rather than completely retire, but the older workers also wanted a flexible schedule and health care benefits. The company also has a plan in which older workers nearing retirement are expected to create a plan to transfer knowledge to as well as to mentor younger workers. The company's retirement project is called, very nicely, "Gray Matters" (King, 2008). Atlantic Health, a company that owns two New Jersey hospitals, has a program called the 1000 Hour Club that permits retirees to work limited hours on flexible schedules. In addition, older workers can take advantage of educational and training opportunities, workshops on health care and retirement planning, and "wellness" programs (Lee, 2008).

These preceding illustrations underscore what one commentator termed "legal astuteness" (Bagley, 2008). That is, when confronted with the requirements of the regulatory law, the astute and ethically egoistic company will move proactively beyond the "letter of the law" in a way that advances its competitive position. The idea is to view government regulation as a way to provide opportunities for profit-making by compelling companies to not only adapt but to innovate. One commentator has termed this viewpoint "strategic compliance" (Bagley, 2008). The objective is to construe the cost of complying with government regulation as not merely a "cost," but as an investment vehicle for the firm, whereby a company can seek out and adopt changes that will enable the firm to convert regulatory constraints into innovative and profit-making opportunities.

Creative Techniques for Managers and Older Workers

Business Week (August 1, 2005) included a special report on the "*Creativity Economy.*" *Business Week* mentioned the "Top 20 Innovative Companies in the World" from a 2005 study conducted by the Boston Consulting Group (BCG). Design strategy (and customer-centric innovation) seems to be the next big things according to the article and "increasing top-line revenue through innovation has become essential to success in their industries" as cited by the 940 senior executives studied in the same BCG study. So, implementing innovative strategies and unleashing the unlimited power of an organization's human resources asset can be a powerful tool in resolving age-related challenges facing older workers in this new economy.

In order to tackle the "ugly faces" of stereotypes regarding older workers, today's workforce along with their managers and organizational leaders can begin "brainstorming" on innovative strategies to have a productive and healthy work environment for all workers. Fred Koury, in his 2005 article entitled *"Creating a winning culture: How to become and stay innovative in a competitive marketplace,"* states that "the key to surviving in a competitive marketplace is innovation." Koury further states that there are many core principles of innovation that companies can benefit from in the twenty-first century's work environment. The manager's challenge is to carefully balance the cost of innovation with its prospective gains. For innovation to occur, a rewarding organizational culture must be created. With the creation of a rewarding organizational culture, innovation can naturally occur from various avenues. Koury (2005) offers four core principles that will help organizations become and stay innovative in the twenty-first century environment; and they are:

- Effective leadership is the key to innovation. It does not matter the size of a company; what matters is who is leading it. The right leadership is essential for the success of any company. Once the CEO has embraced innovation, it allows for the culture of the company to naturally fall into place.
- Encourage new ideas, even if they do not work out. Employees need to feel free to experiment. Do not punish failures, but rather celebrate the attempt at innovation. Encourage managers and employees to speak their minds. Too often, people feel they need to be politically correct or are afraid they will show up a manager. You need to know everything that is on their minds. The best ideas do not always come from the top.
- Calculate the risk vs. the investment. With risk comes reward. Some of the most successful companies today are the ones that allocate the most dollars and resources for research and development. It does not matter the size of the company, there needs to be a certain percentage of revenue, profit or other number you feel comfortable working off of reinvested back into the company for innovation purposes. If one does not have the "dollars" to do so, one probably has not been innovative. With no investment made for innovation, innovation and thus profits will probably be lacking.
- Be patient. The farmer plants the seeds and waits patiently for the rain to fall. He or she is not in control of this element. People must do the same with innovation. Once people have done their best, their customers will determine if the calculated risk was in the right place (Koury, 2005).

Koury (2005) goes on to say that creativity and innovation are not easy. Managers have to invest the time and money to make it happen at all levels of their organization in order to establish an innovative culture. Then, managers and employees can start reaping the benefits of being part of an innovative culture where all employees, regardless of their age, are fairly rewarded for their work. In another article, entitled *"Selling the vision: motivate your managers with more than just money,"* Fred Koury encouraged leaders and managers to recognize, realize, and reward the true value of senior workers and team members in the organization. Some of these senior workers are also managers and thus valuable formal or informal team leaders. Koury (2005) explains that these senior employees are the organization's inner circle of advisers who help guide the company through many difficult decisions. To get the most out of these individuals, leaders must create a motivational work environment for them. Koury also states that engaging senior employees and getting them to take an ownership role can be a difficult but a rewarding task. He explains that the initial steps are the easiest. Monetary rewards and compensation should be tied to the growth goals of the company, and you should also make sure these senior employees get the recognition they deserve. Give them the responsibility that comes with the authority of their positions and levels of expertise. If they are given appropriate levels of freedom to be independent thinkers without them having to worry about obtaining approval for each action, then these senior employees will take more of an ownership role, and, in turn, will empower and develop others around them. So, as good coaches, give senior employees the flexibility to try new things, measure them by performance, not hours worked, and offer steady encouragement. The most important key to motivating senior workers is laying out the vision for the company and having them understand what their role in it is. They need to believe in that vision so they can help the team move the organization forward. According to experts, the best way to "sell" employees on the vision is to involve them in its creation. It is a leader's responsibility and obligation tell employees what the final destination is and let them help in mapping out how to get there. Koury (2005) states: "As part of the vision-making team, each person will intimately know what their responsibilities are and what they committed to. Each one will want to uphold his or her portion of the plan so the team as a whole succeeds." Koury further relates that leaders can be surprised at what happens when employees are truly involved. These senior employees might stretch the leader's vision of where the company can go. So, motivate employees, especially senior or older workers, by involving them to be part of the vision creation, implementation, and execution processes.

Global Management Strategies and Leadership

The combination of an aging workforce globally and a shrinking labor force will materially affect not just the United States, but also many other countries around the world. Consequently, the need for highly skilled and knowledgeable workers may be prompting companies to do more to attract and to retain their older workers. *Business Week* (Edmondson, 2007) reported that a new paradigm shift is occurring in Finland, where companies in that country are now treating older workers as a valuable resource. Instead of coaxing them into early retirement, Finnish firms are now cajoling older employees to work longer by providing them with training, mentoring, health care initiatives, better health benefits, extra weeks of paid vacation, and other "perks," such as fitness clubs, free massages, language training, and theatre tickets. Generally, these benefits are given to workers when they reach age 55. In one manufacturing company cited by *Business Week*, older workers are given an extra 25 days off. These companies, however, are being more than "merely" altruistic or socially responsible; rather, since Finland's workforce is aging more rapidly than any other country (*Business Week* reports that 40% of Finns will reach retirement age by the next 15 years.), companies realize that their self-interest dictates that they will need employees. Moreover, companies realize that their older and more experienced employees are an important source of knowledge and skills, and thereby a key component to productivity. *Business Week* also reported that in Japan, 26% of all workers are over the age of 55; and Spain is set to become the world's oldest country with regard to its population since by 2050 one-half of its population will be older than 55. In the United States, about 19% of the workforce will be 55 or older by 2012. Finland, however, has made the most progress in tackling its older workforce problem. Finnish companies have been helped in large degree by a government program called "age ability," which was started in 1998. The goals of the government program are to assist companies to attract and keep older workers, boost the productivity of older workers, and to increase the country's average retirement age. In one company cited by *Business Week*, the average retirement age of its workforce is now 63 years, up from 58 ages in the late 1990s. Although these older worker initiatives can be expensive, companies believe it is in their long-term self-interest to spend the money in order to maintain a productive workforce. Actually, these initiatives aimed at older workers are working out so well that some companies are now extending them to younger workers.

Global leadership plays a significant role in international business. It is important to have highly skilled leaders in an organization to encourage and train employees. Since global leaders work with people throughout the world, they need to be aware of the cultural differences. Using the same business style as the parent company in another nation might not be a successful method to conduct business. Global leaders ensure that the global organization is operating smoothly and all the subsidiaries are being treated equally. Companies need to send their leaders to foreign nations for them to understand the culture and social standards. Business in the twenty-first century is completely different from prior years, and leaders need to make sure their people are adapting quickly to such changes. Due to the rapid growth of international business, companies require more global leaders and global-minded employees. To develop more global leaders, current leaders need to provide adequate training for the new leaders. The best methodology in developing global leaders is by providing more exposure to the international arena of the organization, and offering training from other experienced global leaders in the company. As stated by Albert Einstein, "Everything should be as simple as possible, but not simpler."

Compared to people working within a country or culture, those who work on international levels have to deal with greater levels of change regarding employment practices because of legal, cultural, social, economical, and environmental differences that exist within and among people of various countries. These international business and non-business people must become aware of subtle differences and nuances in other people's conversations, body gestures, sensitivities, table manners, business dealings, general contracts and agreements, gender differences and perceptions, time management styles, attitudes, values, religious beliefs, and many others that might be more prominent in some cultures than others. The authors conclude that all people deal with change to different degrees, yet everybody goes through the same process in dealing with change. However, how they move through the process may vary based on their subtle differences which could be influenced by personal, organizational, and/or cultural elements. The authors further emphasize that global leaders can use various strategies to initiate, champion, and bring about the needed changes in their employment practices regarding older workers in the right manner and at the right times.

Chapter Summary

In this chapter, appropriate practical recommendations regarding employment issues were offered based on the legal, ethical, and cultural analysis conducted herein. Ethical egoism was underscored as a viable philosophical and practical approach for employers to deal with such complex and difficult international business issues, such as age discrimination in employment. This chapter suggested recommendations, tactics, and strategies to assist managers and business leaders to achieve more efficient and effective operation in small enterprises and multinational corporations. The primary purposes of this chapter were to provide to business leaders and managers practical strategies, tactics, and recommendations to comply with the law and also to maintain fair employment practices. Detailed recommendations were supplied to managers on how to deal with the U.S. Age Discrimination in Employment Act and especially how to avoid legal liability pursuant to this important anti-discrimination statute. Recommendations were also provided on how to deal with and to defend age discrimination lawsuits pursuant to the ADEA. Next, recommendations were offered to managers on how to avoid discriminatory practices – based on age and otherwise – in the workplace. The chapter furnished recommendations to managers on how to deal with the challenges of an aging workforce as well as how to cope with older workers in the workforce. These recommendations were illustrated by U.S. domestic as well as global business examples. As in other important fields, such as education and health care, the law and ethics mean that people must be provided with a true range of employment choices as well as a genuine opportunity to choose; and that people must be afforded the unique consideration and unbiased judgment of their choices. Treating people with dignity and respect and as worthwhile human beings demands no less

Questions for Discussion
1. What practical measures can managers take to ensure that the workplace is free from age discrimination?
2. What practical measures can managers take to avoid age discrimination lawsuits?
3. What recommendations can you offer to enable managers to handle an actual age discrimination lawsuit?
4. Why should business firms in the U.S. and globally be concerned with the recruitment and retention of older workers? Provide examples with explanations thereof.
5. What steps can the proactive employer take to deal with an aging workforce?

6. Do you believe that age discrimination is a culturally conditioned response? Is age discrimination learned in society? Is it learned in the workplace? Why or why not?
7. Is age discrimination legal? Why or why not?
8. Is the rejection of an older person for employment because he or she is "over-qualified" merely a pretext and subterfuge for age discrimination in the workplace? Why or why not?
9. Is age discrimination immoral and unethical? Why or why not?
10. Is it demeaning and thus unethical to call a person "old" or a work colleague an "older worker"? Why or why not?
11. Can age discrimination be "unlearned"? Should it be? Why or why not?
12. What have you learned from this book that you deem important and relevant to your personal life, as well as to your roles as a worker, manager, and/or a professional? Why? Provide examples and illustrations.

CHAPTER 11

SUMMARY AND CASES

This book has attempted to address certain aspects of age discrimination in employment in a comparative academic approach, focusing on several countries, that the authors hope was enlightening intellectually and also efficacious in a realistic business sense. Accordingly, the authors commenced their work with a discussion of the difficult areas of stereotyping and cultural conditioning regarding age discrimination, of course, but also the related and even more problematic area of appearance discrimination. The growing global nature of the increasingly older and more diverse workforce will mean that companies and organizations should intensify diversity and sensitivity training efforts in order to secure employees and also to ensure they are treated with dignity and respect.

Book Summary

The legal "world" in which the global manager exists surely is a perplexing one, as some legal systems, such as the United States, have an extensive corpus of anti-discrimination law, including age discrimination; yet many countries, surprisingly, do not yet have any explicit legal norms or enforceable legal precepts regarding age discrimination in employment. Thus, the global business person who decides to do business in the United States is well-advised to be keenly aware of all the U.S. laws that prohibit and punish discrimination in employment, including age discrimination, of course. Yet, the U.S. business person doing business in a foreign country should not feel secure legally even if the host country lacks anti-discrimination law concerning age or otherwise, as there exists the distinct possibility that the law of the business person's home country, that is, the United States, will have extraterritorial effect. The authors consequently have attempted to delineate the key aspects of U.S. anti-discrimination law, together with a discussion of the extra-territorial application of the law. The authors also pointed out the absence of such age anti-discrimination law generally and in the countries examined, aside from the U.S., of course, although the European Community now is making some strides to further develop its body of anti-discrimination law by addressing age. Thus, ascertaining the legal norms regarding age and the workforce is an important task for the business executive, manager, and entrepreneur; however, determining the law, or the absence thereof, is just the first step.

The prudent business person also must address the moral nature of the subject matter of age discrimination in employment. The serious problem that immediately confronts such a moral examination, as the authors have underscored, is the doctrine of ethical relativism, which treats morality as societal-based, and thus which may allow certain types of discrimination if such practices are the prevailing moral norms of a particular society. The authors presented the research results secured by a professional colleague of the authors which displayed clearly the differing value perceptions in an age and generational study of U.S. and Japanese participants. Nonetheless, despite the varying values and moral norms, the authors have sought to supersede such "relativistic" thinking by emphasizing the intrinsic dignity and worth of human beings that demands that people be treated with fairness and respect, regardless of an absence of laws or the presence of any countervailing societal-based moral norms. Similarly, the authors referred to the "ethics" of the Italian political scientist and philosopher, Niccolo Machiavelli, in an effort to warn the readers of "Machiavellian" practices in business generally and specifically regarding the disparate treatment of employees. Treating employees in a dignified and equable manner, the authors underscored, is not only the moral and socially responsible thing to do, but the smart thing too in an egoistic and strategic business sense. Moreover, businesses and organizations that employ a diverse workforce based on age and other characteristics will have a workforce that will reflect the nature of changing global markets. This "mirror image" result will very likely produce benefits in the form of sustainable competitive advantage over rival firms. Thus, again, the rationale for doing the "right thing" is that it is the "smart thing" to do. That is, the ethical egoistic rationale for diversity – age and otherwise – is that it is in the long-term, economic self-interest of the company or organization to recruit, hire, and retain people of all ages and characteristics.

It is a fact that there are many firms that are in search of wisdom, more specifically, the type of wisdom that comes with age and experience which make companies and organizations successful. It is projected that about 43% of the civilian labor force will be eligible for retirement within the next ten years. Therefore, there will be a shortage of talented and skilled professionals that accompany top leadership. So, companies will have to implement effective strategies for attracting, hiring, developing, and retaining an experienced workforce. In order to accentuate the practical managerial aspect of the book, the authors presented extensive useful material on accommodating workers, enhancing their skills, recruiting and retaining older workers, as well as motivating and satisfying employees. In the twenty-first century work environment, the social responsibility obligation of managers and corporations goes beyond ensuring that people are not discriminated against in the job application process, hiring, discharge, promotion, as well as training opportunities. Social responsibility obligations and reasonable accommodations are about providing resources, if necessary, and training all employees on how to appropriately treat and interact with colleagues of all ages and capabilities. An organization that creates an inclusive environment for individuals of all ages, genders, races, body sizes, disabilities, and ethnicities will benefit in many ways from having diverse employees and diverse customers. There are many excellent practices in attracting and hiring a diverse population of older workers, and the process can start with the elimination of behaviors stemming from one of the most common barriers which are traditional biases and stereotypes toward older workers. The authors, moreover, in an attempt to afford the reader a comprehensive examination, discussed the topic of aging from biological, psychological, and spiritual perspectives.

A very interesting, thought-provoking, and indeed provocative component of the book was the presentation and discussion of the research results obtained by the authors from their initial four country-based survey of employees in Afghanistan, Bahamas, Thailand, Turkey, Jamaica, and the United States. The most prominent research result was the response of the U.S. respondents regarding age discrimination, to wit, the prevalence of such discrimination in the workplace, and this occurrence despite the presence of an extensive body of anti-age discrimination law as well as prevailing societal and personal norms condemning such discrimination as immoral. Based on the comments from the U.S. respondents, the authors concluded that one reason for such illegal and immoral discrimination against older workers may be a perception that older workers lack the necessary technological knowledge and skills and will not readily adapt, change, and learn. Thus, in addition to promulgating more laws, emphasizing the universal moral norm of dignity and respect, and providing workers with diversity and sensitivity training, an employer is well advised to increase the technological education and training of its employees, especially older ones, and the workers, most particularly the older workers, are strongly counseled to take advantage of any knowledge and skill building education and training, above all in the technological field. Applied knowledge truly is power, for the older worker, and for all of people.

Education, thinking, and training on the subject of age discrimination might very well be a harbinger of fairer days for older workers in the future. The hope is that the world will be an even a better place once age discrimination in the workplace is eliminated. The authors hope that the elimination of age discrimination in the workplace comes faster; and, of course, managers can be a critical factor in this process by doing their part to become aware of such biases and not letting inaccurate stereotypes and myths about older workers negatively impact their hiring practices. Eliminating biased thinking and stereotypical practices can best be achieved through the acquisition and application of factual knowledge as well as through conscious decision-making habits that are based on facts, instead of preconceived assumptions. Therefore, as emphasized by the Academy of Management article, "it is incumbent on managers to seize the opportunity to make the workplace a better place for all concerned. And in doing so, companies will be able to increase revenues and retain a competent and committed workforce" (Santora and Seaton, 2008, p. 104).

Yet in addition to the acquisition and application of factual knowledge, managers and leaders should take the time to think about their lives, their attitudes toward others and, most importantly, to determine how they want to live their lives, and how they want to be remembered by their family members, friends, and colleagues. In other words, take the time to determine one's life's purpose, which is really the secret to the "fountain of youth," and that can be the beginning of one's journey to living purposefully. According to Sophia Loren, the actress, "There is a fountain of youth: it is your mind, your talents, the creativity you bring to your life and the lives of the people you love. When you learn to tap this source, you will have truly defeated age."

The globalization of business clearly presents unparalleled opportunities, but also potential problems and dangerous risks for multinational business firms. As the world economies apparently are beginning to blend into a truly global economy, U.S. companies as well as foreign firms, even small ones, are beginning to explore business opportunities overseas. This globalization, though arguably beneficial in the long-term for global society and peoples as a whole, has produced nonetheless in the short-term certain legal, ethical, and cultural clashes as well as practical management problems. The ever-increasing integration of the world's economy in recent years, therefore, has generated a growing demand for international business managers to assure that their firms are in compliance with the various nations' laws, especially employment laws, when business operations take place across borders. As more business firms enter the global marketplace in a material manner, these firms must consider when and to what extent the employment law of the U.S. applies to their overseas workforce. Business decisions now involve not only the analysis of U.S. law and its extraterritorial effect, but also the laws of the host country. The result is that multiple levels of legal analyses must be performed.

Global thinking combined with a local acting mindset has become the norm in today's business world. International joint ventures, mergers, partnerships, and cooperatively working in complementary businesses have become a prevalent mode of business, and are not considered anomalies anymore. The consequent business combinations have been caused by the advent of new technology, global competition, diverse global employees, and the availability of resources around the world in short periods of time. Of course, an abundant amount of information is available, and can be accessed in a matter of five to ten seconds through a telephone, text message, or a computer and the Internet. So, change has become a way of life, and change comes in a variety of shapes, sizes, and forms. Change impacts both young and older workers as well as the employment practices of managers in the workplace. As such, everyone must be properly prepared to effectively deal with these societal changes. Change can be passive or inactive, mandated, self-generated, or proactive. Each type of change may have different affects on people because the variable and elements may be different. However, one knows that successful implementation of international change entails both learning how people go through the stages of the change cycle and learning how to get people excited about change and move them into a brighter future, perhaps more quickly and with less stress in the process. Today's environment demands that each individual becomes a "change agent" and take responsibility for his or her own future by mentally creating it, and then working toward accomplishing it on a daily basis. Once the vision of the future is clear, then a global leader or manager can align the changing world to fit his or her goals and objectives. There is something valuable in each learning experience. At the global or national levels, having a world of wealth means nothing; but having good health means something; however, having integrity and a virtuous character means everything for both younger and older workers of all nations.

Case 1: Age Discrimination and Pilots – U.S. v. International Law

The Miami Herald newspaper reported in November of 2006 that a recent change in an international law regarding the mandatory age of pilots has brought to the attention of the public, the airline industry, and government regulators the always contentious issue of the mandatory retirement age for pilots, which has been established in the U.S., for almost a half a century, by government edit at age 60.

Many pilots, particularly those reaching 60, say that it is time to change the rule, which was promulgated by the Federal Aviation Administration (FAA). The Miami Herald reported that several pilots have been lobbying members of Congress to get the mandatory retirement rule changed. In November of 2006, a new international rule went into effect, which permits foreign pilots to fly up to age 65, as well as to fly into the United States so long as they have co-pilots who are no older than 59. The change was implemented by the International Civil Aviation Organization, which is a United Nations agency. The rule affects pilots in all but four countries: the U.S., France, Pakistan, and Colombia.

Currently, there is legislation pending in Congress that would replicate the international policy for the United States. The proposed law would allow pilots between the ages of 60-65 to fly if their second pilot is younger than 60. As a response to pressure from the pilots as well as from members of Congress, the FAA has commissioned a panel of aviation experts and medical authorities to determine whether the age requirement should be relaxed. Proponents of the rule state that there is a growing body of medical data to indicate that safety risks from older pilots are non-existent. However, opponents of changing the rule contend that any change could be disastrous to the flying public.

What is most interesting is that the retirement issue has produced deep and vocal divisions within the airline industry and even among pilots. American Airlines, for example, as well as the Allied Pilots Association, which represents 10,000 American Airline pilots, oppose the change. Also opposed is the Air Line Pilots Association, which is the nation's largest pilots' union, with 61,000 members from 40 airlines. The communications director for the Allied Pilots Association said the main reason to oppose any change is safety. He explained that since the 60-year-old retirement rule was promulgated, not a single accident has been attributed to the subtle or sudden effect of aging. Moreover, a spokeswoman for American Airlines stated that the rule has served the industry well; and that American Airlines thus does not support changing the rule. However, Southwest Airlines and the 5,300 member Southwest Airlines Pilots Association as well as Jet Blue Airways, with 11,000 crew members, have called for a repeal of the age limit. Southwest's chairman stated that the skills of airline pilots do not arbitrarily end at age 60.

The Miami Herald related that advocates of the repeal have drawn support from research showing that medical advances over the past several decades have considerably improved health and vitality. According to one study noted in the Miami Herald, a male pilot nearing 60 when the FAA rule was enacted could expect to live to nearly 76. Today, the life expectancy for a 60 year old pilot is 80.2 for men and 83.5 for women. A representative for the AARP also noted that the older pilots are the ones with the most experience. However, to complicate matters, many of the pilots are concerned that their pension plans could be adversely affected by changing the retirement age. Also, younger pilots may have a stake in preserving the retirement age since it would remove older pilots, and thereby offer promotion opportunities. The Air Line Pilots Association has officially supported the retirement rule since 1980. However, the Miami Herald related that a poll released in 2005 showed a divided membership, with 56% favoring the current age rule and 42% advocating change.

Questions for Discussion:
1. Should U.S. law be changed to conform to international law regarding the mandatory retirement age for pilots? Why or why not?
2. Is the U.S. law illegal age discrimination? Why or why not?
3. Is the U.S. law immoral age discrimination pursuant to Ethical Relativism? Why or why not?
4. Is it moral pursuant to Utilitarian ethics? Do the good consequences outweigh the bad, or does the bad outweigh the good? Discuss.
5. Is it moral pursuant to Kantian ethics? Why or why not?
6. How would a major airline approach this issue using the principles of Value-Driven Management? Discuss.

Bibliography: Montgomery, Dave, "U.S. pilots battle over low age cap," *The Miami Herald,* November 23, 2006, pp. 1C, 2C.

Case 2: Association Discrimination, Disability, and Age in Employment

The Wall Street Journal revealed in June of 2008 a new, very interesting, complex, and problematical type of discrimination affecting employment, called "association discrimination." This new form of discrimination is related primarily to disability discrimination pursuant to the Americans with Disabilities Act (ADA) but also age discrimination under the Age Discrimination in Employment Act (ADEA). The Wall Street Journal reported that there are two prominent lawsuits now in the U.S. federal courts dealing with "association discrimination," and which are based primarily on a provision of the ADA that protects the jobs of relatives and other care-givers of people who are disabled.

One case involves a hospital employee in Peoria, Illinois, who was fired by her hospital employer because of her disabled husband's extensive medical bills. The other case involves a couple from Wyoming employed by the same company, a utility, which allegedly fired the couple in order to avoid the costs in the treatment of their son, who has a brain tumor. Both lawsuits contend that the plaintiff employees illegally suffered "association discrimination" premised on the employees' association with disabled people.

The Wall Street Journal related that the number of "association discrimination" lawsuits filed with the Equal Employment Opportunity Commission (EEOC) increased to a record level of 253 for 2007, compared to 194 the year before.

Moreover, the Journal quoted the legal counsel of the EEOC who predicted that with the aging population, one should expect to see even more cases of "association discrimination."

The Illinois hospital case, as described by the Journal, arose in 2005 when the plaintiff employee's husband began to receive chemotherapy and radiation for terminal prostate cancer. The employee wife, who was a clinical nursing manager at the hospital, who was hired in 2001, stated that her supervisor asked her if the couple would be switching to less expensive hospice care for her husband. She also stated that the supervisor told her the hospital was self-insured, and consequently could not continue to sustain the substantial medical bills caused by the treatment of her husband. The treatment had cost the hospital about $178,000 the year before. The plaintiff employee was eventually discharged; and she states that she was never told why. The defendant hospital contends that she was fired for insubordination; and also notes that it kept other employees with higher medical costs. The employee's performance evaluations referred to her as an outstanding manager; but the review also said that the employee had a very strong personality and that she could be an intimidating personality. The hospital, as noted, is self-insured, and consequently had to pay the first $250,000 in health care costs for each family. After that amount is expended, the hospital's insurer will pay fully. The hospital keeps a list of all employees who cost the hospital more than $25,000 a year for health care expenditures. Her husband's prostate cancer was diagnosed in 1994, when he was only 42 years of age. In addition to surgery, the husband takes hormone treatments, radiation, and chemotherapy, including the taking of about 20 drugs to combat the cancer, to reduce bone damage, to combat nausea, and for pain relief. The plaintiff employee admits that the treatment for her husband's cancer, which spread to the bones, was very aggressive because her husband wanted to stay alive to see certain milestones, such as their daughter's wedding, their first grandchild, and their son's graduation. The cost of the drugs runs into the thousands per month now. The plaintiff employee contends that their decision to aggressively fight the terminal cancer was a "personal" one that the employer should not have been involved in.

According to the EEOC, as noted by the Journal, the purpose of "association discrimination" is to prevent employers from discriminating against employees based on "unfounded stereotypes and assumptions" regarding people who work with or who care for the infirm and disabled. The Journal provided two examples from the EEOC. First, it would be illegal for a company not to hire a worker who volunteers at an AIDS clinic, due to a fear of contracting the disease. Second, it would be illegal for an employer not to hire an applicant who has a disabled child, based on the assumption that the person would be an unreliable employee.

One possible, and very viable, defense that employers may have is to assert that the employment decisions were strictly based on a desire to cut costs, which the law does allow in certain circumstances. The objective of the plaintiff employee in an "association discrimination" case, therefore, will be to show a nexus, or direct connection, between the relative's or associate's disability covered by the ADA and the employer's actions. If the employer, in addition, cuts costs "across the board," this general type of employment action will make it even more difficult for the plaintiff employee to demonstrate that critical link to the individual associate's disability.

In order to have an "association discrimination" lawsuit, one must first have an associate with a legally recognized "disability," of course. Establishing a legal disability should definitely not be taken for granted. For example, the Wall Street Journal reported a court case in which a person with a well-managed case of multiple sclerosis should not be considered disabled.

Questions for Discussion:
1. Discuss the legal issues involved in the "association discrimination" type of lawsuit? Should the federal courts allow these lawsuits? Why or why not?
2. How would you rule legally on the plaintiff hospital employee's case? Why?
3. Would you sustain the hospital employer's potential defense of uniform cost-cutting? Why or why not?
4. Do you agree with the plaintiff hospital employee's assertion that the decision to aggressively combat the cancer of her husband was a personal one that her employer should be involved with? Why or why not?
5. What is the moral course of action in the hospital case pursuant to Utilitarian ethics? Where does the "greater good" lie? Discuss.
6. Was the hospital's decision a moral one pursuant to Kantian ethics? Why or why not?
7. Utilizing a Value-Driven Management analytical perspective, what is the best value-maximizing course of action for the hospital to take? Why?

Bibliography: Zhang, Jane, "Lawsuits Test Disabilities Act," *The Wall Street Journal,* June 4, 2008, pp. D1, D6.

GLOSSAY OF TERMS

Age Discrimination – discrimination against individuals or groups of people based on stereotypes and generalizations regarding their age.

Age Discrimination in Employment Act (ADEA) – the preeminent civil rights law in the United States promulgated in1967 that protects older workers in the workforce.

Aging – from a medical perspective, the process of growing old or maturing, describing the gradual changes in the structure of a mature organism that occur normally over time and increase the probability of death, inevitably resulting in death; also a combination of environmental, natural, biological, and social factors interacting with each other to produce the effects and signs of the maturation process over time.

American Society on Aging (ASA) – an organization dedicated to enhance the knowledge and skills and to improve the quality of life of older people and their families.

American Association of Retired Persons – political, lobbying, and information sharing organization for older Americans.

Americans with Disabilities Act – principal U.S. federal civil rights law that protects discrimination against disabled workers and also requires an employer to make a reasonable accommodation to the needs of its disabled employees.

Appearance-based Discrimination – appearance based on one's personal appearance, including dress, grooming, and physical appearance.

Baby-Boomers – that portion of the population in the United States that was born in the two decades following the end of World War II.

Bona Fide Occupational Qualification (BFOQ) Exception – a defense to a discrimination lawsuit when the employer can show that a particular job characteristic is reasonably necessary for the normal operations of the job.

Circumstantial Evidence of Discrimination – indirect evidence from which a discriminatory motive or intent can be inferred.

Civil Rights Act – statutory federal law in the United States that forbids discrimination based on race, color, sex, national origin, and religion in employment, public accommodation, and other contexts.

Coaching – developing a trusting relationship with people so that expectations and goals can be clarified jointly, thereby leading to specific action plans for their achievement.

Cognitive Moral Development – one's moral maturity or the ability that one has to make moral determinations based on logic and reasoning from ethical theories and principles; developed by the psychologist Lawrence Kohlberg.

Convergence – the merging of different cultures due to the influence of globalization and other factors that bring them into close contact with each other.

Context – information that surrounds an event and which is directed associated with the meaning of that event.

Crossvergence – the development of a new culture with its own characteristics that result from cultures interacting with each other over time.

Cultural Ally – individuals who intervene or interrupt in order to stop mistreatment or injustice to other people.

Cultural Competency – the capability to function effectively in the context of different cultures, especially in the workforce.

Culture – a way of life that conditions people's behavior toward specific norms, customs, and societal expectations.

Defining Issues Test – a scenario-based survey instrument which indicates one's level of moral maturity or cognitive moral development.

Direct Evidence of Discrimination – evidence that clearly and directly indicates an intent on the part of the employer to discriminate.

Discrimination – making judgments about an individual's or people's behaviors not based on their unique characterizations, but on generalizations and stereotypes.

Disparate Impact Discrimination Case – when the employer's work policies and practices are neutral on their face in the treatment of employees, but they fall more harshly or disproportionately on a protected group of employees.

Disparate Treatment – intentional illegal discrimination, for example, when an employer treats some of its employees less favorably because of a protected characteristic, such as age.

Divergence – the extent to which distinctiveness is exhibited by a specific culture.

Diversity – the presence of a variety of different cultures, religions, races, ethnic backgrounds, and other distinguishing characteristics.

Equal Employment Opportunity Commission – the federal regulatory agency in the United States that administers and enforces civil rights laws as well as promulgates pertinent rules and regulations to implement civil rights laws.

Ethical Egoism – the ethical theory which posits that one should advance one's self-interest in the long-run as the moral course of action.

Ethical Relativism – an ethical theory which posits that morality is determined by what a particular society believes is moral.

Extraterritoriality – when U.S. laws, such as the ADEA and the Civil Rights Act, apply to U.S. companies operating overseas.

Foreign Laws or Foreign Compulsion Defense – a defense for employers operating overseas to civil rights lawsuits when compliance with U.S. anti-discrimination law would cause the employer to violate the law of the foreign host country.

Generation X – people born around 1965-1976.

Generation Y – people born around 1977-1994.

Gerontological Society of American – an information sharing exchange organization for older people.

Hostile Environment – a work or learning environment where inappropriate remarks, conduct, or actions are related to race, color, national origin, gender, age, or disability.

International Management – the process of applying management theories, concepts, and techniques in a global multinational business environment.

Kantian Ethics – the moral philosophy of the German philosopher Immanuel Kant which determines the morality of an action by the form of the action.

Language of Time – a cultural-based time system dealing with the tempo and rhythm of work, scheduling and appointments, and other local time practices.

Mentoring – a developmental, caring, sharing, and helping relationship where the mentor helps the mentee achieve his or her goals.

Monochronic Time – paying attention to and doing only one thing at a time.

Negative Synergy – when two or more people working together produce less than what both of them could produce individually.

Non-Retaliation Provision – a provision in most civil rights laws in the U.S. that makes it unlawful for an employer to retaliate against an employee for opposing discriminatory employment practices.

Older Workers Benefit Protection Act – a 1990 statutory amendment to the ADEA dealing principally with employee benefits and waivers.

Older Worker – according to the law of the United States a worker who is 40 years of age or older.

Polychronic Time – one is involved with many things at one time.

Pretext – when the employee in a discrimination case shows that the employer's proffered reason for different treatment is a phony or fake reason.

Prima Facie Case – the presentment of evidence in a lawsuit which if left unexplained or not contradicted would establish the facts alleged.

Reasonable Factor Other Than Age (RFOA) Defense – an important defense which can be asserted by an employer in an age discrimination lawsuit when the employer can point to a reasonable factor other than age for the employment decision.

Reduction in Force (RIF) – a planned lay-off of employees, usually substantial in nature.

RetirementJobs.Com – career site with an online job board for workers aged 50 years and older.

SHRM – the Society of Human Resource Management.

Silver Surfers – a charitable organization whose mission is to promote the Internet usage by older people in the United Kingdom.

Stereotype – rigid, repetitive, and formalized behavior or thinking in the form of generalizations regarding people or groups; used as the basis for discrimination when employed without factual or evidentiary basis.

Title VII of the Civil Rights Act – section of the U.S. Civil Rights Act that prohibits discrimination in employment based on race, color, sex, national origin, and religion.

Triple-Filter Test – Socrates' test of truth, goodness, and utility.

Unearned Privileges – advantages that are given to some individuals and withheld from others without regard to their efforts or abilities, because of perceived differences, such as being young or old.

BIBLIOGRAPHY

Adams, S. M. (1999). Settling Cross-cultural Disagreements begins with "Where" not "How." *Academy of Management Executive,* Volume.13.

Adamec, Ludwig (2003). *Historical Dictionary of Afghanistan.* Maryland: Rowman & Littlefield.

Administration on Aging (2001). Department of Health and Human Services. [Online]. Retrieved November 13, 2003 from http://www.aoa.dhhs.gov/.

Advantages & Opportunities in Hiring Disabled Workers. (June, 2003). *HR Focus.* Institute of Management and Administration.

Age Discrimination in Employment Act (2005), Sections 621-634. Thompson/West Publishing Company

Age Discrimination in Employment Act of 1967, Public Law 90-202, 29 United States Code, Sections 621-634, http://www.eeoc.gov/policy/adea.html.

Age Discrimination in Employment Act, Help Wanted Notices or Advertisements (2008) 29 Code of Federal Regulations, Section 1625.4. Thomson/West Publishing Company.

Age Discrimination in Employment Act, Employment Applications (2008) 29 Code of Federal Regulations, Section 1625.5. Thomson/West Publishing Company.

Aging with Technology. . . A Way to Stay Independent. *TechConnect.* Retrieved February 3, 2004, from http://www.iltech.org/agingtechnote.htm.

Aging. Retrieved July 23, 2005, from http://www.answers.com/topic/ageing.

Ajzen, I. (1988). *Attitudes, Personality and Behavior.* Chicago, IL: The Dorsey Press.

Ahmed, M. M., Chung, K. Y., and Eichenseher, J. W. (March, 2003). Business Students' Perception of Ethics and Moral Judgment: A Cross-cultural Study. *Journal of Business Ethics,* Volume 43 (Numbers 1/2), p. 89.

Ahmed, S. A., and Rojas, J. (1998). *A Comparative Study of Job Values of North and South American Business Students.* Unpublished manuscript. Downloaded from the web on November 1, 2002 from http://www.sbaer.uca.edu/Research/1998/98sri230.txt.

Akiba, D., and Klub, W. (1999). The Different and the Same: Reexamining East and West in a Cross-cultural Analysis of Values. *Journal of Social Behavior and Personality,* Volume 27, pp. 67-473.

Alaka, Aida M. (2006). Corporate Reorganizations, Job Layoffs, and Age Discrimination: Has Smith v. City of Jackson Substantially Expanded the Rights of Older Workers under the ADEA? *Albany Law Review,* Volume 70, pp. 143f.

Allen, N. J. and Meyer J. P. (1996). Affective, Continuance, and Normative commitment to the Organization: An Examination of Construct Validity. *Journal of Vocational Behavior,* Volume 49, pp. 252-276.

Allport, G. W. (1935). Attitudes. In C. Murchinson (Editor), *Handbook of Social Psychology.* Worchester, MA: Clark University Press.

Allport, G. W. (1954). *The Nature of Prejudice.* Garden City, NY: Doubleday.

Allport, G. W. (1955). *Becoming: Basic Considerations for a Psychology of Personality.* New Haven: Yale University Press, pp. 1-35.

Ang, S.W. (2000). The Power of Money: a Cross-cultural Analysis of Business-related Beliefs. *Journal of World Business,* Volume 35 (1), p. 42. Retrieved March 1, 2005 from the EBSCO Host database.

Anonymous (2005). Diversity at McDonald's: A Way of Life. *Nation's Restaurants News,* Volume 92, p. 3.

Arnold, H. J. and Feldman, D. C. (1982). A Multivariate Analysis of the Determinants of Job Turnover. *Journal of Applied Psychology,* Volume 67, pp. 350-360.

ALPA v. TACA, 748 F.2d 965, 971-72 (5th Cir. 1984), *cert. denied,* 417 U.S. 1100 (1985).

American Association of Retired Persons. Retrieved February 12, 2004 from http://www.aarp.org.

American Banana Company v. United Fruit Company, 213 U.S. 349 (1909).

Anderson, C., Glassman, M., and Pinelli, T. (1997). *A Comparison of Communication Practices among Indian and U.S. Scientists and Engineers.* Working Paper, Old Dominion University.

Ariail, Donald L. (2005). *Personal Values, Moral Development, and Their Relationship: A Study of Certified Public Accountants.* Doctoral Dissertation. The H. Wayne Huizenga School of Business and Entrepreneurship. Nova Southeastern University.

Arthur, Lexine V. (2003). *Ethics in Public Contracting at the General Services Administration.* Doctoral Dissertation. The H. Wayne Huizenga School of Business and Entrepreneurship. Nova Southeastern University.

ASA American Society on Aging Online. Retrieved February 2, 2004, from: http://www.asaging.org.

Avila, A. C., Edward, A., Fitzpatrick, T; Williams, C., and Wohl, J. (2004). *Wal-Mart's Twenty First Century Management Practices.* Graduate team research project presented on March 13th at the Huizenga School of Nova Southeastern University.

Ayguen, A. K., and Imamoglu, E. O. (2002). Value Domains of Turkish Adults and University Students. *Journal of Social Psychology,* Volume 142(3), pp. 333-351.

Babcock, Pamela (September 2008). Elder Care at Work, *HR Magazine, Society for Human Resource Management,* pp. 111-18.

Badaracco, Jr., Joseph L. (1997). *Defining Moments: When Managers Must Choose Between Right and Right.* Boston, Massachusetts: Harvard Business School Press.

Bagley, Constance E. (April 2008). Winning Legally: The Value of Legal Astuteness, *The Academy of Management Review,* Volume 33, Number 2, pp. 378-390.

Basim, H. Nejat, Sesen, Harun, and Sesen, Elif (2007). Are They Equal? Comparison if Turkish and English Job Announcements in Terms of Some Discrimination Factors. *Humanity and Social Sciences Journal,* Volume 2(1), pp. 34-42.

Bailey, A.J. (2001). Molecular Mechanisms of Ageing in Connective Tissues. *Mechanical Ageing Development,* Volume 122, pp.735-755.

Bailey A.J, Sims, T.J, Ebbesen, E.N., Mansell, J.P., Thomsen, J.S., and Moskilde, L. (1999). Age-related Changes in the Biochemical and Biomechanical Properties of Human Bone Collagen: Relationship to Bone Strength. Calcif Tis Res. Volume 65, pp. 203-210.

Barnett, John H, Weathersby, Rita, and Aram, John. (Winter-Spring 1995). American Cultural Values: Shedding Cowboys Ways for Global Thinking. *Business Forum,* Volume 20, Numbers 1-2, p. 9. Retrieved February 8, 2005 from ProQuest database.

Bay v. Times Mirror Magazines, Inc., 936 F.2d 112 (2nd Cir. 1991).

Beard, Marty. Web's Less than Senior Friendly. *New Media.* Retrieved February 5, 2004, from: http://www.medialifemagazine.com/news2002/apr02/apr15/4_thurs/news5thursday.html.

Beauchamp, Tom L. *Philosophical Ethics.* (1982). New York: McGraw-Hill Book Company.

Becker, K. (2000). *Culture and International Business*. Binghamton: International Business Press.

Becker, T. E. (1992). Foci and Bases of Commitment: Are the Distinctions Worth Making? *Academy of Management Journal,* Volume 35, pp. 284-297.

Bennett-Alexander, D. (Second Edition 1998). *Employment Law for Business*. Blacklick, OH: Irwin/McGraw-Hill. Cited in Regulation of Discrimination in Employment, p. 326.

Bentley, Michael (2007). How American Employers (Almost) Learned to Respect Their Elders: Smith v. City of Jackson and the Availability of the Disparate Impact Theory under the Age Discrimination in Employment Act. *Mississippi College Law Review,* Volume 26, pp. 347f.

Bernbach, M. J. (1996). *Job Discrimination: How to Fight, How to Win.* New York: Crown Trade Paperbacks.

Bhuian, S. N., Al-Shammari, E. S., and Jefri, O. A. (1996). An Extension and Evaluation of Job Characteristics, Organizational Commitment and Job Satisfaction in an Expatriate, Guest worker, Sales setting. *International Journal of Commerce and Management,* pp. 57-80.

Bibby, Courtney L. (April 2008). Should I Stay or Should I Leave? Perceptions of Age Discrimination, Organizational Justice, and Employee Attitudes on Intentions to Leave. *Journal of Applied Management and Entrepreneurship,* Volume 12, No. 2, pp. 63-86.

Biesada, A. (2004). Wal-Mart Stores, Inc. Hoover's On-Line. Retrieved January 18, 2004 from http://www.hoovers.com/wal-mart/--ID_11600--/free-co-factsheet.html.

Birk, Mary (April 2008). RIFs: Use Statistical Analysis To Avoid Disparate Impact Based on Age. *Legal Report, Society for Human Resource Management,* pp. 5-8.

Bitter, Adam (2007). Smith v. City of Jackson, Solving an Age-Old Problem? *Catholic University Law Review,* Volume 56, pp. 647f.

Black, S., Morrison, A. and Gregersen, H. (1999). *Global Explorers.* New York & London: Routledge , pp. 6-8.

Bloom, D. E., Mahal, A., King, D., Henry-Lee, A., and Castillo, P. (February 21, 2001). Globalization, Liberalization and Sustainable Human Development: Progress and Challenges in Jamaica. *UNCTAD/ UNDP,* Kingston, Jamaica.

Bluedorn, A.C. (1982). A unified model of turnover from organizations. *Human Relations,* Volume 35, pp. 135-153.

Bluedorn, A.C. (1982). The Theories of Turnover: Causes, Effects, and Meaning. *Research in the Sociology of Organization,* Volume 1, pp. 75-128.

Bond, M. H. (1994). Finding Universal Dimensions of Individual Variation in Multicultural Studies of Values: The Rokeach and Chinese Value surveys. In Bill Apuka (Editor) (1994). *New Research on Moral Development: Moral Development aCcompendium,* Volume 5, pp. 385-391. New York, NY: Garland Publishing, Inc.

Bond, M. H. (1996). Chinese Values. In Michael Bond (Editor). *The Handbook of Chinese Psychology,* pp. 208-226). New York, NY: Oxford University Press.

Bonner, B. (January 4, 2004). Inner Grove Heights, Minn., Wal-Mart to open despite intense local opposition. *Knight Ridder Tribune Business News.* Retrieved April 8, 2004 from http://www.proquest.umi.com.novacat.nova.edu.

Bravin, J. (March 31, 2005). Court Expands Age Bias Claims for Work Force. *The Wall Street Journal,* pp. B1, B3.

Bravin, Jess (February 28, 2008). Age Case Splits Conservatives. *The Wall Street Journal,* p. A12.

Bravin, Jess (May 28, 2008). Top Court Backs Workers Who Report Discrimination. *The Wall Street Journal,* p. A3.

Bravin, Jess and Sataline, Suzanne (June 30, 2009). *Ruling Upends Race's Role in Hiring.* The Wall Street Journal, pp. A1, A4.

Brettle, Oliver, and Dowling, Donald C. Jr. (October-November, 2007). The EEAR: Not Your Uncle Sam's ADEA, *Legal Report, Society for Human Resource Management*, pp. 3-4.

Brown, LaToya S. (2007). The Title VII Tug-of-War: Application of U.S. Employment Discrimination Law Extraterritoriality. *Vanderbilt Journal of Transactional Law,* Volume 40, pp. 833-857.

Brinton, Crane (1990). *A History of Western Morals.* New York: Paragon House.

Bronowski, J. and Mazlish, Bruce (1962). *The Western Intellectual Tradition.* New York: Harper and Row.

Brunetto, Y., & Wharton, R. (2002). Using social identity theory to explain the job satisfaction of public sector employees. *International Journal of Public Sector Management,* Volume 15, pp. 534-552.

Bucher, Richard D. (2000). *Diversity Consciousness: Opening Our Minds to People, Cultures and Opportunities.* Upper Saddle River, NJ: Prentice-Hall.

Bureau of Labor Statistics, 2002. *Occupational Outlook Handbook.* 2002-2003 Edition. Washington D.C.: U.S. Department of Labor.

Burrit, Chris (March 31, 1996). Upgrading Southern Skills. *The Atlanta Constitution,* p C1.

Business Briefs (February 28, 2008). U.S. Supreme Court: FedEx workers can sue. *The Miami Herald,* p. 1C.

Business Wire. New York. (February 3, 2005). *ACLJ Encouraged by President Bush's Remarks on Values Issues in State of Union Address.* Retrieved February. 8, 2005 from ProQuest database.

Cabrillo College (2001). *Older Workers in the Labor Market: A Report from the Congressional Research Service* (Online). Available at http://www.cabrillo.cc.ca.us/.

Cannon, Carol (2001). *Does Education Increase Moral Development? A re-examination of the Moral Reasoning Abilities of Working Adult Learners.* Doctoral Dissertation. The H. Wayne Huizenga School of Business and Entrepreneurship. Nova Southeastern University.

Cant, A.G. (Sep 2004). Internationalizing the Business Curriculum: Developing Intercultural Competence. *Journal of American Academy of Business,* Volume 5, Issues 1-2, p. 177. Retrieved Feb. 6, 2005 from ProQuest database.

Carpenter, Dave (November 2, 2008). More Being Forced Out of Retirement. *Sun-Sentinel,* p. 4D.

Cavalier, Robert J. (Editor), Govinlock, James (Editor), and Sterba, James P. (Editor), (1989). *Ethics in the History of Western Philosophy.* New York: St. Martin's Press.

Cavico, Frank J. and Mujtaba, Bahaudin G. (2006). Age Discrimination in Employment: Cross Cultural Comparison and Management Strategies. BookSurge Publishing (An Amazon.com Company, USA).

Cavico, Frank J. and Mujtaba, Bahaudin G. (2009). Business Ethics: The Moral Foundation for Effective Leadership, Management, and Entrepreneurship. Pearson/Prentice Hall.

Cavico, Frank J. and Mujtaba, Bahaudin G. (2005). Business Ethics: Transcending Requirements through Moral Leadership. Pearson Custom Publications.

Cavico, Frank J. and Mujtaba, Bahaudin G. (2008). Legal Challenges for the Global Manager and Entrepreneur. Dubuque, Iowa: Kendall Hunt Publishing Company.

Cavico, Frank J. and Mujtaba, Bahaudin G. (2004). Machiavellian Values "The Prince": Bullying, Begulling, Backstabbing, and Bargaining in the Twenty First Century Management. The Association on Employment Practices and Principles (AEPP) Proceedings. 12th Annual International Conference.

Chang, C. M. (1997). A Three Generation Assessment of Strengths and Needs of African-American, Caucasian, Hispanic and Chinese Grand-parents. *Dissertation Abstracts-International Section-A: Humanities and Social Sciences,* Volume 57(7-A): 2862.

Chang, W. C., Wong, W. K., and Koh, J. B. K. (2003). Chinese Values in Singapore: Traditional and Modern. *Asian Journal of Social Psychology.* Volume 6(1), pp. 5-29. Cileli, M., and Tezer, E. (1998). Life and Value Orientations of Turkish University Students. *Adolescence,* Volume 33(129), pp. 219-228.

Chappell, Tom (1993). The Soul of a Business: Managing for Profit and the Common Good. New York: Bantam Books.

Chavez, Joseph (2003). *Morality and Moral Reasoning in the Banking Industry: An Ethical and Cognitive Moral Development Examination.* Doctoral Dissertation. The H. Wayne Huizenga School of Business and Entrepreneurship. Nova Southeastern University.

Cheng, K. (March/April 2003). Silent Minority: Reaching Employees and Consumers with Mental-Health Concerns. *Diversity Inc.* New Jersey. Diversity Inc. Media, LLC.

Civil Rights Act of 1991 (2005), 105 U.S. Statutes, Sections 1071, 2000. Thomson/West Publishing Company.

Clark, K., (2003). Judgment Day. *Money and Business. U.S.News.com.* Retrieved on January 13, 2003 from: http://www.usnews.com/usnews/biztech/articles/030113/.

Colias, Mike (2005). McDonald's plans to continue healthy focus. *The Associated Press/Chicago,* pp. 1-2.

Community Affairs v. Burdine (1981). 450 U.S. 248.

Complaints, (January 17, 2004). Number of Complaints Suggest Wal-Mart Disrespects Workers, Laws. *St. Louis Post.* Retrieved April 1, 2004 from Nova Southeastern University's ProQuest database.

Comtex (2003). *McDonalds Targets Older Workers.* Retrieved October 30, 2003 from Infotrac.

Connor, P. E., Becker, B. W., and Kakuyama, Y. (1993). A Cross-national Comparative Study of Managerial Values: United States, Canada and Japan. *Advances in International Comparative Studies,* Volume 8, pp. 3-11.

Connor, P. E., Becker, R. W., Kakuyama, T. and Moore, L. F. (1993). A Cross-national Comparative Study of Managerial Values: United States, Canada and Japan. In S. B. Prasad and R. B. Peterson (1993) *Advances in International Comparative Management,* Volume 8. Greenwich, CO: Jai Press, Inc.

Cook, C. (2005). Wall Street Project on Social Responsibility. *Wall Street Journal,* pp. 1-2.

Cooper, Phillip J. (2007). *Public Law & Public Administration (4th Edition).* Belmont California: Thompson-Wadsworth Publishers.

Cornell Law School (2001). *Age Discrimination in Employment.* As cited in United States Code; Title 29 (Labor), Chapter 14. Available at http://www.law.cornell.edu/.

Colarelli, S. M. (1984). Methods of Communication and Mediating Processes in Realistic Job Previews. *Journal of Applied Psychology,* Volume 69, pp. 633-642.

Cook, J. D., Hepworth, S. J., Wall, T. D., and Warr, P. B. (1981). *The Experience of Work.* California: Academic Press, Inc.

Corbin, Peter Reed and Duvail, John E. (2008). Eleventh Circuit Survey: January 1, 2007 - December 31, 2007: Article: Employment Discrimination. *Mercer Law Review,* Volume 59, pp. 1137f.

Corbin, Peter Reed, and Duvail, John E. (2007) Employment Discrimination. *Mercer Law Review,* Volume 58, pp. 1187f.

Critchley, R. K. (2002). Rewired, Rehired, or Retired? *A Global Guide for the Experienced Worker.* San Francisco: Jossey-Bass/Pfeiffer.

Dalton, M., Ernest, C., Deal, J., and Leslie, J. (2002). Success for the New Global Manager: What You Need to Know to Work Across Distances, Countries, and Cultures. San Francisco: Jossey-Bass, A Wiley Company.

Dastoor, B., Roofe, E., and Mujtaba, B. (March 2005). Value Orientation of Jamaicans Compared to Students in the United States of America. *International Business and Economics Research Journal,* Volume 4, Number 3, pp. 43-52.

David, P. (2003). National Jeweler, Volume. 97, Issue 7, p.30. Retrieved February 14, 2005 from the Business Source Premier database.

DeGrazia, Sebastian (1989). *Machiavelli in Hell.* Princeton, New Jersey: Princeton University Press.

Demby, E. R. (February 2004). *Two* Stores Refuse to Join the Race to the Bottom for Benefits and Wages. *Workforce Management,* pp. 57-59.

DeMooij, M. 1998). *Global Marketing and Advertising: Understanding Cultural Paradoxes.* Thousand Oaks, CA: Sage Publications.

Denty v. SmithKline Beecham Corporation, 109 F.3d 147 (3rd Circuit 1997).

DiDomenico, N. & Mujtaba, B. (October 2004). *Tempered Radicals: The Leadership Style for Making Changes Quietly.* The Association on Employment Practices and Principles. Published in the AEPP Proceedings, pages 86-91.

D'Innocenzio, A. (September 21, 2003). Wal-Mart Suppliers Flocking to Arkansas. *The State and Wire Service Sources.* Retrieved February 20, 2004 from http://retailindustry.

Disability Discrimination. (2002). EEOC. http://www.eeoc.gov/types/ada/html

Di-ve.com (2005). Run for Fun: The McDonald's Olympic Day Run 2005. *www.di-ve.com,* 1-2.

Dorfman, P. W., Howell, J. P. (1998). Dimensions of National Culture and Effective leadership Patterns: Hofstede Revisited. In R.N. Farmer and E.C. McGoun (Editors), Advances in International Comparative Management, Volume 3, pp. 127-150.

Dougherty, L. (2004). *Immigration to America.* Retrieved November 23, 2004, from Northwest High School Library Media Center Web Site: http://www.kn.pacbell.com/wired/fil/pages/ listimmigratli.html.

Dowling, D. (1996). From the Social Charter to the Social Action Program 1995-1997: European Employment Law Comes Alive, *Cornell International Law Journal,* Volume 29(43), pp. 60f.

Downes, A (2003). *Productivity and Competitiveness in the Jamaican Economy.* Inter American Development Bank, Washington DC, USA.

Downes, M., Thomas, A. S., and Singley, R. B. (2002). Predicting Expatriate Job Satisfaction: The Role of Firm Internationalization. *Career Development International,* Volume 7, pp. 24-36.

Doyle, Michael (June 30, 2009). *Ruling backs white firefighters.* The Miami Herald, p. 3A.

Dworkin, G. (2002). *Paternalism.* The Stanford Encyclopedia of Philosophy. Edward N. Zalta (Editor.). Retrieved on November 11, 2003 from http://plato.stanford. Edu/archives/win2002/entries/paternalism/perspective. *Journal of Economic Issues,* Volume 34(2), pp. 393-401.

Ebeling, Ashlea (September 28, 2008). Here's a Plan: Work Longer. *Forbes,* pp. 96-103.

Eccles, S. (2003). The Relationship between Job Satisfaction and Organizational Commitment as Perceived by Irrigation Workers in a Quasi-irrigation Company in Jamaica. Michigan: Proquest Information and Learning Company. (UMI No. 3096346).

Edmondson, Gail (September 17, 2007). We're Not Finnished With You Yet. *Business Week,* p. 62.

EEOC v. Arabian American Oil Company, 499 U.S. 244 (1991).

EEOC Compliance Manual (October 20, 1993). EEOC Enforcement Guidance on Application of Title VII to Conduct Overseas and to Foreign Employers Discriminating in the U.S., Notice 915.002, p. 2169.

Elashmawi, F. and Harris, P. R. (1993). *Multicultural Management.* Houston, Texas: Gulf Publishing.

Elderly get a taste of the net. *BBCNews.* Retrieved February 5, 2004 from http://news.bbc.co.uk/2/hi/technology/3020719.stm.

Elkhouly, S. M. E. and Buda, R. (1997). A Cross-cultural Comparison of Value Systems of Egyptians, Americans, Africans and Arab Executives. *International Journal of Commerce and Management*, Volume 7, pp. 102-199.

England, G. W. (1967a). Personal Value System of American Managers. *Academy of Management Journal*, Volume 10, pp. 53-68.

England, G. W. (1967b). Organizational Goals and Expected Behavior of American Managers. *Academy of Management Journal*, Volume 10, pp. 101-117.

England, G. W. (1978). Managers and their Value Systems: A Five Country Comparative Study. *Columbia Journal of World Business*, Volume 13, pp. 35-44.

Eskilson, A., and Wiley, M. (1999). Solving for the X: Aspirations and Expectations of College Students. *Journal of Youth and Adolescence*, 28-1; 51-70.

Eskin, M. (2003). Self-reported Assertiveness in Swedish and Turkish Adolescents: A Cross-cultural Comparison. *Scandinavian Journal of Psychology*, Volume 44(1), pp. 7-12.

Ethics and Excellence: Cooperation and Integrity in Business (1992). New York: Oxford University Press.

Equal Employment Opportunity Commission (2008). Age Discrimination. Retrieved May 28, 2008 from http://www.eeoc.gov/types/age.html.

Equal Employment Opportunity Commission (2008). Employee Rights When Working for Multinational Employers. Retrieved May 28, 2008 from http://www.eeoc.gove/facts/multi-employers.html.

Equal Employment Opportunity Commission (2008). Employers and Other Entities Covered by EEO Laws. Retrieved May 28, 2008 from http://www.eeoc.gov/abouteeo/overview_coverage.html.

Equal Employment Opportunity Commission (March 11, 2009). EEOC Reports Job Bias Charges Hit Record High of Over 95,000 in Fiscal Year 2008. *EEOC Press Release.* Retrieved March 20, 2009 from http://www.eeoc.gov/press.

Equal Employment Opportunity Commission (2008). The Equal Employment Opportunity Responsibilities of Multinational Employers. Retrieved May 28, 2008 from http://www.eeoc.gov/facts/multi-employers.html.

Evans, Kelly (May 9-10, 2009). Ranks of Older Workers Swell as Losses Shorten Retirement. *The Wall Street Journal, p. A2.*

Farber, M. L. (1955). *English and Americans: Values in the Socialization Process.* In D. C. McClelland (Editor), *Studies in Motivation*, pp. 323-330. New York, NY: Appleton-Century-Crofts.

Feather, N. T. (1970). Educational Choice and Student Attitudes in Relation to Terminal and Instrumental Values. *Australian Journal of Psychology*, Volume 22(2), pp. 127-143.

Feather, N. T. (1975). Value Systems and Delinquency: Parental and Generational Discrepancies in Value Systems and Delinquent and Non-delinquent Boys. *British Journal of Social and Clinical Psychology*, Volume 14(2), pp. 117-129.

Feather, N. T. (1979). Human Values and the Work Situation: Two studies. *Australian Psychologist*, Volume 14(2), pp. 131-141.

Feather, N. T. (1982). Reasons for Entering Medical School in Relation to Value Priorities and Sex of Student. *Journal of Occupational Psychology*, Volume 55, pp. 119-128.

Feather, N. T. (1984). Protestant Ethic, Conservatism and Values. *Journal of Personality and Social Psychology*, Volume 46(5), pp. 1132-1141.

Feather, N. T. (1988). Value Systems across Cultures: Australia and China. *International Journal of Psychology*, Volume 21, pp. 697-715.

Feather, N. T. (1999). *Values, Achievement andJjustice: Studies in the Psychology of Deservingness*. New York, NY: Kluwer Academic/Plenum Publishers.

Feather, N. T. and Mckee, L. R. (1993). Global Self-esteem and Attitudes toward High Achievers for Australian and Japanese Students. *Social Psychology Quarterly*, Volume 56-1, pp. 65-76.

Federal Laws Prohibiting Job Discrimination Questions and Answers. The U.S. Equal Employment Opportunity Commission. Retrieved on October 04, 2003 from: http://www.eeoc.gov/facts/qanda.html

Fein, Richard (June 27, 2008). Job-Seeking Baby Boomers. *The New York Times*, p. A18.

Finn, Jeffrey (2004). Aging and Information Technology: The Promise and the Challenge. *ASA: Generations Journal*. Retrieved February 3, 2004, from http://www.gener ationsjournal.org/index.cfm?page=gen-21-3/gen-21-3-toc.html

Firoz, N. M. & Ramin, T. (2004). Understanding Cultural Variables is Critical to Success in International Business. *International Journal of Management*, Volume *21*, pp. 307-324.

Fishman, C. (2003). The Wal-Mart You Don't Know. *Fast Company* (77). Retrieved March 30, 2004 from http://fastcompany.com/magazine/77/walmart.html.

Fleischer, Randy A. (July 13, 2009). Another bad right turn by the Supreme Court. *The Miami Herald, p. 7G.*

Floyd, M. (August 24, 2008). Job Bias Lawsuits on the Increase Rise may be Due to Economy and Easier Online Access to EEOC. Retrieved on September 3 2008 from: http://www.chron.com/disp/story.mpl/front/5962605.html.

Foley Bros. Inc. v. Filardo, 336 U.S. 281, 285 (1949).

Fordahl, Matthew. "Elderly Reach for the Digital Age" *Associated Press.* Retrieved February 2, 2004 from http://www.globalaging.org/elderrights/us/digitalage.htm.

Forever Young. (2005). Retrieved July 25, 2005 from http://www.leoslyrics.com/listlyrics.php?hid=Wxj%2BxWLcwrg%3D.

Formal Interest Group. Technology & Aging. *Gerontological Society of America (GSA)*. Retrieved February 3, 2004, from http://www.gsa-tag.org/1999 /mainsymposium.html.

Fournet, L. M. (1996). A Three Generation Assessment of Strengths and Needs of Africa American, Caucasian and Hispanic Grandparents. *Abstracts-International Section-A: Humanities and Social Sciences,* Volume 57(5-B): 3421.

Fowler – Hermes, J. (April 2001). Appearance-based Discrimination Claims Under EEO Laws. *The Florida Bar Journal*, pp 32f.

Frankena, William K. (Second Edition 1973). *Ethics*. Englewood Cliffs, New Jersey: Prentice-Hall.

Fraser, B. (2005). Corporate Social Responsibility. *Internal Auditor*, Volume 62(1), pp. 42-47. Retrieved March 1, 2005 from the EBSCO Host database.

Freeman, William J. (2007). *Moral Maturity and the Knowledge Management Firm. Doctoral Dissertation.* The H. Wayne Huizenga School of Business and Entrepreneurship. Nova Southeastern University.

Friedman, M. (1970).The Social Responsibility of Business is to Increase its Profits. In Hoffman W. and Moore J. (1990), *Business Ethics, Readings and Cases in Corporate Morality*, pp. 153-157. NY: McGraw-Hill.

Furnham, A. and Albhai, N. (1985). Value Differences in Foreign Students. *International Journal of Intercultural Relations*, Volume 9, pp. 365-375.

Fyock, C. D. & Dorton, A. M. (1994). UnRetirement: A Career Guide for the Retired…the Soon-to-be-Retired…the Never-Want-to-be-Retired. New York: Amacom.

Galla, Donna (2006). *Moral Reasoning of Finance and Accounting Professionals: An Ethical and Cognitive Moral Development Examination.* Doctoral Dissertation. The H. Wayne Huizenga School of Business and Entrepreneurship. Nova Southeastern University.

Gale Group (1999, Oct). Associates Keystone to Structure (Wal-Mart). Retrieved March 19, 2004 from http://www.findarticles.com/cf_dls/m3092/1999_Oct/57578936/print.html.

Gardner, Marilyn (November 5, 2007). Retired? Not for long. *The Christian Science Monitor*, p. 13.

Garfield, Leslie Yalof (2008). *The Glass Half Full: Envisioning The Future of Race Preference Policies*. New York University Annual Survey of American Law, Volume 63, pp. 385f.

Garver, Eugene (1987). *Machiavelli and the History of Prudence*. Madison, Wisconsin: The University of Wisconsin Press.

General Dynamics Land Systems, Inc. v. Cline, 540 U.S. 581, 592 (2004).

Gender interests divide silver surfers" *BBCNews*. Retrieved February 4, 2004 from http://news.bbc.co.uk/2/hi/technology/2205941.stm.

Ghobar, M.G.M. (1967). Afghanistan dar Masir-e Tarikh, Volume I. Kabul, Afghanistan.

Gibson, J., Ivancevich, J. and Donnelly, J. (1991). *Organizations: Behavior, Structures, Processes.* Homewood, Illinois: Irwin.

Girlando, A. P. (1998). A Study of the Influence of National Culture on Russian Students in the United States.

Gosden, R. (1996). *Cheating Time: Science, Sex, and Aging*. W.H. Freeman & Co.: New York.

Greene, Kelly (February 14-15, 2009). There Goes Retirement. *The Wall Street Journal*, pp. D1, D4.

Green, Heather (December 15, 2008). The Unretired. *Business Week*, pp. 47-49.

Green, Ronald M. (1993). *The Ethical Manager: A New Method for Business Ethics*. New York: Macmillan Publishing Company.

Greenhouse, Linda (June 20, 2008). Justices, in Bias Case, Rule for Older Workers. *The New York Times*, p. A15.

Greenhouse, Linda (May 28, 2008). Justices Say Law Bars Retaliation Over Bias Claims. *The New York Times,* pp. A1, A18.

Greenhouse, Seven (June 30, 2009). For Employers, Ruling Offers Little Guidance on How to Make Their Hiring Fair. The New York Times, p. A13.

Gregorian, Vartan. (1969). *The Emergence of Modern Afghanistan*. California: Stanford University Press.

Gregory, F. R. (2001). *Age Discrimination in the American Workplace: Old at a Young Age.* New Brunswick, New Jersey: Rutgers University Press.

Griest, G. (January 2004). *Kmart Posts $250 Million Profit, 13.5 Percent Drop in Sales.* Retrieved March 29, 2004 from http://0-proquest.umi.com.novacat.nova.edu/pqweb?index+13&sis= 1&srchmode=1&vins.

Griggs v. Duke Power (1971). 401 U.S. 424.

Gross, Daniel (June 16, 2008). Eighty Is the New Fifty. *The Money Culture, Newsweek*, p. 18.

Grossman, Robert J. (May 2009). Defusing Discrimination Claims. *HR Magazine*, pp. 47-51.

Grossman, Robert J. (May 2008) Keep Pace with Older Workers. *HR Magazine*, pp. 39-46.

Grossman, Robert J. (June 2008). Older Workers: Running to the Courthouse? *HR Magazine*, pp. 63-70.

Guy, V. and Mattock, J. (1995). The International Business Book: All the Tools, Tactics, and Tips You Need for doing Business across Cultures. Lincolnwood: NTC Business Books.

Haas, Mark L. (August 2008). Pax Americana Geriatrica. *Miller-McCune*, pp. 31-39.

Hale, R. L. (1995). *Systat: Statistical Applications*. Cambridge, MA: Course Technology.

Hall, E. T. and Hall, M. R., (1987). *Understanding Cultural Differences*. Intercultural Press, Inc. USA.

Hamann, R., Agbazue, T., Kapelus, P., and Hein, A. (2005). Universalizing Corporate Social Responsibility? South African Challenges to the International Organization for Standardization's New Social Responsibility Standard. Retrieved March 1, 2005 from the EBSCO Host database.

Hambrick, D. C., Canney D. S., Snell, S. A., and Snow, C, C., (1998). When Groups Consist of Multiple Nationalities: Towards a New Understanding of the Implications. *Organizational Studies*, Volume 19, pp. 181-205.

Hamlyn, D.W. (1988). *A History of Western Philosophy*. London: Penguin Books.

Hampshire, Stuart (1983). *Morality and Conflict*. Cambridge, Massachusetts: Harvard University Press.

Hanna, Thomas M. (2007). *The Employer's Legal Advisor*. New York: AMACON (The American Management Association).

Harper, Thomas G. (Editor) (August 2008). Supreme Court Update, Alphabet soup: Does BFOQ trump RFOA under ADEA? *Florida Employment Law Letter*, Volume 20, Number. 6, pp. 4-5.

Harris, P. R., Moran, R. T., and Moran, S. V. (2004). *Managing Cultural Differences: Global Leadership Strategies for the 21st Century* (6th Edition.). Burlington, VT: Elsevier Butterworth-Heinemann.

Harvard Business Review (2001). *HBR on Managing Diversity*. Harvard Business School Publications.

Harvey, Carol P. and Allard, M. June (Second Edition 2002). *Understanding and Managing Diversity: Readings Cases and Exercises*. Prentice Hall.

Hayflick, L. (1994). *How and Why We Age*. New York: Ballantine Books.

Henke, H. (1999). Jamaica's Decision to Pursue a Neoliberal Development Strategy: Realignment in the State-Business – Class Triangle. *Latin American Perspectives*, Volume 108(26), pp. 7-33.

Heller, Agnes (1981). *Renaissance Man*. New York: Schocken Books.

Henderson, Verne E. (1992). *What's Ethical in Business*. New York: McGraw-Hill.

Heron, W. Thomas (2006). An Examination of the Moral Development and Ethical Decision-making of Information Technology Professionals. Doctoral Dissertation. The H. Wayne Huizenga School of Business and Entrepreneurship. Nova Southeastern University.

Herzberg, F. (Second Edition 1968). One More Time: How do you Motivate Employees? In S. J. Ott (Editor.), *Classical Readings in Organizational Behavior*. Orlando, Florida: Harcourt Brace & Company.

Hickman, Melissa S. (2008). The Religiousity and Ethical Reasoning in Accounting Students. Doctoral Dissertation. The H. Wayne Huizenga School of Business and Entrepreneurship. Nova Southeastern University.

Highlights from Good Morning American, Andrew Cuomo Reporting (July 13, 2009). *Older Workers Face Job Discrimination*. Retrieved July 13, 2009 from http://abcnews.go.com.

Hoecklin, L (1995). Managing Cultural Differences: Strategies for Competitive Advantages. New York: Addison-Wesley Publishing.

Hoffman, J., J. (1998). Evaluating International Ethical Climates: A Goal-programming Model. *Journal of Business Ethics*, Volume 17, pp. 1861-1869.

Hofstede, G. (2001). Culture's Consequences: Comparing Values, Behaviors, Institutions and Organizations Across Nations, 2nd edition. Thousand Oaks, CA: Sage Publications.

Hofstede, G. (2003). *Geert Hofstede Cultural Dimensions*. Downloaded on September 9, 2003 from ITIM website: http:// geert-hofstede.com/218ofstede_united_states.shtml.

Hofstede, G. (1997). *Cultures and Organization: Software of the Mind*. London: McGraw Hill.

Hofstede, G. (1993). Cultural Constraints in Management Theories. *Academy of Management Executive*, Volume 7(1), pp. 81-90.

Hofstede, G. (1984). *Culture's Consequences: International Differences in Work-Related Values* (Abridged Edition). Newbury Park, CA: Sage Publishing Company.

Hofstede, G. (1983). National Cultures in Four Dimensions: a Research-based Theory of Cultural Differences among Nations. *International Studies of Management and Organization*, Volume 13, pp. 46-74.

Hofstede, G. (1980). *Culture's Consequences: International Differences in Work-related Values*. Beverly Hills, CA: Sage Publications.

Hofstede, G., Neuijen, B., Ohayv, D.D., and Sander, G. (1990). Measuring Organizational Cultures: a Qualitative and Quantitative Study across 20 Cases. *Administrative Science Quarterly*, Volume 35, pp. 286-316.

Hofstede, G. and Bond, M. (1984). Hofstede's Culture Dimensions: An Independent Validation using Rokeach's Value Survey. *Journal of Cross-cultural Psychology*, Volume 15(4), pp. 417-433.

Hodgetts, R. M., and Luthans, F. (Fifth edition 2002). *International Management: Culture, Strategy, and Behavior*. New York: McGraw-Hill/Irwin.

Holt, D. H., Ralston, D. & Terpstra, R., H. (1994). Constraints on capitalism in Russia: The managerial psyche. *California Management Review*, pp. 124-141.

Hosseini, Khaled (2003). *The Kite Runner*. Riverhead Books, New York. ISBN: 1-59448-000-1.

Howard, L. (2005). *Global Balanced Lifestyles*. Associated Press and NewsCom, pp. 1-2.

Howard, A., Shudo, K., and Umeshima, M. (1983). Motivation and Values among Japanese and American managers. *Personnel Psychology*, Volume 36(4), pp. 883-898.

HR Guide to the Internet: Disparate Treatment. Retrieved on July 5, 2009 from: http://www.hr-guide.com/data/G701.htm.

Hsu, J. C. (2002). *Does organizational commitment affect turnover in China's internet industry?* Michigan: ProQuest Information and Learning Company. (UMI No. 3042263).

Huang, Chunlong (2006). Cross-Cultural Ethics: A Study of Cognitive Moral Development and Moral Maturity of U.S. and Japanese Expatriate Managers in Taiwan and Taiwanese Managers. Doctoral Dissertation. The H. Wayne Huizenga School of Business and Entrepreneurship. Nova Southeastern University.

Hulliung, Mark (1983). *Citizen Machiavelli*. Princeton, New Jersey: Princeton University Press.

Hunt, S. D., Chonko, L. B., and Wood, V. R. (2003). Organizational Commitment and Marketing. *Journal of Marketing*. Volume 49, pp. 112-126.

Hymowitz, Carol (March 8, 2005). When Meeting Targets Becomes the Strategy, CEO Is on Wrong Path. *The Wall Street Journal*, p. B1.

Hyppolite, Aranck Aurel (2003). *The Influence of Organizational Culture, Ethical Views and Practices in Local Government: A Cognitive Moral Development Study*. Doctoral

218

Dissertation. The H. Wayne Huizenga School of Business and Entrepreneurship. Nova Southeastern University.

Hsu, Tiffany (May 4, 2009). Age a hurdle for unemployed. Sun-Sentinel, p. 5D.

Imamoglu, E. O., and Ayguen, Z. K. (1999). Value Preferences from the 1970s to 1990s: Cohort, Generation and Gender Differences at a Turkish University. *Turk-Psikoloji-Dergisi*, Volume 14(44), pp. 1-22.

Introduction to the Americans with Disabilities Act. (2003). Available at: http://www.usdoj.gov/crt/ada/adaintro/htm

Isbell v. Allstate Insurance Company, 418 F.3d 788 (7th Circuit 1995), *certiorari denied*, 126 S.Ct. 1590 (2006).

Ivancevich, J. and Matterson, M. (1990). *Organizational Behavior and Management.* Homewood, IL: Irwin.

Jackall, Robert (1988). *Moral Mazes: The World of Corporate Managers.* New York: Oxford University Press.

Jacobs, J. (2005). *Global Balanced Lifestyles.* Associated Press and NewsCom, pp. 1-2.

Jamaican Handbook (2001). *The Jamaican Handbook for the Elderly.* A Blue Cross of Jamaica Sponsored Publication.LMH Publishing Limited. ISBN: 976-8184-26-4.

James, Heather R. (2008). If you are attractive and you know it, please apply: Appearance based discrimination and employers' discretion. *Valparaiso University Law Review*, Volume 42, pp. 629f.

Jamrog, J. and McCAnn, J. (2003). *Blindsided: Working through the Coming Knowledge Crisis* (Working Paper). Tampa, FL: Human Resource Institute, The University of Tampa.

Job Applicants and the Americans with Disabilities Act. (2003). Available at EEOC.gov/facts/jobapplicant.html.

Johnson, A. (June/July 2003). Americans with Disabilities Act: Is Your Company Compliant? *Diversity Inc.* New Jersey: Diversity Inc. Media, LLC.

Johnson, A. (October/November 2003). They Had No Idea What to Say to Me. *Diversity Inc.* New Jersey: Diversity Inc. Media, LLC.

Johnson, T. (February 9, 2005). Taking Care of Older Parents is Law of the Land. *The Miami Herald*, p.17A.

Johnson, William and Weinstein, Art (2004). *Superior Customer Value in the New Economy: Concepts and Cases.* Boca Raton, FL: CRC Press LLC.

Jones, G. and George, J. (Third Edition 2003). *Contemporary Management.* New York: McGraw-Hill.

Kaczorek, Mary (Summer 2008). 'No Country for Old Men:' AARP v. EEOC and Age Discrimination in Employer-Sponsored Retiree Health Benefits. *Law and Inequality: A Journal of Theory and Practice Law and Inequality, Law & Inequality Journal*, Volume 26, pp. 435f.

Kahle, L. R. (1984). Attitudes and Social Adaptation: A Person-Situation Interaction Approach. *International Series in Experimental Social Psychology*, Volume 8, Pergamon Press.

Kaiser, E. (January 24, 2004). *U.S. Retailers give Wal-Mart a Head Start on RFID. USA TODAY.* Retrieved April 1, 2004 from http://www.usatoday.com/tech/news/techinnovations/2004-01-27-walmart-pioneers-rfid_x.htm.

Kanfer, R. and Ackerman, P. L. (2004). *Aging, Adult Development, and Work Motivation.* Academy of Management Review, Volume. 29, No. 3, pp. 440-458.

Keller, Dennison (2006). Older, Wiser and More Dispensable: ADEA Options Available Under Smith v. Jackson; Desperate Times Call for Desperate Impact. *Northern Kentucky Law Review*, Volume 33, pp. 259f.

Kelley, Debbie (October 15, 2007). Expert Advises Preparing for Aging Workforce. *The Miami Herald, Business Monday*, p. 1.

Kelly, E. P., (2003). Ethical Perspectives on Layoffs of Highly Compensated Workers and Age Discrimination in Employment. *The Journal of Applied Management and Entrepreneurship,* Volume 8, No. 3, pp. 84-97.

Kennedy, Joseph William (2003). A Study of the Moral Reasoning Skills of Proactive and Reactive Organizational Management. Doctoral Dissertation. The H. Wayne Huizenga School of Business and Entrepreneurship. Nova Southeastern University.

Kern v. Dynalectron Corporation, 577 F. Supp. 1196 (N. Tex. 1983), affirmed 746 F.2d 810 (5th Cir. 1984).

Kalakota and Robinson (August 2003). From e-Business to Services: Why and Why Now? Retrieved April5, 2004 from http://www.informit.com/isapi/product.

Khan, Ali, Liaquat (2009). Temporality of Law. *McGeorge Law Review*, Volume 40, pp. 55-106.

Khan, S.Y. (2003). *Desperately Seeking Older Employees.* Retrieved October 1, 2003, from Infotrac.

King, Marsha (April 9, 2008). Meeting Halfway between Employment, Retirement, Companies Find Ways to Retail Expertise of Valuable Older Workers. *The Seattle Times*, p. A 1.

Kluckhohn, C. (1951). *The Study of Values*. In D. N. Barrett (Editor.), *Values in Transition*, pp. 17-45). Notre Dame, IN: University of Notre Dame Press.

Kluckhohn, C. M. (1962). Values and Value-Orientations in the Theory of Action. In T. Parsons and E. A. Shils (Editors), *Toward a General Theory of Action*, pp. 388-433. New York: Harper and Row.

Kmart Corporation (2004). Hoover's Company Information. Retrieved March 19, 2004 from http://cobrands.hoovers.com/global/cobrands/proquest/factsheet. xhtml?COID= 10830.

Kmart Corporation (2004). *About Kmart*. Retrieved April 3, 2004 from http://www.kmartcorp.com/corp/.

Konovsky, M. and Haynie, B.G. (2001). Performance Criteria in RIF and their Impact on Age Discrimination Lawsuits. *Employee Rights Quarterly*. Autumn. Retrieved October 1, 2003 from Infotrac.

Koury, F. (July 2005). Selling the Vision: Motivate your Managers with More than Just Money. *Smart Business*, Retrieved on July 26, 2005 from: http://broward.sbnonline.com/marticle.asp?periodicalKey=23&particleKey=9821.

Koury, F. (January 2005). Creating a Winning Culture: How to Become and Stay Innovative in a Competitive Marketplace. *Smart Business*. Retrieved July 26, 2005 from http://broward.sbnonline.com/marticle.asp?periodicalKey=23&particleKey=9135.

Krome, Margaret (April 30, 2008). Retire or Not? It's Nobody's Business But Yours. *Madison Capital Times*, p. 42.

Labriola, Donald J. (2009). "But I'm Denny Crane!": Age Discrimination in the Legal Profession After Sidley. *Albany Law Review,* Volume 72, pp. 367-386.

Laluk, Susan S. and Stiller, Sharon P. (2008). 2006-2007 Survey of New York Law: Employment Law. *Syracuse Law Review*, Volume 58, pp. 955f.

Lambert, E. G. (2001). To Stay or Quit: A Review of the Literature on Correctional Officer Turnover. *American Journal of Criminal Justice,* Volume 26, pp. 61-76.

Lambert , E., Hogan, N. L., and Barton, S. M. (2002). Satisfied Correctional Staff: A Review of the Literature on the Correlates of Correctional Staff Job Satisfaction. *Criminal Justice and Behavior,* Volume 29, pp. 115-143.

Lau, S. (1988). The value orientations of Chinese university students in Hong Kong. *International Journal of Psychology*, Volume 23(5), pp. 583-596.

Lau, S. (1992). Collectivism's Individualism: Value Preference, Personal Control, and the Desire for Freedom among Chinese in Mainland China, Hong Kong, and Singapore. *Personality and Individual Differences*, Volume 13(3), pp. 361-366.

Lau, S., and Wong, A. (1992). Value and Sex-role Orientation of Chinese Adolescents. *International Journal of Psychology*, Volume 27(1), pp. 3-17.

Laukaran VH, Winikoff B, Myers D. (1986). The Impact of Health Services on Breastfeeding: Common Themes from Developed and Developing Worlds. In Jeliffe A. and Jeliffe, L. (Editors). *Advances in International Maternal and Child Health*, pp. 121-128.

Lavelle, John (Winter 2007). On Workforce Architecture, Employment Relationship, and Lifecycles: Explaining the Purview of Workforce Planning and Management. *Public Personnel Man*agement, Volume 36, No. 4, pp. 371f.

Leininger M. (1985). Transcultural Care, Diversity and Universality: a Theory of Nursing.

Lee, Evelyn (2006). New Jersey Retirees Age Getting Back to Work. *NUBIZ*, Volume 21, Issue 8, pp. 15-16.

Leonard, Dorothy (2005). *Knowledge Management: How To Salvage Your Company's Deep Smarts*. Retrieved August 3, 2005 from harvardbusinessonline.hbsp.harvard.edu.

Lee, Janet (September 1, 1996). 50 Plus Advises Older Job-seekers on What 'Curve-balls' to Expect. *Boulder County Business Report*, Volume 15, Issue 9, p. 12.

Lee, K. (1991). The Problem of Appropriateness of the Rokeach Value Survey in Korea. *International Journal of Psychology*, Volume 26(3), pp. 299-310.

Legislation (June 19, 2009), "High court makes age discrimination harder to prove," *The Miami Herald*, p. 3C.

Levitz, Jennifer and Shishkin, Philip (March 11, 2009). More Workers Cite Age Bias After Layoffs. *The Wall Street Journal*, pp. D1, D2.

Liptak, Adam (June 30, 2009). *Supreme Court Finds Bias Against White Firefighters*. The New York Times, pp. A1, A13.

Locke, E. A. (1976). The Nature and Consequences of Job Satisfaction. In M. D. Dunnette (Editor), *Handbook of Industrial and Organizational Psychology*. Chicago: Rand-McNally.

Lomax, A. (2005). McDonald's Fun Fast Food. *The Motley Fool.com*, pp. 1-2.

Lowry, Tom (September 8, 2008). Extreme Experience. *Business Week*, pp. 46-51.

Maass, P. (2005). Niger Delta Dispatch Road to Hell. *The New Republic*, Volume 232 (3), p. 15. Retrieved from the EBSCO Host database.

MacDonald, Jay (June 30, 2008). Is retiring early unpatriotic? *Yahoo! Finance Online*. Retrieved July 11, 2008.

Machiavelli, Niccolo (1977). *The Prince* (Translated and Edited by Adams, Robert M.). New York: W.W. Norton Company.

Machiavelli, Niccolo (Second Edition 1998). The Prince (translated and edited by Mansfield, Harvey C.). Chicago: The University of Chicago Press.

MacIntyre, Alasdair (1966). *A Short History of Ethics*. New York: Macmillan Publishing Company.

Mackie, J.L. (1990). *Ethics: Inventing Right and Wrong*. New York: Penguin Books.

Macoby, L.(January/February 2005). Creating Moral Organizations. *Research Technology Management*, Volume .48, Issue 1, p. 59. Retrieved Feb. 6, 2005 from ProQuest database.

Mahoney v. RFE/RL, Inc., 47 F.3rd 447 (D.C. Cir. 1995).

Mansfield, E. D. (1995). A Comparison of More and Less Generative Adults according to Psychological Variables, Demographic Characteristics, and Generativity Types. Dissertation Abstracts International, Section A, Humanities and Social Sciences, Volume 56(3-A): 0870.

Mansfield, Harvey C. (1995). *Machiavelli's Virtue*. Chicago: University of Chicago Press.

March, J. G. and Simon, H. A. (1958). *Organizations*. New York: Wiley.

Marquardt, M. and Berger, N. (2000). *Global Leaders for the 21ˢᵗ Century*. Albany, New York: State University of New York Press, pp. 1-32, 175-189.

Martinez- Carbonell, Karelia (2002). *Examination of the Moral Maturity Levels Based on Kohlberg's Six Stages of Moral Reasoning: A Study of School Administrators*. Doctoral Dissertation. The H. Wayne Huizenga School of Business and Entrepreneurship. Nova Southeastern University.

Maslow, A. H. (Second Edition 1943). A Theory of Human Motivation. In S. J. Ott (Editor), *Classical Readings in Organizational Behavior*. Orlando, Florida: Harcourt Brace & Company.

Mathieu, J. E. and Zajac, D. (1990). A Review and Meta-analysis of the Antecedents, Correlates, and Consequences of Organizational Commitment. *Psychological Bulletin*, Volume 108, pp. 171-194.

Mayton, D. and Furnham, A. (1994). Value Underpinnings of Antinuclear Political Activism: A Cross-national Study. *Journal of Social Issues*, Volume 50(4), pp. 117-128.

McFarlane, D.A., and Mujtaba, B. (2005). Gender Issues in the Corporate World. In Mujtaba, B. (2005). *The Art of Mentoring Diverse Professionals: Employee Development and Retention Practices for Entrepreneurs and Multinational Corporations*. Aglob Publishing Inc.

McGeary, J. (2001). Death Stalks a Continent. *Time Magazine*. Retrieved July 25, 2005, from http://www.time.com/time/2001/aidsinafrica/cover.html.

McMichael, S. H. (2000). *The X Factor in Air Traffic Control Training at Travis Air Force Base*. Graduate Research Project Master's Thesis, Embry Riddle Aeronautical University, Travis Academic Center, California.

McQuarrie, E. (1989). The Impact of a Discontinuous Innovation: Outcomes Experienced by Owners of Home Computers. *Computers in Human Behavior*, Volume 5(4), pp. 227-240.

McShane, M., Williams F., and McClaine, K. (1991). Early Exits: Examining Employee Turnover. *Corrections Today*, Volume 53, pp. 220-225.

Mattingly, Garrret (1965). "Machiavelli" in *Renaissance Profiles*. Plumb, J.H. (Editor). New York: Harper and Row.

Maurer, T.J. and Rafuse, N.E. (2001). *Learning, not Litigating: Managing Employee Development and Avoiding Claims of Age Discrimination*. Academy Management Executive. Retrieved September 12, 2003 from AgeLine.

McDonnel Douglas Corp. v. Green (1973). 411 U.S. 792.

Meacham v. Knolls Atomic Power Laboratory (2008). 128 Supreme Court 2395.

Medina, J. (1996). The Clock of Ages. Why We Age – How We Age – Winding Back the Clock. Cambridge University Press.

Meglino, B. M. (May-June 1998). Individual Values in Organizations: Concepts, Controversies and Research. *Journal of Management*. Downloaded from www.findarticles.com.

Melbin, M. (1961). Organization Practice and Individual Behavior: Absenteeism among Psychiatric Aides. *American Sociological Review*, Volume 26, pp. 14-23.

Meyer, J. P. and Allen, N. J. (1984). Testing the "Side-bet theory" of Organizational Commitment: Some Methodological Considerations. *Journal of Applied Psychology*, Volume 69, pp. 372-378.

Meyer, J. P. and Allen, N. J. (1997). *Commitment in the Workplace: Theory, Research, and Application*. California: Sage Publications.

Mendenhall, M., Kuhlmann, T. and Stahl, G. (2001). *Developing Global Business Leaders: Policies, Processes, and Innovations*, pp. 2-16, 54-55, and 75-80.

Microsoft Encarta (1993-2000). *Age Discrimination* (Computer Software). Microsoft Encarta Encyclopedia 2000: Microsoft Corporation.

Michaels, C. E. & Spector, P. E. (1982). Causes of Employee Turnover: A Test of the Mobley, Griffeth, Hand, and Meglino Model. *Journal of Applied Psychology,* Volume 67, pp. 53-59.

Miller, Susan E. (February 23, 1998). Senior Workers Filling Employment Gaps. *Tribune Business Weekly,* Volume 8, Issue 45, p. 1.

Mitchell, O., Mackenzie, D. L., Styve G. J., and Gover, A. R. (2000). The Impact of Individual, Organizational, and Environmental Attributes on Voluntary Turnover among Juvenile Correctional Staff Members. *Justice Quarterly,* Volume 17, pp. 333-357.

Mobley, Sandra E. Ford (2002). The Study of Lawrence Kohlberg's Stages of Moral Development Theory and Ethics: Considerations in Public Administration Practices. Doctoral Dissertation. The H. Wayne Huizenga School of Business and Entrepreneurship. Nova Southeastern University.

Mobley, W. H. (1977). Intermediate Linkages in the Relationship between Job Satisfaction and Employee Turnover. *Journal of Applied Psychology,* Volume 62, pp. 237-240.

Mobley, W. H., Griffeth, R. W., Hand, H. H., and Meglino, B. M. (1979). Review and Conceptual Analysis of the Employee Turnover Process. *Psychological Bulletin,* Volume 86, pp. 493-522.

Mobley, W. H. (1982). *Employee Turnover: Causes, Consequences, and Control.* Philippines: Addison-Wesley Publishing Company, Inc.

Mojo, J. (2004). Convenience is Good Business. *Brandweek,* Volume 45, p. 16.

Moncur, Michael (1994-2004). *The Quotations Page.* Retrieved Feb 6, 2005, from www.thequotationspage.com.

Moore, S. (2004, February 18, 2004). Beaumont, California approves Wal-Mart; Critics say small businesses will suffer. *Knight Ridder Tribune Business news.* Retrieved April 11, 2004 from Nova Southeastern University's ProQuest database http://0-proquest.umi.com.

Moos, Bob (March 9, 2008). Millions Spend Golden Years Making Green. *The Pittsburg Post-Gazette,* p. J 1.

Morelli v. Cedel, 141 F.3d 39, 42-43 (2nd Cir. 1998).

Morris, Tom (1997). If Aristotle Ran General Motors: The New Soul of Business. New York: Henry Holt and Company.

Morrow, P. C. (1993). *The Theory and Measurement of Work Commitment.* Greenwich, CT: JAI Press.

Mowday, R. T., Porter, L. W., and Steers, R. M. (1982). *Employee-organization Linkages: The Psychology of Commitment, Absenteeism, and Turnover.* New York: Academic Press.

Mowrey, Megan E. (2007). Establishing Retaliation for Purposes of Title VII. *Penn State Law Review,* Volume 111, pp. 893f.

Mujtaba, B. G. and McCartney, T. (2010). *Managing Workplace Stress and Conflict amid Change, 2nd edition.* ILEAD Academy Publications; Davie, Florida, United States.

Mujtaba, B. G. (2010). *Workplace Diversity Management: Challenges, Competencies and Strategies (2nd edition).* ILEAD Academy Publications; Davie, Florida, United States.

Mujtaba, B. G. (2008). *Coaching and Performance Management: Developing and Inspiring Leaders.* ILEAD Academy Publications; Davie, Florida, USA.

Mujtaba, B. G. (2007). *Cross Cultural Management and Negotiation Practices.* ILEAD Academy Publications; Florida, United States.

Mujtaba, B. G. (2007). *AFGHANISTAN: Realities of war and rebuilding (2nd edition).* ILEAD Academy, LLC, Davie, Florida; United States.

Mujtaba, Bahaudin G. (2007). *The ethics of management and leadership in Afghanistan (2nd edition)*. ILEAD Academy. Davie, Florida USA.

Mujtaba, B. G. (2007). *Mentoring Diverse Professionals (2nd edition)*. Llumina Press. Davie, Florida, United States.

Mujtaba, Bahaudin G. (1996). *Business Ethics Survey of Supermarket Managers and Employees.* Doctoral Dissertation. The H. Wayne Huizenga School of Business and Entrepreneurship. Nova Southeastern University.

Mujtaba, Bahaudin G.; Cavico, F.; Edwards, R. M.; and Oskal, C. (January 2006). Age Discrimination in the Workplace: Cultural Paradigms Associated with Age in Afghanistan, Jamaica, Turkey, and the United States. *Journal of Applied Management and Entrepreneurship,* Volume 11, Number 1.

_____ and Cavico, Frank J. (2006). *Age Discrimination in Employment: Cross Cultural Comparison and Management Strategies.* BookSurge Publishing – An Amazon.com Company, USA.

_____ and Cavico, Frank J., McCartney, Timothy O., and DiPaolo, Peter T. (May/June 2009). Ethics and Retail Management: An Examination of Age, Education, and Experience Values. *American Journal of Business Education, Vol. 2, No. 3, pp. 13-25.*

_____ and Rhodes, J., (2006). The Aging Workface: Best Practices in Recruiting and Retaining Older Workers at Publix. *The 2006 Pfeiffer Annual: Human Resource Management* (Edited by Robert C. Preziosi), pp. 87-95. ISBN: 0-7879-7824-8.

_____ and Hinds, R. M. (November 3-4, 2004). Quality Assurance through Effective Faculty Training and Development Practices in Distance Education: The Survey of Jamaican Graduates. THE CARIBBEAN AREA NETWORK FOR QUALITY ASSURANCE IN TERTIARY EDUCATION (CANQATE) Conference. Ocho Rios, Jamaica.

_____and Richardson, W., and Blount, P. (April 2003). Age Discrimination and Means of Avoiding It in the Workplace! Presented and published in SAM International Conference Proceedings on *"Trust, Responsibility, and Business."* Orlando, Florida.

Mullman, J. (2005). Ronald McDonald Houses, Charity Unite. *Crain's Chicago Business*, Volume 28(10), p. 18.

Munson, M. J. (1980). Concurrent Validity of a Modified Rokeach Value Survey in Discriminating More Successful from Less Successful Students. *Educational and Psychological Measurement*, Volume 40(2), pp. 479-485.

Munson, M. J. and McIntyre, S. H. (1980). Developing Practical Procedures for the Measurement of Personal Values in Cross-cultural Marketing. *Journal of Marketing Research*, Volume 16-1, 48-52.

Munson, M. J. and Posner, B. Z. (1980a). The Factorial Validity of a Modified Rokeach Value Survey for Four Diverse Samples. *Educational and Psychological Measurement*, Volume 40(4), pp. 1073-1079.

Munson, M. J. and Posner, B. Z. (1980b). Concurrent Validation of Two Value Inventories in Predicting Job Classification and Success for Organizational Personnel. *Journal of Applied Psychology*, Volume 65(5), pp. 536-542.

Murphy, E. F. Jr., Gordon, J.D., and Anderson, T.L. (2003). *An Examination of Cross-Cultural Age and Generation-based Value Differences between the United States and Japan.* Proceeding of the Southern Academy of Management 2003 Conference.

Murphy, E. F. Jr. (1994). Military Organizational Culture: An investigation of sex and gender differences in the values, sex role stereotype attitudes, and situational leadership II behaviors of Air Force middle-level managers. Doctoral Dissertation, Nova Southeastern University. University Microfilms International UMI No. 9525247.

Murphy, E. F. Jr. and Anderson, T. (May 2003). A Longitudinal Study Exploring Value Changes during the Cultural Assimilation of Japanese Student Pilot Sojourners in the United States. *International Journal of Value Based Management*, Volume 16(2), pp. 111-129.

Murphy, E. F., Jr., Eckstat, A., and Parker, T. (1995). Sex and Gender Differences in Leadership. *The Journal of Leadership Studies,* Volume 2, pp. 116-131.

Murphy, E. F., Jr., Snow, W. A., Carson, P. P., and Zigarmi, D. (1997). Values, Sex Differences and Psychological Androgyny. *International Journal of Value-Based Management,* Volume 10, pp. 69-99.

Murphy, S. A. (2001). A Study of Career Values by Generation and Gender. *Dissertation Abstracts-International Section-A: Humanities and Social Sciences,* Volume 61(9-A): 3781.

Nail, T. and Scharringer, D. (2002). Guidelines on Interview and Employment Application Questions. *HR Magazine.* Virginia: HR Press

Nash, Laura L. (1990). Good Intentions Aside: A Manager's Guide to Resolving Ethical Problems. Boston: Harvard Business School Press.

Neumark, David (2008). Reassessing the Age Discrimination in Employment Act. *Research Report #2008-09.* AARP Public Policy Institute, Washington, D.C.

Ng, A. H. (1993). Exploring Country Values and Information Technology Adoption in Business Schools. *Proceedings of the Academy of Management, Poster Sessions*, p. 418. Atlanta, GA.

Nicholson, J.D., Stephina, L.P., and Hochwarter, W. (1990). Psychological Aspects of Expatriate Training and Effectiveness. In G. Ferris & K. Rowland (Editors), *Research in Personnel and Human Resource Management,* Supplement 2, pp. 127-145. Greenwich, CT: JAI Press.

Nobile, R.J. (1998). *Essential Facts: Employment (Age Discrimination).* Warren, Gorham & Lamont: Boston, Massachusetts, Section 6.4, pp 6-12-13.

Noelle, Christine (1997). *State and Tribe in Nineteenth-Century Afghanistan.* Great Britain: Curzon Press.

Norman, Richard (1991). *The Moral Philosophers: An Introduction to Ethics.* Oxford: Clarendon Press.

Notable & Quotable, (June 30, 2009). From Justice Anthony Kennedy's majority opinion in the case of Ricci v. DeStefano. The Wall Street Journal, p. A15.

Nunally, J. C. (1978). *Psychometric Theory.* New York: McGraw-Hill. *Nurse and Health Care*, Volume 6, pp. 209-212.

Nuttall, Jon (1992). *Moral Questions: An Introduction to Ethics.* Cambridge: Polity Press.

O'Connor v. Consolidated Coin Caterers Corp, 116 U.S. 1307 (1996).

Offermann, L. R. and Hellmann, P. S. (1997). Culture's Consequences for Leadership behavior: National values in action. *Journal of Cross-Cultural Psychology*, pp. 342-351.

Older Workers Benefit Protection Act (2008). Public Law 101-433. Retrieved May 28, 2008 from http://www.eeoc.gov/policy/adea.html.

Olson, W. (1999). *Kansas Journal of Law and Public Policy,* Volume 8(32), p. 7. West Publishing Company.

Olshansky, S.J., Hayflick, L., and Carnes, B.A. (2004). *Position Statement on Human Aging.* Retrieved July 25, 2005, from http://www.quackwatch.org/01QuackeryRelatedTopics/antiagingpp.html.

O'Reilly, C. A., and Chatman J. (1986). Organizational Commitment and Psychological Attachment: The Effects of Compliance, Identification, and Internalization on Prosocial Behavior. *Journal of Applied Psychology,* Volume 71, pp. 492-499.

Orzel v. City of Wauwatosa Fire Department, 697 F.2d 743 (7th Cir. 1983).

Osgood, Rosalind (2002). *A Study of the Cognitive Moral Development Theory and Ethics in Municipal Government*. Doctoral Dissertation. The H. Wayne Huizenga School of Business and Entrepreneurship. Nova Southeastern University.

Palmquist, Matt (August 2008). Old Without Wheels. *Miller-McCune*, pp. 18-19.

Pounds, Marcia Heroux (April 30, 2009). Job Discrimination Claims Have Risen Dramatically in South Florida. Sun-Sentinel, pp. 1D, 2D.

Quirk, Barbara (May 7, 2008). Don't Let 'Em Call You An Old Fart. *Madison Capital Times*, p. 42.

Quirk, J. (1993). A Brief Overview of the Age Discrimination in Employment Act A (ADEA). Reviewed June 1999. Available online at http://my.shrm.org/whitepapers/documents~agediscrimination.

Parents Involved in Community Schools v. Seattle School District No. 1 et al. (2007). 551 U.S. 701.

Patten R. (September/October, 2004). From Implicit to Explicit: Putting Corporate Values and Personal Accountability Front and Centre. *Ivey Business Journal Online*, p. H1.

Pear, Robert (December 27, 2007). U.S. Ruling Backs Benefit Cut at 65 in Retiree Plans. *The New York Times*, pp. A1, A24.

Peters, L. H., Jackofsky, E. F., and Salter, J. R. (1981). Predicting Turnover: a Comparison of Part-time and Full-time employees. *Journal of Occupational Behavior*, Volume 2, pp. 89-98.

Pohlman, R. and Gardiner, G. (2000). Value Driven Management: How to Create and Maximize Value Over Time for Organizational Success. New York: AMACOM.

Pollock, T., Whitbred, R., and Contractor, N. (2000). Social Information Processing and Job Characteristics: a Simultaneous Test of Two Theories with Implications for Job Satisfaction. *Human Communication Research*, Volume 26, pp. 292-330.

Pope, Lucetta D. (2006). Employment Law: Recent Developments in Employment Law. *Indiana Law Review*, Volume 39, pp. 925f.

Porter, L. W., Steers, R. M., Mowday, R. T. & Boulian, P. V. (1974). Organizational Commitment, Job Satisfaction, and Turnover among Psychiatric Technicians. *Journal of Applied Psychology*, Volume 59, pp. 603-609.

Porter, L. W., Crampon, W. J., and Smith, F. J. (1976). Organizational Commitment and Managerial Turnover: A Longitudinal Study. *Organizational Behavior and Human Performance*, Volume 15, pp. 87-98.

Postal, Lawrence R. (January 2009). ADAAA Will Result in Renewed Emphasis on Reasonable Accommodation. *Legal Report, Society for Human Resource Management*, pp. 1-6.

Posthuma, Richard and Campion, Russell (2009). Age Stereotypes in the Workplace: Common Stereotypes, Moderators, and Future Research Directions. *Journal of Management*, Volume 35, pp. 158-88.

Pounds, Marcia Heroux (March 12, 2009). Keep right attitude, be 'ageless' to thrive in today's workplace. *The Sun-Sentinel*, pp. 1D, 2D.

Preziosi, R. (August 2005). The Fuel of Business: 8 Ways to Light the Fires of Creativity and Innovation. *Smart Business*, Volume 1, Number 12. Retrieved on August 30, 2005 from http://broward.sbnonline.com/marticle.

Preziosi, C. and Gooden, D. (October 2003). *Machiavelli Revisited: MBA Students' Perspectives*. International Business and Economics Conference Proceedings, Las Vegas, Nevada.

Primus (2003). *Equal Protection and Disparate Impact: Round Three*. Harvard Law Review, Volume 117, pp. 493f.

Publix Careers (2004). Retrieved on August 18 2004 from:
http://www.publix.com/about/careers/Careers.do.

Publix (2004). Publix News Release. Retrieved on August 20th from:
http://www.publix.com/about/newsroom/NewsReleaseItem.do.

Publix Awards (2005). Retrieved on August 20th 2005 from http://www.publix.com/.

Rachels, James (1986). *The Elements of Moral Philosophy*. New York: McGraw-Hill.

Rakich, J., Longest, B., and Darr, K. (1992). *Managing Health Service Organizations*.
Baltimore, MD: Health Professional Press.

Ralston, D. A., Gustafson, D. J., Cheung, F. M., and Terpstra, R. H. (1993). Differences in
Managerial Values: A Study of U. S., Hong Kong and PRC Managers. *Journal of
International Business Studies*, Volume 24 (2), pp. 249-275.

Ramlall, S. (2004). A Review of Employee Motivation Theories and their Implications for
Employee Retention within Organizations. *Journal of American Academy of
Business,* Volume 5, pp. 52-63.

Randall, D. M. (1993). Cross-cultural Research on Organizational Commitment: A Review and
Application of Hofstede's Value Survey Module. *Journal of Business Research,*
Volume 26, pp. 91-110.

Recruiting Seniors (2004). Why Hire Seniors and Retirees? Retrieved from
http://www.recruitersnetwork.com/articles/seniors.htm.

Redding, S.G., Norman, A, and Schlander, A. (1994). The Nature of Individual Attachment to
Theory: A Review of East Asian Variations. In H.C. Triandis, M.D. Dunnett, and
L.M. Hough (Editors.), Handbook of Industrial and Organizational Psychology,
Volume 4, pp. 674-688. Palo Alto, CA: Consulting Psychology Press.

Reidenbach, R.E. and Robin D.P. (1989). *Ethics and Profits.* New York: Prentice-Hall.

Reid, Maise E. (2004). Doctoral Dissertation. *An Empirical Examination of Organization
Ethical Climate and the Cognitive Moral Development of Health Care
Professionals*. The H. Wayne Huizenga School of Business and Entrepreneurship.
Nova Southeastern University.

Reyes-Ganoan v. North Carolina Growers Association 250 F.3d 861(4th Cir. 2001), cert.
denied, 122 S.Ct. 463 (2001).

Reynolds, T. J., and Olson, J. C. (Editors) (2001). *Understanding Consumer Decision- making:
The Means-end Approach to Marketing and Advertising Strategy*. Mahwah, NJ:
Lawrence Erlbaum Associates.

Ricci v. DeStefano (2009). 2009 U.S. Lexis 4945.

Ricks, D. A., Toyne, B, and Martinez, Z. (1990). Recent Developments in International
Management Research. *Journal of Management*, Volume 16, pp. 219-252.

Rice, A. K., Hill, J. M., and Trist, E. L. (1950). The Representation of Labor Turnover as a
Social Process. *Human Relation,* Volume, 3, pp. 349-372.

Rioux, M. (2003, Mar). Lessons Learned from Kmart. *IDEA Article*. Retrieved April 9, 2004
from http://www.naedtechnolgyinformer.com/feature_archive_4-04-03-2.html.

RMHC (2005). Ronald McDonald House Charities. *Ronald McDonald House Charities, Inc.*,
pp. 1-3.

Roberts, Kathy (2007). Correcting Culture: Extraterritoriality and U.S. Employment
Discrimination Law. *Hofstra Labor and Employment Law Journal*, Volume 24, pp.
295-331.

Robertson, C. J. and Hoffman, J. J. (2000). How Different are we? An Investigation of
ConfucianV in the United States. *Journal of Managerial Issues*, Volume 12(1), pp.
34-48.

Roscoe, B. and Peterson, K. (1989). Age-appropriate Behaviors: A Comparison across Three
Generations of Females. *Adolescence*, Volume 24(93), pp. 167-178.

Rokeach, M. (1973). *The Nature of Human Values*. New York: Free Press.

Rokeach, M. (1977). Can computers change human values? *Revista Latinoamericana de Psicologia*, Volume 9(3), pp. 449-458.

Rokeach, M. (1979). *Understanding Human Values: Individual and Societal*. New York: Free Press.

Rokeach, M. (1986). *Beliefs, Attitudes and Values: A Theory of Organization and Change*. San Francisco, CA: Jossey-Bass Publishers.

Rokeach, M. and Ball-Rokeach, S. J. (1989). Stability and Change in American Value Priorities. *American Psychologist*, Volume 44, pp. 775-784.

Rokeach, M. and Regan, J. F. (May 1980). The Role of Values in the Counseling Situation. *Personnel and Guidance Journal*, pp. 576-588.

Rose, G. M. 1997). Cross-cultural Values Research: Implications for International Advertising. In L. R. Kahle and L. Chiagouris (Editors). *Values, Lifestyles and Psychograhics*. New Jersey: Lawrence Erlbaum.

Rugabar, Christopher S. (July 3, 2009). Older job seekers fight assumptions about age. *Sun-Sentinel*, p. 3D.

Russell, Bertrand (1972). *A History of Western Philosophy*. New York: Simon and Schuster.

Schwartz, S.A. (1999). A Theory of Cultural Values and Some Implications for Work. *Applied Psychology: An International Review*, Volume 48(1), pp. 23-47.

Sadat, Mir Hekmatullah, (2004). *Afghan History:Kite Flying, Kite Running and Kite Banning*. June. Retrieved June 2, 2004 from http://www.afghanmagazine.com/2004_06/articles/hsadat.shtml.

St. Mary's Honor Center v. Hicks (1993). 509 U.S. 502.

Salter, Chuck (2001). Attention, Class! 16 Ways to Be a Smarter Teacher. *Fast Company*. Retrieved March 5, 2004 from http://www.fastcompany.com/magazine/53/teaching.html.

Samuelson, Robert J. (January 26, 2009). Boomers Versus the Rest. *Newsweek*, p. 77.

Santora, Joseph C. and Seaton, William J. (May 2008). Age Discrimination: Alive and Well in the Workplace? *The Academy of Management Perspectives*, Volume 22, Number 2, pp. 103-04.

Sargeant, M. (June 2004). Age As An Equality Issue: Legal and Policy Perspectives. Book Review. *Industrial Law Journal*, Volume 33, p. 208.

Saunderson, R. (2004). Survey Findings of the Effectiveness of Employee Recognition in the Public Sector. *Public Personnel Management*, Volume 33, pp. 255-275.

Savage, David G. (June 20, 2008). Court Backs Strong Age Bias Protection. *The Houston Chronicle*, p. 6.

Schramm, Jennifer (2005). The Future of Retirement. *Visions*, No. 2-2005. Society of Human Resource Managers.

Schneider, J. D., (2004). *The Psychology of Stereotyping*. New York: The Guilford Press.

Schwartz, Martin A. (2009). Twentieth Annual Supreme Court Review: Civil Rights Litigation from the October 2007 Term. *Touro Law Review*, Volume 25, pp. 679-694.

Scrivano, K. (2004). Global Balanced Lifestyles. *Associated Press and NewsCom*, pp. 1-2.

Segrave, Kerry (2001). *Age Discrimination by Employers*. Jefferson, North Carolina, and London, England: McFarland & Company, Inc., Publishers.

Senior Journal, 2004. *Website Helping Seniors Find Jobs Adds 12 New Employers*. Retrieved August 8, 2004 from http://www.seniorjournal.com/NEWS/WebsWeLike/4-02-09Jobs.htm.

Shackman, G, Liu, Y. and Wang, G. X. (2003). *Global Social Change reports*. Retrieved July 24, 2005, from http://gsociology.icaap.org/reports.html.

Shapiro, Phil, (2004). Computer Use and the Elderly. *Washing Apple Pi Journal.* Retrieved
    February 1, 2004, from http://www.his.com/~pshapiro/computers.and elderly.html.
Sherman, Mark (February 18, 2008). Court to Rule on Age Bias. *The Miami Herald.* p. 3A.
Sherman, Mark (February 18, 2008). Justices to Hear Plenty on Age Bias. *Madison Capital
    Times*, p. A 4.
Sherman, Mark (February 18, 2008). Supreme Court Mulls Five Age Discrimination Cases.
    Tulsa World, p. A 24.
SHRM (2002). *School-to-Work Program Survey.* Alexandria, VA: Society of Human Resource
    Management.
Sikula, A, Sr. and Costa, Adelmiro, D. (1994). Are age and ethics related? *The Journal of
    Psychology*, Volume 6(128), pp. 659-689.
Silver surfers are taking to the net. *BBCNews.* Retrieved February 5, 2004 from
    http://news.bbc.co.uk/2/hi/science/nature/1899354.stm.
Silver Surfers Day. *Silver Surfers.* Retrieved February 4, 2004 from
    http://www.silversurfersday.org.
Silver surfers do well at Westminster. *BBCNews.* Retrieved February 4, 2004
    from http://news.bbc.co.uk/2/hi/technology/2581103.stm.
Silverheib, Alan (2008). Age an issue in the 2008 campaign. *CNN Politics.com.* Retrieved June
    15, 2008 from http://www.cnn.com/2008/POLITICS/0615/mccain.age./index.html.
Simon, S. (2005). *Phyllis Diller: Still Out for a Laugh.* Retrieved July 25, 2005 from
    http://www.npr.org/templates/story/story.php?storyId=4764906.
Singhapakdi, Marta and Rawwas, Ahmed (1999). A Cross-cultural Study of Consumer
    Perceptions about Marketing Ethics. *Journal of Consumer Marketing,* Volume
    16(3), p. 257.
Singhapakdi, M. and Vitell, S. J. (1993b). Personal and Professional Values Underlying the
    Ethical Judgments of Marketers. *Journal of Business Ethics,* Volume 12, p. 528.
Smith Evans, Pamela K. (2004). *A Study of Cognitive Moral Development Theory and Moral
    Maturity of African-American Business Professionals.* Doctoral Dissertation. The H.
    Wayne Huizenga School of Business and Entrepreneurship. Nova Southeastern
    University.
Smith v. City of Jackson, Mississippi, 125 S. Ct. 1536, 544 U.S. 228 (2005).
Smith, Richard M. (June 30, 2008). In the Driver's Seat: The CEO of Nissan and Renault on
    turnarounds. *Enterprise-Leadership, Newsweek*, p. E10.
Soeters, J. L. and Recht, R. (2001). Convergence or Divergence in the Classroom? Experience
    from the Military. *International Journal of Intercultural Relations.*
Solomon, Robert C. (1993). *Ethics: A Short Introduction.* Dubuque, Iowa: Brown and
    Benchmark.
Sonnenberg. (2002). Mental Disabilities in the Workplace. *Workforce.* ACC Communications
    Inc.
Soule, Alexander (December 3, 2007). Silver Lining for a Graying Work Force. *Fairfield
    County Business Journal,* Volume. 46, Issue 49, p. 17.
Spector, P. E. (1997). *Job Satisfaction: Application, Assessment, Causes, and Consequences.*
    California: Sage Publications.
Stamberg, Susan (July 26, 2005). Miss Lilly Keeps Them Talking in Paris. *Morning Edition*,
    National Public Radio. Retrieved from:
    http://www.npr.org/templates/story/story.php?storyId=4770776.
Steinhauser, S. (1998). *Age Bias: Is Your Corporate Culture in Need of an Overhaul?*
    Available online: http://my.shrm.org/hrmagazine/articles/default.asp~htm.
Strategis (2005). *Corporate Social Responsibility.* Retrieved March 1, 2005, from
    http://strategis.ic.gc.ca/epic/internet/incsr-rse.nsf/en/Home.

Stoddard, S., Jans, L., Ripple, J., and Kraus, L. (1998) Chartbook on Work and Disability in the United States, 1998. *An InfoUse Report*. Washington, D.C.: U.S. National Institute on Disability and Rehabilitation Research.

Strauss, Leo, (1958). *Thoughts on Machiavelli*. Chicago: University of Chicago Press.

Sturgeon, Jessica (2007). Smith v. City of Jackson: Setting An Unreasonable Standard. *Duke Law Journal*. Volume 56, pp. 1377-1402.

Sunstein, C. (2002). Switching the Default Rule. *New York University Law Review,* Volume 77, pp. 106-107.

Sural, Nathan (2009). Labor Law in the Eastern Mediterranean Employment Discrimination: Anti-Discrimination Rules and Policies in Turkey. *Comparative Labor Law and Policy Journal.* Volume 30, pp. 245-271.

Tajfel, S. and Turner, S. (Second Edition 1987). The social identity theory of intergroup behavior. In Worchel, S. & Austin, W. (Editors.), *Psychology of intergroup relations*. Chicago, Illinois: Nelson Hall.

The ADA: Your Responsibilities as an Employer (2003). Equal Employment Opportunity Commission. Retrieved on June 23, 2005 from http://www.eeoc.gov/facts/ada17/html.

The Family & Medical Leave Act Compliance Guide (2003). *Business & Legal Reports, Inc.* www.hr.blr.com/article.ctm/nav/1.0.0.0.28997#6.

The Sunday Gleaner (March 6, 2005), Kingston, Jamaica, p. 16.

Thernstron, Abigall (July 1, 2009). *The Supreme Court Says No To Quotas*. The Wall Street Journal, p. A13.

Thompson, R.W. (January 2000). Tight Labor Market Seen as Boon for Older Execs. *HR Magazine*, p.10.

Thomson West (2005a). Age Discrimination in Employment Act, *United States Code Annotated*, Volume *29*, Sections 621-634.

Thomson West (2005b). Civil Rights Act. *United States Code Annotated,* Title 42, Sections 2000e, 12101b.

Thomas, G. and Mujtaba, B. (2004). *Effective Global Leadership in the Twenty First Century and Preventing Disasters from Occurring in Developing Nations.* The Association on Employment Practices and Principles. Proceedings of Twelfth Annual AEPP International

Tinkler, H. (November 16, 2004). *Ethics in business – the heart of the matter*.

Triandis, H.C. (1982). Review of Cultural Consequences. International Differences in Work Related Values. *Human Organization*, Volume 41, pp. 86-90.

Twin, A. (December 2003). 2003's Biggest Losers. *CNN Money*. Retrieved March 30, 2004 from http://money.cnn.com/2003/12/12/markets/yir_biglosers03/.

Trevor, C. O. (2001). Interactions among Actual Ease-of-movement Determinants and Job Satisfaction in the Prediction of Voluntary Turnover. *Academy of Management Journal*, Volume 44, pp. 621-638.

Tuna, Carl, Koppel, Nathan, and Sanserino, Michael (July 1, 2009). *Job-Test Ruling Cheers Employers*. The Wall Street Journal, p. B1.

Tymkovichfm, Timothy M. (2008). The Problem with Pretext. *Denver University Law Review*, Volume 85, pp. 503-29.

Uchitelle, L. (September 10, 2003). As Jobs Shrink, Older Workers Thrive. *International Herald Tribune*. Retrieved October 1, 2003, from Infotrac.

UNAIDS (2003). *HIV and Aids in Africa*. Retrieved July 25, 2005, from http://www.aidsandafrica.com/.

United Nations (1948). Universal Declaration of Human Rights, December 10, 1948, Article 2.

Upbin, Bruce (April 12, 2004). Wall to Wall Wal-Mart: The Retailer Conquered America and Made it Look Easy. The Rest of the World is a Tougher Battleground. *Forbes: The World's 2000 Leading Companies.*

U.S. Bureau of the Census, 2002. Population : *Older Americans 2000: Key Indicators of Well-Being.* Retrieved April 3, 2003 from http://www.agingstats.gov/chartbook2002/population.

U.S. Bureau of the Census (1996). Current Population Reports, P25-1130, "Population Projections of the United States, by Age, Sex, and Hispanic Origin: 1995 to 2050," February 1996; and "U.S. Population Estimates, by Age, Sex, Race, and Hispanic Origin: 1990 to 1994."

Vandenberg, R. J. and Lance, C. E. (1992). Examining the Causal Order of Job Satisfaction and Organizational Commitment. *Journal of Management,* Volume 18, pp. 153-167.

Vandenberg, R. J. and Nelson, J. B. (1999). Disaggregating the Motives Underlying Turnover Intentions: When Do Intentions Predict Turnover Behavior? *Human Relations,* Volume 52, pp. 1313-1336.

Vanderveen, Don (September 6, 1994). Over-age 50 Workforce Getting Help. *Grand Rapids Business Journal,* Volume 12, Issue 36, Section A, p. 1.

Venezia, Chiulien Chuang (2004). *The Ethical Reasoning Abilities of Accounting Students: Comparison between the U.S. and Taiwan.* Doctoral Dissertation. The H. Wayne Huizenga School of Business and Entrepreneurship. Nova Southeastern University.

Verschoor, Curtis C. (December 2004). Strategic Finance. *Montvale,* Volume 86, Issue 6, p. 15.

VSA Partners (2004). *McDonald's Worldwide.* McDonald's Corporation, pp. 1-83.

Wadhwa, Vivek (January 15, 2008). High-Tech Hiring: Youth Matters. *Business Week Online.* Retrieved July 11, 2008.

Wal-Mart Corporation (2004). Hoover's Company Information. Retrieved April 10, 2004 from http://cobrands.hoovers.com/global/cobrands/proquest/ops. xhtml?

Wal-Mart Corporation (October 29, 2003). Wal-Mart Named America's Largest Corporate Cash Giver. *Wal-Mart News.* Retrieved March 30, 2004 from http://www.walmartstores.com/ wmstore/wmstores.

Wal-Mart Stores (2004). Home page. Retrieved April 9, 2004 from http://www.walmartstores.com/wmstore/wmstores/HomePage.jsp.

Walsh, L. (July 5, 2003). *Older, Wiser and Still Enjoying the Rat Race.* Europe Intelligence Wire. Retrieved October 1, 2003, from Infotrac.

Walton, S. and Huey, J. (1992). *Made in America.* New York: Doubleday.

Watson, Charles E. (1991). *Managing with Integrity.* New York: Praeger Publishers.

Weinberg, S. J. (1986). Decision Making Style of Japanese and American Managers. *Asian American Psychological Association Journal,* pp. 62-64.

Weinstein, J. (Spring 2002). A Survey in Changes in United States Litigation. *St. John's Law Review,* Volume 76, p. 379.

Welford, R. (September 18, 2004). *Unocal Decision Impacts Shell, Coca-cola, Exxon, and Gap.* CSR Asia. Retrieved March 1, 2004 from http://www.csr-asia.com/index.php/archives/2004/09/18/unocal-decision-impacts-shell-coca-cola-exxon-and-gap/

White, Erin (January 14, 2008). The New Recruits: Older Workers. *The Wall Street Journal,* p. B3.

Wick, G., Jansen-Durr, P., Berger, P., Blasko I, and Grubeck-Loebenstein, B. (2000). Diseases of Aging. *Vaccine,* Volume 18, pp. 1567-1583.

Williams, R. M., Jr. (1979). Change and Stability in Values and Value Systems: A Sociological Perspective. In M. Rokeach (Editor), *Understanding Human Values: Individual and Societal.* New York: Free Press.

Wilson Web (2005). Social Responsibility: An Ongoing Mission for a Good Corporate Citizen. *Nation's Restaurant News*. Volume 39, p. 15.

Wodgemuth, Liz (May 28, 2008). How and Older Worker Can Get the Interview. *U.S. News and World Report Online*. Retrieved July 3, 2008.

Workplace Trends (2008). An Overview of the Findings of the Latest SHRM Workplace Forecast. *Workplace Visions, Society for Human Resource Management*, No. 3, pp. 1-8.

Yeatts, D.E., Folts, W., and Knapp, J. (2000). *Older Workers' Adaptation to a Changing Workplace: Employment Issues for the 21st Century.* Retrieved October 1, 2003 from Biomedical Reference Collection: Comprehensive.

Yost, Pete (February 27, 2008). Peers' Testimony to Age Bias Eyed. *The Miami Herald*, p. 3A.

Zeffane, R. M. (1994). Understanding Employee Turnover: The Need for a Contingency Approach. *International Journal of Manpower,* Volume 15, pp. 22-38.

Age and Cultural Values Questionnaire

This study is primarily concerned with the view of age from the perspective of individuals socialized in different cultures. You are not required to record your name and the information you provide will be totally confidential. Please check/circle the appropriate sections; and your cooperation deserves heart-felt thanks and gratitude.

Part I - Demographics

A.   What is your gender?   1.____Male   2._____Female

B.   What is your age?
     1.____16 – 25   2.____26 – 39   3.____40 -49
     4.____50 – 59   5.____60 or above

C.   How would you describe yourself?
     1____White,   2____Black,   3____Hispanic
     4____Asian/Pacific Islander
     5____American Indian/Alaskan Native
     6____Other (please specify) _____

D.   Which country have you lived in most of your life?
     1.____USA   2.____Jamaica   3.____Turkey
     4.____Afghanistan   5.____Other (*specify*): _____.

E.   How many years have you lived in the United States of America?
     1.____Never lived in the USA   2.____1 - 5 years
     3.____6 – 10 years   4.____11 – 19 years
     5.____20 or more years

F.   What is the highest academic schooling you have acquired until the present time?
     1.____Less than twelve years
     2.____High School Diploma or Equivalent.
     3.____Bachelors Degree – *Specify discipline*: _____.

     4.____Masters Degree – *Specify discipline*: _____.
     5.____Doctorate Degree – *Specify discipline*: _____.
     6.____Other (please specify)_____

G.   Which country do you currently reside in?
     1.____USA   2.____Jamaica   3.____Turkey
     4.____Afghanistan   5.____Other (*specify*): _____.

H.   How long have you worked with your current employer?
     1.____Less than one year   2.____1 – 5 years   3.____6 – 15 years
     4.____16 -29 years.   5.____30 or more years

I.   What industry do you work for currently?
        1.___Educatation
        2.___Government
        3.___Private sector
        4.___Retail
        5.___Health
        6.___Other (please specify)_____

J.   Have you ever any had diversity training (workshop) with your past or current employers?
        1.___Yes   2.___No

K.   Have you ever had any ethics training (workshop) with your past or current employers?
        1.___Yes   2.___No

L.   Have you ever had an ethics course in an academic setting (community college, college, graduate school, professional school, etc)?
        1.___Yes   2.___No

Part II - Perceptions of Age
Please answer based on the perspective of the country where you have lived most of your life. For example, if you have lived in Jamaica, Turkey, or Afghanistan most of your life, but are currently living in the USA, then answer these questions from the perspective of Jamaica, Turkey, or Afghanistan. Please keep in mind that for the purpose of research in the USA, "older workers" are those individuals who are 40 years of age or older.

1. Do "older workers" get more respect than "younger workers" in your country?
    Yes_____.
    No _____.

2. Do "older workers" get more respect than "younger workers" from managers and employers in your country?
    Yes_____.
    No _____.

3. Do you prefer to work with:
    • "Older workers" (those who are 40 years of age or above) _____.
    • Younger workers (those who are less 40 years of age) _____.
    • All workers – I have no preference on age _____.

4. Do most managers in your culture prefer to work with:
    - "Older workers" (those who are 40 years of age or above) _____.
    - Younger workers (those who are less 40 years of age) _____.
    - All workers – They have no preference on age _____.

5. Based on your observations, do most managers in your country believe:
    - "Older workers" are more productive than younger workers _____.
    - Younger workers are more productive than "older workers" _____.
    - All workers are equally productive _____.

6. Is it more difficult for "older workers" to find jobs in your country?
    Yes_____.
    No _____.

7. Is it more difficult for "younger workers" to find jobs in your country?
    Yes_____.
    No _____.

8. Have you ever seen evidence of age discrimination toward "older workers" by managers in your country?
    Yes_____.
    No _____.

9. Have you ever seen evidence of age discrimination toward "younger workers" by managers in your country?
    Yes_____.
    No _____.

10. Is age discrimination against "older workers" legally wrong in your country?
    Yes_____.
    No_____.
    Do not know_____.

11. Is age discrimination against "younger workers" legally wrong in your country?
    Yes_____.
    No_____.
    Do not know_____.

12. Is age discrimination against "older workers" regarded as morally or ethically wrong in your country?
    Yes_____.
    No_____.
    Do not know_____.

13. Is age discrimination against "younger workers" regarded as morally or ethically wrong in your country?
    Yes____ .
    No_____ .
    Do not know____ .

14. Is age discrimination against "older workers" regarded by you personally as morally or ethically wrong?
    Yes____ .
    No_____ .

15. Is age discrimination against "younger workers" regarded by you personally as morally or ethically wrong?
    Yes____ .
    No_____ .

Comments:
Do you have any comments on age issues, discrimination, and older workers that you would like to share?

Index

Biographies of the Authors

Bahaudin G. Mujtaba

Dr. Bahaudin G. Mujtaba is an Associate Professor in Nova Southeastern University's H. Wayne Huizenga School of Business and Entrepreneurship in Fort Lauderdale, Florida. Bahaudin has worked as an internal consultant, trainer, and teacher in the corporate arena. He also worked in retail management for 16 years. As a consultant, he coaches, trains, educates, and develops managers. In his capacity as a consultant and trainer, Bahaudin has worked with various firms in the areas of management, diversity management, cross-cultural communication, customer value/service, and cultural competency. His doctorate degree, from the H. Huizenga School of Business and Entrepreneurship of Nova Southeastern University, is in Management, and he completed his dissertation research on the topic of business ethics in management. He has two post-doctorate specialties: one in Human Resource: Management and another in International Management. He has been listed in the publications of *Who's Who in America, Who's Who in Management,* and *Who's Who in the World.* Bahaudin is the author and coauthor of over sixteen professional and academic books. During the past 25 years he has had the pleasure of working in the United States, Brazil, Bahamas, Afghanistan, Pakistan, St. Lucia, Grenada, Thailand, and Jamaica. He was born in Khoshie of Logar province and raised in Kabul, Afghanistan. Bahaudin and his family moved to Pakistan for one year during the Soviet invasion of Afghanistan in the early 1980s and then moved to the United States when he was a teenager. This diverse exposure has provided him many insights in ethics, culture, leadership, and management from the perspectives of different firms, people, and countries. He is grateful for such opportunities in the past years and looks forward to learning each and every day.

Frank J. Cavico

Dr. Frank J. Cavico is a Professor of Business Law and Ethics at the H. Wayne Huizenga School of Business and Entrepreneurship of Nova Southeastern University in Ft. Lauderdale, Florida. He has been associated with the University as a full-time faculty member since 1988, and as an adjunct since 1985. He has been involved in an array of teaching responsibilities, at the undergraduate, master's, and doctoral levels, encompassing such subject matter areas as business law, government regulation of business, constitutional law, administrative law and ethics, labor law and labor relations, health care law, and business ethics. He was the principal faculty member for the creation of the required Huizenga School MBA law and ethics course: "The Values of Legality, Morality, and Social Responsibility in Business"; and he presently serves as Lead Professor for that course. In 2000, he was awarded the Excellence in Teaching Award by the Huizenga School; and in 2007, he was awarded the Faculty Member of the Year Award by the Huizenga School. His fine record is manifested by numerous research endeavors, principally law review articles, in the broad sectors of business law and ethics. His most recent law review publications examined trade secret law, the law of intentional interference with contract, a comparative legal and ethical analysis of "whistleblowing" in the private sector, the tort of intentional infliction of emotional distress in the private employment sector, and the covenant of good faith and fair dealing in the franchise business relationship. In addition to their first age book - Age Discrimination in Employment book, in 2005, he published, together with his faculty colleague and co-author, Dr. Bahaudin Mujtaba, a textbook on business ethics, Business Ethics: Transcending Requirements Through Moral Leadership. That ethics book is now in its second edition, and is called Business Ethics: The Moral Foundation of Effective Leadership, Management, and Entrepreneurship. Since then, he and Dr. Mujtaba have published two other books: Legal Challenges for the Global Manager and Entrepreneur, and Business Law for the Entrepreneur and Manager. They also have published several scholarly articles. Dr. Cavico discharges substantial service responsibilities at the Huizenga School, principally by serving as the Chair of the Faculty Executive Committee and Chair of the Faculty Rank, Reappointment, and Promotion Committee, as well as Supervisory Professor and Lead Professor for several law and ethics courses. Drs. Cavico and Mujtaba have created a scholarship at the Huizenga School of Business, The Business Ethics and Global Corporate Social Responsibility Scholarship, to which they donate a portion of their royalties from the sale of all their books, which sum is matched by their university. Dr. Cavico holds a J.D. degree from St. Mary's University School of Law and a B.A. from Gettysburg College. He also possesses a Master of Laws degree from the University of San Diego School of Law and a Master's degree in Political Science from Drew University. Dr. Cavico is licensed to practice law in the states of Florida and Texas. He has worked as a federal government regulatory attorney and as counsel for a labor union; and he has practiced general civil law and immigration law in South Florida. Dr. Cavico is married; and he and his wife, Nancy, a Registered Nurse and adjunct nursing professor, reside in Lauderdale-by-the Sea, Florida. Nancy holds a BSN degree as well as a Legal Assistant Certificate from Nova Southeastern University. They co-authored a law review article on nursing malpractice law as well as one on the nursing profession and the employment at will doctrine.

Stay "Forever Young" – by Rod Stewart

May the Good Lord be with ya down every road you roam
And may sunshine and happiness surround you when you're far from home
And may you grow to be proud, dignified, and true
And do unto others as you would have done to you

Be courageous and be brave
And in my heart you'll always stay
Forever young (forever young)
Forever young (forever young)

May good fortune be with you, may your guiding light be strong
Build a stairway to heaven with a prince or vagabond

And may you never love in vain
And in my heart you will remain
Forever young (forever young)
Forever young (forever young)

For ever young
For ever young
Yeah!

And when you fin'lly fly away I'll be hopin' that I served ya well
For all the wisdom of a lifetime no one can ever tell

But whatever road ya choose
I'm right behind you, win or lose
Forever young (forever young)
Forever young (forever young)

For ever young
For ever young
For! For! Ever young
For ever young!

(Written by Kevin Stuart, James Savigar, James Cregan, Rod Stewart, and
Bob Dylan)